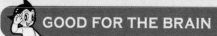

GOOD FOR THE BRAIN

EDU·MANGA™

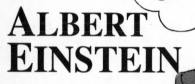

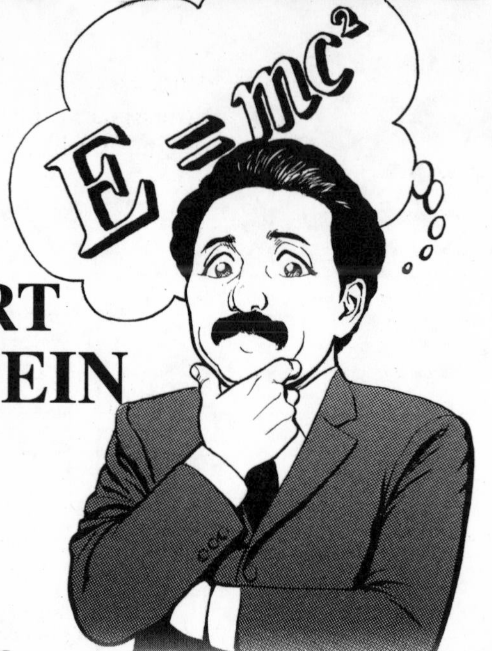

$E = mc^2$

ALBERT EINSTEIN

CONTENTS

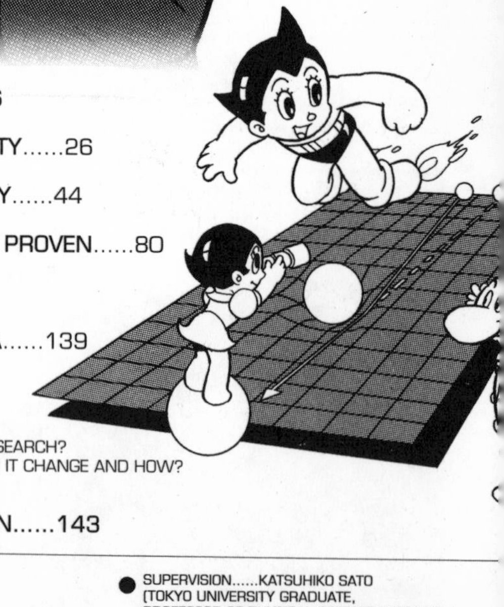

● SCRIPT......ISAO HIMURO

● MANGA......KOTARO IWASAKI

● INTRODUCTORY MANGA, ILLUSTRATIONS......
TEZUKA PRODUCTIONS

● SUPERVISION......KATSUHIKO SATO
(TOKYO UNIVERSITY GRADUATE,
PROFESSOR OF PHYSICAL SCIENCE RESEARCH)

● ARTICLES......TADAMASA YOSHIDA

● DESIGN......KOZO KAKEI (KAKEI GRAPHICS)

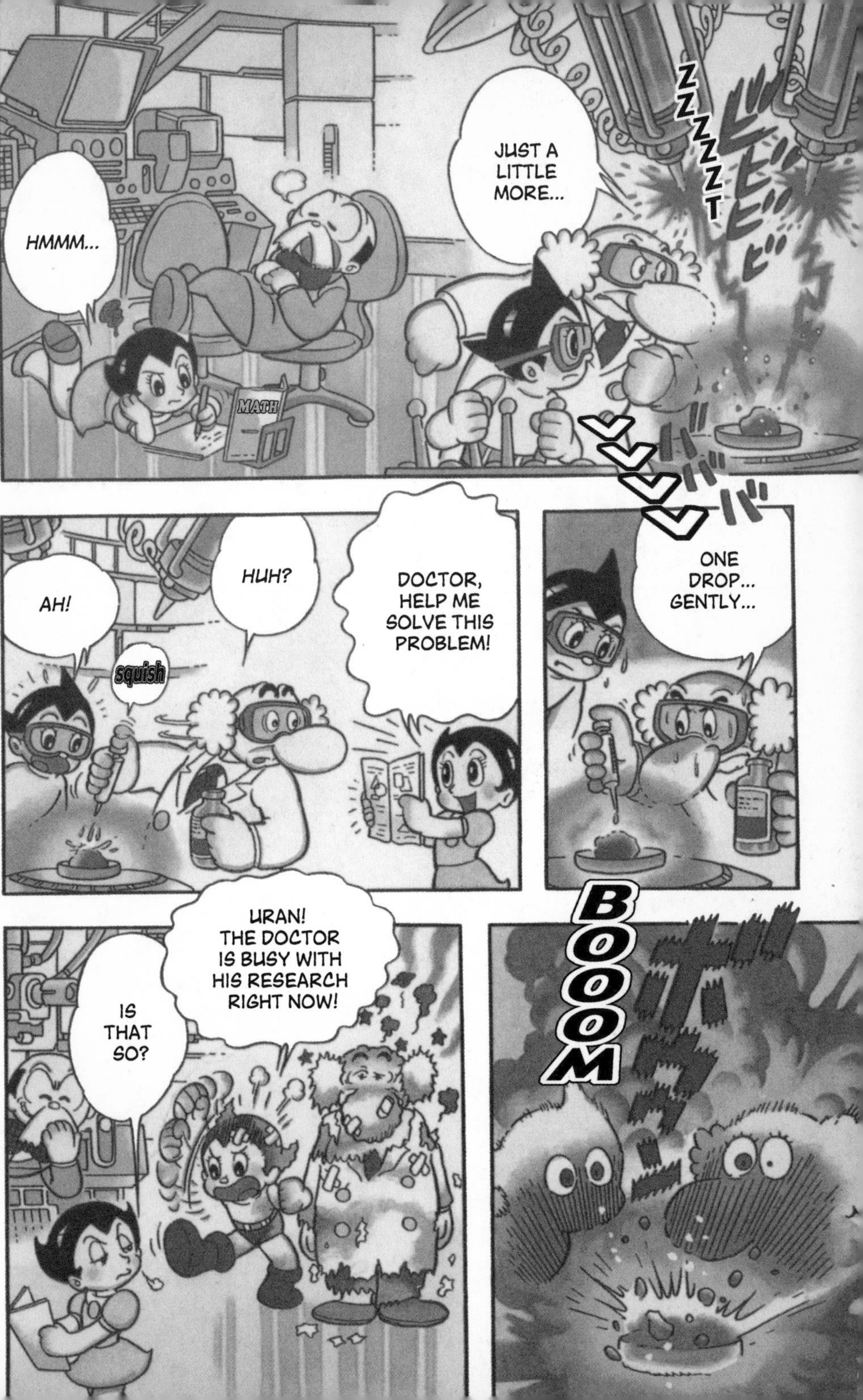
ZZZZZT
JUST A LITTLE MORE...
HMMM...
VVVVV
ONE DROP... GENTLY...
DOCTOR, HELP ME SOLVE THIS PROBLEM!
HUH?
squish
AH!
MATH
BOOOOM
URAN! THE DOCTOR IS BUSY WITH HIS RESEARCH RIGHT NOW!
IS THAT SO?

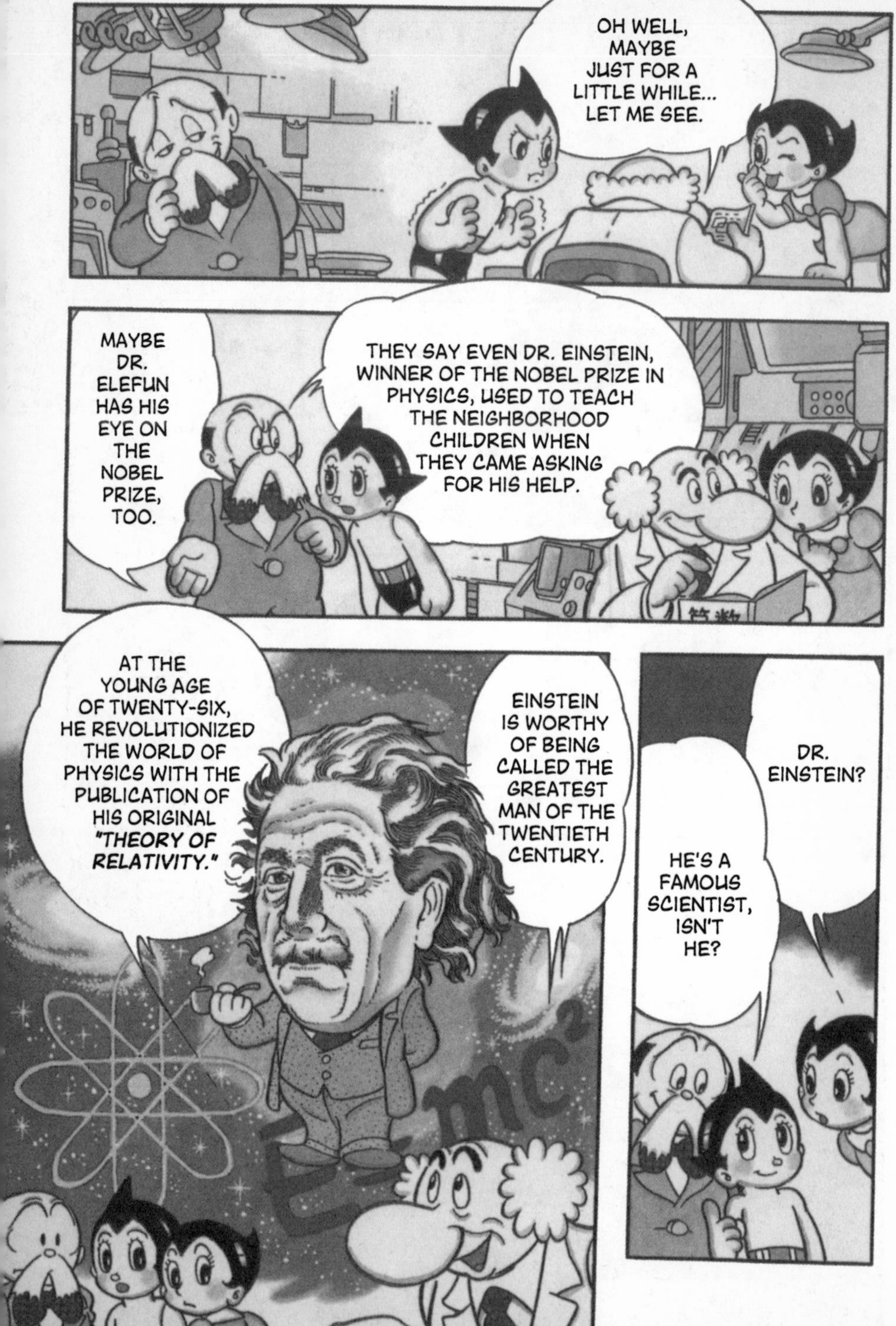
OH WELL, MAYBE JUST FOR A LITTLE WHILE... LET ME SEE.
THEY SAY EVEN DR. EINSTEIN, WINNER OF THE NOBEL PRIZE IN PHYSICS, USED TO TEACH THE NEIGHBORHOOD CHILDREN WHEN THEY CAME ASKING FOR HIS HELP.
MAYBE DR. ELEFUN HAS HIS EYE ON THE NOBEL PRIZE, TOO.
DR. EINSTEIN?
HE'S A FAMOUS SCIENTIST, ISN'T HE?
EINSTEIN IS WORTHY OF BEING CALLED THE GREATEST MAN OF THE TWENTIETH CENTURY.
AT THE YOUNG AGE OF TWENTY-SIX, HE REVOLUTIONIZED THE WORLD OF PHYSICS WITH THE PUBLICATION OF HIS ORIGINAL "THEORY OF RELATIVITY."

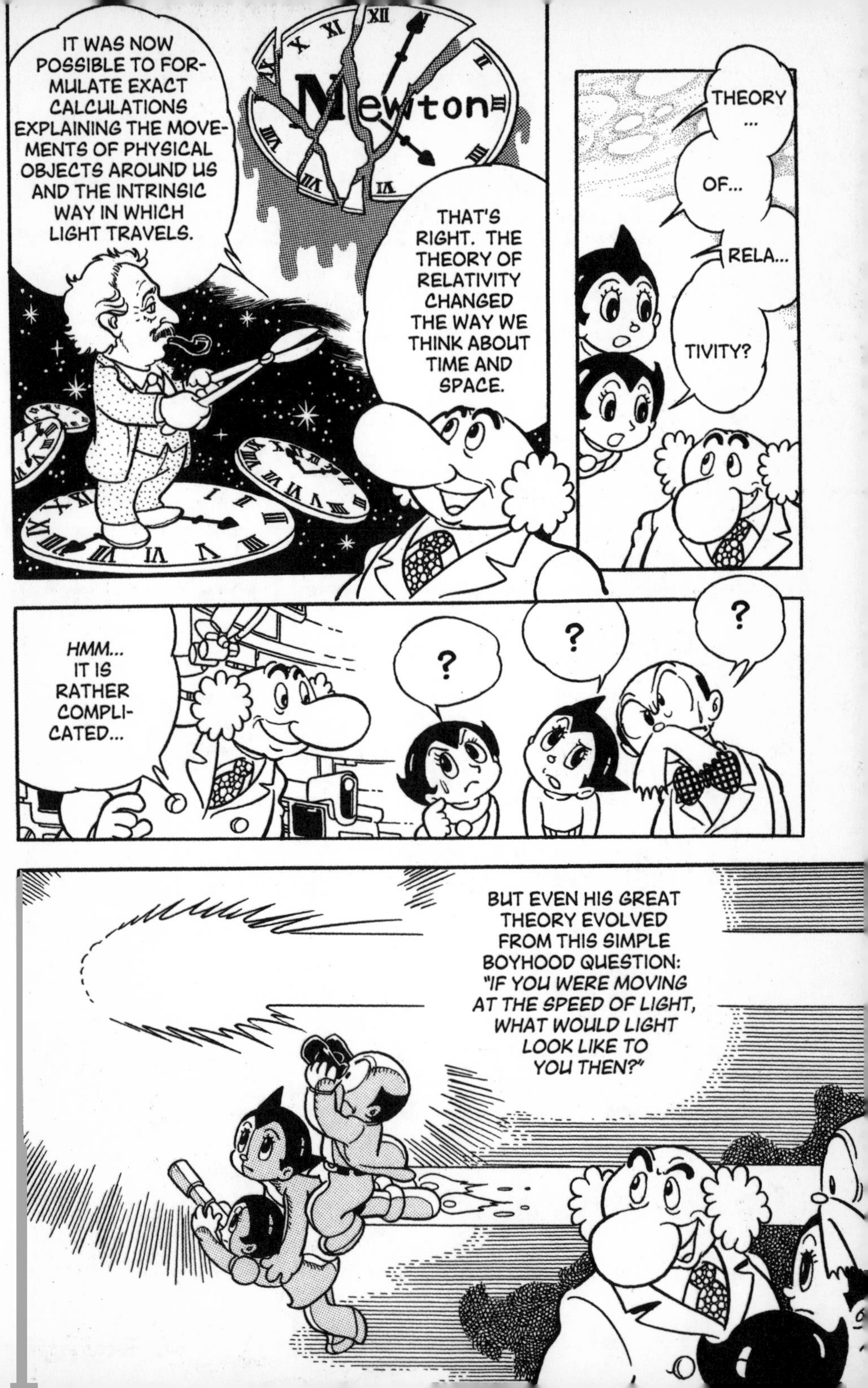
THEORY ...
OF...
RELA...
TIVITY?
Newton
IT WAS NOW POSSIBLE TO FORMULATE EXACT CALCULATIONS EXPLAINING THE MOVEMENTS OF PHYSICAL OBJECTS AROUND US AND THE INTRINSIC WAY IN WHICH LIGHT TRAVELS.
THAT'S RIGHT. THE THEORY OF RELATIVITY CHANGED THE WAY WE THINK ABOUT TIME AND SPACE.
?
?
?
HMM... IT IS RATHER COMPLICATED...
BUT EVEN HIS GREAT THEORY EVOLVED FROM THIS SIMPLE BOYHOOD QUESTION: "IF YOU WERE MOVING AT THE SPEED OF LIGHT, WHAT WOULD LIGHT LOOK LIKE TO YOU THEN?"

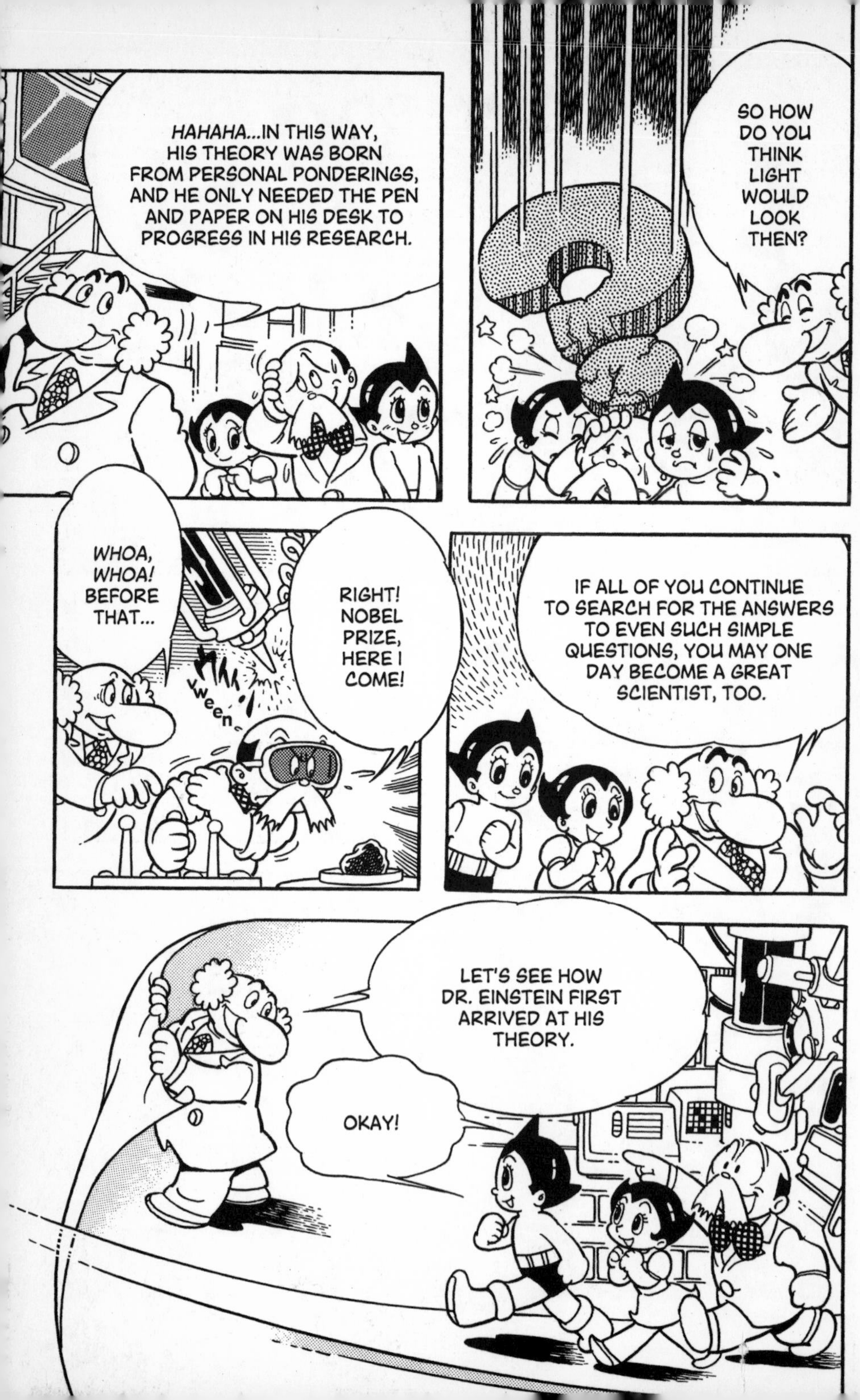

SO HOW DO YOU THINK LIGHT WOULD LOOK THEN?
HAHAHA...IN THIS WAY, HIS THEORY WAS BORN FROM PERSONAL PONDERINGS, AND HE ONLY NEEDED THE PEN AND PAPER ON HIS DESK TO PROGRESS IN HIS RESEARCH.
IF ALL OF YOU CONTINUE TO SEARCH FOR THE ANSWERS TO EVEN SUCH SIMPLE QUESTIONS, YOU MAY ONE DAY BECOME A GREAT SCIENTIST, TOO.
RIGHT! NOBEL PRIZE, HERE I COME!
WHOA, WHOA! BEFORE THAT...
vween
LET'S SEE HOW DR. EINSTEIN FIRST ARRIVED AT HIS THEORY.
OKAY!

CHAPTER 1
THE SHY BOY

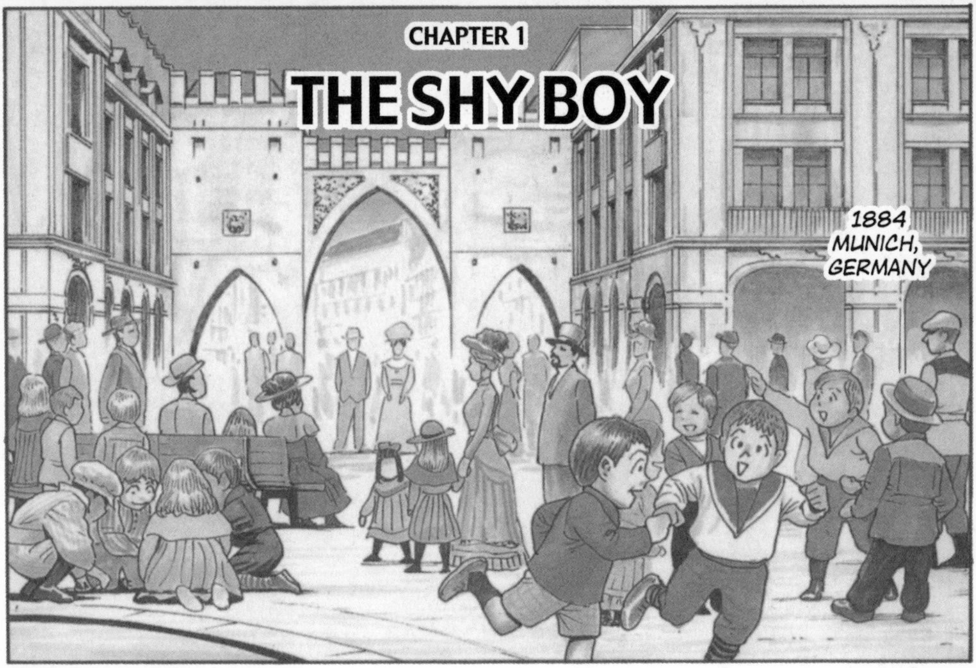
1884
MUNICH,
GERMANY

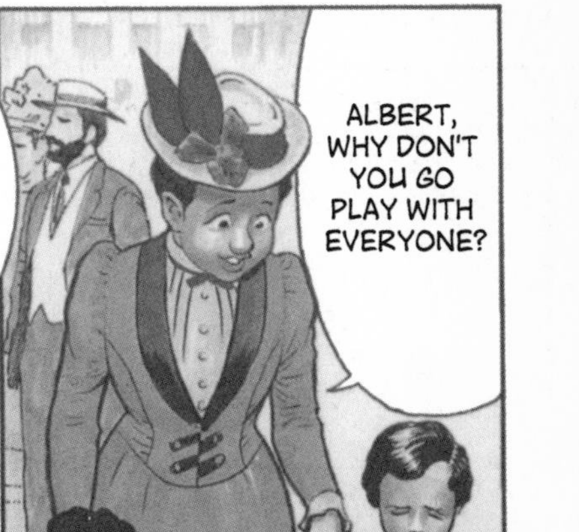
ALBERT, WHY DON'T YOU GO PLAY WITH EVERYONE?

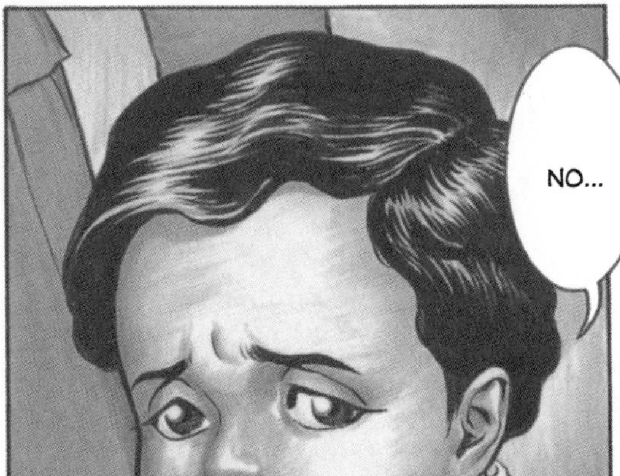
NO...

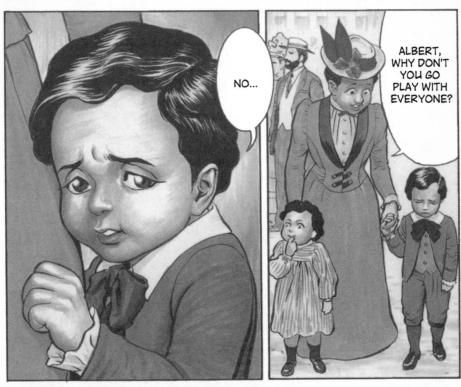

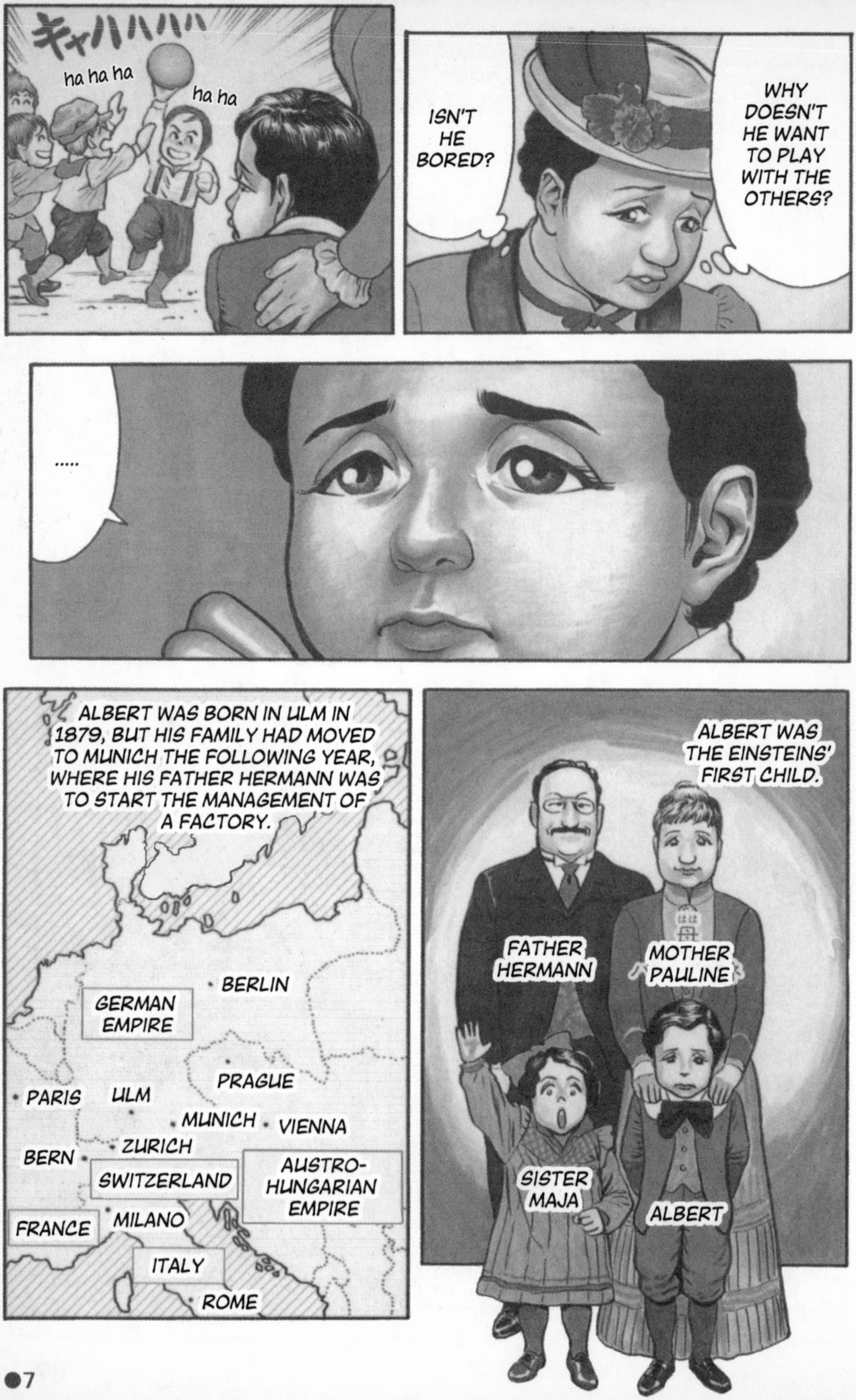
WHY DOESN'T HE WANT TO PLAY WITH THE OTHERS?
ISN'T HE BORED?
キャハハハ
ha ha
ha ha ha
.....
ALBERT WAS THE EINSTEINS' FIRST CHILD.
MOTHER PAULINE
FATHER HERMANN
ALBERT
SISTER MAJA
ALBERT WAS BORN IN ULM IN 1879, BUT HIS FAMILY HAD MOVED TO MUNICH THE FOLLOWING YEAR, WHERE HIS FATHER HERMANN WAS TO START THE MANAGEMENT OF A FACTORY.
BERLIN
GERMAN EMPIRE
PRAGUE
PARIS
ULM
MUNICH
VIENNA
ZURICH
BERN
SWITZERLAND
AUSTRO-HUNGARIAN EMPIRE
FRANCE
MILANO
ITALY
ROME

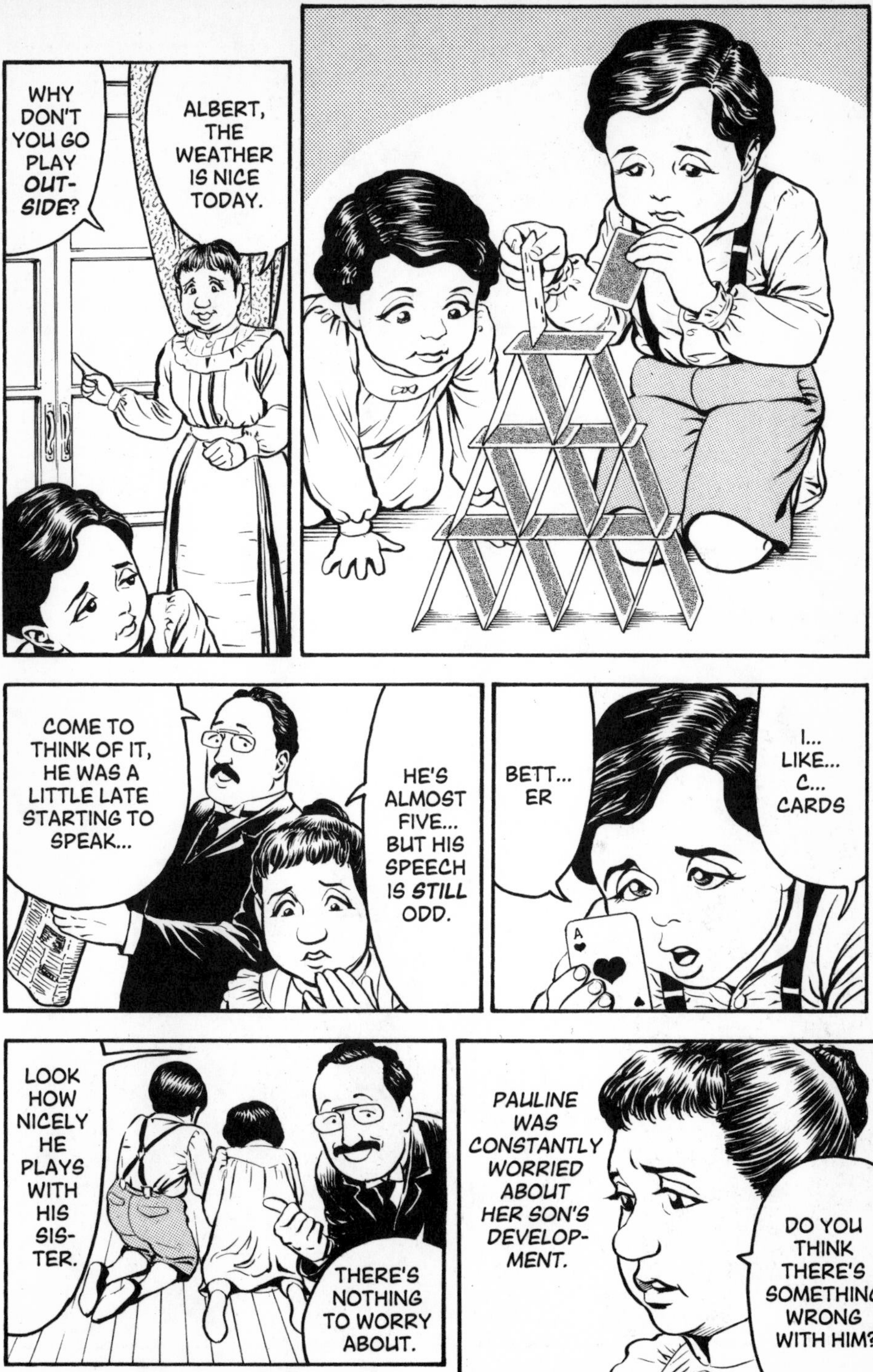
ALBERT, THE WEATHER IS NICE TODAY.
WHY DON'T YOU GO PLAY OUT-SIDE?
I... LIKE... C... CARDS
BETT... ER
HE'S ALMOST FIVE... BUT HIS SPEECH IS STILL ODD.
COME TO THINK OF IT, HE WAS A LITTLE LATE STARTING TO SPEAK...
PAULINE WAS CONSTANTLY WORRIED ABOUT HER SON'S DEVELOP-MENT.
DO YOU THINK THERE'S SOMETHING WRONG WITH HIM?
LOOK HOW NICELY HE PLAYS WITH HIS SIS-TER.
THERE'S NOTHING TO WORRY ABOUT.

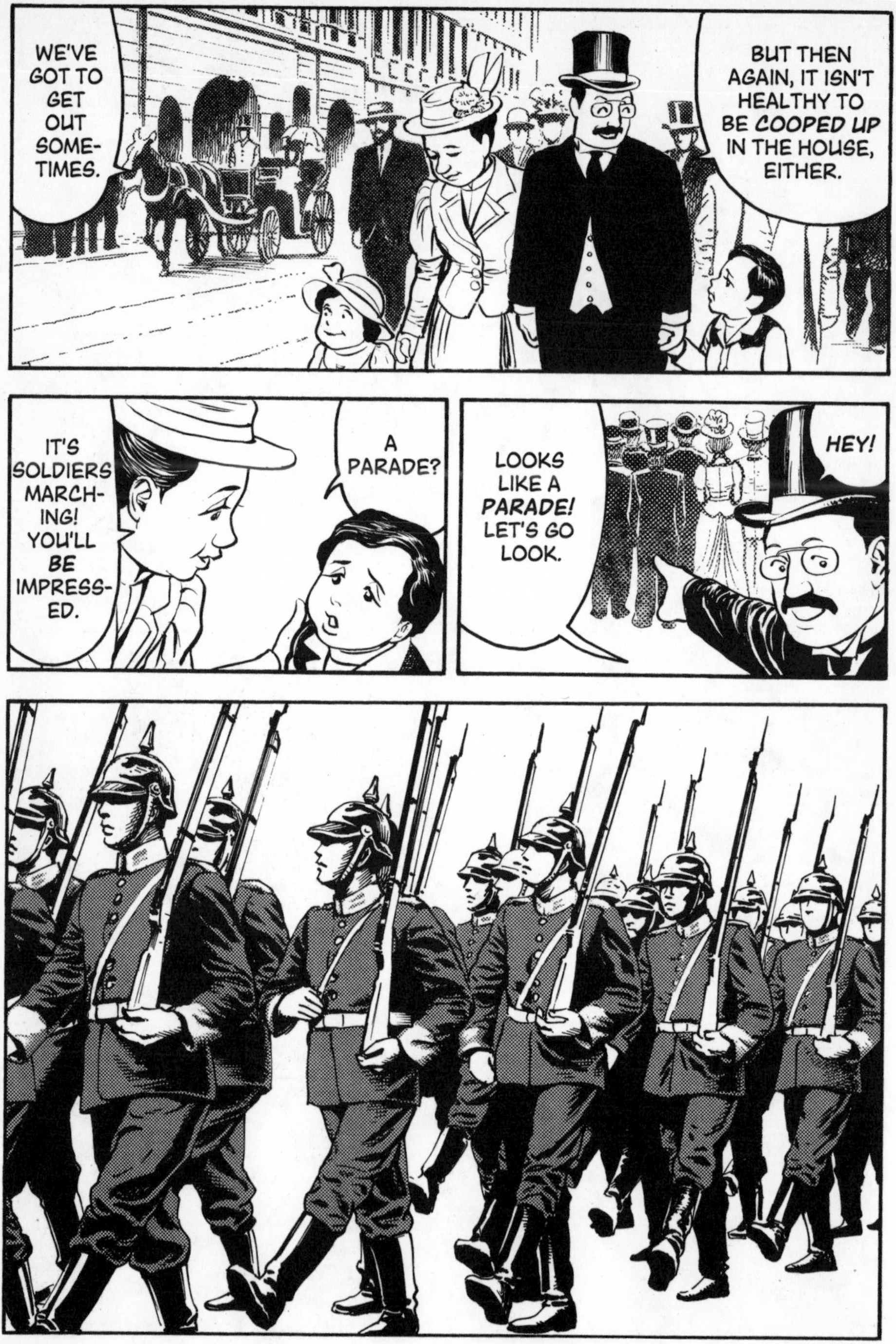
BUT THEN AGAIN, IT ISN'T HEALTHY TO BE *COOPED UP* IN THE HOUSE, EITHER.
WE'VE GOT TO GET OUT SOME-TIMES.
HEY!
LOOKS LIKE A *PARADE!* LET'S GO LOOK.
A PARADE?
IT'S SOLDIERS MARCH-ING! YOU'LL *BE* IMPRESS-ED.

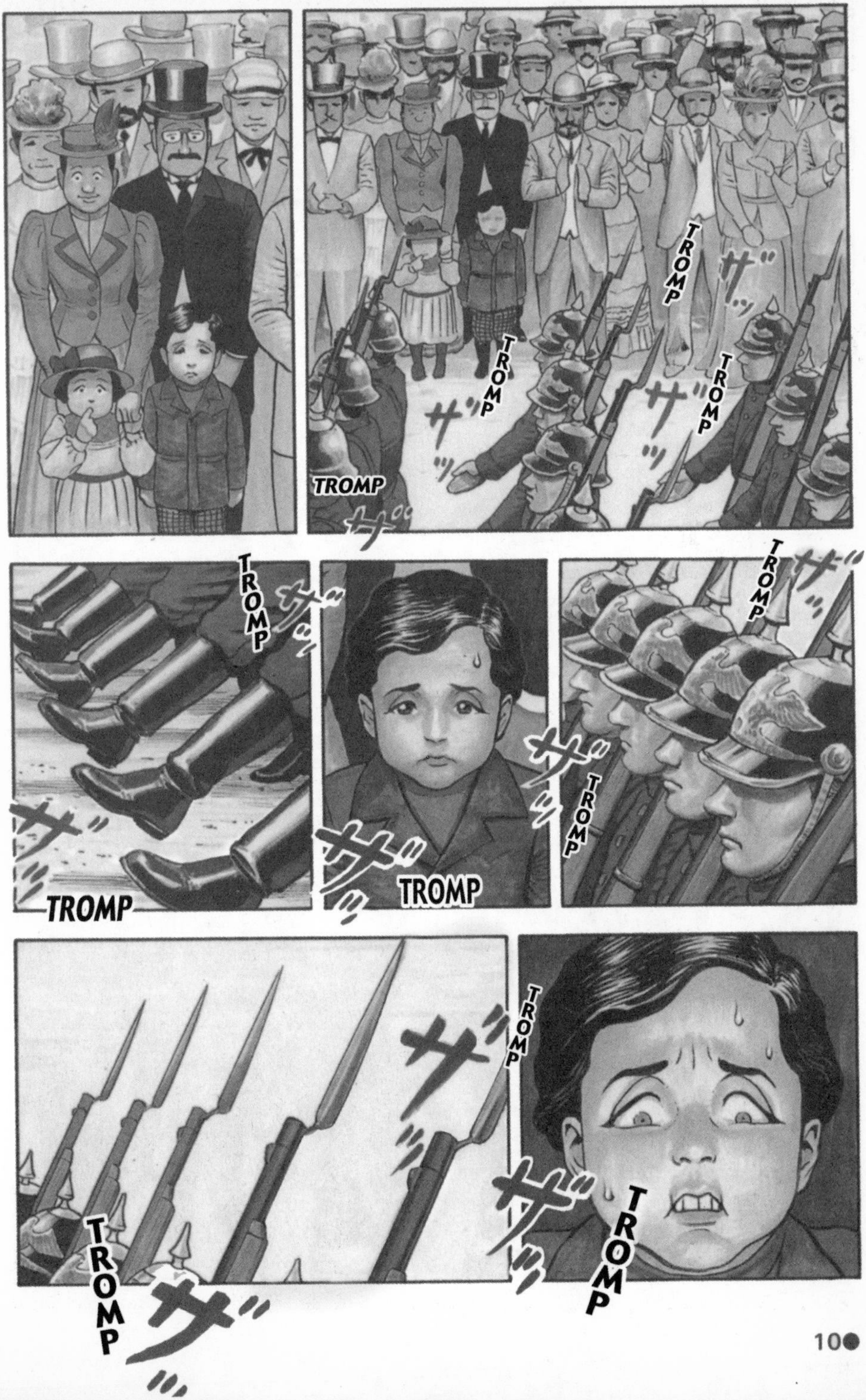
TROMP
ザッ
TROMP
ザッ
TROMP
ザッ
TROMP
ザッ
TROMP
ザッ
TROMP
ザッ
TROMP
ザッ
TROMP
ザッ
TROMP
ザッ
TROMP
ザッ
TROMP
ザッ
TROMP
ザッ
TROMP
ザッ
TROMP

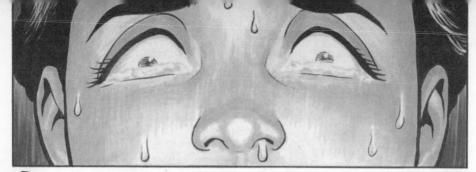

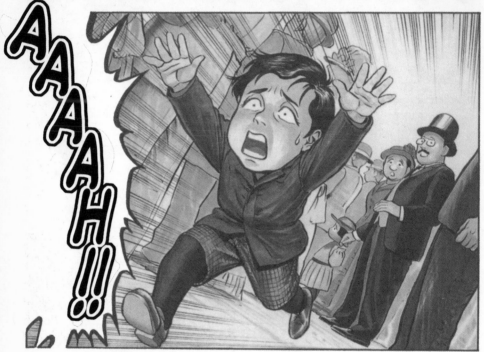

AAAAH!!

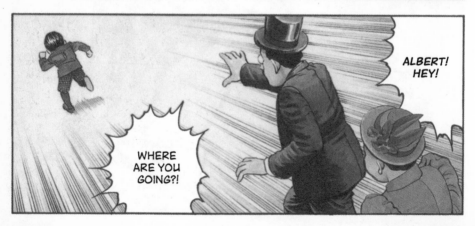

ALBERT! HEY!

WHERE ARE YOU GOING?!

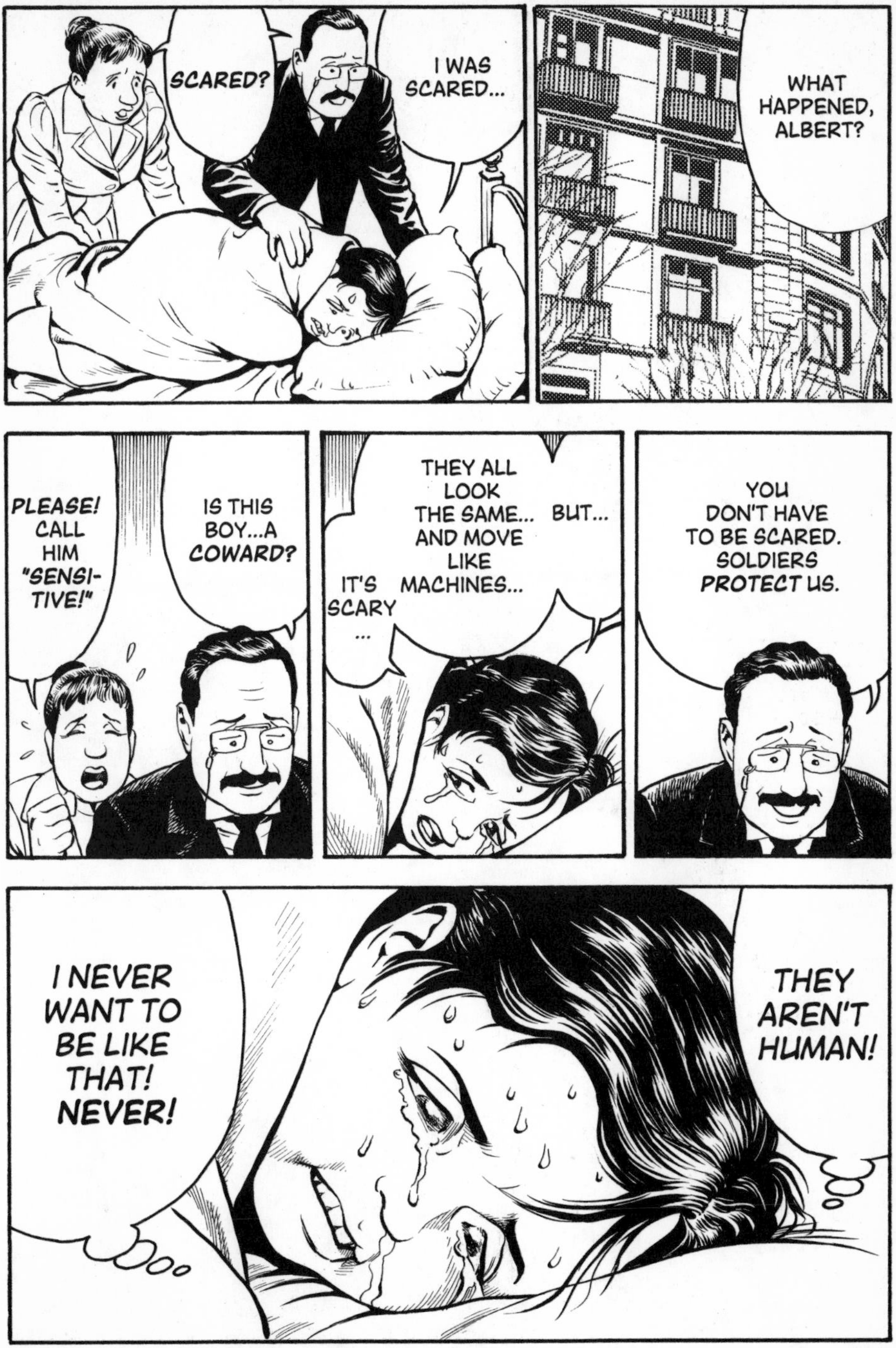
WHAT HAPPENED, ALBERT?
I WAS SCARED...
SCARED?
YOU DON'T HAVE TO BE SCARED. SOLDIERS PROTECT US.
BUT...
THEY ALL LOOK THE SAME... AND MOVE LIKE MACHINES...
IT'S SCARY ...
IS THIS BOY...A COWARD?
PLEASE! CALL HIM "SENSITIVE!"
THEY AREN'T HUMAN!
I NEVER WANT TO BE LIKE THAT! NEVER!

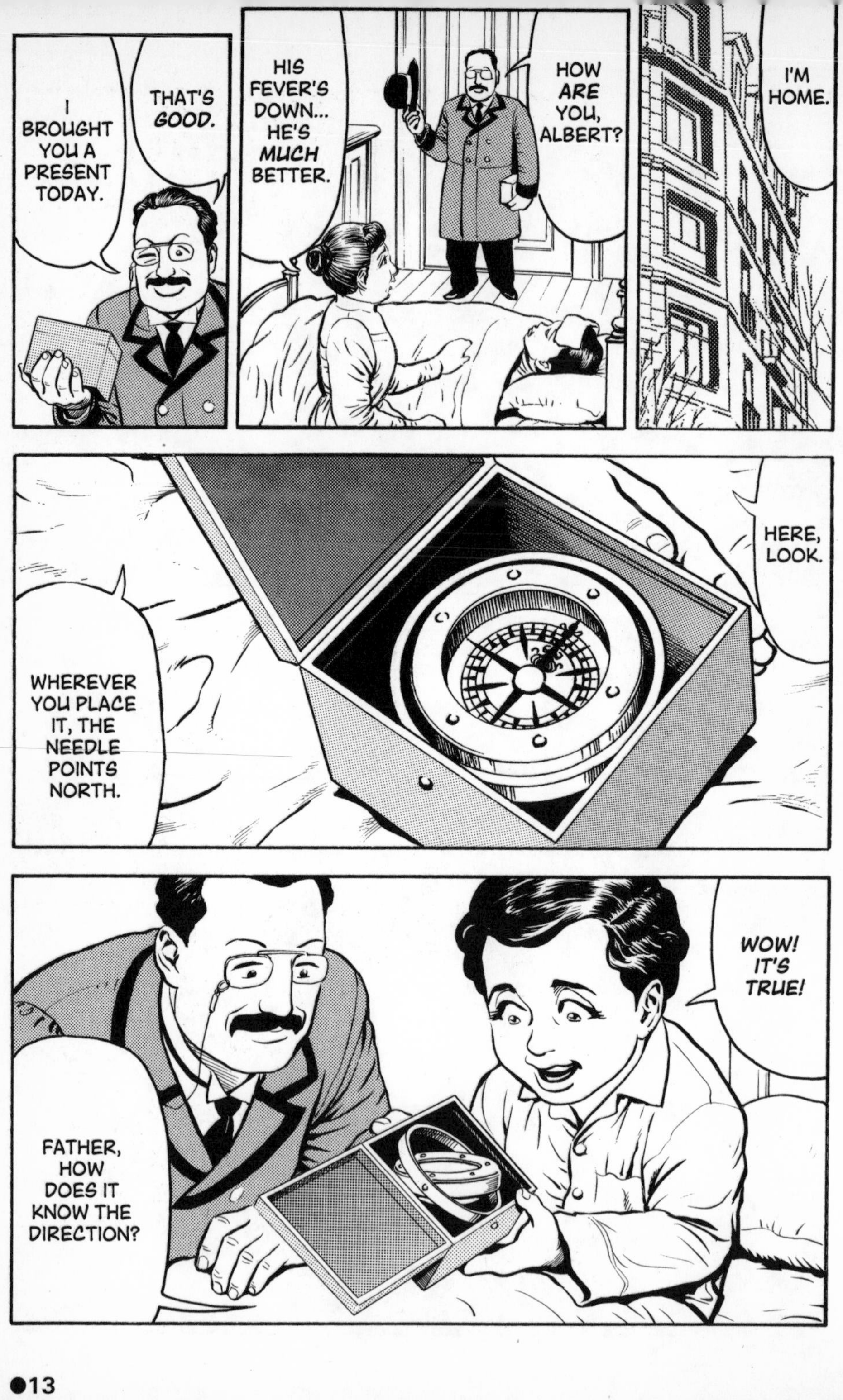
I'M HOME.
HOW ARE YOU, ALBERT?
HIS FEVER'S DOWN... HE'S MUCH BETTER.
THAT'S GOOD.
I BROUGHT YOU A PRESENT TODAY.
HERE, LOOK.
WHEREVER YOU PLACE IT, THE NEEDLE POINTS NORTH.
WOW! IT'S TRUE!
FATHER, HOW DOES IT KNOW THE DIRECTION?

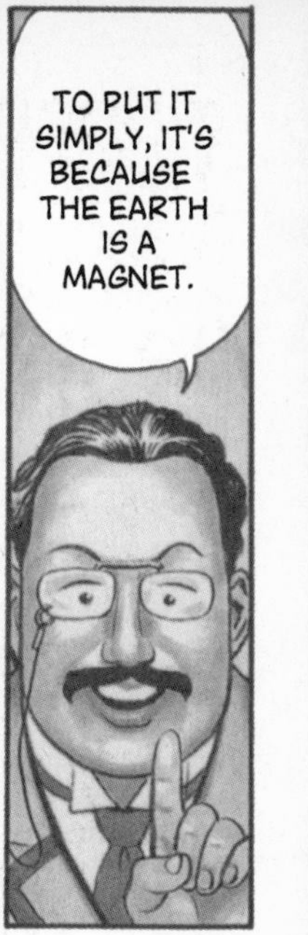
TO PUT IT SIMPLY, IT'S BECAUSE THE EARTH IS A MAGNET.
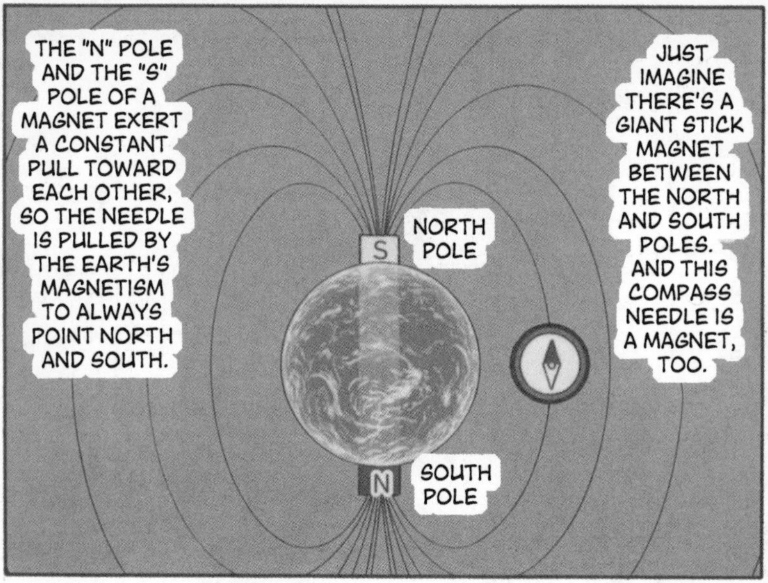
JUST IMAGINE THERE'S A GIANT STICK MAGNET BETWEEN THE NORTH AND SOUTH POLES. AND THIS COMPASS NEEDLE IS A MAGNET, TOO.
NORTH POLE
S
N
SOUTH POLE
THE "N" POLE AND THE "S" POLE OF A MAGNET EXERT A CONSTANT PULL TOWARD EACH OTHER, SO THE NEEDLE IS PULLED BY THE EARTH'S MAGNETISM TO ALWAYS POINT NORTH AND SOUTH.
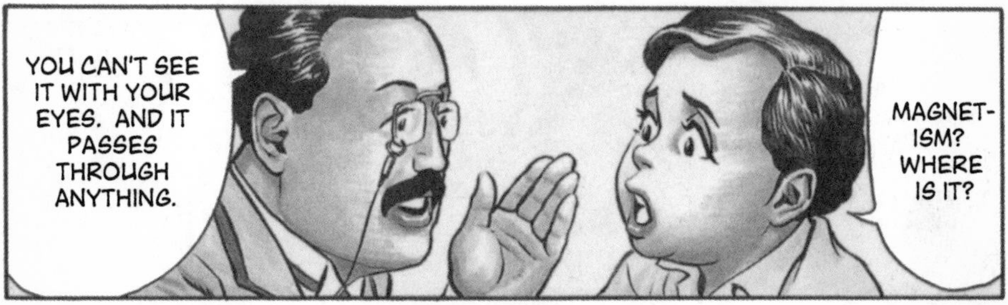
MAGNET-ISM? WHERE IS IT?
YOU CAN'T SEE IT WITH YOUR EYES. AND IT PASSES THROUGH ANYTHING.
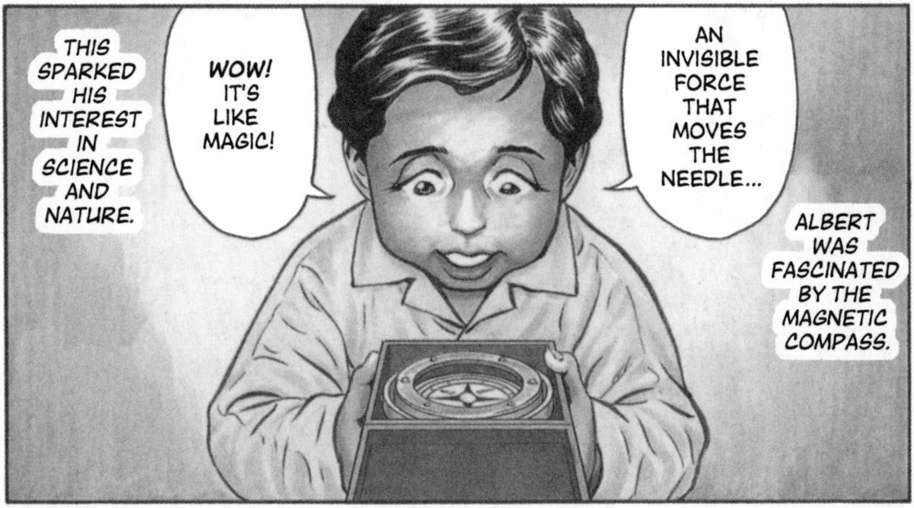
AN INVISIBLE FORCE THAT MOVES THE NEEDLE...
WOW! IT'S LIKE MAGIC!
ALBERT WAS FASCINATED BY THE MAGNETIC COMPASS.
THIS SPARKED HIS INTEREST IN SCIENCE AND NATURE.

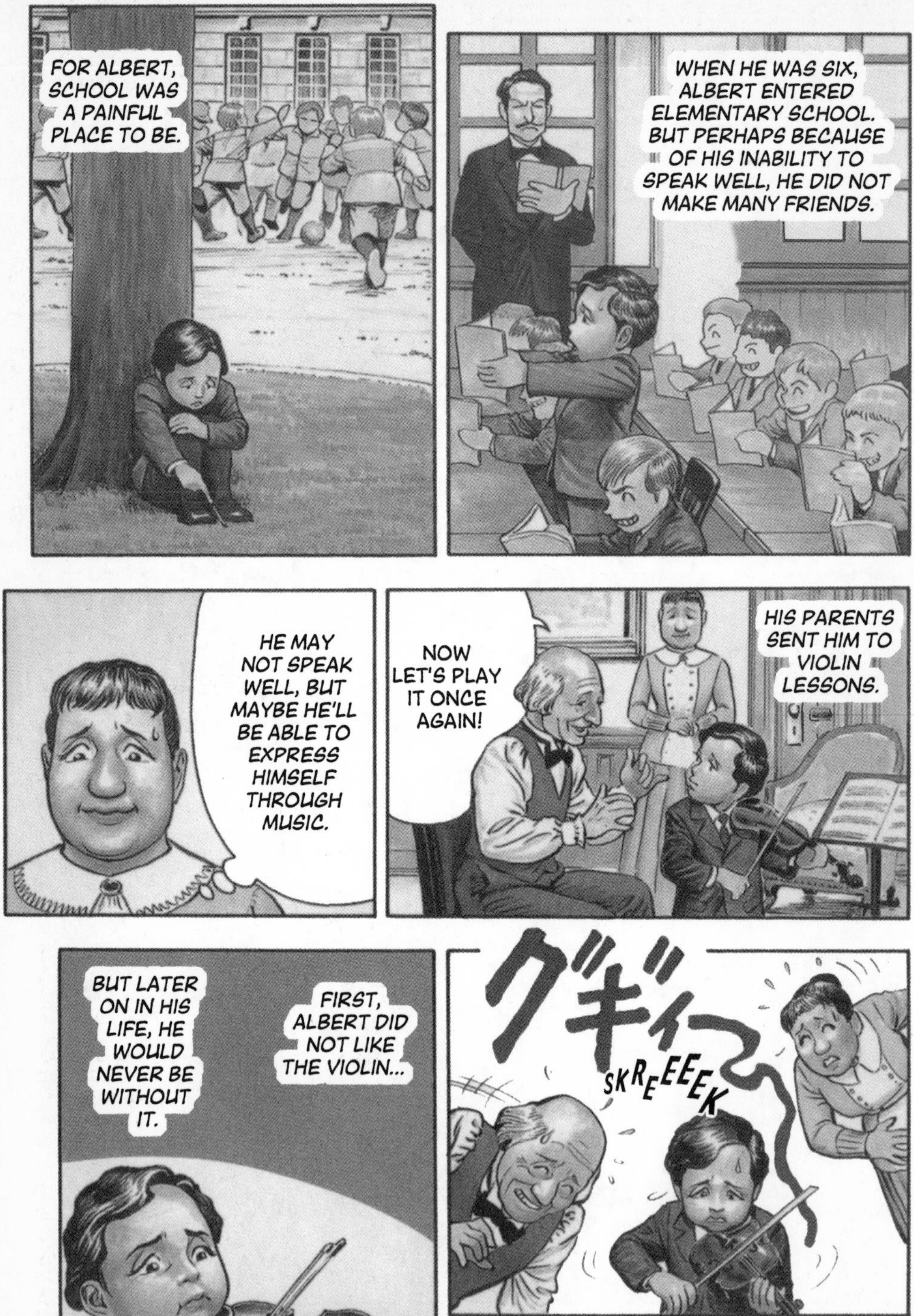
WHEN HE WAS SIX, ALBERT ENTERED ELEMENTARY SCHOOL. BUT PERHAPS BECAUSE OF HIS INABILITY TO SPEAK WELL, HE DID NOT MAKE MANY FRIENDS.
FOR ALBERT, SCHOOL WAS A PAINFUL PLACE TO BE.
HIS PARENTS SENT HIM TO VIOLIN LESSONS.
NOW LET'S PLAY IT ONCE AGAIN!
HE MAY NOT SPEAK WELL, BUT MAYBE HE'LL BE ABLE TO EXPRESS HIMSELF THROUGH MUSIC.
グギイー
SKREEEEK
FIRST, ALBERT DID NOT LIKE THE VIOLIN...
BUT LATER ON IN HIS LIFE, HE WOULD NEVER BE WITHOUT IT.

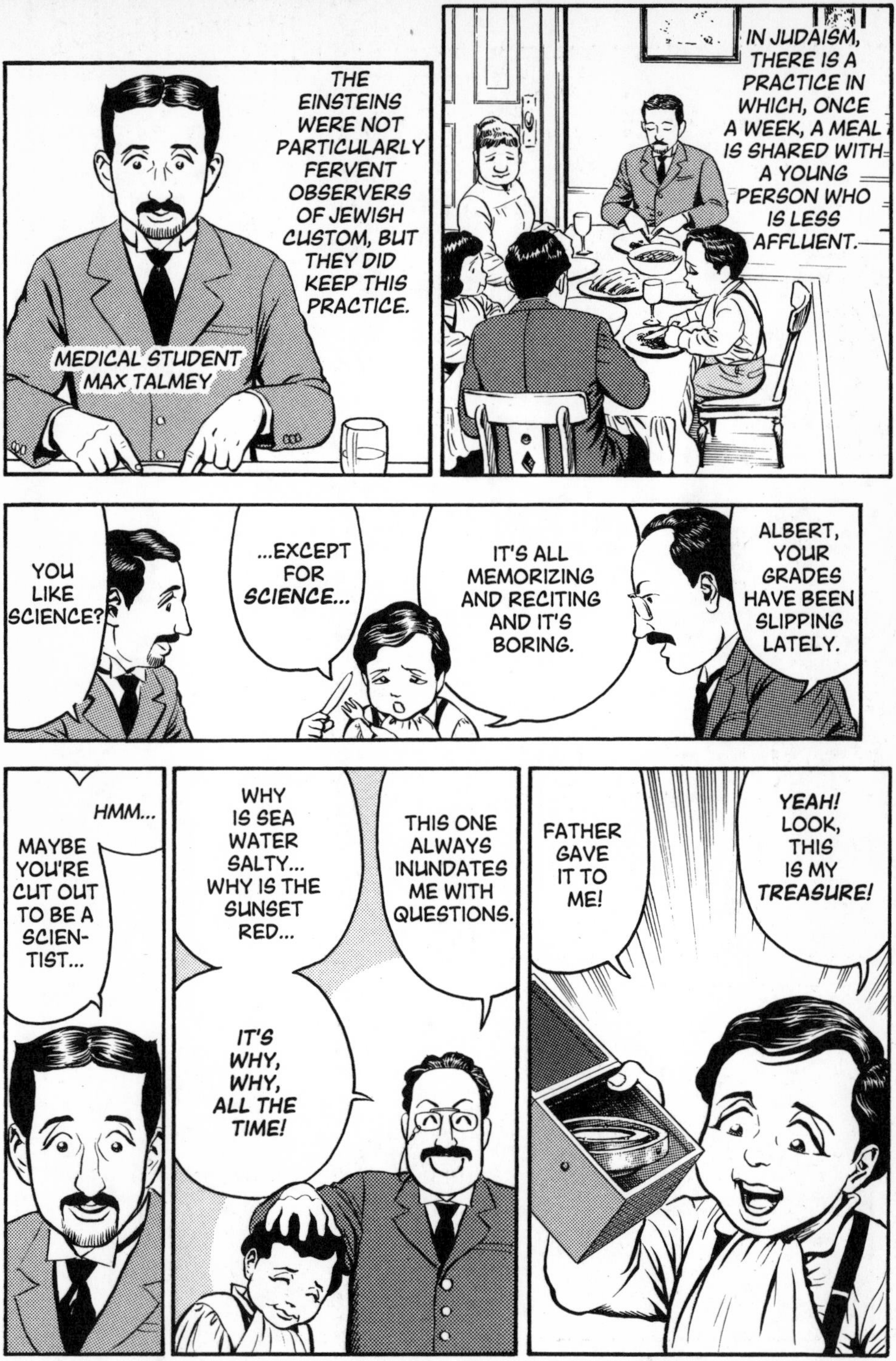
IN JUDAISM, THERE IS A PRACTICE IN WHICH, ONCE A WEEK, A MEAL IS SHARED WITH A YOUNG PERSON WHO IS LESS AFFLUENT.
THE EINSTEINS WERE NOT PARTICULARLY FERVENT OBSERVERS OF JEWISH CUSTOM, BUT THEY DID KEEP THIS PRACTICE.
MEDICAL STUDENT MAX TALMEY
ALBERT, YOUR GRADES HAVE BEEN SLIPPING LATELY.
IT'S ALL MEMORIZING AND RECITING AND IT'S BORING.
...EXCEPT FOR SCIENCE...
YOU LIKE SCIENCE?
YEAH! LOOK, THIS IS MY TREASURE!
FATHER GAVE IT TO ME!
THIS ONE ALWAYS INUNDATES ME WITH QUESTIONS.
WHY IS SEA WATER SALTY... WHY IS THE SUNSET RED...
IT'S WHY, WHY, ALL THE TIME!
HMM...
MAYBE YOU'RE CUT OUT TO BE A SCIEN-TIST...

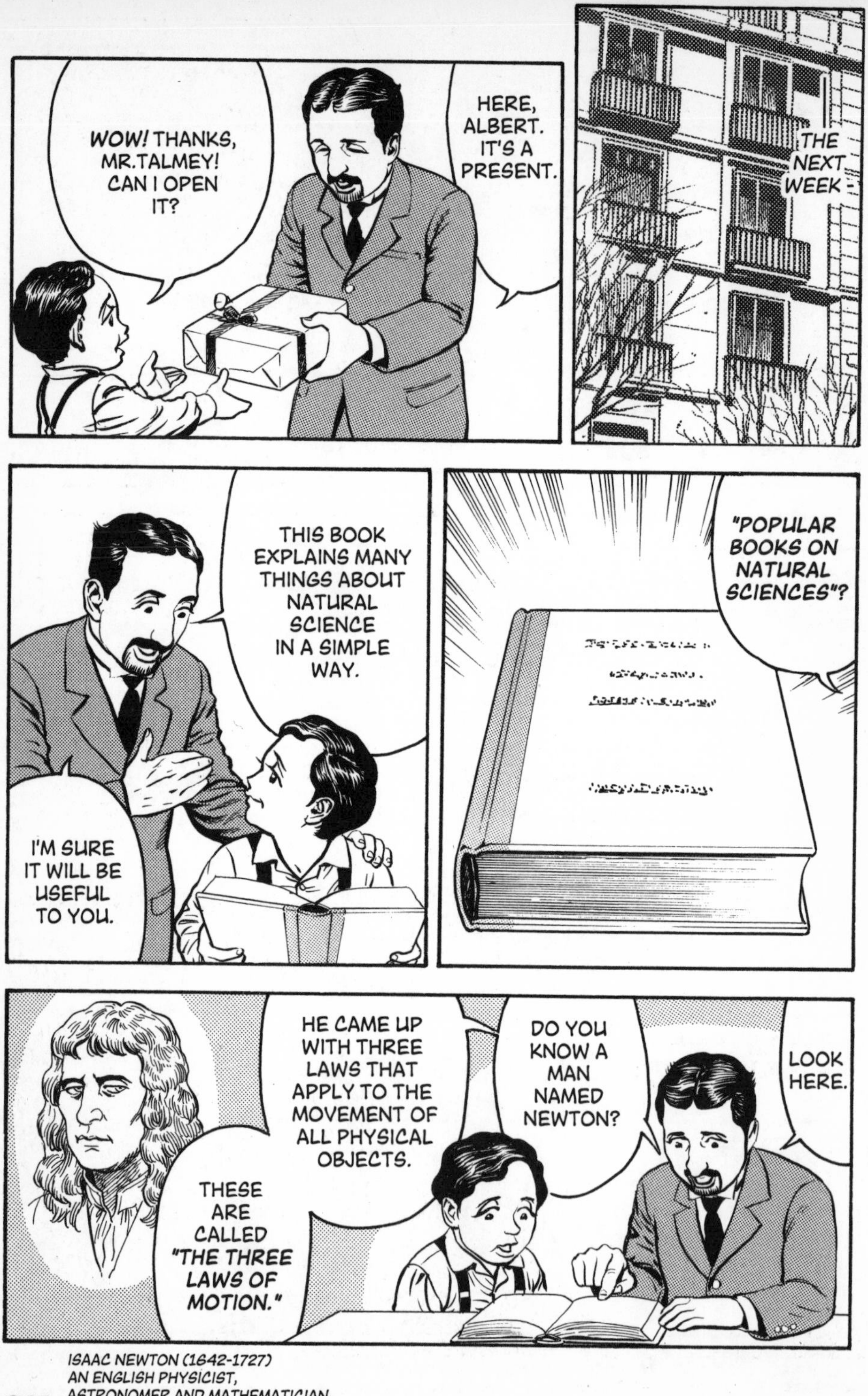
THE NEXT WEEK -
HERE, ALBERT. IT'S A PRESENT.
WOW! THANKS, MR.TALMEY! CAN I OPEN IT?
"POPULAR BOOKS ON NATURAL SCIENCES"?
THIS BOOK EXPLAINS MANY THINGS ABOUT NATURAL SCIENCE IN A SIMPLE WAY.
I'M SURE IT WILL BE USEFUL TO YOU.
LOOK HERE.
DO YOU KNOW A MAN NAMED NEWTON?
HE CAME UP WITH THREE LAWS THAT APPLY TO THE MOVEMENT OF ALL PHYSICAL OBJECTS.
THESE ARE CALLED "THE THREE LAWS OF MOTION."

ISAAC NEWTON (1642-1727)
AN ENGLISH PHYSICIST,
ASTRONOMER AND MATHEMATICIAN.

THE LAW OF INERTIA (THE FIRST LAW OF MOTION)

A PHYSICAL OBJECT PERSISTS IN MAINTAINING ITS PRESENT STATE OF MOTION.
THIS IS CALLED "INERTIA."
FOR THIS REASON, IF NO ADDITIONAL FORCE IS APPLIED,
THERE WILL BE NO CHANGE IN MOVEMENT.
A BODY AT REST WILL REMAIN AT REST, AND A BODY IN MOTION
WILL CONTINUE IN MOTION, IN A STRAIGHT LINE, AT THE SAME SPEED.

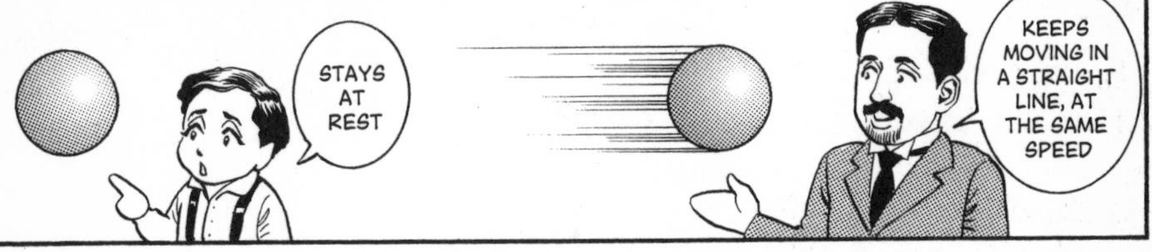
KEEPS MOVING IN A STRAIGHT LINE, AT THE SAME SPEED
STAYS AT REST

THE LAW OF ACCELERATION (THE SECOND LAW OF MOTION)

1 - WHEN FORCE IS APPLIED TO A PHYSICAL OBJECT,
THE OBJECT'S STATE OF MOVEMENT WILL CHANGE.
2 - DEPENDING ON THE DIRECTION IN WHICH THE FORCE IS APPLIED,
THE OBJECT'S SPEED AND DIRECTION OF MOVEMENT WILL CHANGE.
3 - THE GREATER THE FORCE APPLIED TO THE OBJECT,
THE GREATER THE INCREASE IN SPEED (ACCELERATION).
4 - IF THE AMOUNT OF FORCE APPLIED IS EQUAL, THE HEAVIER THE OBJECT,
THE SMALLER THE INCREASE IN SPEED (ACCELERATION).

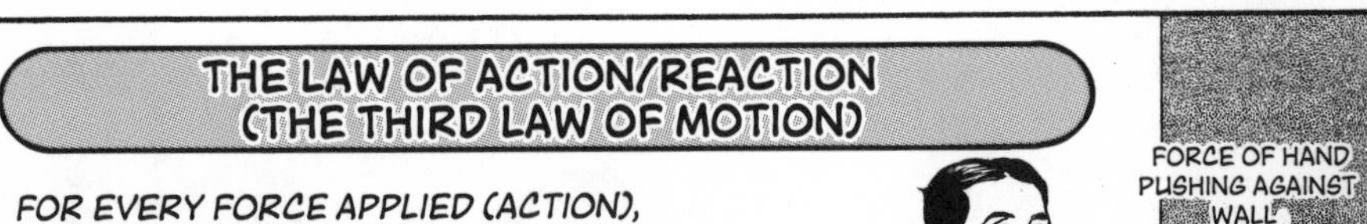
FORCE
HEAVIER OBJECT, SMALLER CHANGE IN SPEED
FORCE
BIG FORCE, BIG CHANGE IN SPEED

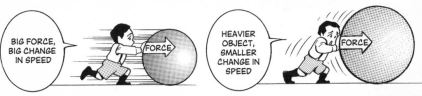

THE LAW OF ACTION/REACTION (THE THIRD LAW OF MOTION)

FOR EVERY FORCE APPLIED (ACTION),
THERE IS AN EQUAL AND OPPOSITE
FORCE AT WORK (REACTION).

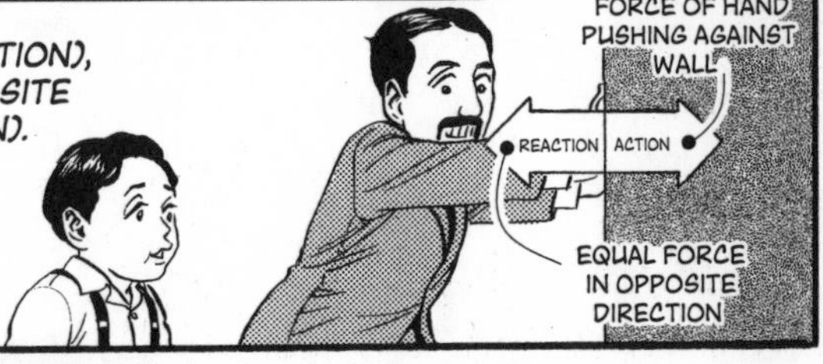
FORCE OF HAND PUSHING AGAINST WALL
REACTION
ACTION
EQUAL FORCE IN OPPOSITE DIRECTION

ACCELERATION...DEGREE OF CHANGE IN VELOCITY WITH TIME.
ACCELERATION INCREASES IN PROPORTION TO THE FORCE APPLIED (PROPORTIONAL TO FORCE), DECREASES WHEN THE OBJECT BEOMES HEAVY, AND INCREASES WHEN THE OBJECT BECOMES LIGHT (INVERSELY PROPORTIONAL TO MASS).

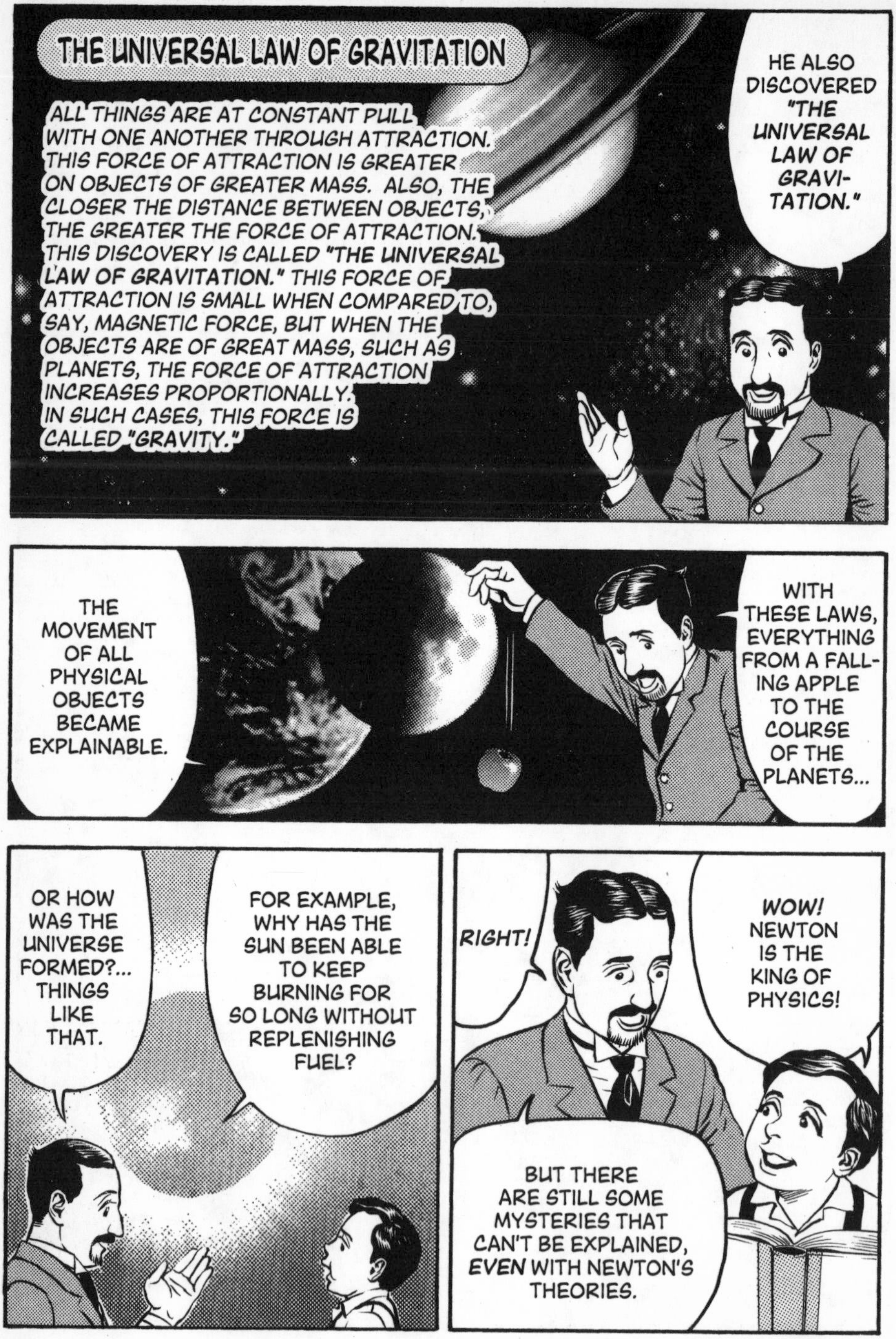
HE ALSO DISCOVERED "THE UNIVERSAL LAW OF GRAVITATION."
THE UNIVERSAL LAW OF GRAVITATION
ALL THINGS ARE AT CONSTANT PULL WITH ONE ANOTHER THROUGH ATTRACTION. THIS FORCE OF ATTRACTION IS GREATER ON OBJECTS OF GREATER MASS. ALSO, THE CLOSER THE DISTANCE BETWEEN OBJECTS, THE GREATER THE FORCE OF ATTRACTION. THIS DISCOVERY IS CALLED "THE UNIVERSAL LAW OF GRAVITATION." THIS FORCE OF ATTRACTION IS SMALL WHEN COMPARED TO, SAY, MAGNETIC FORCE, BUT WHEN THE OBJECTS ARE OF GREAT MASS, SUCH AS PLANETS, THE FORCE OF ATTRACTION INCREASES PROPORTIONALLY. IN SUCH CASES, THIS FORCE IS CALLED "GRAVITY."
WITH THESE LAWS, EVERYTHING FROM A FALLING APPLE TO THE COURSE OF THE PLANETS...
THE MOVEMENT OF ALL PHYSICAL OBJECTS BECAME EXPLAINABLE.
WOW! NEWTON IS THE KING OF PHYSICS!
RIGHT!
BUT THERE ARE STILL SOME MYSTERIES THAT CAN'T BE EXPLAINED, *EVEN* WITH NEWTON'S THEORIES.
FOR EXAMPLE, WHY HAS THE SUN BEEN ABLE TO KEEP BURNING FOR SO LONG WITHOUT REPLENISHING FUEL?
OR HOW WAS THE UNIVERSE FORMED?... THINGS LIKE THAT.

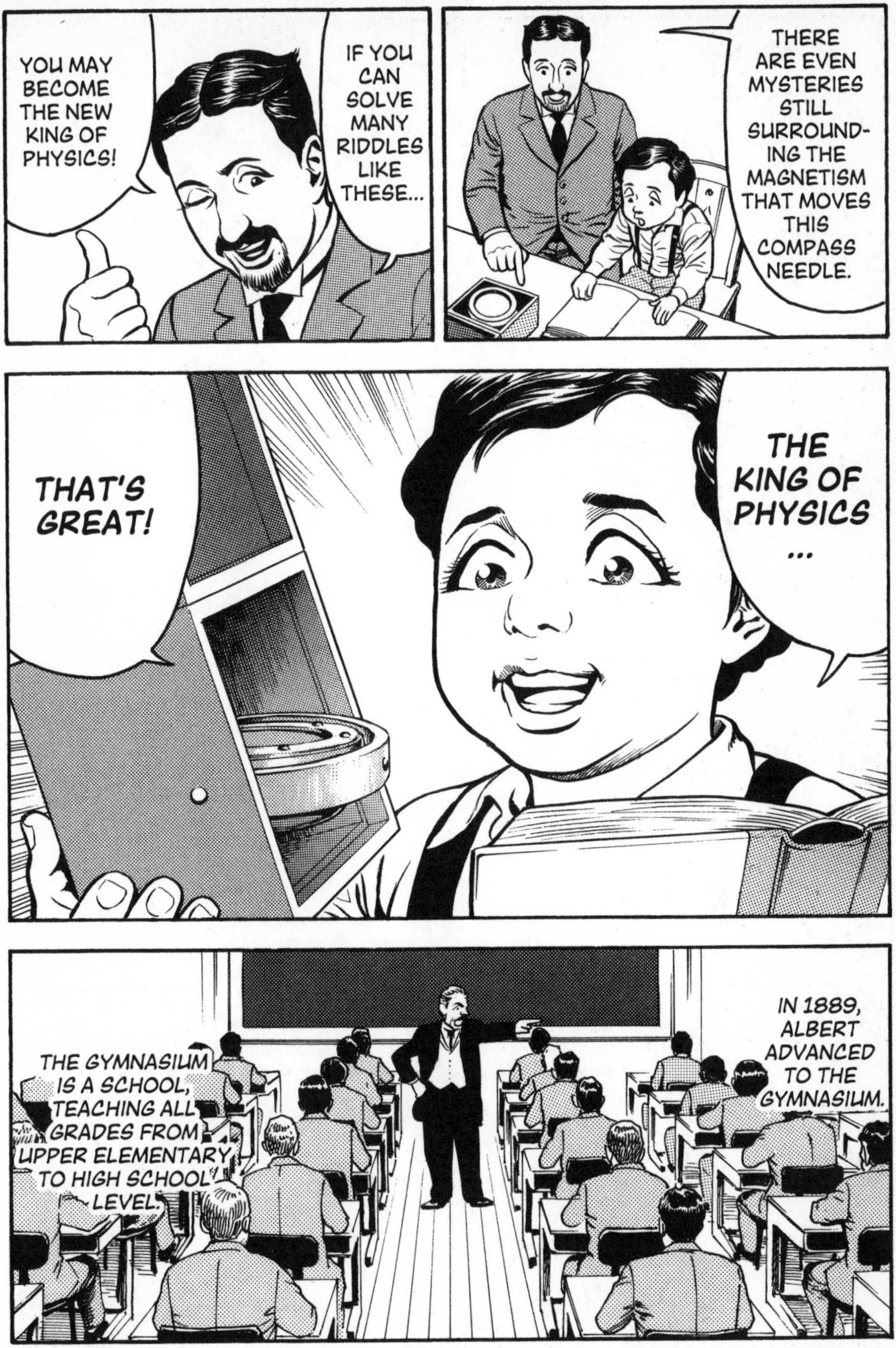
THERE ARE EVEN MYSTERIES STILL SURROUND-ING THE MAGNETISM THAT MOVES THIS COMPASS NEEDLE.
IF YOU CAN SOLVE MANY RIDDLES LIKE THESE...
YOU MAY BECOME THE NEW KING OF PHYSICS!
THE KING OF PHYSICS ...
THAT'S GREAT!
IN 1889, ALBERT ADVANCED TO THE GYMNASIUM.
THE GYMNASIUM IS A SCHOOL, TEACHING ALL GRADES FROM UPPER ELEMENTARY TO HIGH SCHOOL LEVEL.

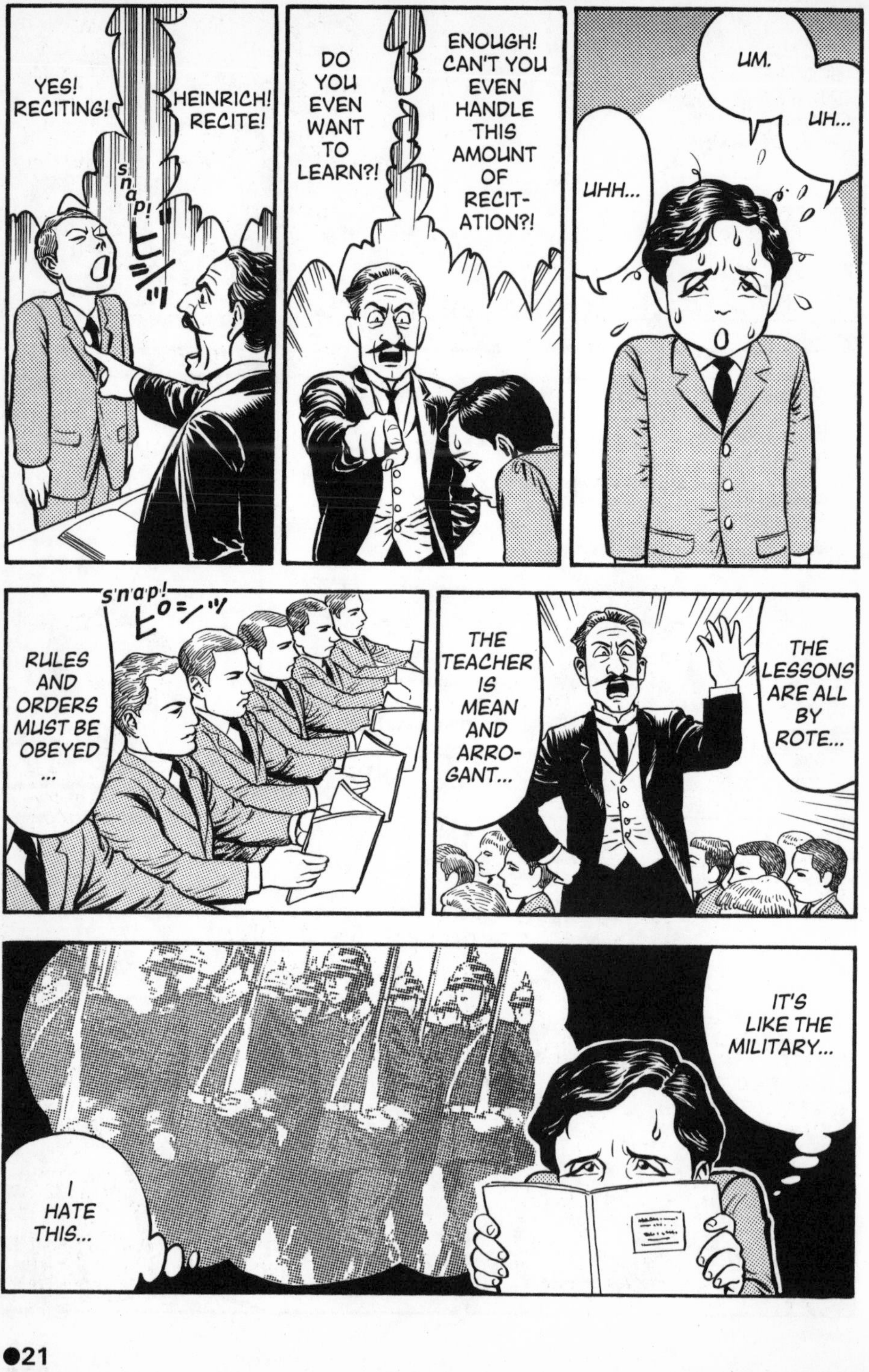
UM.
UH...
UHH...
ENOUGH! CAN'T YOU EVEN HANDLE THIS AMOUNT OF RECIT-ATION?!
DO YOU EVEN WANT TO LEARN?!
HEINRICH! RECITE!
YES! RECITING!
snap!
ビシッ
THE LESSONS ARE ALL BY ROTE...
THE TEACHER IS MEAN AND ARRO-GANT...
snap!
ピシッ
RULES AND ORDERS MUST BE OBEYED ...
IT'S LIKE THE MILITARY...
I HATE THIS...

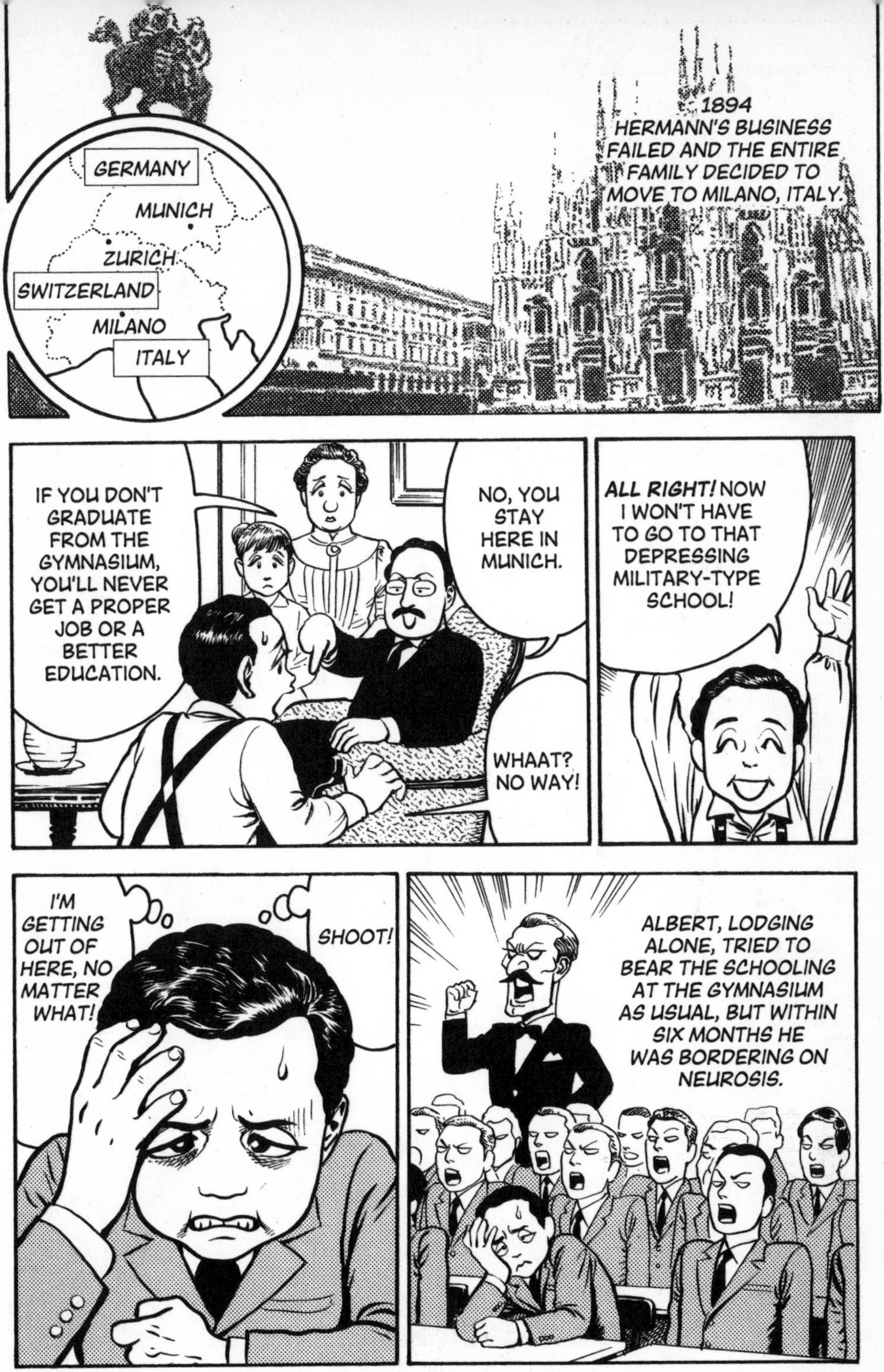
1894
HERMANN'S BUSINESS FAILED AND THE ENTIRE FAMILY DECIDED TO MOVE TO MILANO, ITALY.
GERMANY
MUNICH
ZURICH
SWITZERLAND
MILANO
ITALY
ALL RIGHT! NOW I WON'T HAVE TO GO TO THAT DEPRESSING MILITARY-TYPE SCHOOL!
NO, YOU STAY HERE IN MUNICH.
IF YOU DON'T GRADUATE FROM THE GYMNASIUM, YOU'LL NEVER GET A PROPER JOB OR A BETTER EDUCATION.
WHAAT? NO WAY!
ALBERT, LODGING ALONE, TRIED TO BEAR THE SCHOOLING AT THE GYMNASIUM AS USUAL, BUT WITHIN SIX MONTHS HE WAS BORDERING ON NEUROSIS.
SHOOT!
I'M GETTING OUT OF HERE, NO MATTER WHAT!

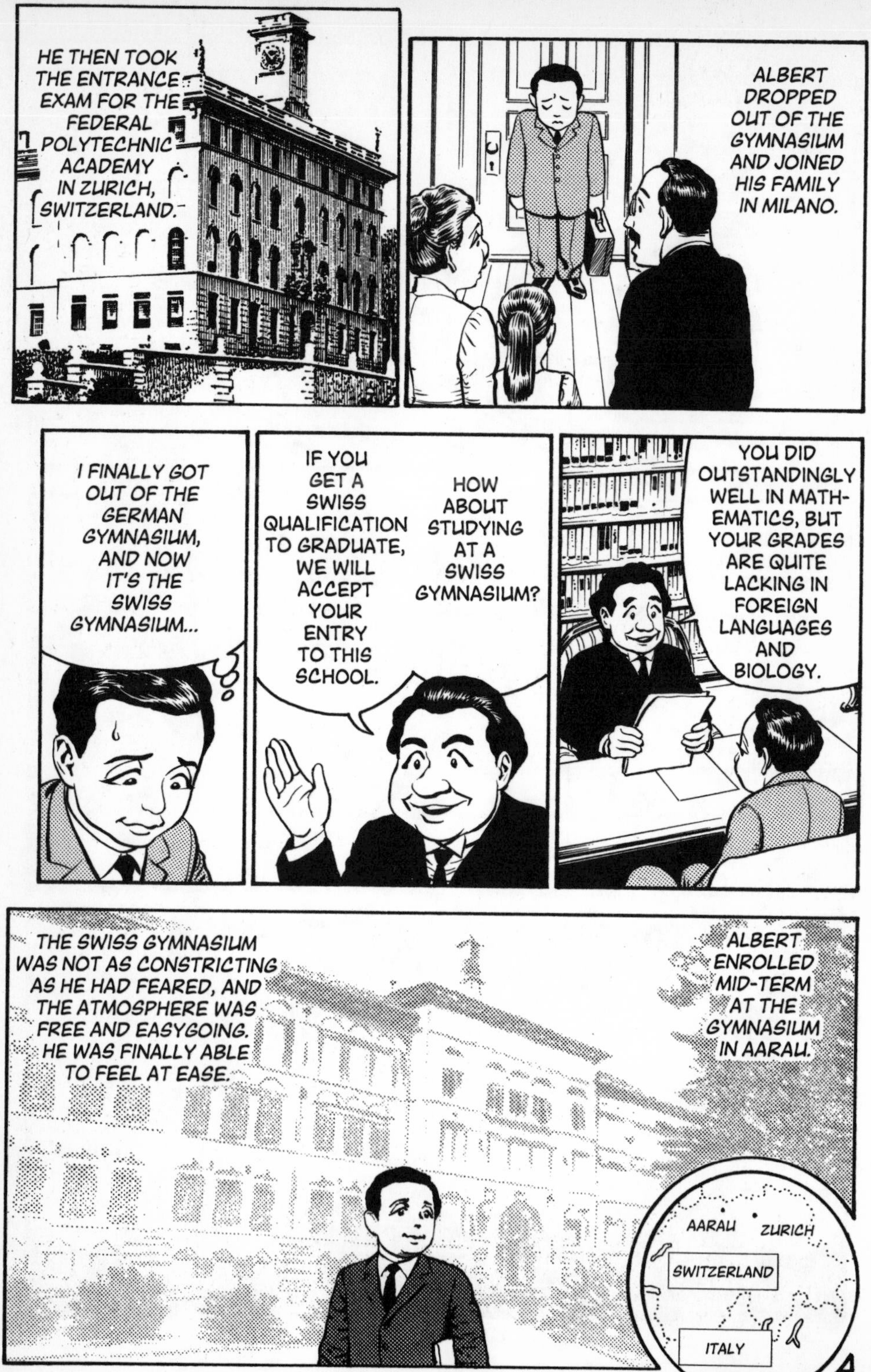
ALBERT DROPPED OUT OF THE GYMNASIUM AND JOINED HIS FAMILY IN MILANO.
HE THEN TOOK THE ENTRANCE EXAM FOR THE FEDERAL POLYTECHNIC ACADEMY IN ZURICH, SWITZERLAND.
YOU DID OUTSTANDINGLY WELL IN MATH-EMATICS, BUT YOUR GRADES ARE QUITE LACKING IN FOREIGN LANGUAGES AND BIOLOGY.
HOW ABOUT STUDYING AT A SWISS GYMNASIUM?
IF YOU GET A SWISS QUALIFICATION TO GRADUATE, WE WILL ACCEPT YOUR ENTRY TO THIS SCHOOL.
I FINALLY GOT OUT OF THE GERMAN GYMNASIUM, AND NOW IT'S THE SWISS GYMNASIUM...
ALBERT ENROLLED MID-TERM AT THE GYMNASIUM IN AARAU.
THE SWISS GYMNASIUM WAS NOT AS CONSTRICTING AS HE HAD FEARED, AND THE ATMOSPHERE WAS FREE AND EASYGOING. HE WAS FINALLY ABLE TO FEEL AT EASE.
AARAU
ZURICH
SWITZERLAND
ITALY
MILANO

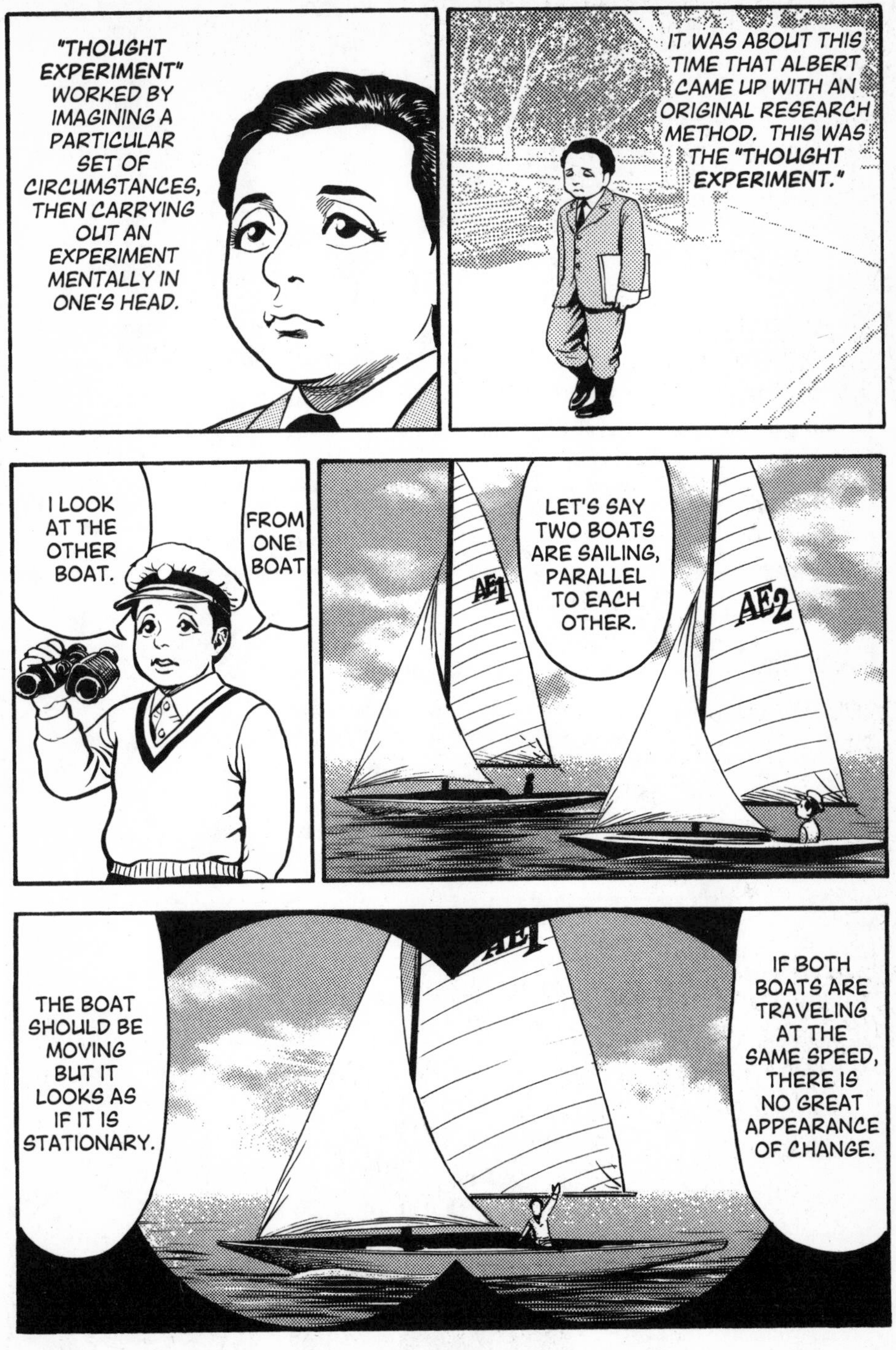
IT WAS ABOUT THIS TIME THAT ALBERT CAME UP WITH AN ORIGINAL RESEARCH METHOD. THIS WAS THE "THOUGHT EXPERIMENT."
"THOUGHT EXPERIMENT" WORKED BY IMAGINING A PARTICULAR SET OF CIRCUMSTANCES, THEN CARRYING OUT AN EXPERIMENT MENTALLY IN ONE'S HEAD.
LET'S SAY TWO BOATS ARE SAILING, PARALLEL TO EACH OTHER.
AE2
AE1
FROM ONE BOAT
I LOOK AT THE OTHER BOAT.
IF BOTH BOATS ARE TRAVELING AT THE SAME SPEED, THERE IS NO GREAT APPEARANCE OF CHANGE.
THE BOAT SHOULD BE MOVING BUT IT LOOKS AS IF IT IS STATIONARY.

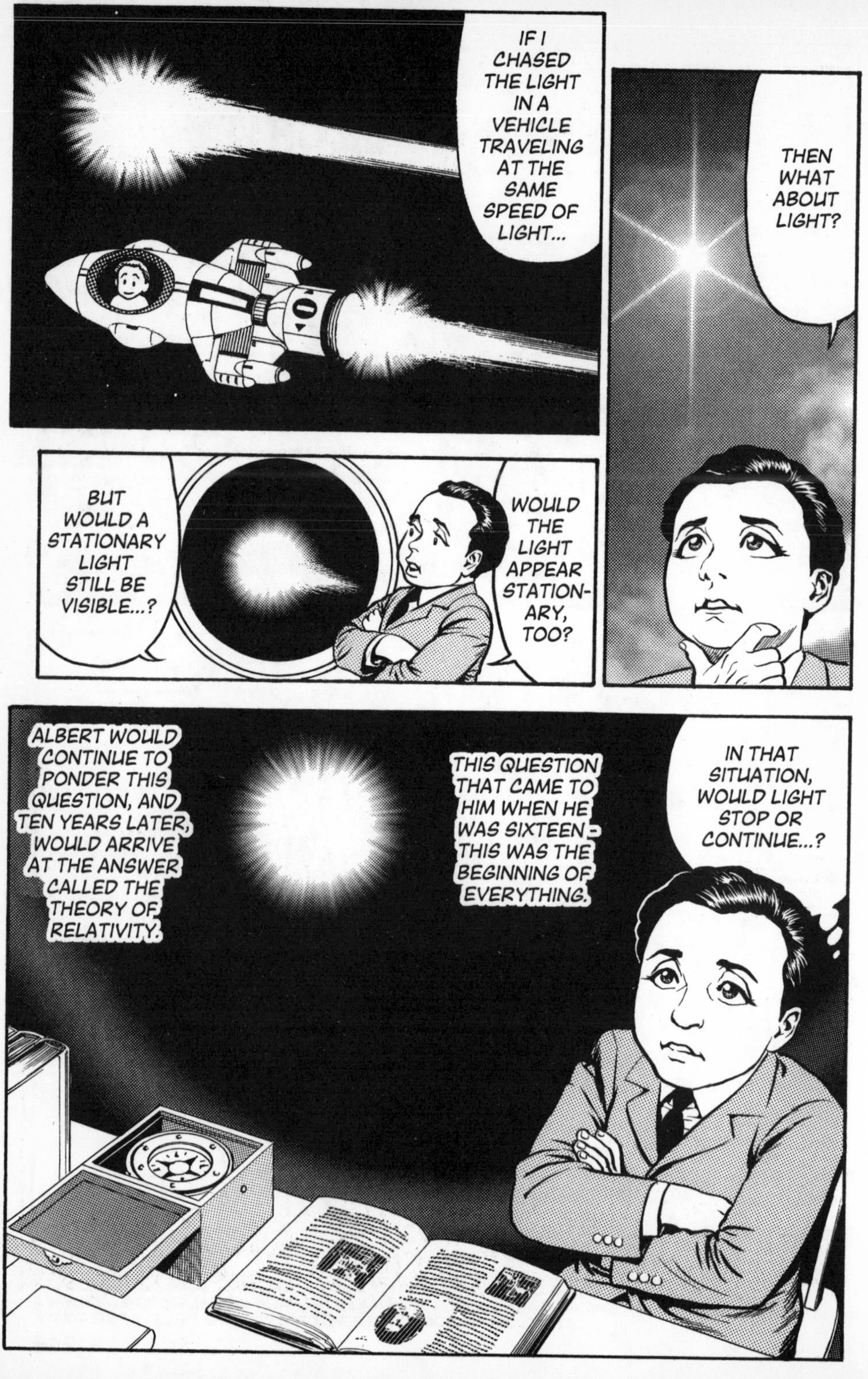
THEN WHAT ABOUT LIGHT?
IF I CHASED THE LIGHT IN A VEHICLE TRAVELING AT THE SAME SPEED OF LIGHT...
WOULD THE LIGHT APPEAR STATION-ARY, TOO?
BUT WOULD A STATIONARY LIGHT STILL BE VISIBLE...?
IN THAT SITUATION, WOULD LIGHT STOP OR CONTINUE...?
THIS QUESTION THAT CAME TO HIM WHEN HE WAS SIXTEEN - THIS WAS THE BEGINNING OF EVERYTHING.
ALBERT WOULD CONTINUE TO PONDER THIS QUESTION, AND TEN YEARS LATER, WOULD ARRIVE AT THE ANSWER CALLED THE THEORY OF RELATIVITY.

CHAPTER 2

DAYS OF OBSCURITY

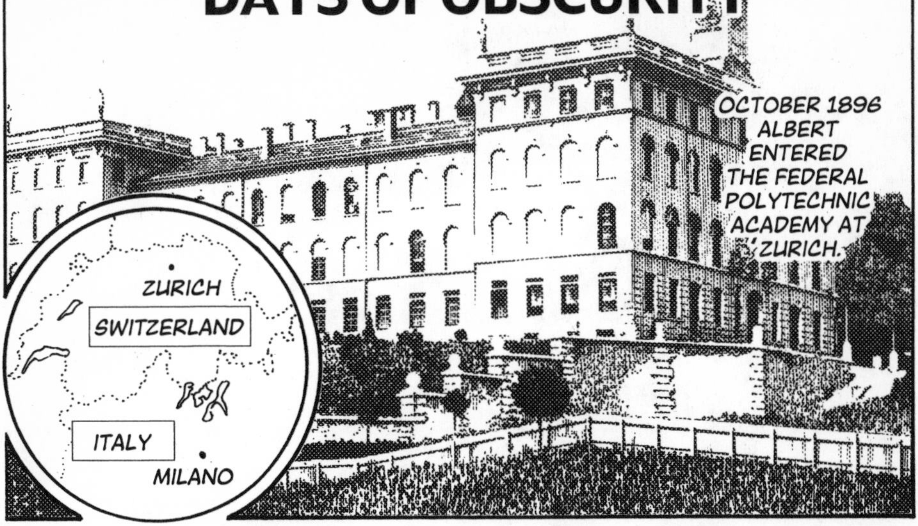
OCTOBER 1896 ALBERT ENTERED THE FEDERAL POLYTECHNIC ACADEMY AT ZURICH.
ZURICH
SWITZERLAND
ITALY
MILANO

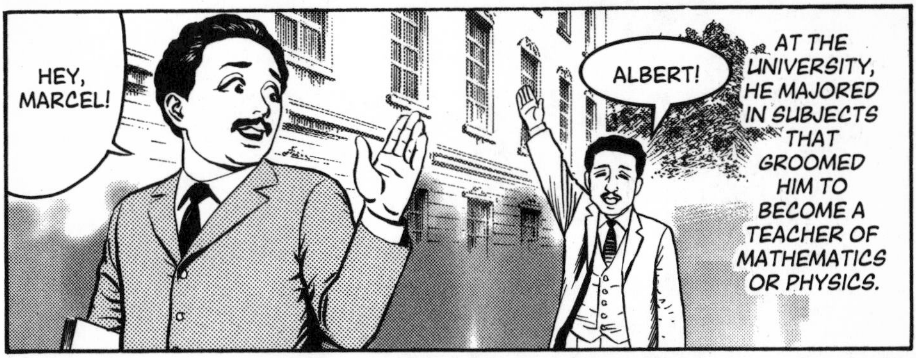
AT THE UNIVERSITY, HE MAJORED IN SUBJECTS THAT GROOMED HIM TO BECOME A TEACHER OF MATHEMATICS OR PHYSICS.
ALBERT!
HEY, MARCEL!

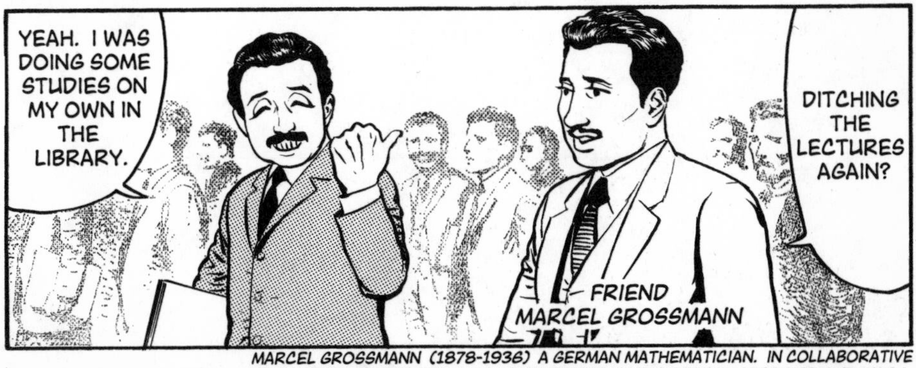
DITCHING THE LECTURES AGAIN?
FRIEND MARCEL GROSSMANN
YEAH. I WAS DOING SOME STUDIES ON MY OWN IN THE LIBRARY.

MARCEL GROSSMANN (1878-1936) A GERMAN MATHEMATICIAN. IN COLLABORATIVE THEORIES WITH EINSTEIN, HE HANDLED THE MATHEMATICAL SECTIONS, AND WAS A GREAT CONTRIBUTOR TO THE DEVELOPMENT OF THE THEORY OF RELATIVITY.

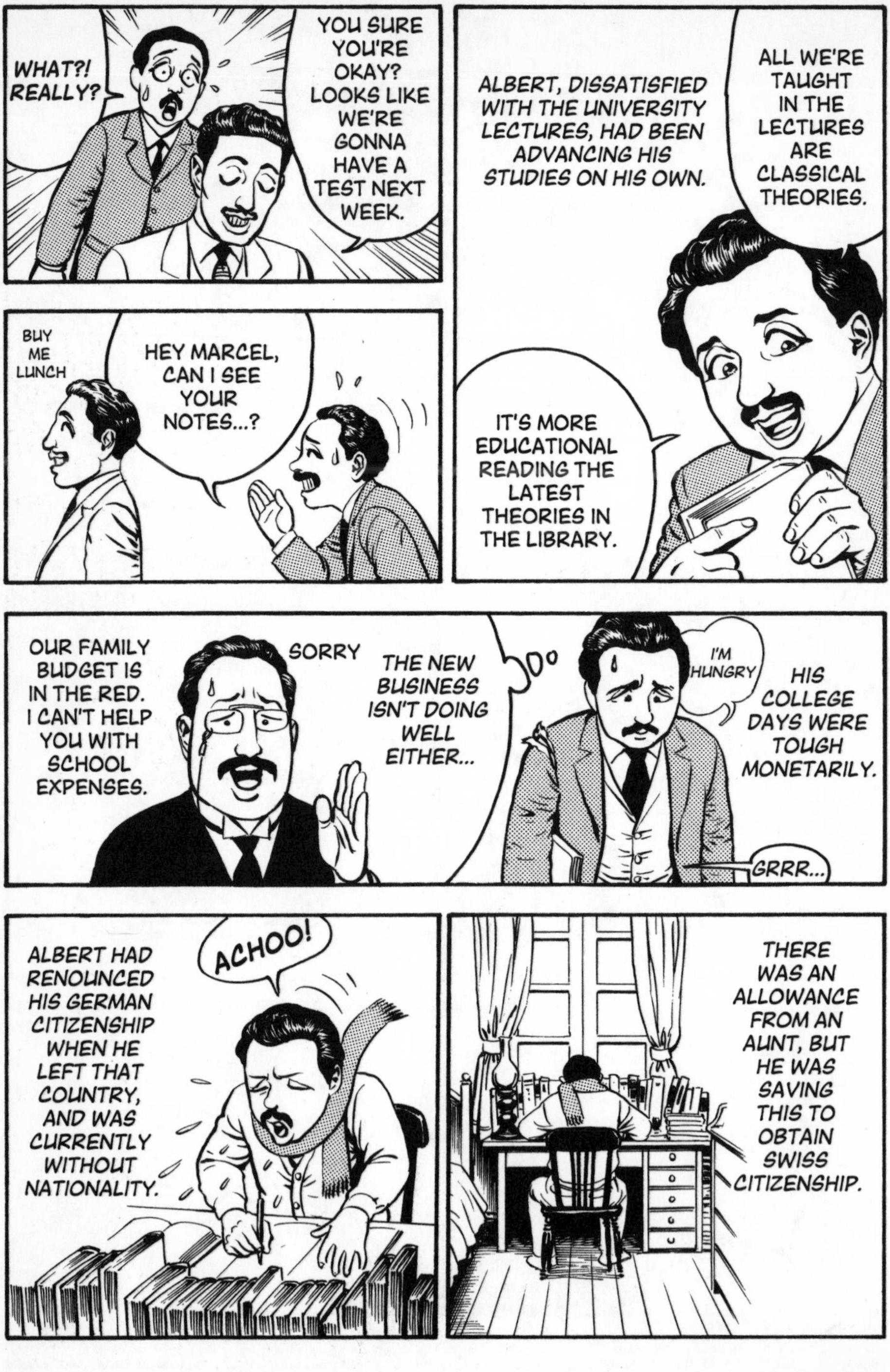
ALL WE'RE TAUGHT IN THE LECTURES ARE CLASSICAL THEORIES.
ALBERT, DISSATISFIED WITH THE UNIVERSITY LECTURES, HAD BEEN ADVANCING HIS STUDIES ON HIS OWN.
IT'S MORE EDUCATIONAL READING THE LATEST THEORIES IN THE LIBRARY.
YOU SURE YOU'RE OKAY? LOOKS LIKE WE'RE GONNA HAVE A TEST NEXT WEEK.
WHAT?! REALLY?
HEY MARCEL, CAN I SEE YOUR NOTES...?
BUY ME LUNCH
HIS COLLEGE DAYS WERE TOUGH MONETARILY.
I'M HUNGRY
GRRR...
THE NEW BUSINESS ISN'T DOING WELL EITHER...
SORRY
OUR FAMILY BUDGET IS IN THE RED. I CAN'T HELP YOU WITH SCHOOL EXPENSES.
THERE WAS AN ALLOWANCE FROM AN AUNT, BUT HE WAS SAVING THIS TO OBTAIN SWISS CITIZENSHIP.
ACHOO!
ALBERT HAD RENOUNCED HIS GERMAN CITIZENSHIP WHEN HE LEFT THAT COUNTRY, AND WAS CURRENTLY WITHOUT NATIONALITY.

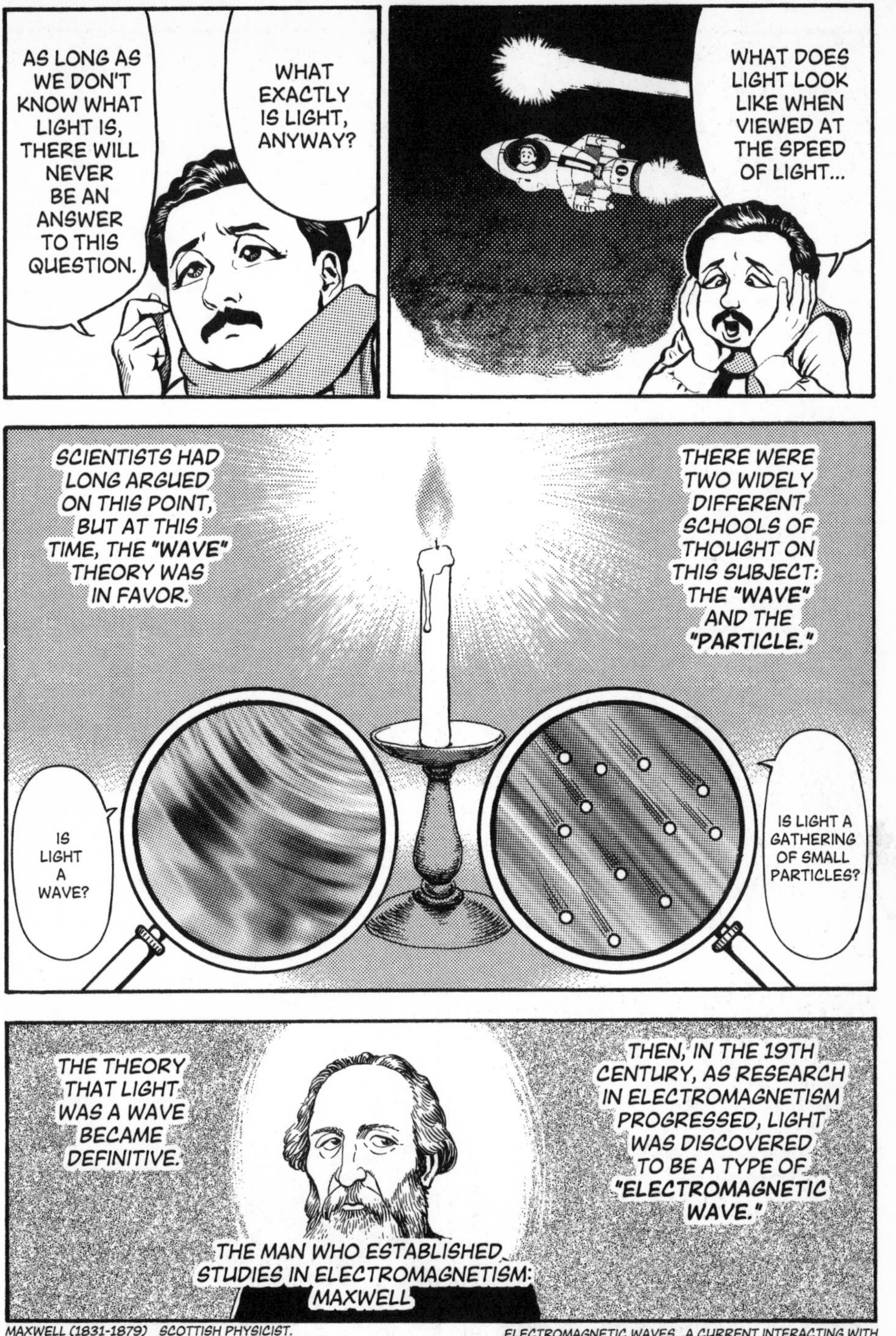
WHAT DOES LIGHT LOOK LIKE WHEN VIEWED AT THE SPEED OF LIGHT...
WHAT EXACTLY IS LIGHT, ANYWAY?
AS LONG AS WE DON'T KNOW WHAT LIGHT IS, THERE WILL NEVER BE AN ANSWER TO THIS QUESTION.
THERE WERE TWO WIDELY DIFFERENT SCHOOLS OF THOUGHT ON THIS SUBJECT: THE "WAVE" AND THE "PARTICLE."
SCIENTISTS HAD LONG ARGUED ON THIS POINT, BUT AT THIS TIME, THE "WAVE" THEORY WAS IN FAVOR.
IS LIGHT A GATHERING OF SMALL PARTICLES?
IS LIGHT A WAVE?
THEN, IN THE 19TH CENTURY, AS RESEARCH IN ELECTROMAGNETISM PROGRESSED, LIGHT WAS DISCOVERED TO BE A TYPE OF "ELECTROMAGNETIC WAVE."
THE THEORY THAT LIGHT WAS A WAVE BECAME DEFINITIVE.
THE MAN WHO ESTABLISHED STUDIES IN ELECTROMAGNETISM: MAXWELL

MAXWELL (1831-1879) SCOTTISH PHYSICIST. THE FOUNDER OF ELECTROMAGNETIC THEORY WHO DEMONSTRATED THAT ELECTRIC AND MAGNETIC FORCES,WHICH AT THE TIME WERE THOUGHT TO BE ENTIRELY SEPARATE, ARE TWO COMPLEMENTARY ASPECTS OF ELECTROMAGNETISM.

ELECTROMAGNETIC WAVES...A CURRENT INTERACTING WITH THE MAGNETIC FIELD, TRAVELING IN THE FORM OF OSCILLATING WAVES THROUGH SPACE. A GENERIC TERM FOR ELECTRICITY. OTHER EXAMPLES INCLUDE TELEVISION BROADCAST WAVES, ULTRAVIOLET RAYS, INFRARED RAYS AND X-RAYS.

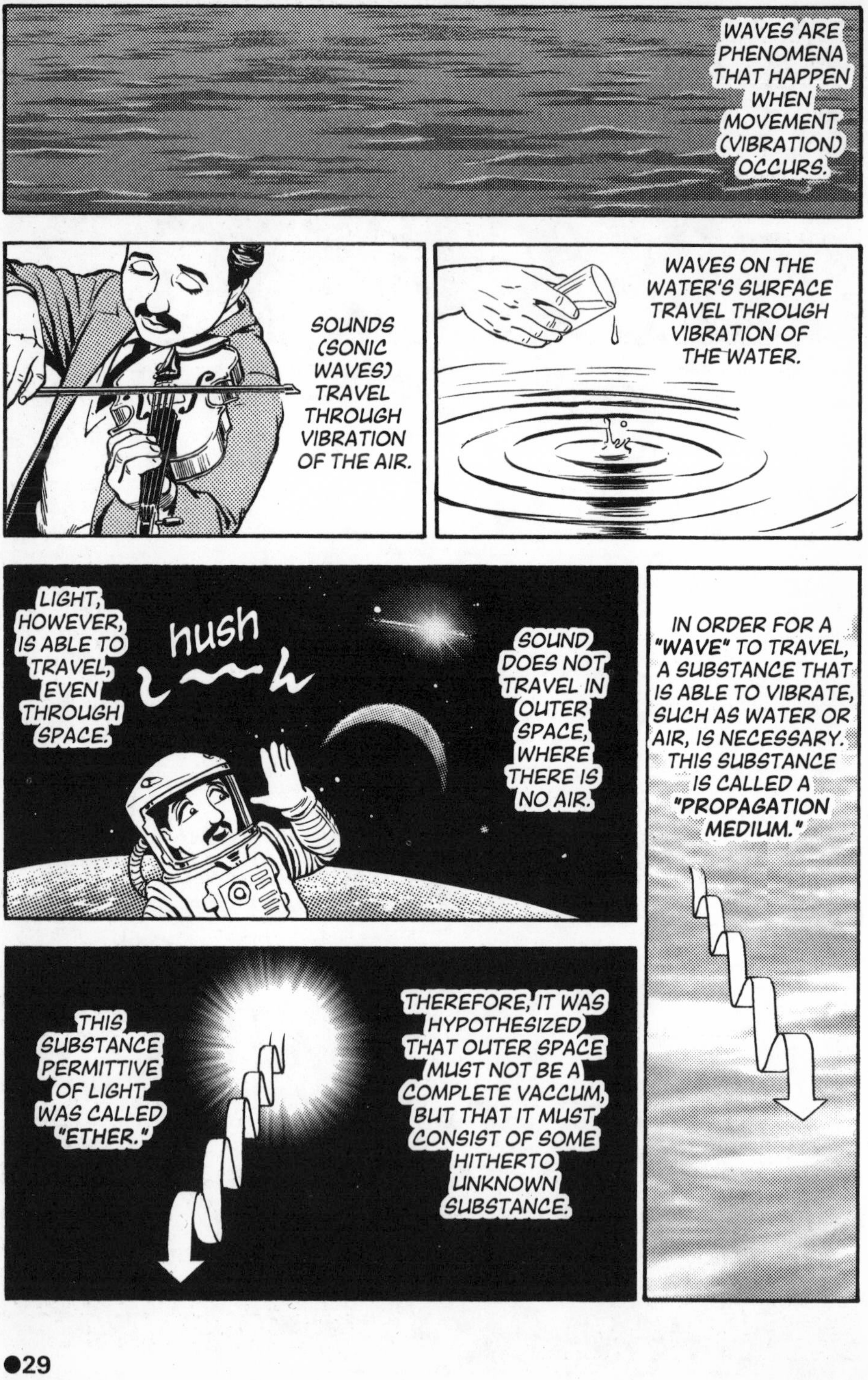
WAVES ARE PHENOMENA THAT HAPPEN WHEN MOVEMENT (VIBRATION) OCCURS.
WAVES ON THE WATER'S SURFACE TRAVEL THROUGH VIBRATION OF THE WATER.
SOUNDS (SONIC WAVES) TRAVEL THROUGH VIBRATION OF THE AIR.
IN ORDER FOR A "WAVE" TO TRAVEL, A SUBSTANCE THAT IS ABLE TO VIBRATE, SUCH AS WATER OR AIR, IS NECESSARY. THIS SUBSTANCE IS CALLED A "PROPAGATION MEDIUM."
SOUND DOES NOT TRAVEL IN OUTER SPACE, WHERE THERE IS NO AIR.
hush
LIGHT, HOWEVER, IS ABLE TO TRAVEL, EVEN THROUGH SPACE.
THEREFORE, IT WAS HYPOTHESIZED THAT OUTER SPACE MUST NOT BE A COMPLETE VACCUM, BUT THAT IT MUST CONSIST OF SOME HITHERTO UNKNOWN SUBSTANCE.
THIS SUBSTANCE PERMITTIVE OF LIGHT WAS CALLED "ETHER."

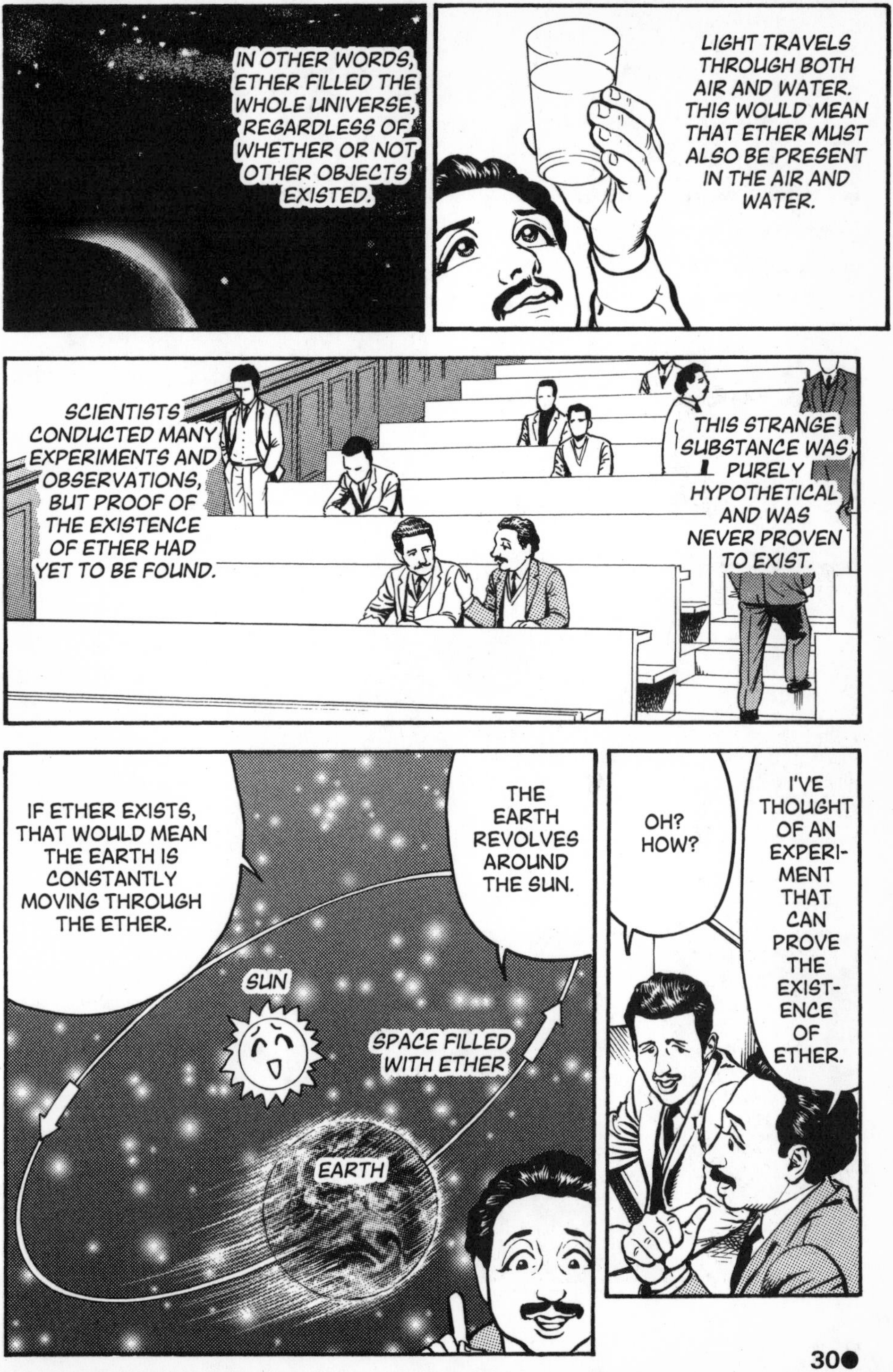
LIGHT TRAVELS THROUGH BOTH AIR AND WATER. THIS WOULD MEAN THAT ETHER MUST ALSO BE PRESENT IN THE AIR AND WATER.
IN OTHER WORDS, ETHER FILLED THE WHOLE UNIVERSE, REGARDLESS OF WHETHER OR NOT OTHER OBJECTS EXISTED.
THIS STRANGE SUBSTANCE WAS PURELY HYPOTHETICAL AND WAS NEVER PROVEN TO EXIST.
SCIENTISTS CONDUCTED MANY EXPERIMENTS AND OBSERVATIONS, BUT PROOF OF THE EXISTENCE OF ETHER HAD YET TO BE FOUND.
I'VE THOUGHT OF AN EXPERI-MENT THAT CAN PROVE THE EXIST-ENCE OF ETHER.
OH? HOW?
THE EARTH REVOLVES AROUND THE SUN.
IF ETHER EXISTS, THAT WOULD MEAN THE EARTH IS CONSTANTLY MOVING THROUGH THE ETHER.
SUN
SPACE FILLED WITH ETHER
EARTH

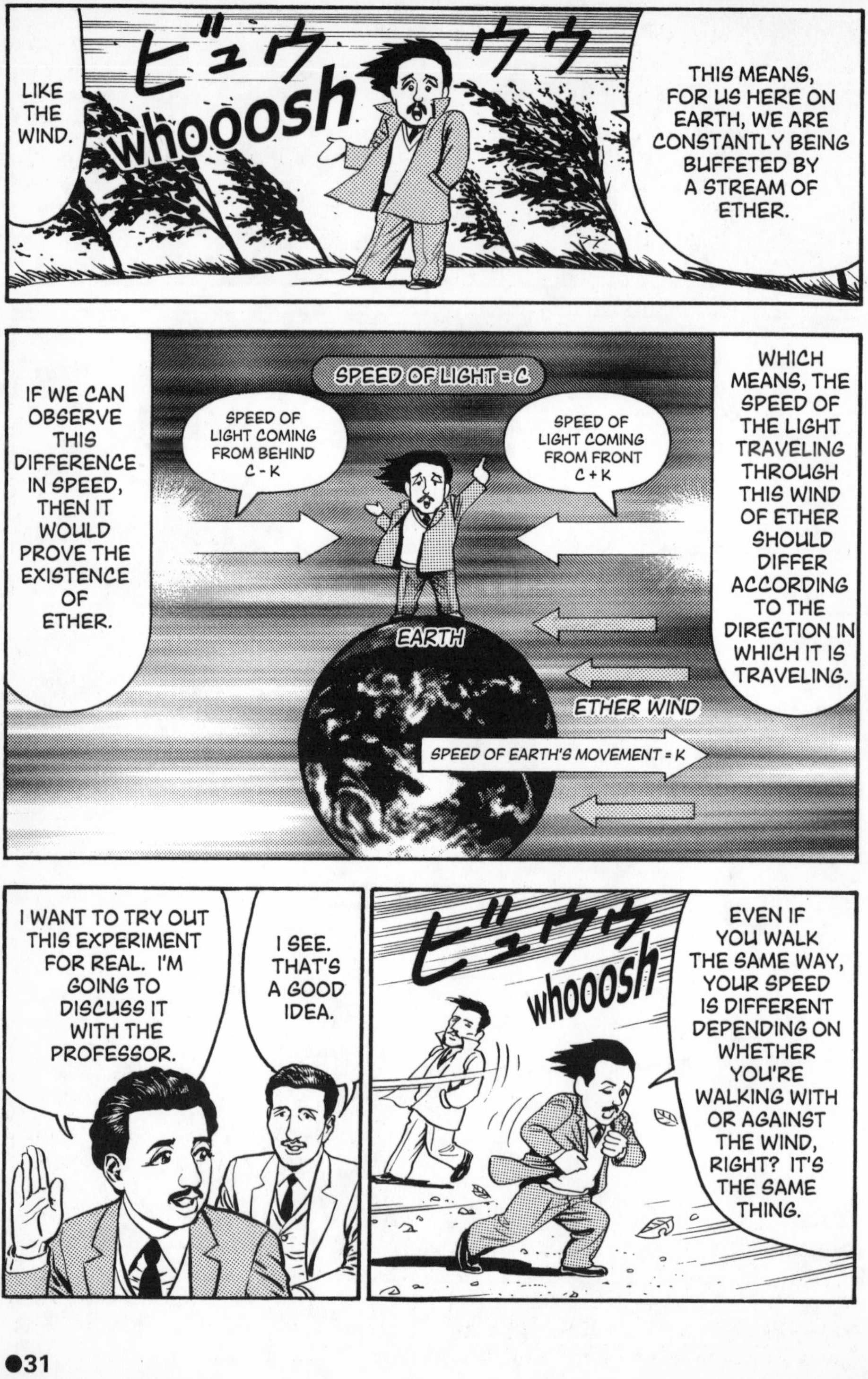
THIS MEANS, FOR US HERE ON EARTH, WE ARE CONSTANTLY BEING BUFFETED BY A STREAM OF ETHER.
ビュウ ウウ
whooosh
LIKE THE WIND.
WHICH MEANS, THE SPEED OF THE LIGHT TRAVELING THROUGH THIS WIND OF ETHER SHOULD DIFFER ACCORDING TO THE DIRECTION IN WHICH IT IS TRAVELING.
SPEED OF LIGHT = C
SPEED OF LIGHT COMING FROM FRONT C + K
SPEED OF LIGHT COMING FROM BEHIND C - K
EARTH
ETHER WIND
SPEED OF EARTH'S MOVEMENT = K
IF WE CAN OBSERVE THIS DIFFERENCE IN SPEED, THEN IT WOULD PROVE THE EXISTENCE OF ETHER.
ビュウウ
whooosh
EVEN IF YOU WALK THE SAME WAY, YOUR SPEED IS DIFFERENT DEPENDING ON WHETHER YOU'RE WALKING WITH OR AGAINST THE WIND, RIGHT? IT'S THE SAME THING.
I SEE. THAT'S A GOOD IDEA.
I WANT TO TRY OUT THIS EXPERIMENT FOR REAL. I'M GOING TO DISCUSS IT WITH THE PROFESSOR.

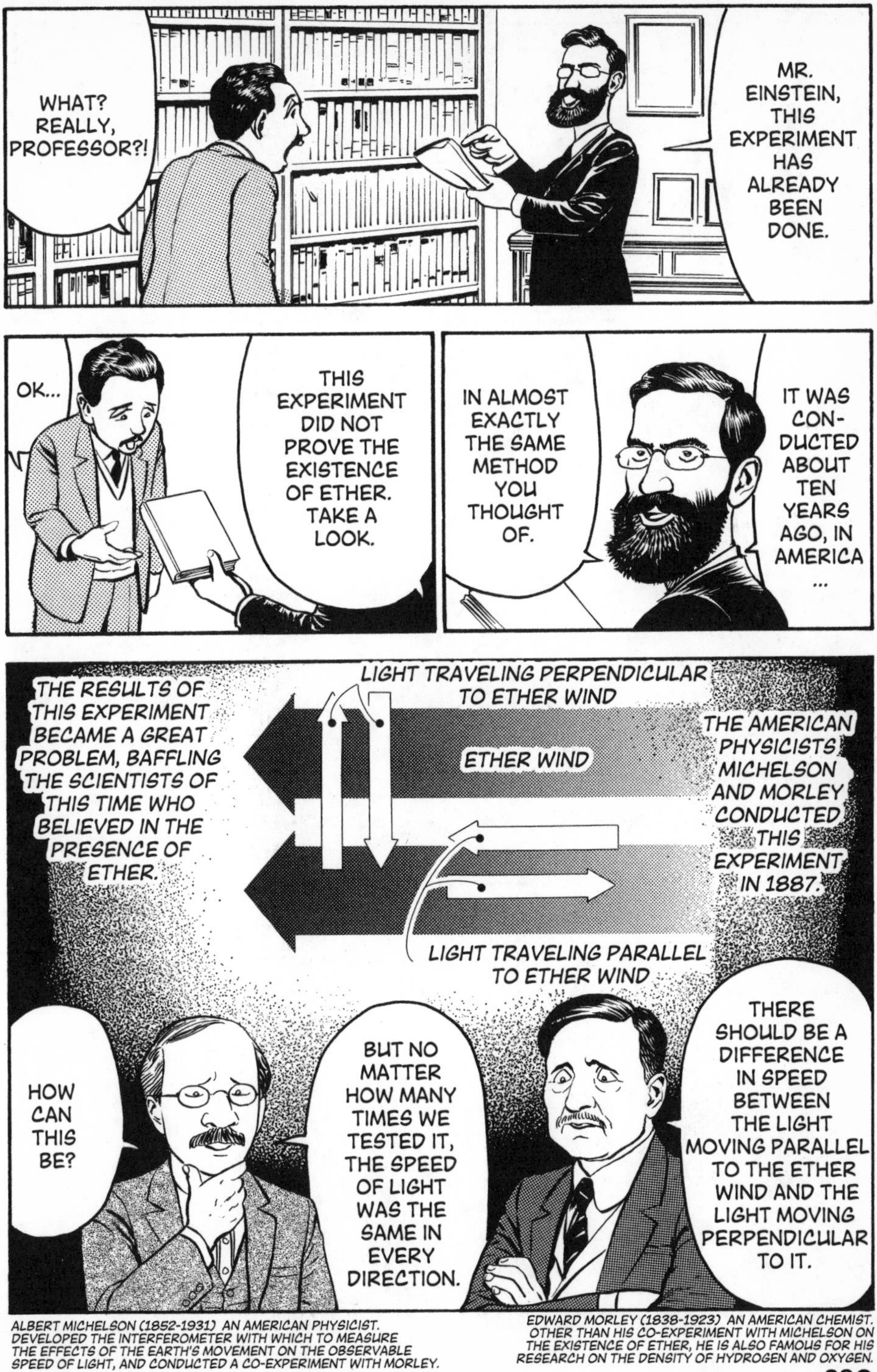
MR. EINSTEIN, THIS EXPERIMENT HAS ALREADY BEEN DONE.
WHAT? REALLY, PROFESSOR?!
IT WAS CON-DUCTED ABOUT TEN YEARS AGO, IN AMERICA ...
IN ALMOST EXACTLY THE SAME METHOD YOU THOUGHT OF.
THIS EXPERIMENT DID NOT PROVE THE EXISTENCE OF ETHER. TAKE A LOOK.
OK...
THE AMERICAN PHYSICISTS MICHELSON AND MORLEY CONDUCTED THIS EXPERIMENT IN 1887.
LIGHT TRAVELING PERPENDICULAR TO ETHER WIND
ETHER WIND
LIGHT TRAVELING PARALLEL TO ETHER WIND
THE RESULTS OF THIS EXPERIMENT BECAME A GREAT PROBLEM, BAFFLING THE SCIENTISTS OF THIS TIME WHO BELIEVED IN THE PRESENCE OF ETHER.
THERE SHOULD BE A DIFFERENCE IN SPEED BETWEEN THE LIGHT MOVING PARALLEL TO THE ETHER WIND AND THE LIGHT MOVING PERPENDICULAR TO IT.
BUT NO MATTER HOW MANY TIMES WE TESTED IT, THE SPEED OF LIGHT WAS THE SAME IN EVERY DIRECTION.
HOW CAN THIS BE?

ALBERT MICHELSON (1852-1931) AN AMERICAN PHYSICIST. DEVELOPED THE INTERFEROMETER WITH WHICH TO MEASURE THE EFFECTS OF THE EARTH'S MOVEMENT ON THE OBSERVABLE SPEED OF LIGHT, AND CONDUCTED A CO-EXPERIMENT WITH MORLEY.

EDWARD MORLEY (1838-1923) AN AMERICAN CHEMIST. OTHER THAN HIS CO-EXPERIMENT WITH MICHELSON ON THE EXISTENCE OF ETHER, HE IS ALSO FAMOUS FOR HIS RESEARCH ON THE DENSITY OF HYDROGEN AND OXYGEN.

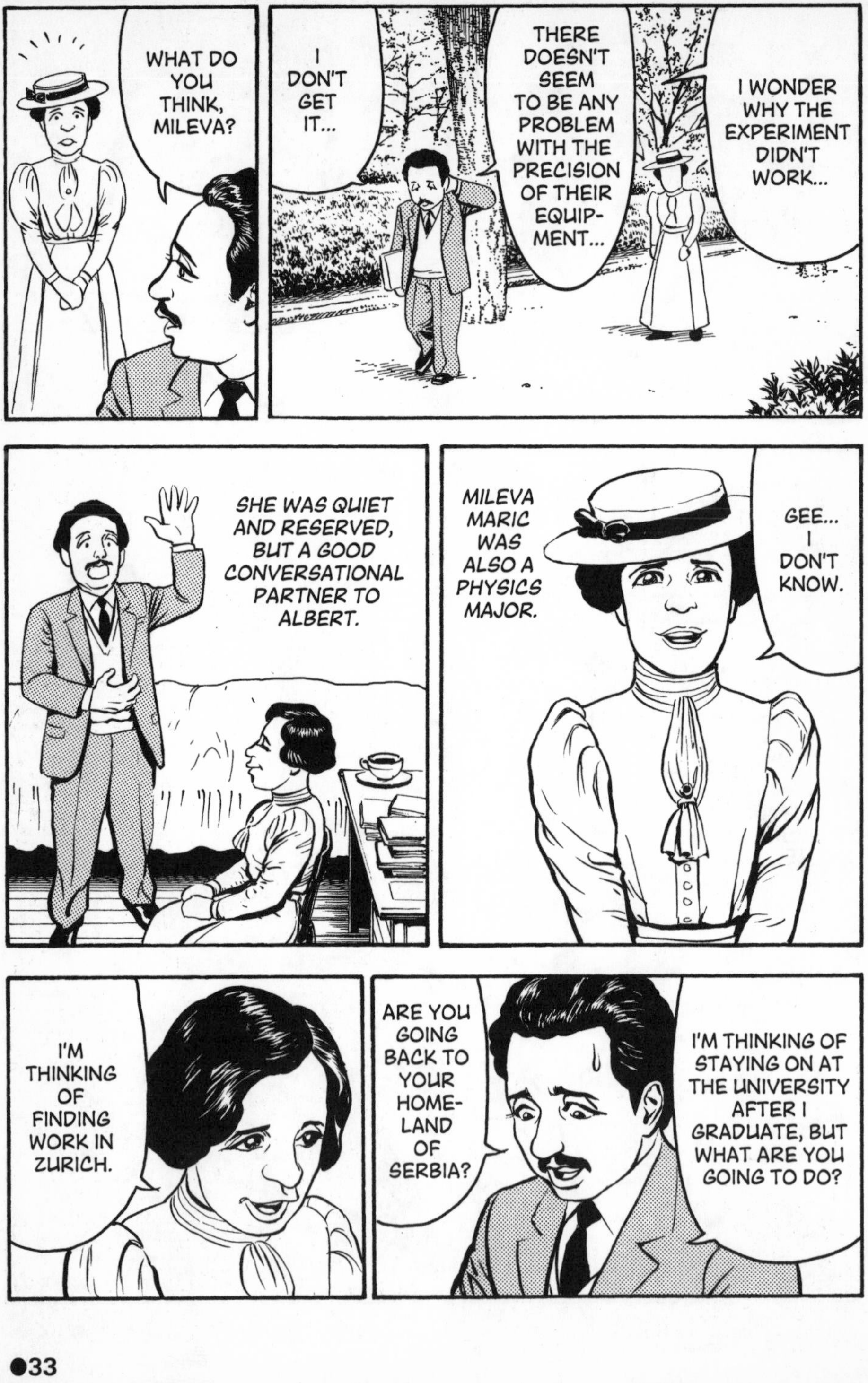
I WONDER WHY THE EXPERIMENT DIDN'T WORK...
THERE DOESN'T SEEM TO BE ANY PROBLEM WITH THE PRECISION OF THEIR EQUIP-MENT...
I DON'T GET IT...
WHAT DO YOU THINK, MILEVA?
GEE... I DON'T KNOW.
MILEVA MARIC WAS ALSO A PHYSICS MAJOR.
SHE WAS QUIET AND RESERVED, BUT A GOOD CONVERSATIONAL PARTNER TO ALBERT.
I'M THINKING OF STAYING ON AT THE UNIVERSITY AFTER I GRADUATE, BUT WHAT ARE YOU GOING TO DO?
ARE YOU GOING BACK TO YOUR HOME-LAND OF SERBIA?
I'M THINKING OF FINDING WORK IN ZURICH.

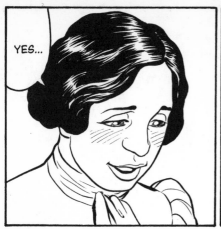

THEN I'LL SEE YOU AGAIN?
YOU WILL SEE ME AGAIN, WON'T YOU?
YES...
OH... GOOD...
fidget fidget
もじもじ
もじもじ
I KNOW!
LISTEN! I'LL DEDICATE A TUNE TO YOU.
THE TWO WOULD LATER MARRY.

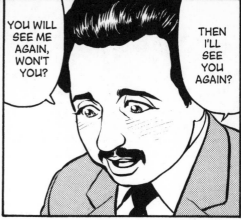

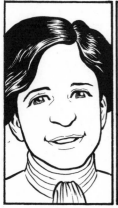

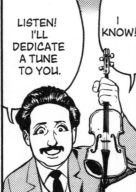

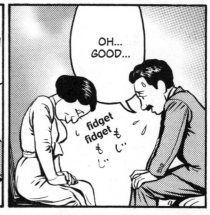

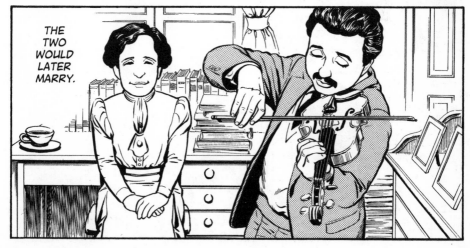

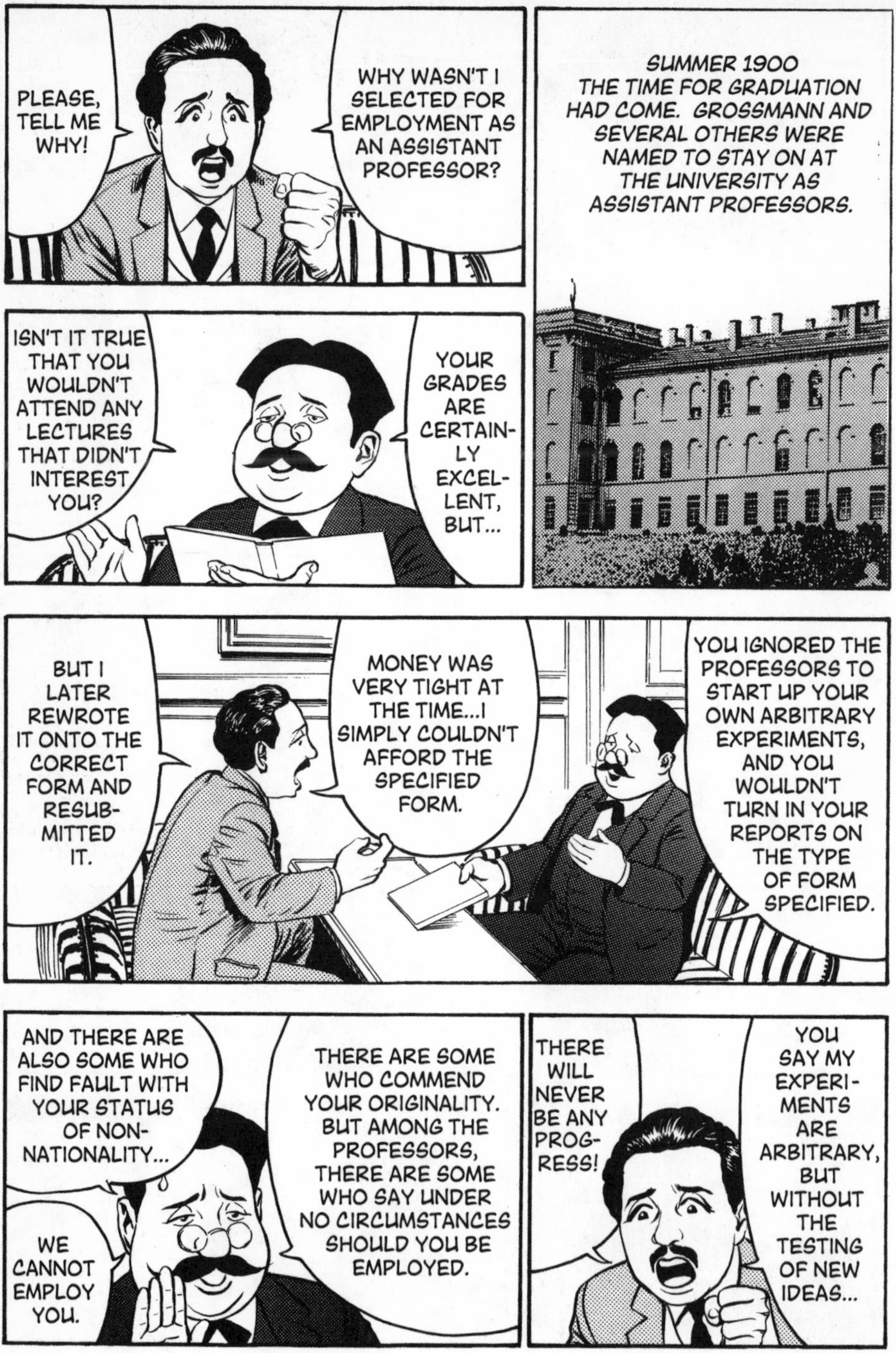
SUMMER 1900 THE TIME FOR GRADUATION HAD COME. GROSSMANN AND SEVERAL OTHERS WERE NAMED TO STAY ON AT THE UNIVERSITY AS ASSISTANT PROFESSORS.
WHY WASN'T I SELECTED FOR EMPLOYMENT AS AN ASSISTANT PROFESSOR?
PLEASE, TELL ME WHY!
YOUR GRADES ARE CERTAIN-LY EXCEL-LENT, BUT...
ISN'T IT TRUE THAT YOU WOULDN'T ATTEND ANY LECTURES THAT DIDN'T INTEREST YOU?
YOU IGNORED THE PROFESSORS TO START UP YOUR OWN ARBITRARY EXPERIMENTS, AND YOU WOULDN'T TURN IN YOUR REPORTS ON THE TYPE OF FORM SPECIFIED.
MONEY WAS VERY TIGHT AT THE TIME...I SIMPLY COULDN'T AFFORD THE SPECIFIED FORM.
BUT I LATER REWROTE IT ONTO THE CORRECT FORM AND RESUB-MITTED IT.
YOU SAY MY EXPERI-MENTS ARE ARBITRARY, BUT WITHOUT THE TESTING OF NEW IDEAS...
THERE WILL NEVER BE ANY PROG-RESS!
THERE ARE SOME WHO COMMEND YOUR ORIGINALITY. BUT AMONG THE PROFESSORS, THERE ARE SOME WHO SAY UNDER NO CIRCUMSTANCES SHOULD YOU BE EMPLOYED.
AND THERE ARE ALSO SOME WHO FIND FAULT WITH YOUR STATUS OF NON-NATIONALITY...
WE CANNOT EMPLOY YOU.

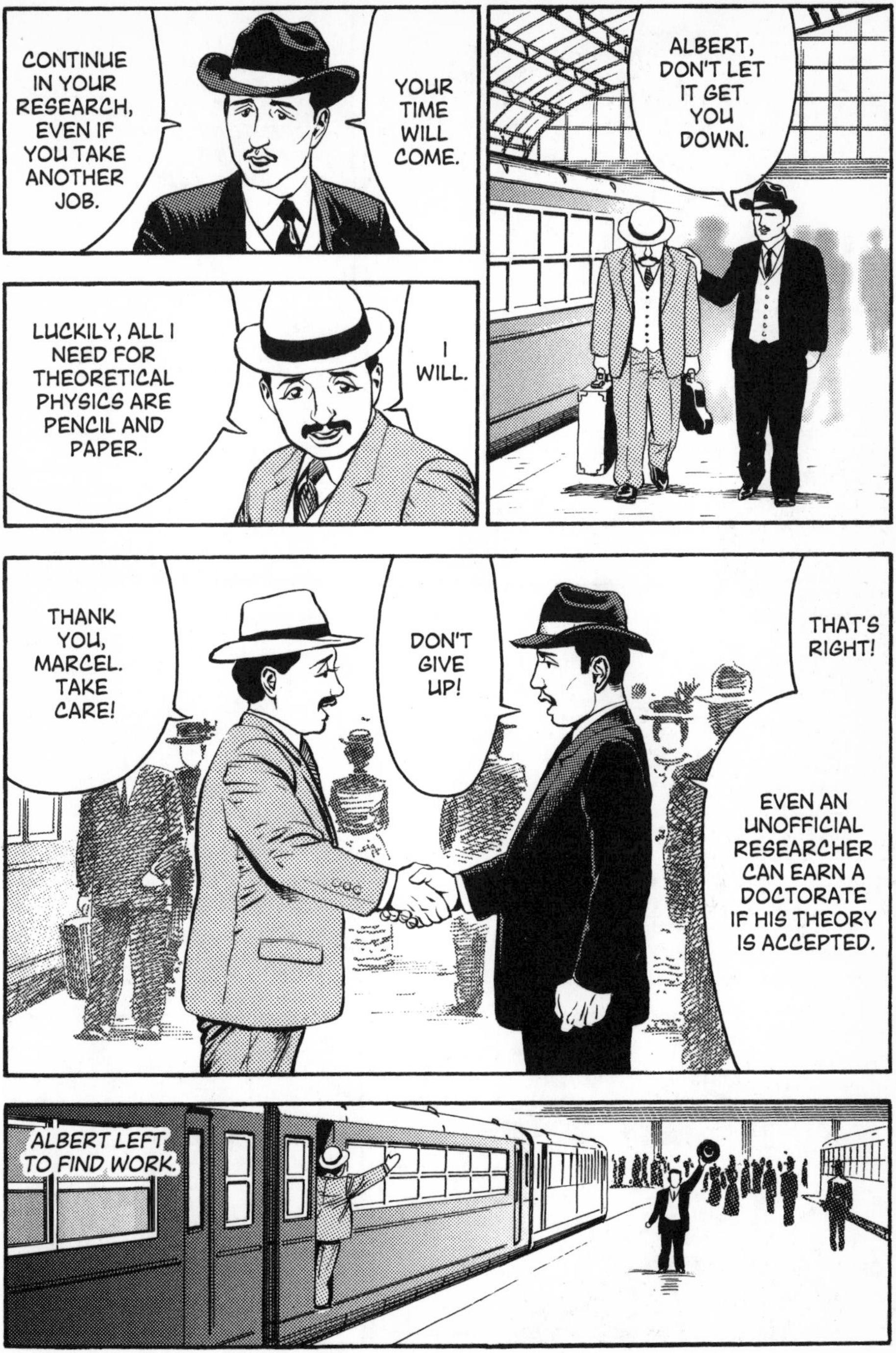
ALBERT, DON'T LET IT GET YOU DOWN.
YOUR TIME WILL COME.
CONTINUE IN YOUR RESEARCH, EVEN IF YOU TAKE ANOTHER JOB.
I WILL.
LUCKILY, ALL I NEED FOR THEORETICAL PHYSICS ARE PENCIL AND PAPER.
THAT'S RIGHT!
EVEN AN UNOFFICIAL RESEARCHER CAN EARN A DOCTORATE IF HIS THEORY IS ACCEPTED.
DON'T GIVE UP!
THANK YOU, MARCEL. TAKE CARE!
ALBERT LEFT TO FIND WORK.

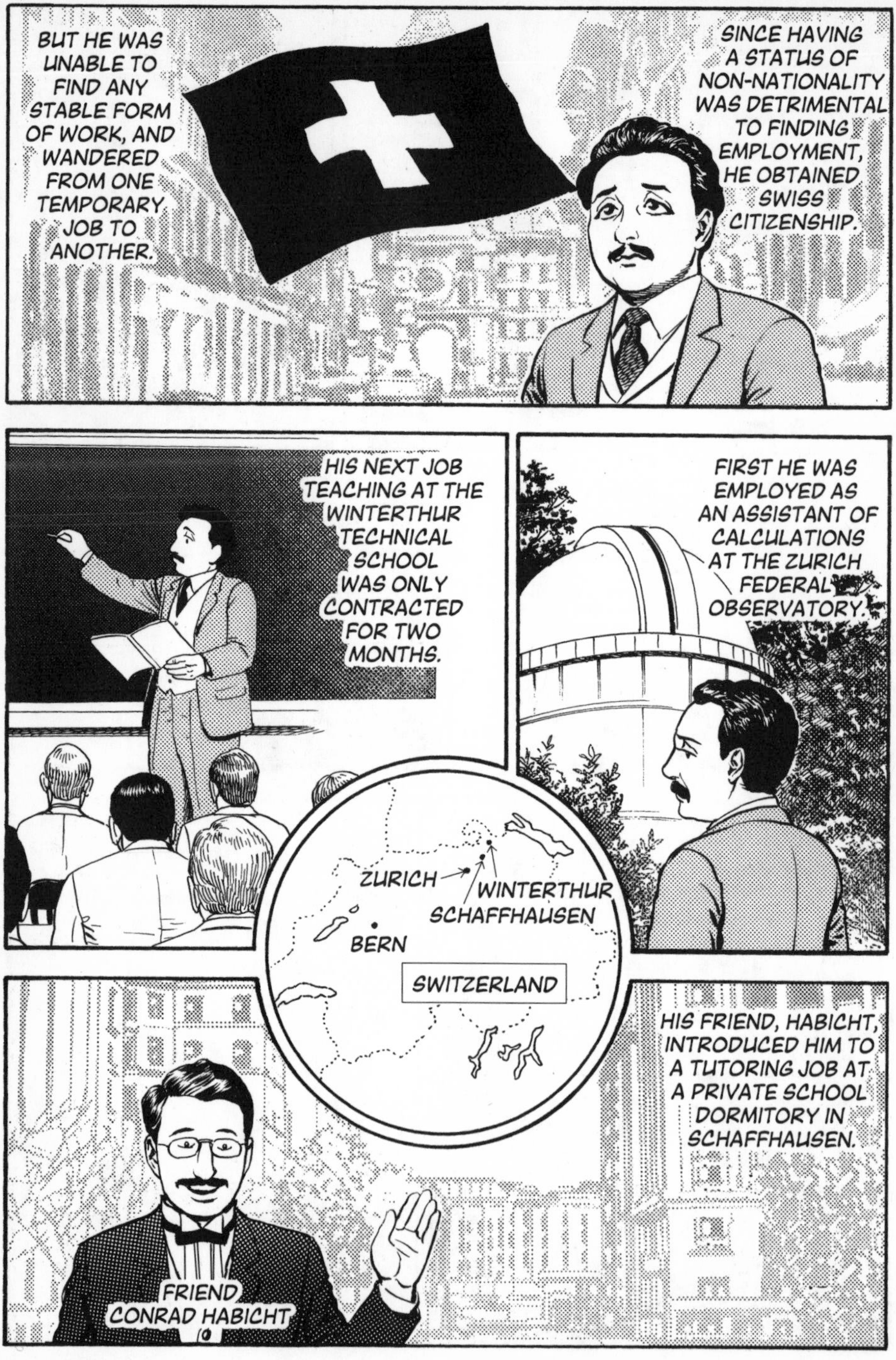
SINCE HAVING A STATUS OF NON-NATIONALITY WAS DETRIMENTAL TO FINDING EMPLOYMENT, HE OBTAINED SWISS CITIZENSHIP.
BUT HE WAS UNABLE TO FIND ANY STABLE FORM OF WORK, AND WANDERED FROM ONE TEMPORARY JOB TO ANOTHER.
FIRST HE WAS EMPLOYED AS AN ASSISTANT OF CALCULATIONS AT THE ZURICH FEDERAL OBSERVATORY.
HIS NEXT JOB TEACHING AT THE WINTERTHUR TECHNICAL SCHOOL WAS ONLY CONTRACTED FOR TWO MONTHS.
ZURICH
WINTERTHUR
SCHAFFHAUSEN
BERN
SWITZERLAND
HIS FRIEND, HABICHT, INTRODUCED HIM TO A TUTORING JOB AT A PRIVATE SCHOOL DORMITORY IN SCHAFFHAUSEN.
FRIEND CONRAD HABICHT

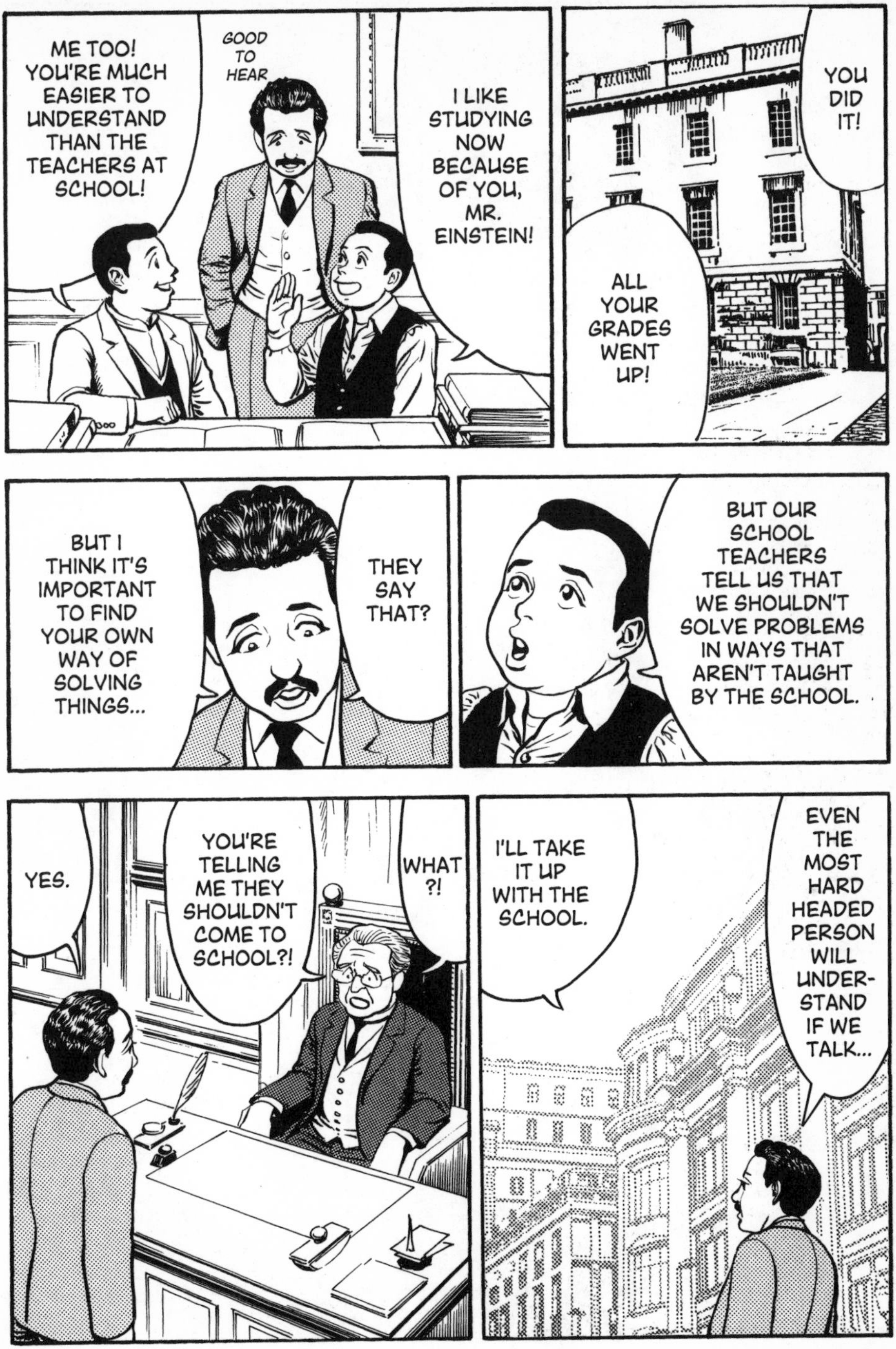
YOU DID IT!
ALL YOUR GRADES WENT UP!
I LIKE STUDYING NOW BECAUSE OF YOU, MR. EINSTEIN!
GOOD TO HEAR
ME TOO! YOU'RE MUCH EASIER TO UNDERSTAND THAN THE TEACHERS AT SCHOOL!
BUT OUR SCHOOL TEACHERS TELL US THAT WE SHOULDN'T SOLVE PROBLEMS IN WAYS THAT AREN'T TAUGHT BY THE SCHOOL.
THEY SAY THAT?
BUT I THINK IT'S IMPORTANT TO FIND YOUR OWN WAY OF SOLVING THINGS...
EVEN THE MOST HARD HEADED PERSON WILL UNDER-STAND IF WE TALK...
I'LL TAKE IT UP WITH THE SCHOOL.
WHAT?!
YOU'RE TELLING ME THEY SHOULDN'T COME TO SCHOOL?!
YES.

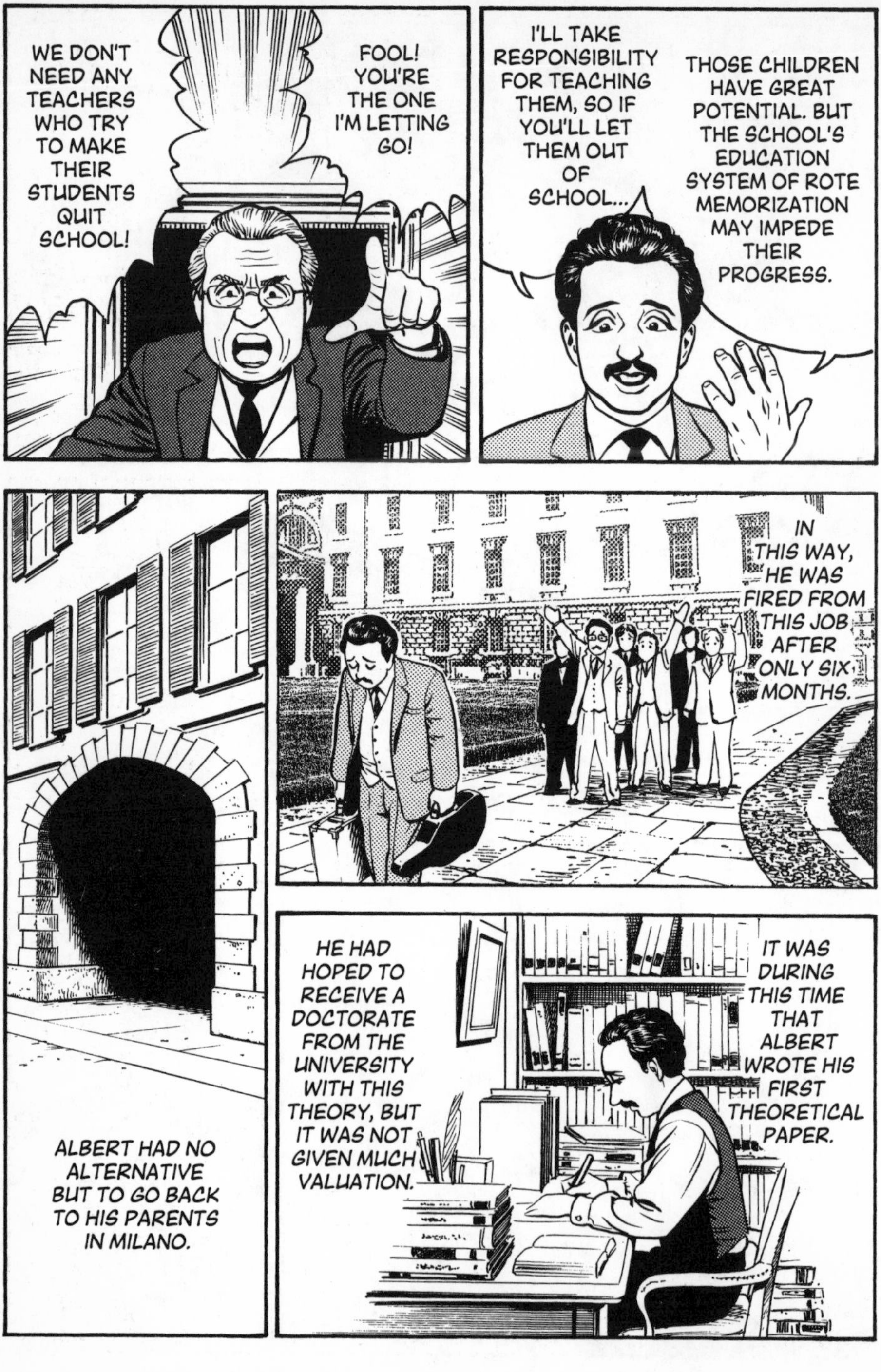
THOSE CHILDREN HAVE GREAT POTENTIAL. BUT THE SCHOOL'S EDUCATION SYSTEM OF ROTE MEMORIZATION MAY IMPEDE THEIR PROGRESS.
I'LL TAKE RESPONSIBILITY FOR TEACHING THEM, SO IF YOU'LL LET THEM OUT OF SCHOOL...
FOOL! YOU'RE THE ONE I'M LETTING GO!
WE DON'T NEED ANY TEACHERS WHO TRY TO MAKE THEIR STUDENTS QUIT SCHOOL!
IN THIS WAY, HE WAS FIRED FROM THIS JOB AFTER ONLY SIX MONTHS.
IT WAS DURING THIS TIME THAT ALBERT WROTE HIS FIRST THEORETICAL PAPER.
HE HAD HOPED TO RECEIVE A DOCTORATE FROM THE UNIVERSITY WITH THIS THEORY, BUT IT WAS NOT GIVEN MUCH VALUATION.
ALBERT HAD NO ALTERNATIVE BUT TO GO BACK TO HIS PARENTS IN MILANO.

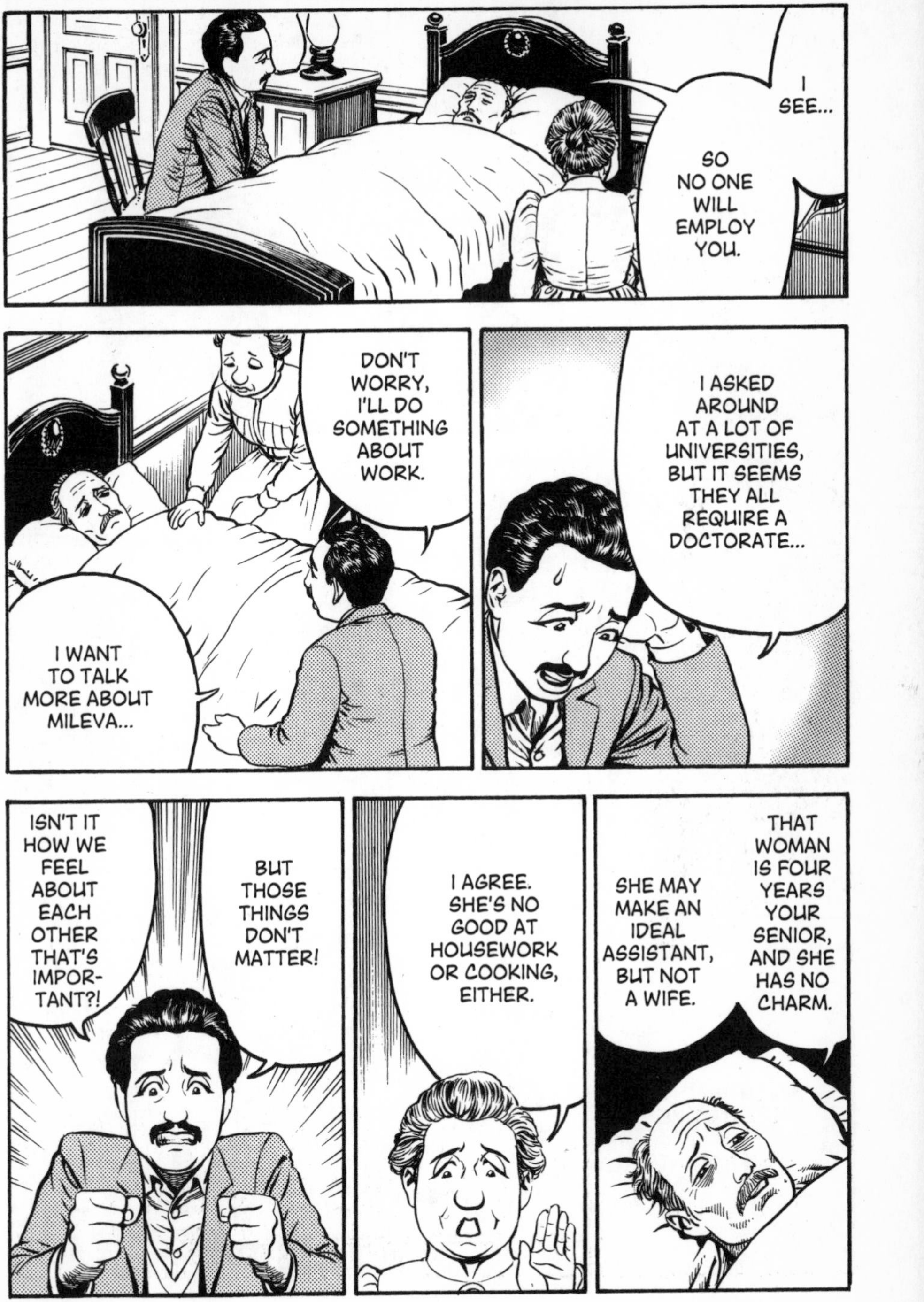
I SEE...
SO NO ONE WILL EMPLOY YOU.
I ASKED AROUND AT A LOT OF UNIVERSITIES, BUT IT SEEMS THEY ALL REQUIRE A DOCTORATE...
DON'T WORRY, I'LL DO SOMETHING ABOUT WORK.
I WANT TO TALK MORE ABOUT MILEVA...
THAT WOMAN IS FOUR YEARS YOUR SENIOR, AND SHE HAS NO CHARM.
SHE MAY MAKE AN IDEAL ASSISTANT, BUT NOT A WIFE.
I AGREE. SHE'S NO GOOD AT HOUSEWORK OR COOKING, EITHER.
BUT THOSE THINGS DON'T MATTER!
ISN'T IT HOW WE FEEL ABOUT EACH OTHER THAT'S IMPORTANT?!

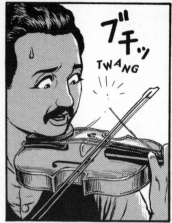

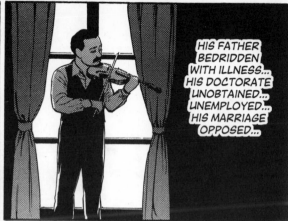

HIS FATHER BEDRIDDEN WITH ILLNESS... HIS DOCTORATE UNOBTAINED... UNEMPLOYED... HIS MARRIAGE OPPOSED...
ブチッ
TWANG
THE FUTURE WAS BLEAK -
SWISS FEDERAL PATENT OFFICE
HM... IS HE THAT GOOD?
THIS MAN EINSTEIN...
PATENT OFFICE DIRECTOR FRIEDRICH HARREL

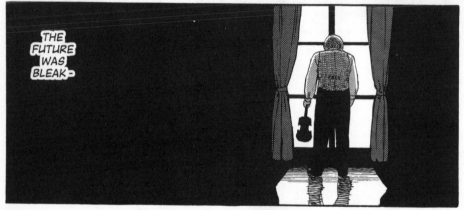

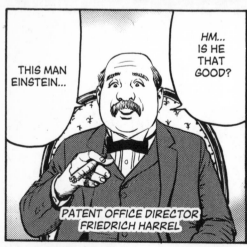

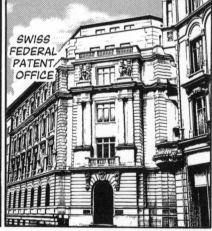

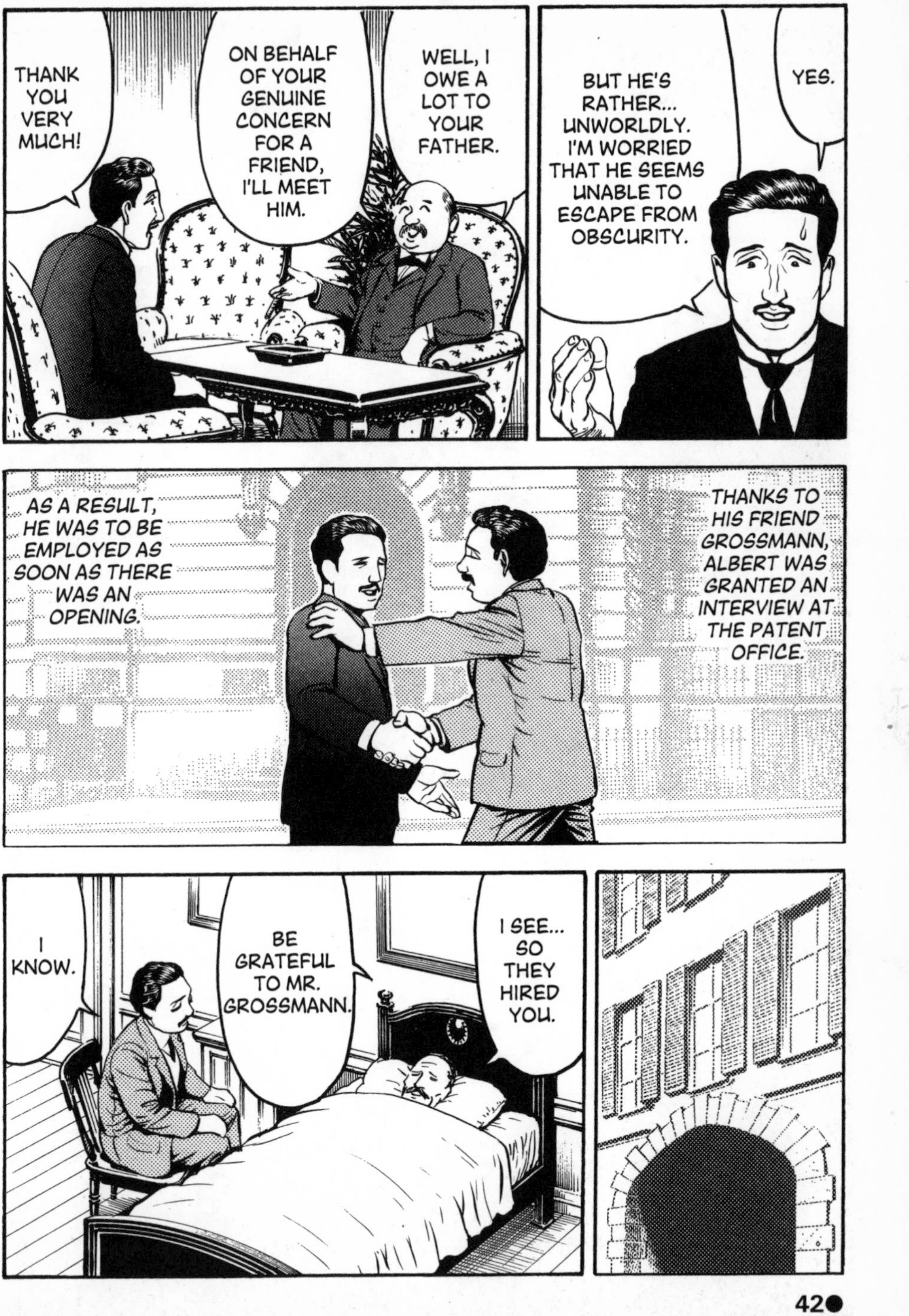
YES.
BUT HE'S RATHER... UNWORLDLY. I'M WORRIED THAT HE SEEMS UNABLE TO ESCAPE FROM OBSCURITY.
WELL, I OWE A LOT TO YOUR FATHER.
ON BEHALF OF YOUR GENUINE CONCERN FOR A FRIEND, I'LL MEET HIM.
THANK YOU VERY MUCH!
THANKS TO HIS FRIEND GROSSMANN, ALBERT WAS GRANTED AN INTERVIEW AT THE PATENT OFFICE.
AS A RESULT, HE WAS TO BE EMPLOYED AS SOON AS THERE WAS AN OPENING.
I SEE... SO THEY HIRED YOU.
BE GRATEFUL TO MR. GROSSMANN.
I KNOW.

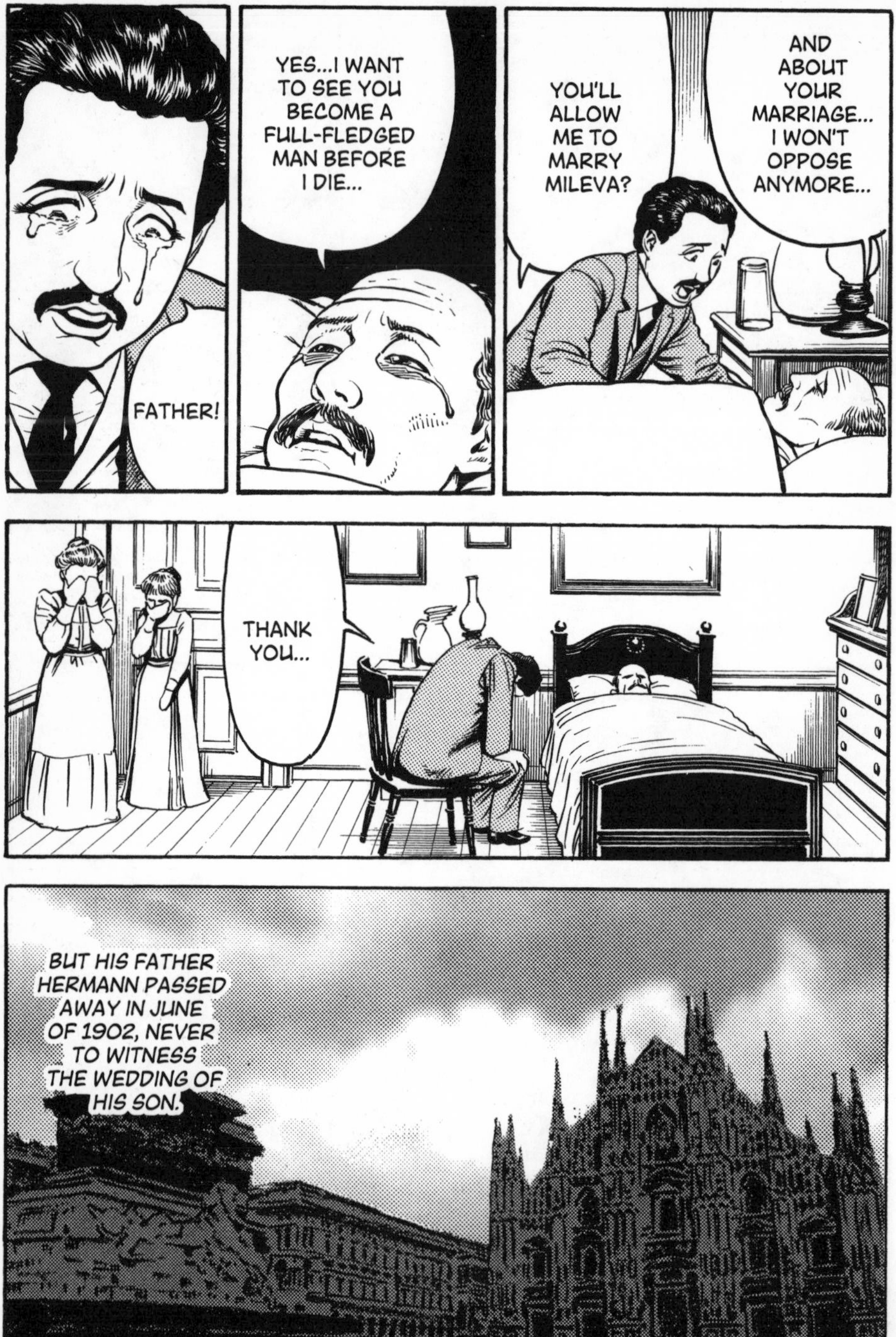
FATHER!
YES...I WANT TO SEE YOU BECOME A FULL-FLEDGED MAN BEFORE I DIE...
YOU'LL ALLOW ME TO MARRY MILEVA?
AND ABOUT YOUR MARRIAGE... I WON'T OPPOSE ANYMORE...
THANK YOU...
BUT HIS FATHER HERMANN PASSED AWAY IN JUNE OF 1902, NEVER TO WITNESS THE WEDDING OF HIS SON.

CHAPTER 3
OLYMPIA ACADEMY

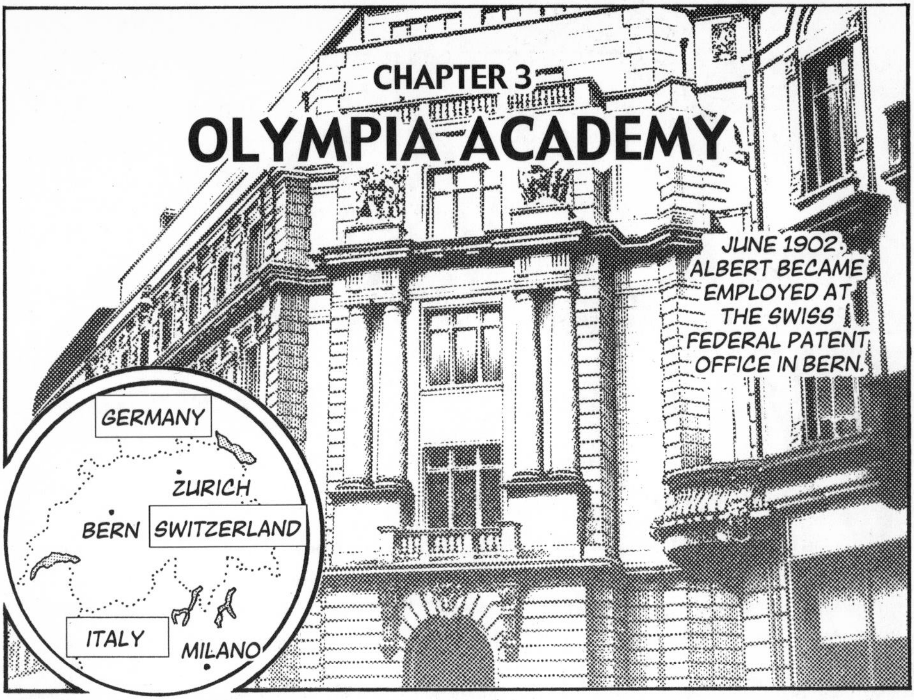

JUNE 1902. ALBERT BECAME EMPLOYED AT THE SWISS FEDERAL PATENT OFFICE IN BERN.
GERMANY
ZURICH
BERN
SWITZERLAND
ITALY
MILANO

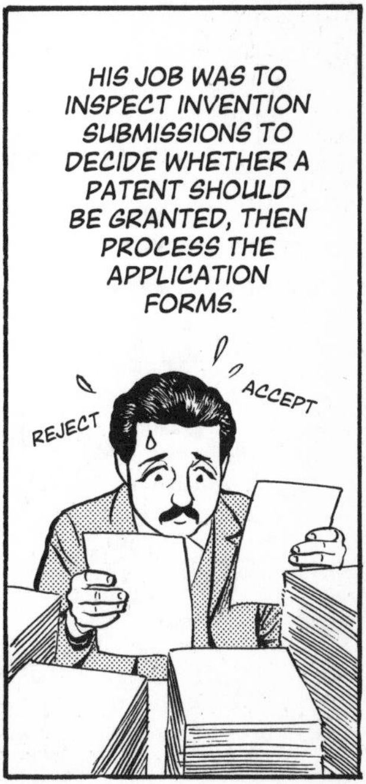

HIS JOB WAS TO INSPECT INVENTION SUBMISSIONS TO DECIDE WHETHER A PATENT SHOULD BE GRANTED, THEN PROCESS THE APPLICATION FORMS.
ACCEPT
REJECT

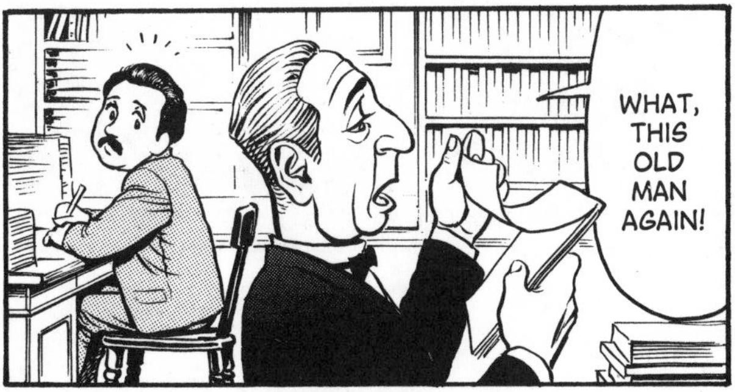

WHAT, THIS OLD MAN AGAIN!

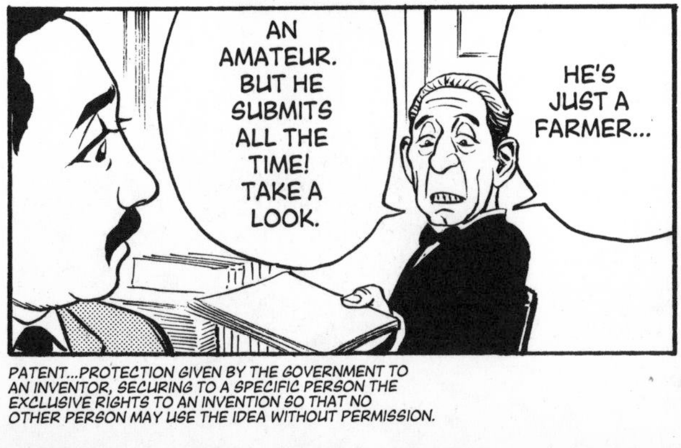

HE'S JUST A FARMER...
AN AMATEUR. BUT HE SUBMITS ALL THE TIME! TAKE A LOOK.

PATENT...PROTECTION GIVEN BY THE GOVERNMENT TO AN INVENTOR, SECURING TO A SPECIFIC PERSON THE EXCLUSIVE RIGHTS TO AN INVENTION SO THAT NO OTHER PERSON MAY USE THE IDEA WITHOUT PERMISSION.

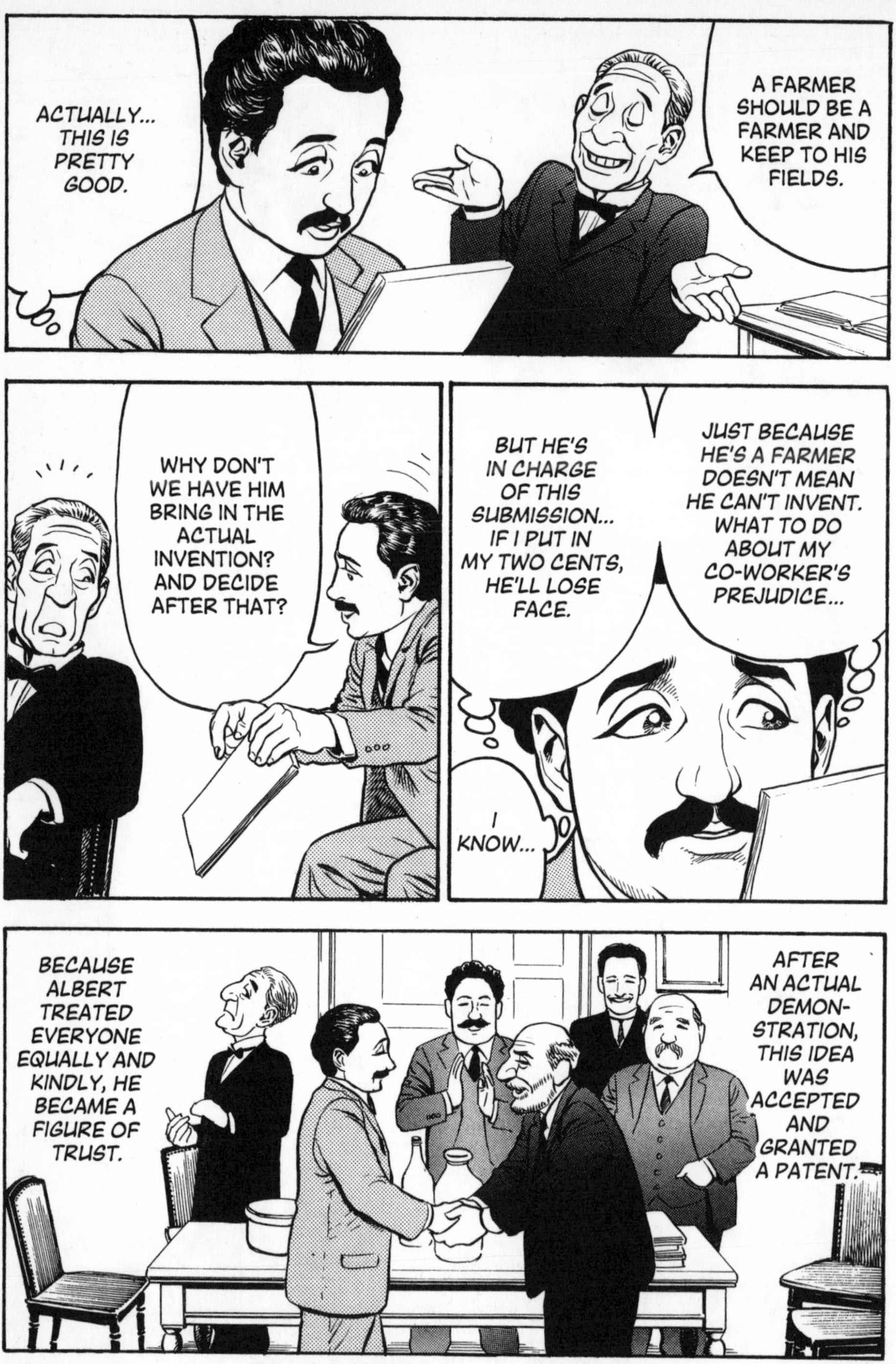
A FARMER SHOULD BE A FARMER AND KEEP TO HIS FIELDS.
ACTUALLY... THIS IS PRETTY GOOD.
JUST BECAUSE HE'S A FARMER DOESN'T MEAN HE CAN'T INVENT. WHAT TO DO ABOUT MY CO-WORKER'S PREJUDICE...
BUT HE'S IN CHARGE OF THIS SUBMISSION... IF I PUT IN MY TWO CENTS, HE'LL LOSE FACE.
I KNOW...
WHY DON'T WE HAVE HIM BRING IN THE ACTUAL INVENTION? AND DECIDE AFTER THAT?
AFTER AN ACTUAL DEMON-STRATION, THIS IDEA WAS ACCEPTED AND GRANTED A PATENT.
BECAUSE ALBERT TREATED EVERYONE EQUALLY AND KINDLY, HE BECAME A FIGURE OF TRUST.

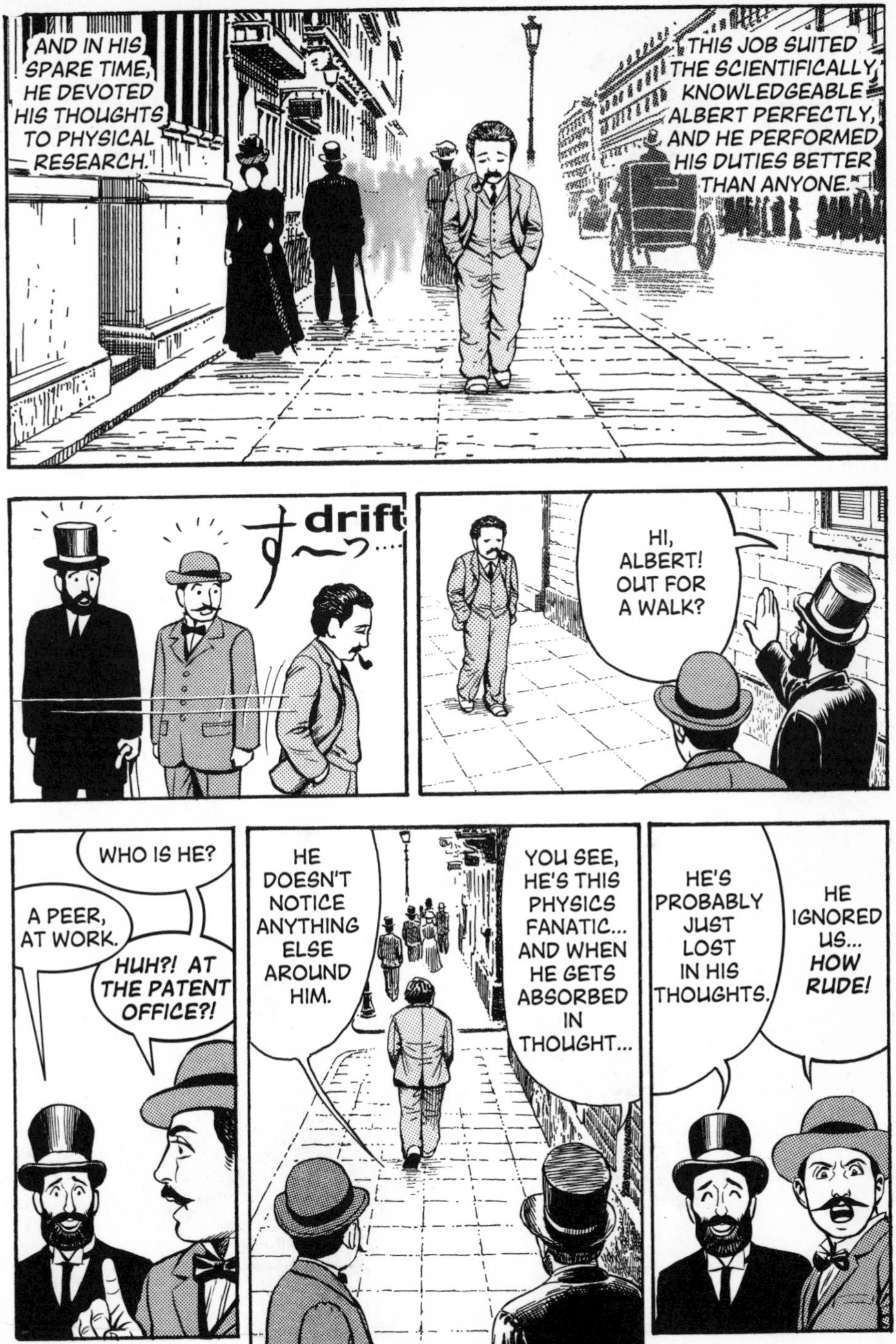
THIS JOB SUITED THE SCIENTIFICALLY KNOWLEDGEABLE ALBERT PERFECTLY, AND HE PERFORMED HIS DUTIES BETTER THAN ANYONE.
AND IN HIS SPARE TIME, HE DEVOTED HIS THOUGHTS TO PHYSICAL RESEARCH.
HI, ALBERT! OUT FOR A WALK?
す〜っ drift
HE IGNORED US... HOW RUDE!
HE'S PROBABLY JUST LOST IN HIS THOUGHTS.
YOU SEE, HE'S THIS PHYSICS FANATIC... AND WHEN HE GETS ABSORBED IN THOUGHT...
HE DOESN'T NOTICE ANYTHING ELSE AROUND HIM.
WHO IS HE?
A PEER, AT WORK.
HUH?! AT THE PATENT OFFICE?!

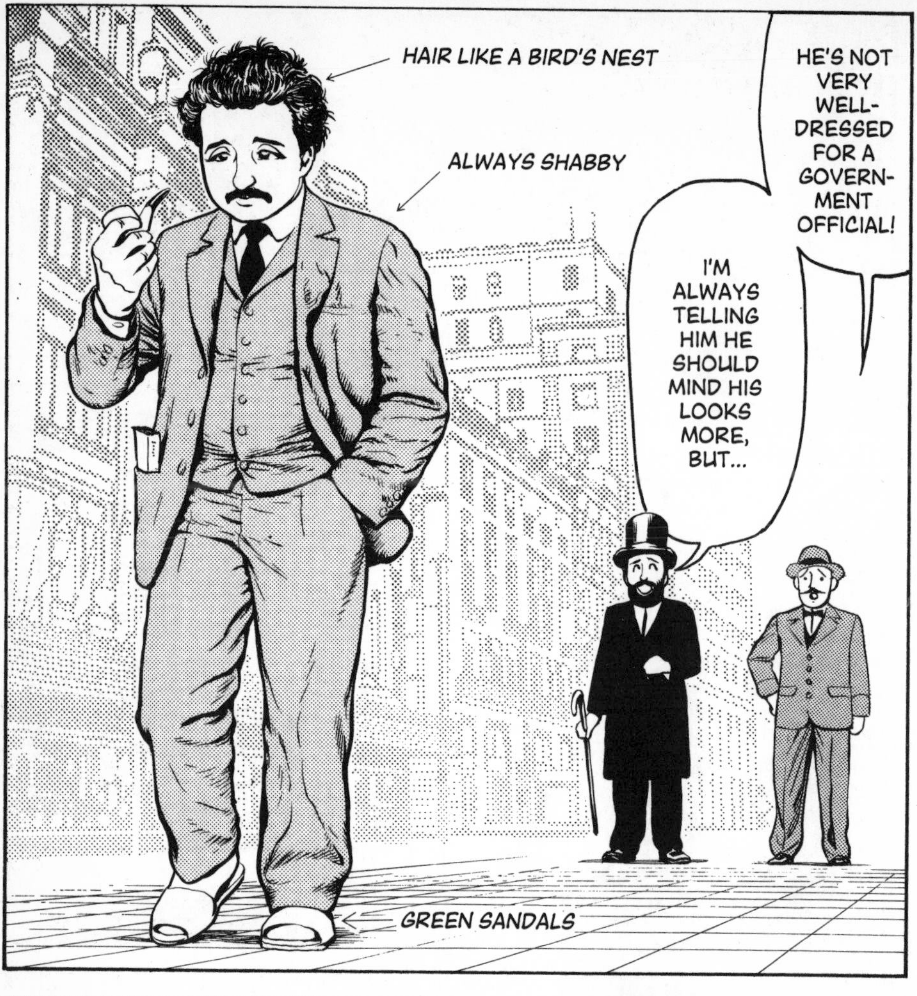
HE'S NOT VERY WELL-DRESSED FOR A GOVERNMENT OFFICIAL!
I'M ALWAYS TELLING HIM HE SHOULD MIND HIS LOOKS MORE, BUT...
HAIR LIKE A BIRD'S NEST
ALWAYS SHABBY
GREEN SANDALS
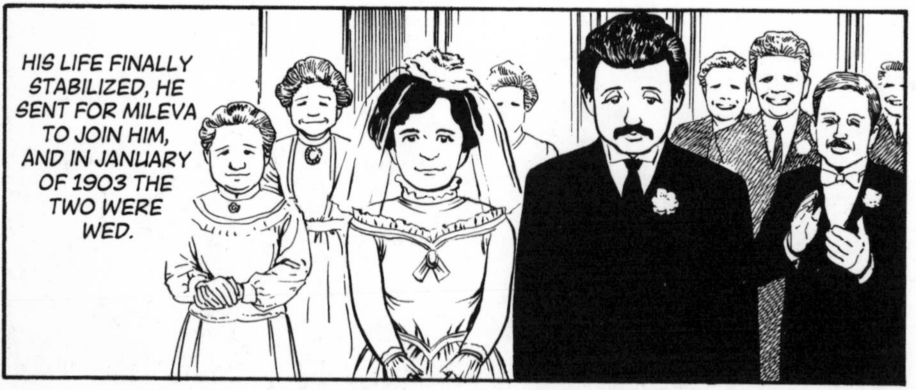
HIS LIFE FINALLY STABILIZED, HE SENT FOR MILEVA TO JOIN HIM, AND IN JANUARY OF 1903 THE TWO WERE WED.

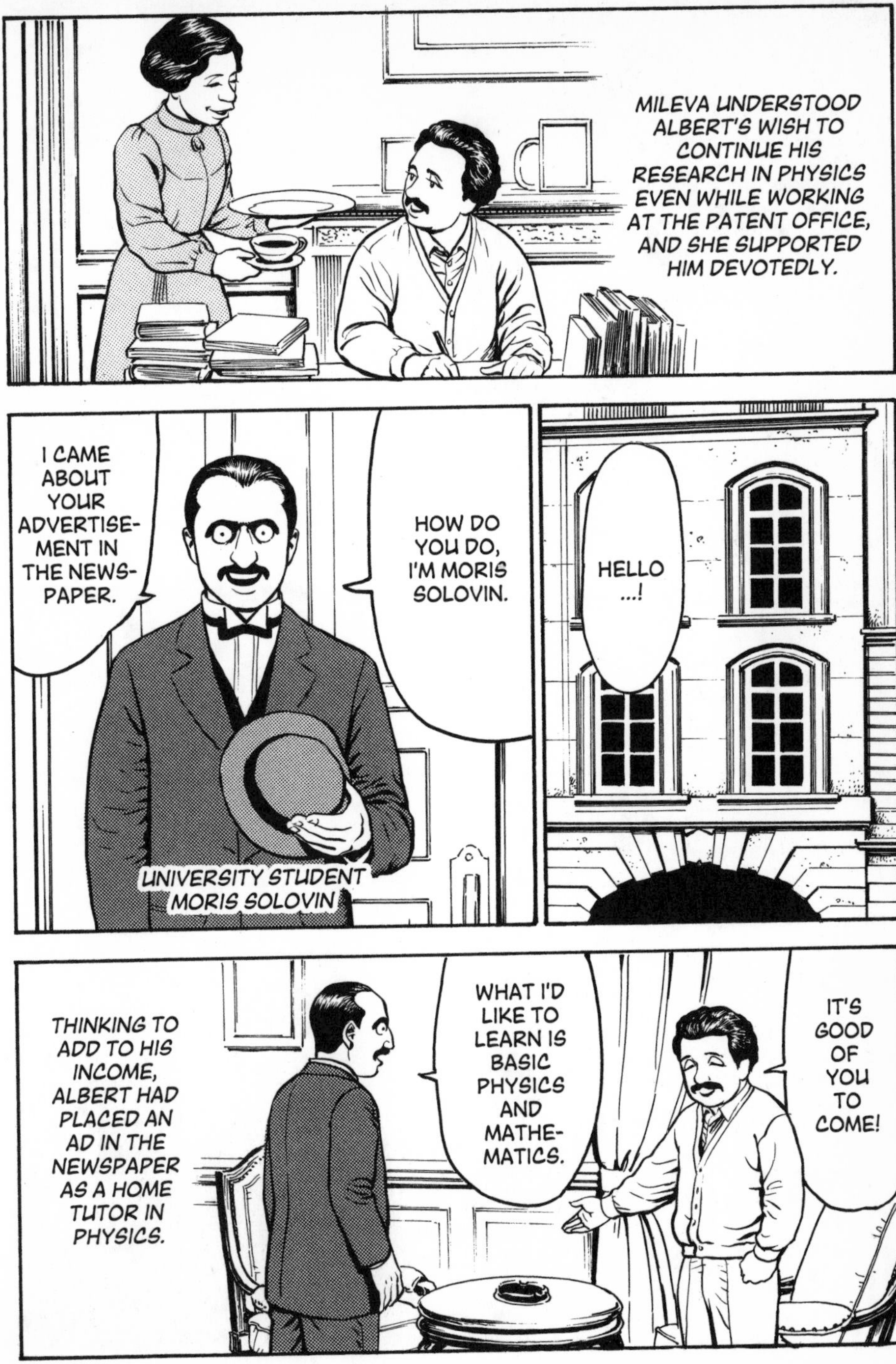
MILEVA UNDERSTOOD ALBERT'S WISH TO CONTINUE HIS RESEARCH IN PHYSICS EVEN WHILE WORKING AT THE PATENT OFFICE, AND SHE SUPPORTED HIM DEVOTEDLY.
HELLO ...!
HOW DO YOU DO, I'M MORIS SOLOVIN.
I CAME ABOUT YOUR ADVERTISEMENT IN THE NEWSPAPER.
UNIVERSITY STUDENT MORIS SOLOVIN
IT'S GOOD OF YOU TO COME!
WHAT I'D LIKE TO LEARN IS BASIC PHYSICS AND MATHEMATICS.
THINKING TO ADD TO HIS INCOME, ALBERT HAD PLACED AN AD IN THE NEWSPAPER AS A HOME TUTOR IN PHYSICS.

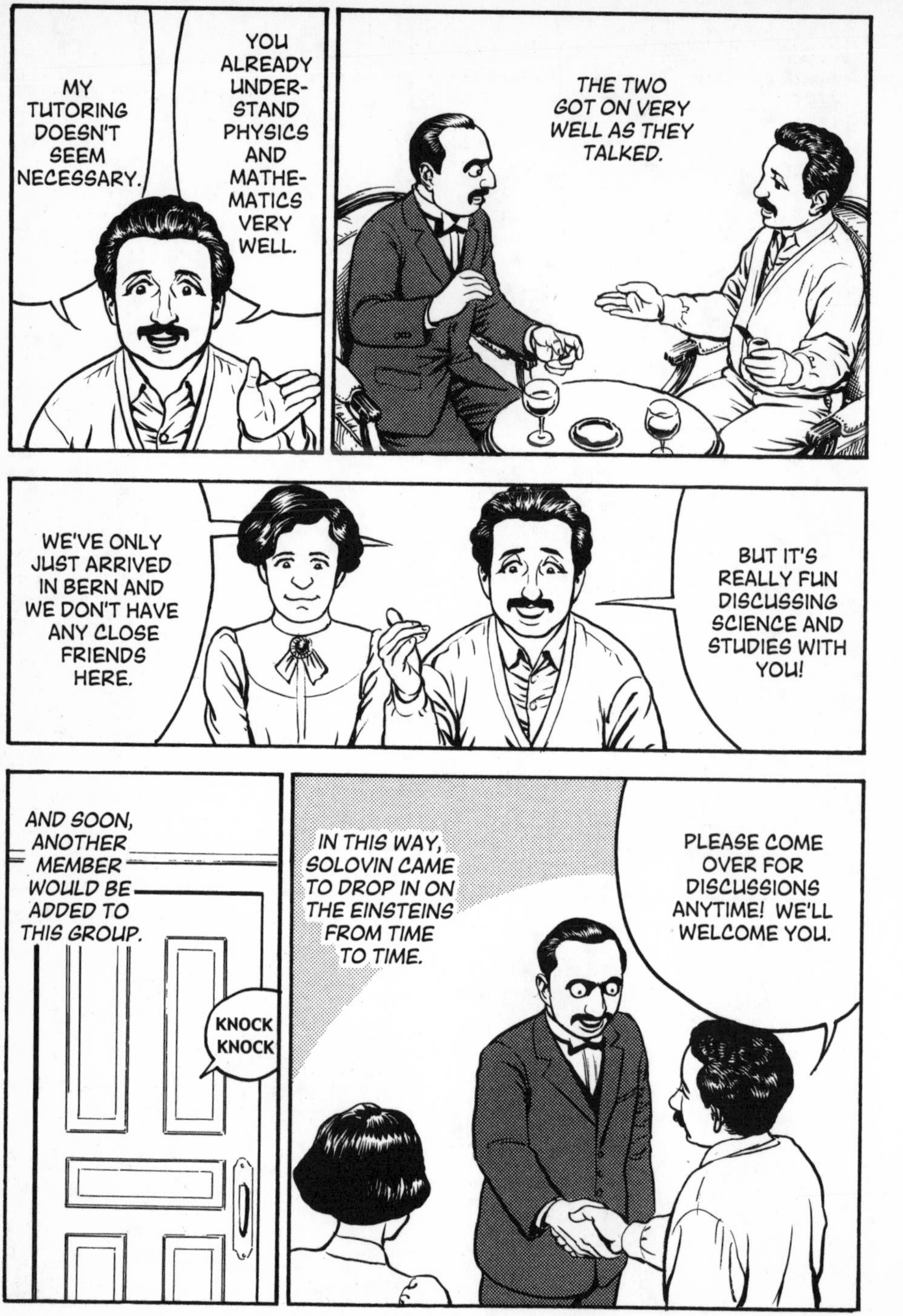
THE TWO GOT ON VERY WELL AS THEY TALKED.
YOU ALREADY UNDER-STAND PHYSICS AND MATHE-MATICS VERY WELL.
MY TUTORING DOESN'T SEEM NECESSARY.
WE'VE ONLY JUST ARRIVED IN BERN AND WE DON'T HAVE ANY CLOSE FRIENDS HERE.
BUT IT'S REALLY FUN DISCUSSING SCIENCE AND STUDIES WITH YOU!
PLEASE COME OVER FOR DISCUSSIONS ANYTIME! WE'LL WELCOME YOU.
IN THIS WAY, SOLOVIN CAME TO DROP IN ON THE EINSTEINS FROM TIME TO TIME.
AND SOON, ANOTHER MEMBER WOULD BE ADDED TO THIS GROUP.
KNOCK KNOCK

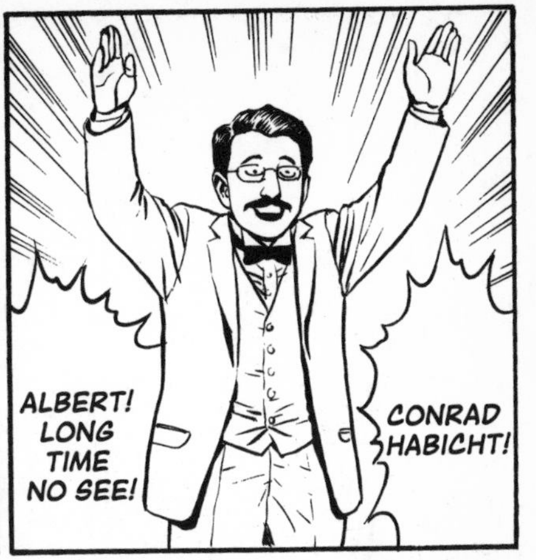
CONRAD HABICHT!
ALBERT! LONG TIME NO SEE!

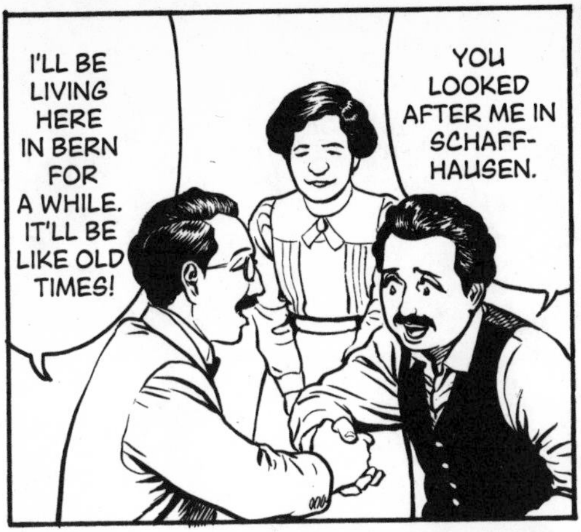
YOU LOOKED AFTER ME IN SCHAFF-HAUSEN.
I'LL BE LIVING HERE IN BERN FOR A WHILE. IT'LL BE LIKE OLD TIMES!

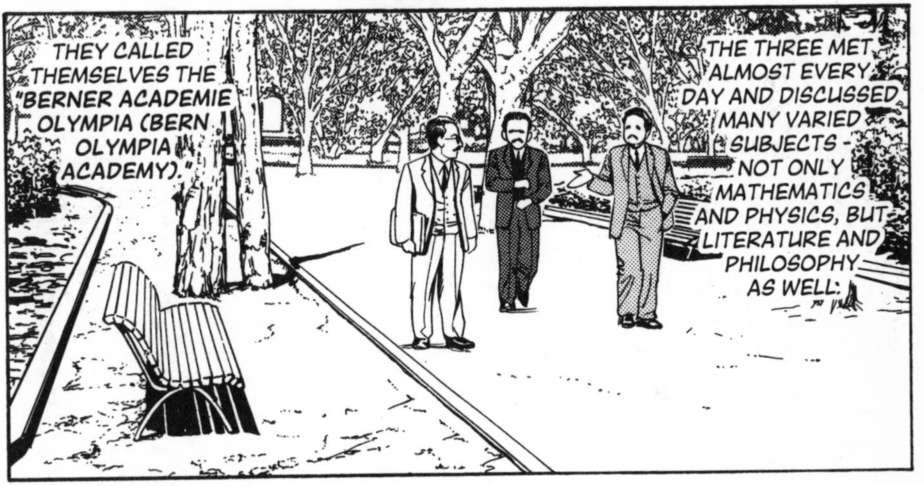
THE THREE MET ALMOST EVERY DAY AND DISCUSSED MANY VARIED SUBJECTS - NOT ONLY MATHEMATICS AND PHYSICS, BUT LITERATURE AND PHILOSOPHY AS WELL.
THEY CALLED THEMSELVES THE "BERNER ACADEMIE OLYMPIA (BERN OLYMPIA ACADEMY)."

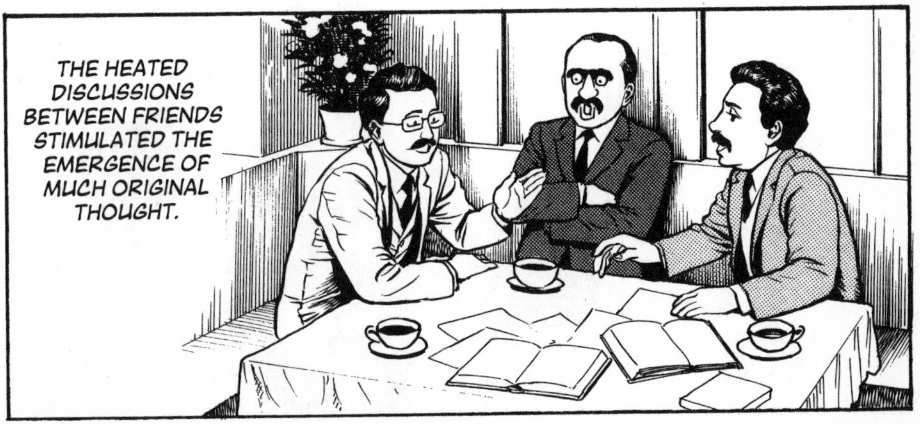
THE HEATED DISCUSSIONS BETWEEN FRIENDS STIMULATED THE EMERGENCE OF MUCH ORIGINAL THOUGHT.

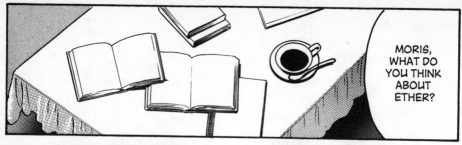

MORIS, WHAT DO YOU THINK ABOUT ETHER?
THE PROPAGATION MEDIUM FOR LIGHT?
IT FILLS THE ENTIRE UNIVERSE, AND REMAINS UNMOVING.
PHYSICAL OBJECTS MOVE THROUGH IT.
BUT ETHER IS ONLY *THOUGHT* TO EXIST, AND HAS NEVER BEEN ACTUALLY PROVEN.
EVEN THE MICHELSON-MORLEY EXPERIMENT COULDN'T PROVE ITS EXISTENCE...
I WONDER WHY THE EXPERIMENT FAILED?
THAT METHOD *SHOULD* HAVE PROVEN THE EXISTENCE OF ETHER...

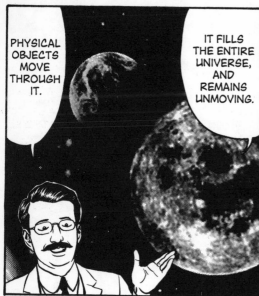

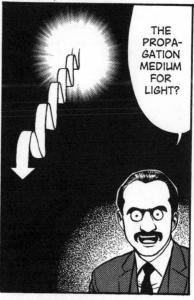

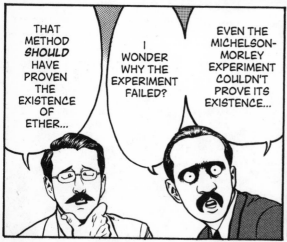

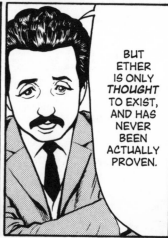

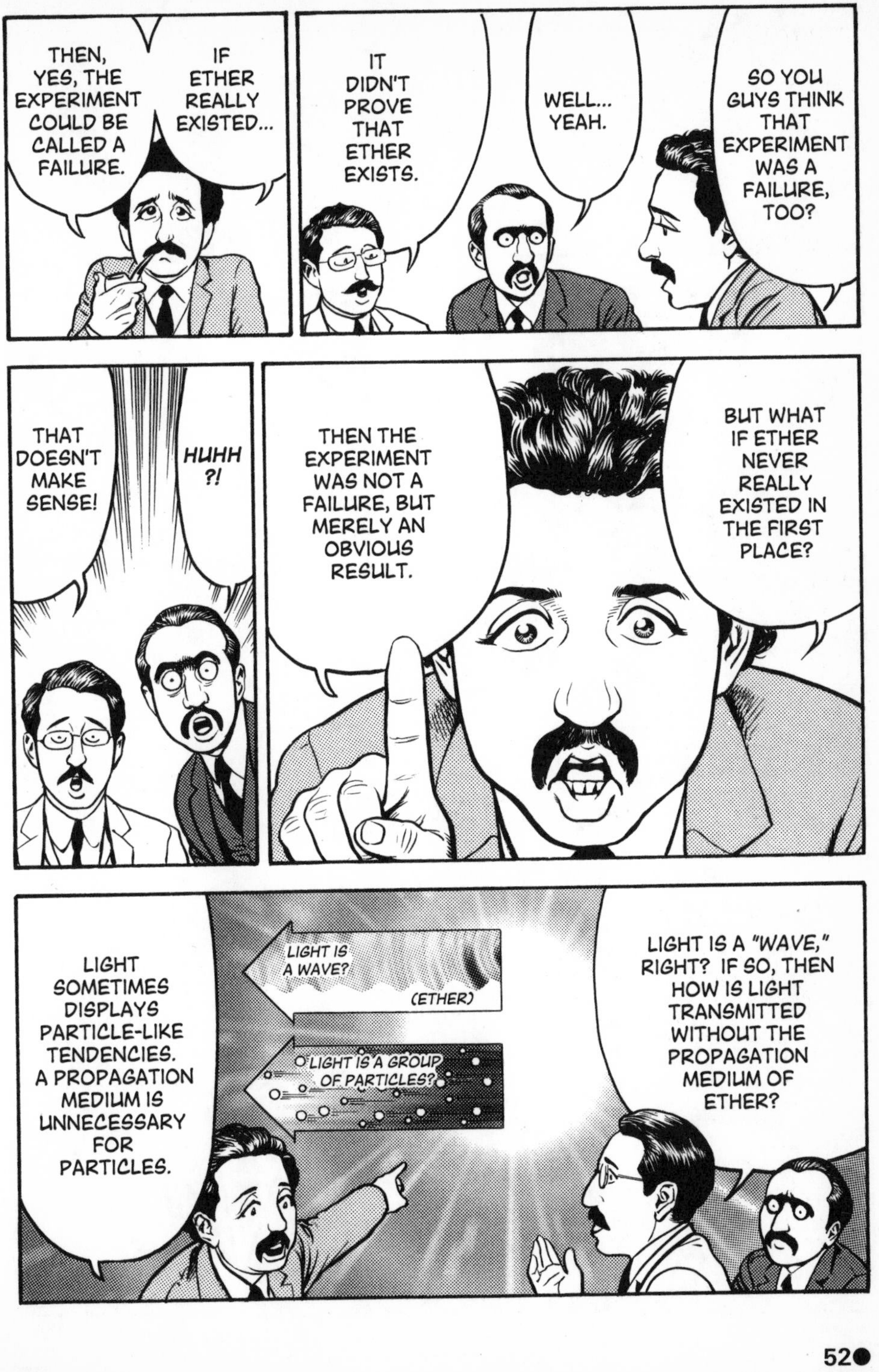
SO YOU GUYS THINK THAT EXPERIMENT WAS A FAILURE, TOO?
WELL... YEAH.
IT DIDN'T PROVE THAT ETHER EXISTS.
IF ETHER REALLY EXISTED...
THEN, YES, THE EXPERIMENT COULD BE CALLED A FAILURE.
BUT WHAT IF ETHER NEVER REALLY EXISTED IN THE FIRST PLACE?
THEN THE EXPERIMENT WAS NOT A FAILURE, BUT MERELY AN OBVIOUS RESULT.
HUHH ?!
THAT DOESN'T MAKE SENSE!
LIGHT IS A "WAVE," RIGHT? IF SO, THEN HOW IS LIGHT TRANSMITTED WITHOUT THE PROPAGATION MEDIUM OF ETHER?
LIGHT IS A WAVE?
(ETHER)
LIGHT IS A GROUP OF PARTICLES?
LIGHT SOMETIMES DISPLAYS PARTICLE-LIKE TENDENCIES. A PROPAGATION MEDIUM IS UNNECESSARY FOR PARTICLES.

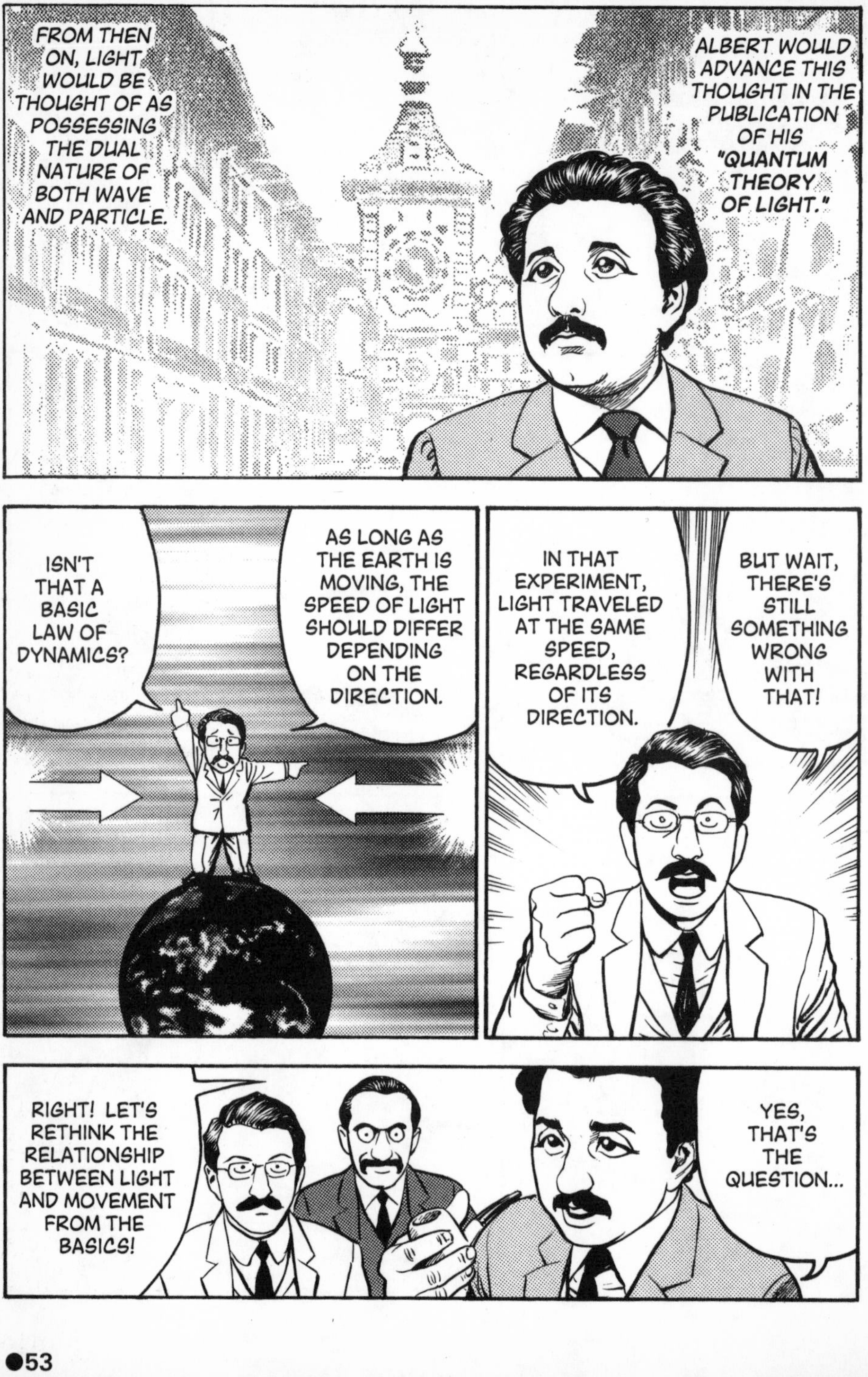

ALBERT WOULD ADVANCE THIS THOUGHT IN THE PUBLICATION OF HIS "QUANTUM THEORY OF LIGHT."
FROM THEN ON, LIGHT WOULD BE THOUGHT OF AS POSSESSING THE DUAL NATURE OF BOTH WAVE AND PARTICLE.
BUT WAIT, THERE'S STILL SOMETHING WRONG WITH THAT!
IN THAT EXPERIMENT, LIGHT TRAVELED AT THE SAME SPEED, REGARDLESS OF ITS DIRECTION.
AS LONG AS THE EARTH IS MOVING, THE SPEED OF LIGHT SHOULD DIFFER DEPENDING ON THE DIRECTION.
ISN'T THAT A BASIC LAW OF DYNAMICS?
YES, THAT'S THE QUESTION...
RIGHT! LET'S RETHINK THE RELATIONSHIP BETWEEN LIGHT AND MOVEMENT FROM THE BASICS!

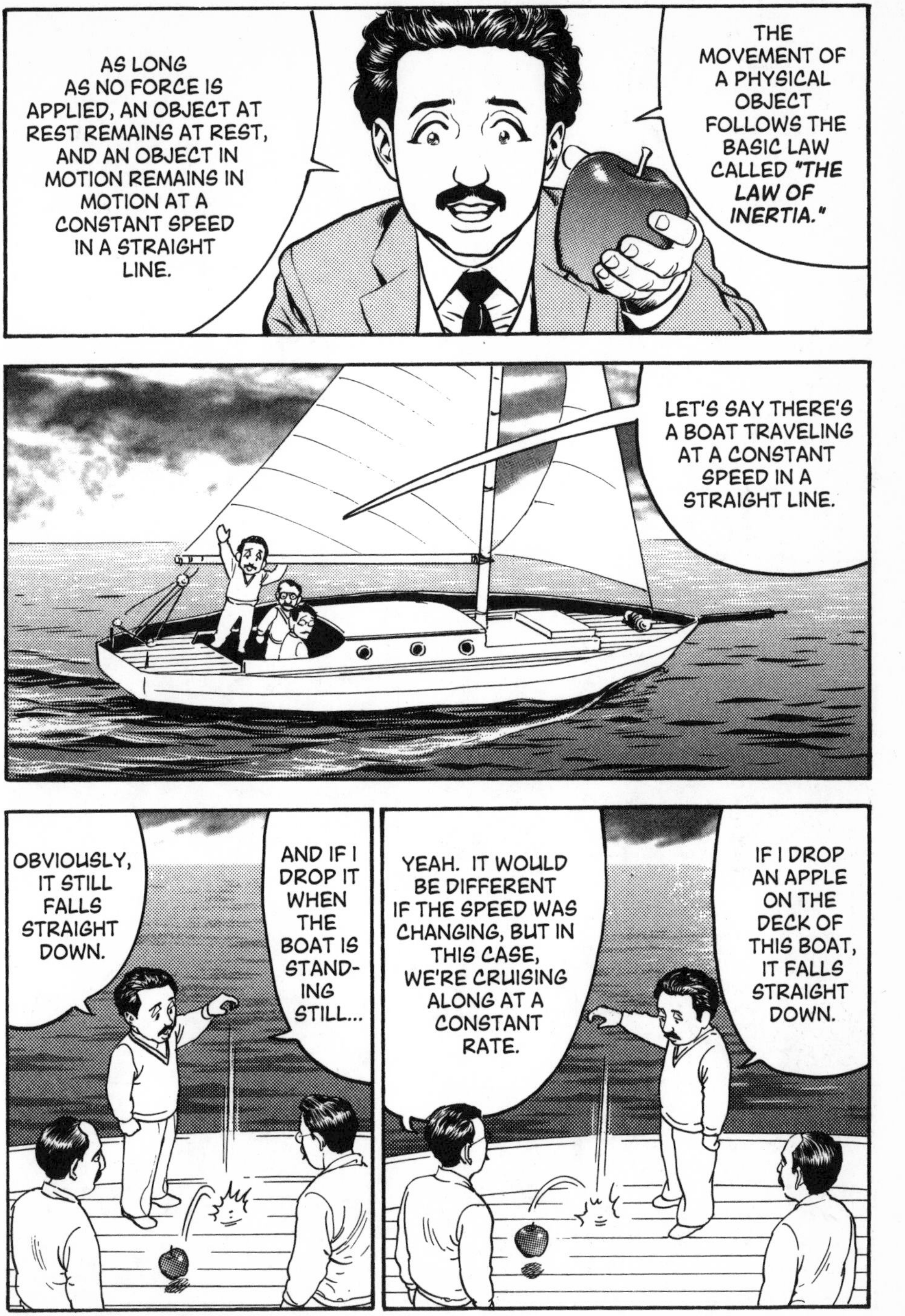
THE MOVEMENT OF A PHYSICAL OBJECT FOLLOWS THE BASIC LAW CALLED "THE LAW OF INERTIA."
AS LONG AS NO FORCE IS APPLIED, AN OBJECT AT REST REMAINS AT REST, AND AN OBJECT IN MOTION REMAINS IN MOTION AT A CONSTANT SPEED IN A STRAIGHT LINE.
LET'S SAY THERE'S A BOAT TRAVELING AT A CONSTANT SPEED IN A STRAIGHT LINE.
IF I DROP AN APPLE ON THE DECK OF THIS BOAT, IT FALLS STRAIGHT DOWN.
YEAH. IT WOULD BE DIFFERENT IF THE SPEED WAS CHANGING, BUT IN THIS CASE, WE'RE CRUISING ALONG AT A CONSTANT RATE.
AND IF I DROP IT WHEN THE BOAT IS STAND-ING STILL...
OBVIOUSLY, IT STILL FALLS STRAIGHT DOWN.

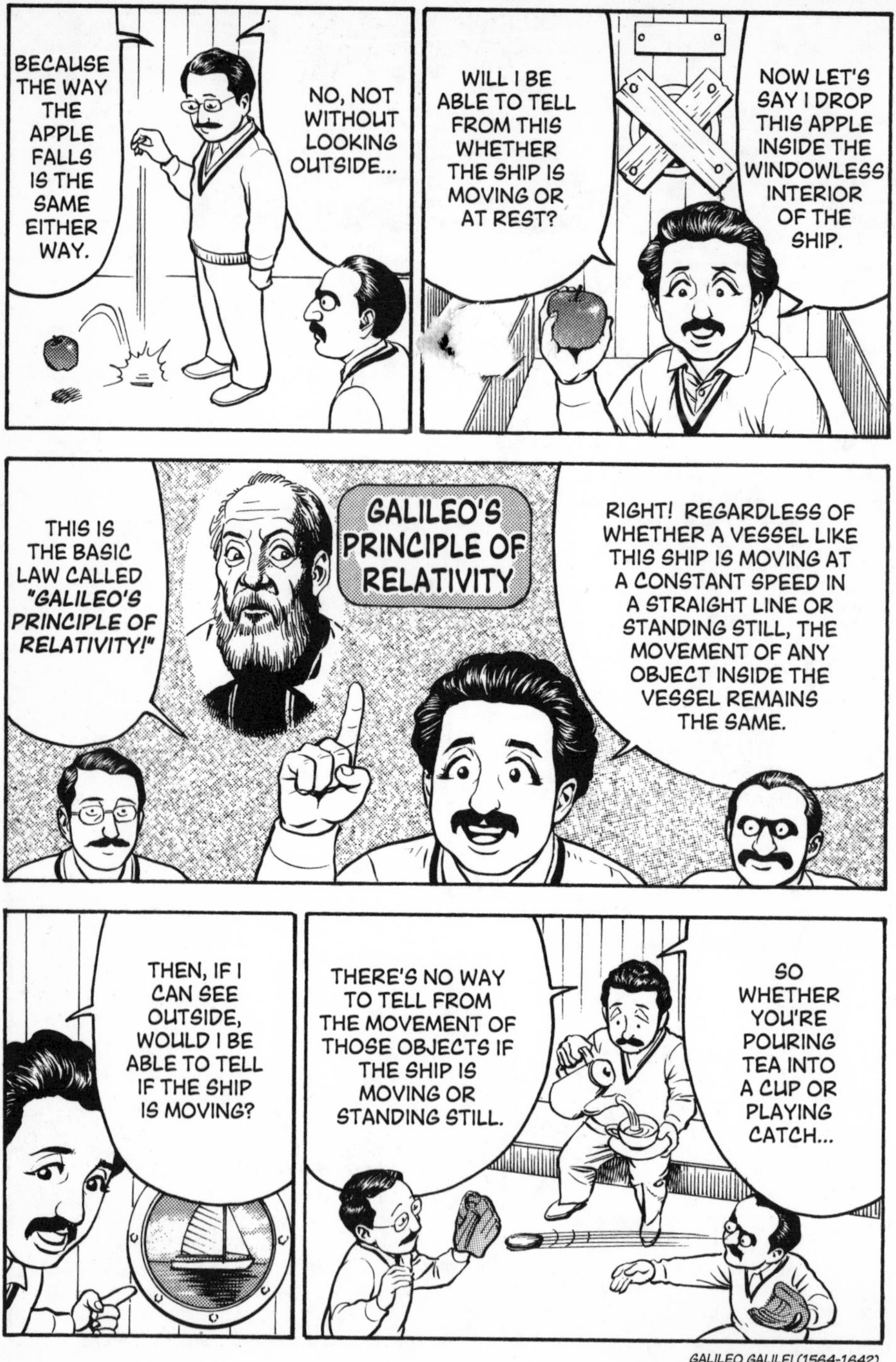
NOW LET'S SAY I DROP THIS APPLE INSIDE THE WINDOWLESS INTERIOR OF THE SHIP.
WILL I BE ABLE TO TELL FROM THIS WHETHER THE SHIP IS MOVING OR AT REST?
NO, NOT WITHOUT LOOKING OUTSIDE...
BECAUSE THE WAY THE APPLE FALLS IS THE SAME EITHER WAY.
RIGHT! REGARDLESS OF WHETHER A VESSEL LIKE THIS SHIP IS MOVING AT A CONSTANT SPEED IN A STRAIGHT LINE OR STANDING STILL, THE MOVEMENT OF ANY OBJECT INSIDE THE VESSEL REMAINS THE SAME.
GALILEO'S PRINCIPLE OF RELATIVITY
THIS IS THE BASIC LAW CALLED "GALILEO'S PRINCIPLE OF RELATIVITY!"
SO WHETHER YOU'RE POURING TEA INTO A CUP OR PLAYING CATCH...
THERE'S NO WAY TO TELL FROM THE MOVEMENT OF THOSE OBJECTS IF THE SHIP IS MOVING OR STANDING STILL.
THEN, IF I CAN SEE OUTSIDE, WOULD I BE ABLE TO TELL IF THE SHIP IS MOVING?

GALILEO GALILEI (1564-1642)
AN ITALIAN PHYSICIST AND ASTRONOMER.
MADE DISCOVERIES IN THE BASIC LAWS
OF DYNAMICS, SUCH AS THE LAW OF
INERTIA AND RELATIVITY OF MOTION.

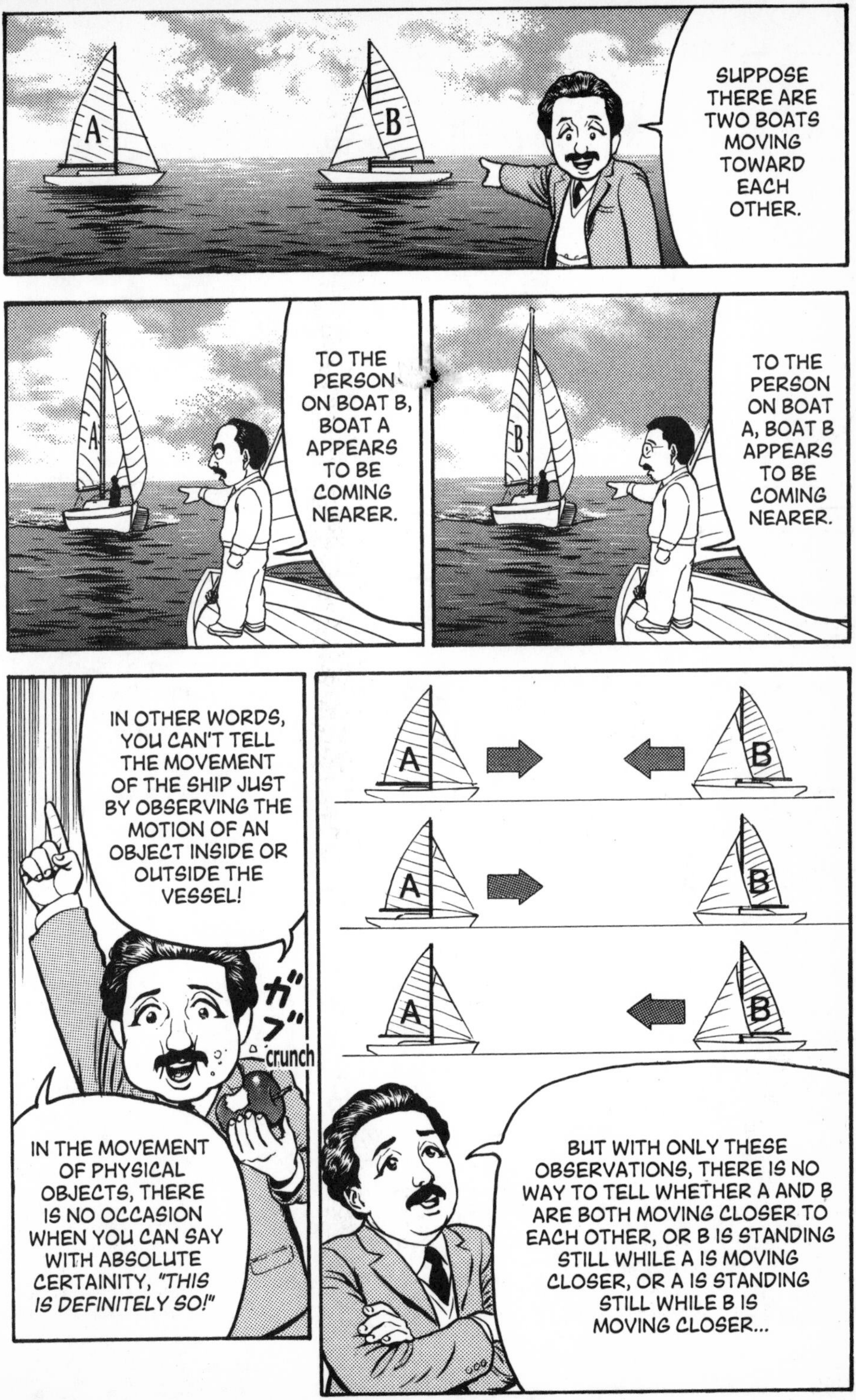
A
B
SUPPOSE THERE ARE TWO BOATS MOVING TOWARD EACH OTHER.
B
TO THE PERSON ON BOAT A, BOAT B APPEARS TO BE COMING NEARER.
A
TO THE PERSON ON BOAT B, BOAT A APPEARS TO BE COMING NEARER.
A
B
A
B
A
B
BUT WITH ONLY THESE OBSERVATIONS, THERE IS NO WAY TO TELL WHETHER A AND B ARE BOTH MOVING CLOSER TO EACH OTHER, OR B IS STANDING STILL WHILE A IS MOVING CLOSER, OR A IS STANDING STILL WHILE B IS MOVING CLOSER...
IN OTHER WORDS, YOU CAN'T TELL THE MOVEMENT OF THE SHIP JUST BY OBSERVING THE MOTION OF AN OBJECT INSIDE OR OUTSIDE THE VESSEL!
ガブ
crunch
IN THE MOVEMENT OF PHYSICAL OBJECTS, THERE IS NO OCCASION WHEN YOU CAN SAY WITH ABSOLUTE CERTAINITY, "THIS IS DEFINITELY SO!"

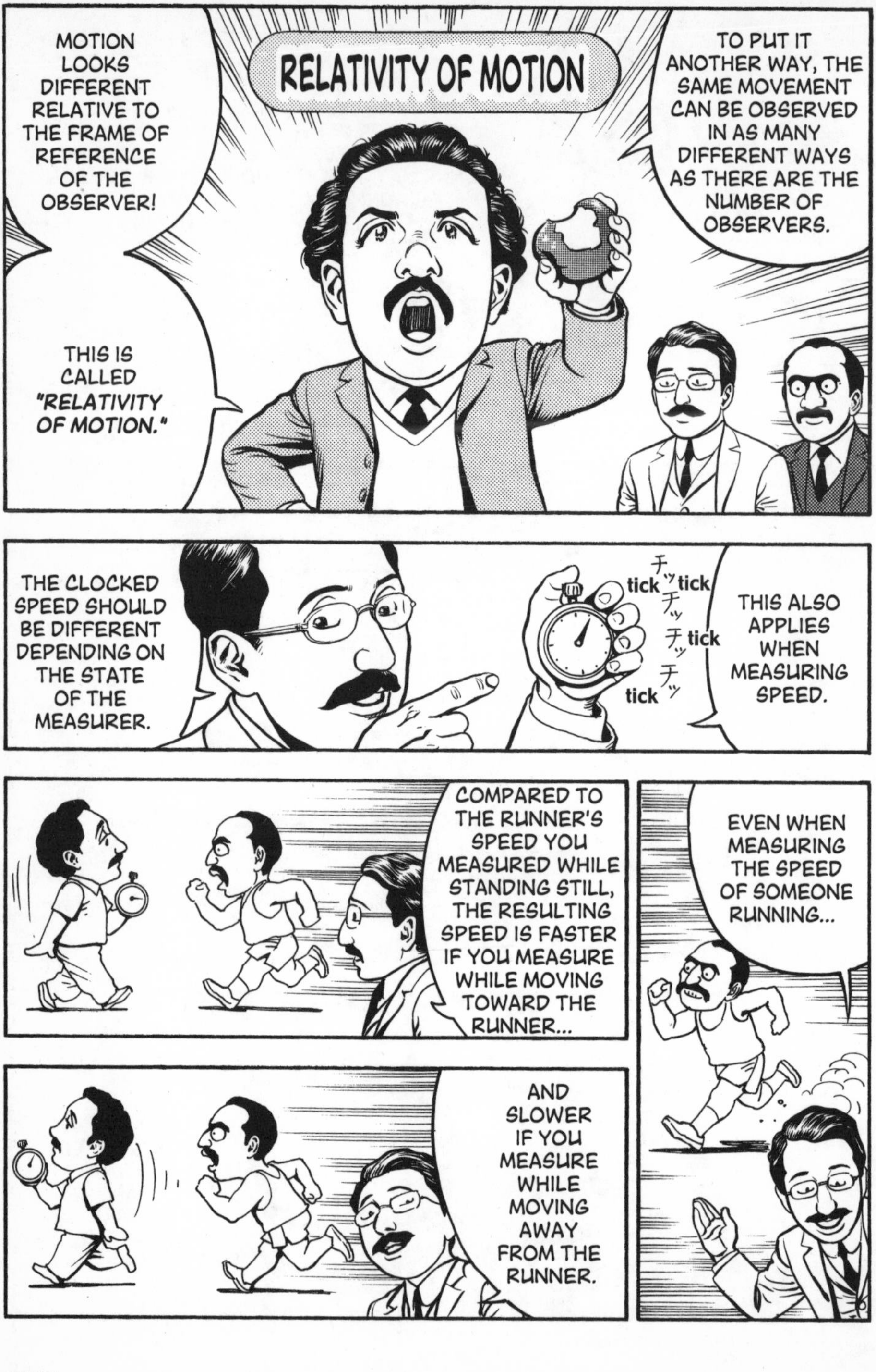
RELATIVITY OF MOTION
MOTION LOOKS DIFFERENT RELATIVE TO THE FRAME OF REFERENCE OF THE OBSERVER!
TO PUT IT ANOTHER WAY, THE SAME MOVEMENT CAN BE OBSERVED IN AS MANY DIFFERENT WAYS AS THERE ARE THE NUMBER OF OBSERVERS.
THIS IS CALLED "RELATIVITY OF MOTION."
THIS ALSO APPLIES WHEN MEASURING SPEED.
tick tick tick tick
チッ チッ チッ チッ
THE CLOCKED SPEED SHOULD BE DIFFERENT DEPENDING ON THE STATE OF THE MEASURER.
EVEN WHEN MEASURING THE SPEED OF SOMEONE RUNNING...
COMPARED TO THE RUNNER'S SPEED YOU MEASURED WHILE STANDING STILL, THE RESULTING SPEED IS FASTER IF YOU MEASURE WHILE MOVING TOWARD THE RUNNER...
AND SLOWER IF YOU MEASURE WHILE MOVING AWAY FROM THE RUNNER.

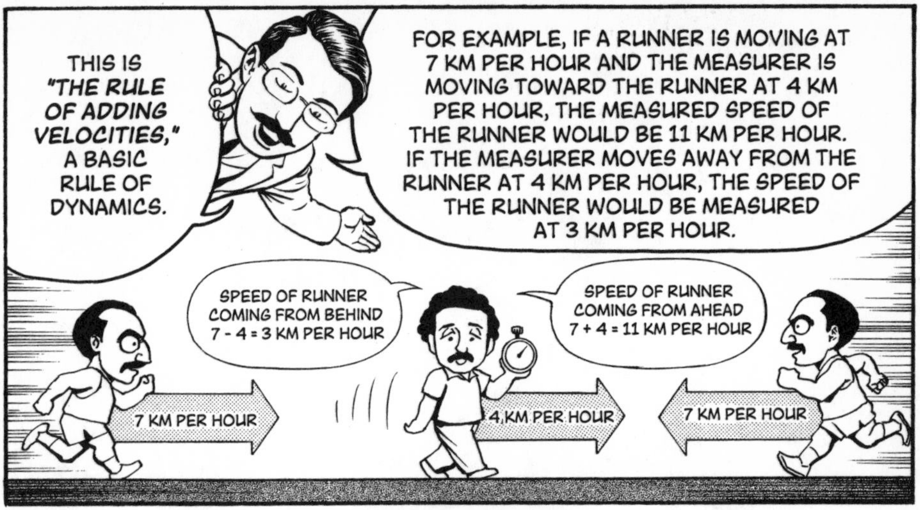
THIS IS "THE RULE OF ADDING VELOCITIES," A BASIC RULE OF DYNAMICS.
FOR EXAMPLE, IF A RUNNER IS MOVING AT 7 KM PER HOUR AND THE MEASURER IS MOVING TOWARD THE RUNNER AT 4 KM PER HOUR, THE MEASURED SPEED OF THE RUNNER WOULD BE 11 KM PER HOUR. IF THE MEASURER MOVES AWAY FROM THE RUNNER AT 4 KM PER HOUR, THE SPEED OF THE RUNNER WOULD BE MEASURED AT 3 KM PER HOUR.
SPEED OF RUNNER COMING FROM BEHIND 7 - 4 = 3 KM PER HOUR
SPEED OF RUNNER COMING FROM AHEAD 7 + 4 = 11 KM PER HOUR
7 KM PER HOUR
4 KM PER HOUR
7 KM PER HOUR

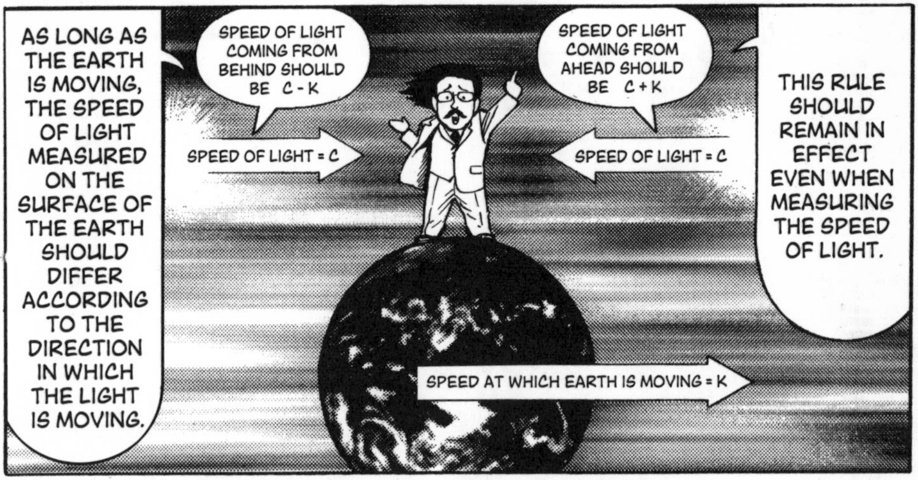
AS LONG AS THE EARTH IS MOVING, THE SPEED OF LIGHT MEASURED ON THE SURFACE OF THE EARTH SHOULD DIFFER ACCORDING TO THE DIRECTION IN WHICH THE LIGHT IS MOVING.
SPEED OF LIGHT COMING FROM BEHIND SHOULD BE C - K
SPEED OF LIGHT COMING FROM AHEAD SHOULD BE C + K
SPEED OF LIGHT = C
SPEED OF LIGHT = C
THIS RULE SHOULD REMAIN IN EFFECT EVEN WHEN MEASURING THE SPEED OF LIGHT.
SPEED AT WHICH EARTH IS MOVING = K

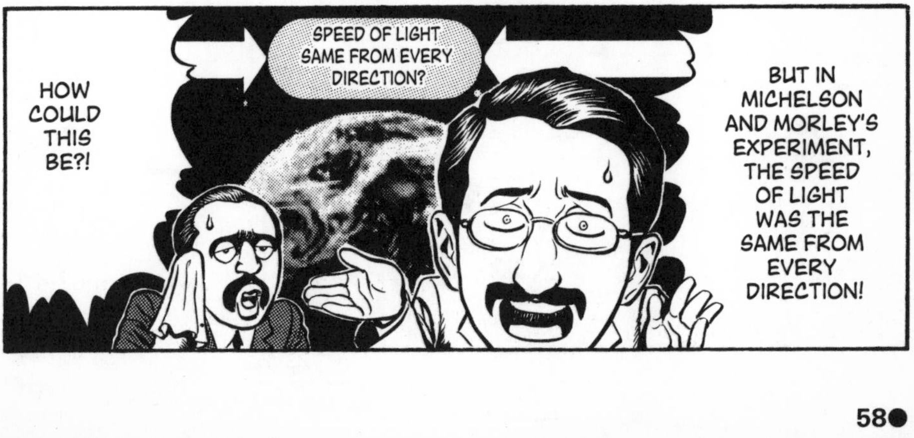
BUT IN MICHELSON AND MORLEY'S EXPERIMENT, THE SPEED OF LIGHT WAS THE SAME FROM EVERY DIRECTION!
SPEED OF LIGHT SAME FROM EVERY DIRECTION?
HOW COULD THIS BE?!

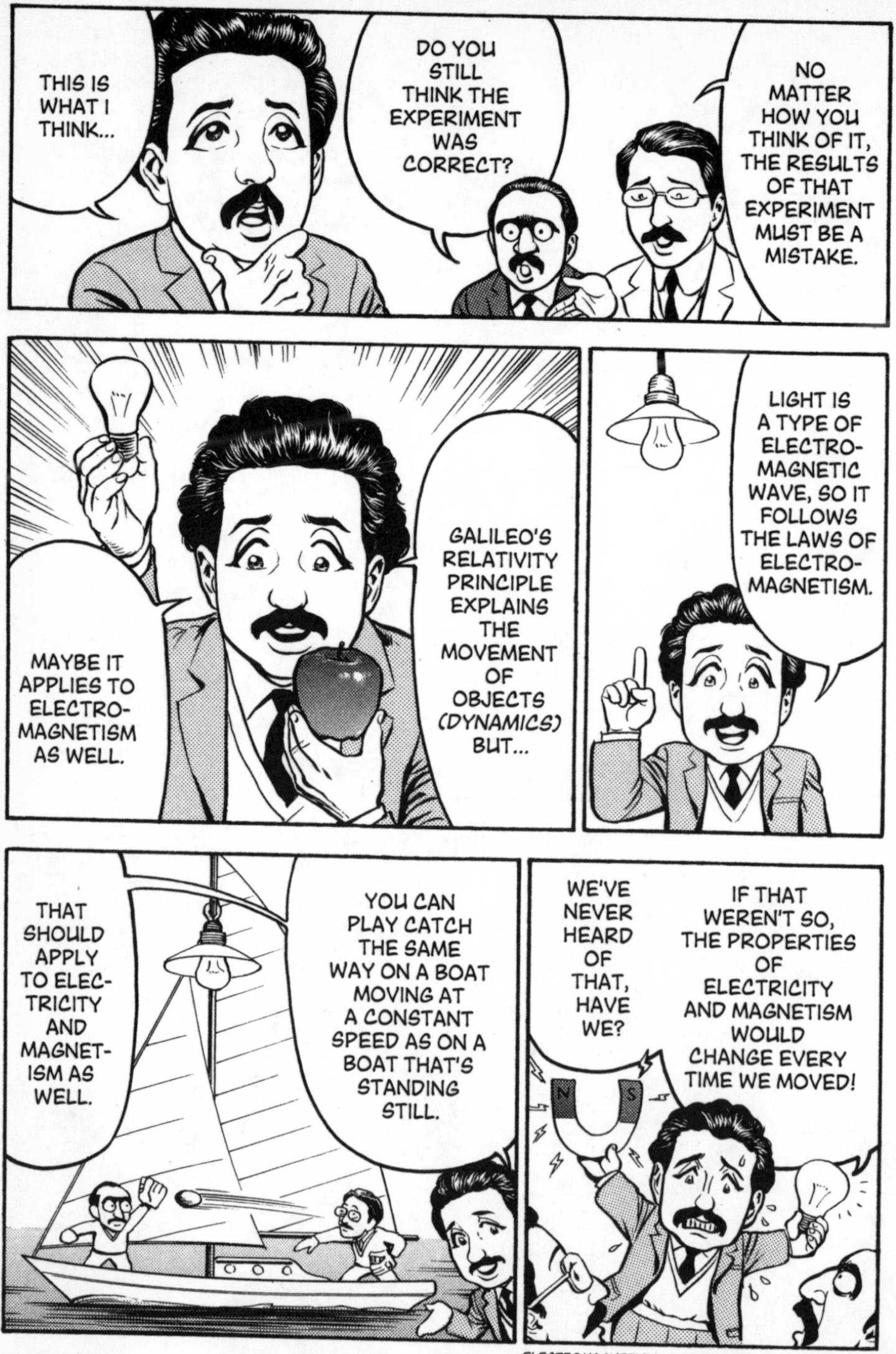
NO MATTER HOW YOU THINK OF IT, THE RESULTS OF THAT EXPERIMENT MUST BE A MISTAKE.
DO YOU STILL THINK THE EXPERIMENT WAS CORRECT?
THIS IS WHAT I THINK...
LIGHT IS A TYPE OF ELECTRO-MAGNETIC WAVE, SO IT FOLLOWS THE LAWS OF ELECTRO-MAGNETISM.
GALILEO'S RELATIVITY PRINCIPLE EXPLAINS THE MOVEMENT OF OBJECTS (DYNAMICS) BUT...
MAYBE IT APPLIES TO ELECTRO-MAGNETISM AS WELL.
IF THAT WEREN'T SO, THE PROPERTIES OF ELECTRICITY AND MAGNETISM WOULD CHANGE EVERY TIME WE MOVED!
WE'VE NEVER HEARD OF THAT, HAVE WE?
N
S
YOU CAN PLAY CATCH THE SAME WAY ON A BOAT MOVING AT A CONSTANT SPEED AS ON A BOAT THAT'S STANDING STILL.
THAT SHOULD APPLY TO ELEC-TRICITY AND MAGNET-ISM AS WELL.

ELECTROMAGNETISM...A SECTION OF PHYSICS STUDYING ALL PHENOMENA RELATED TO ELECTRICITY AND MAGNETISM

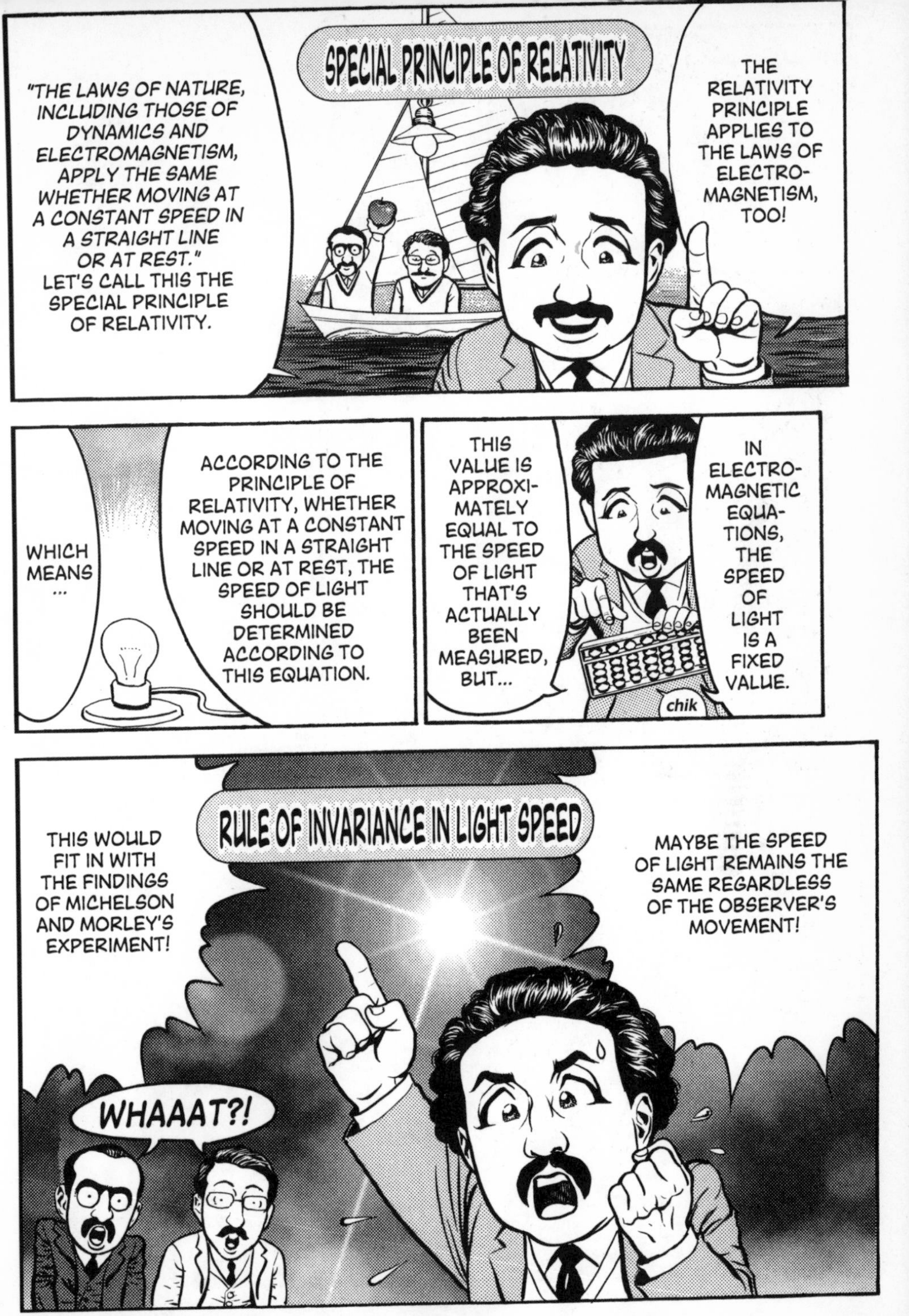
SPECIAL PRINCIPLE OF RELATIVITY
THE RELATIVITY PRINCIPLE APPLIES TO THE LAWS OF ELECTRO-MAGNETISM, TOO!
"THE LAWS OF NATURE, INCLUDING THOSE OF DYNAMICS AND ELECTROMAGNETISM, APPLY THE SAME WHETHER MOVING AT A CONSTANT SPEED IN A STRAIGHT LINE OR AT REST." LET'S CALL THIS THE SPECIAL PRINCIPLE OF RELATIVITY.
IN ELECTRO-MAGNETIC EQUA-TIONS, THE SPEED OF LIGHT IS A FIXED VALUE.
THIS VALUE IS APPROXI-MATELY EQUAL TO THE SPEED OF LIGHT THAT'S ACTUALLY BEEN MEASURED, BUT...
chik
ACCORDING TO THE PRINCIPLE OF RELATIVITY, WHETHER MOVING AT A CONSTANT SPEED IN A STRAIGHT LINE OR AT REST, THE SPEED OF LIGHT SHOULD BE DETERMINED ACCORDING TO THIS EQUATION.
WHICH MEANS ...
RULE OF INVARIANCE IN LIGHT SPEED
MAYBE THE SPEED OF LIGHT REMAINS THE SAME REGARDLESS OF THE OBSERVER'S MOVEMENT!
THIS WOULD FIT IN WITH THE FINDINGS OF MICHELSON AND MORLEY'S EXPERIMENT!
WHAAAT?!

LIGHT SPEED...IN A VACCUM, APPROXIMATELY 300,000 KILOMETERS PER SECOND.

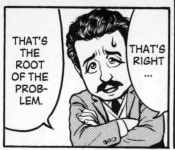

BUT EVEN THE RULE OF INVARIANCE IN LIGHT SPEED IS BASED ON THE PRINCIPLE OF RELATIVITY.
WHY WOULD THE RESULT BE DIFFER-ENT?
THAT'S RIGHT ...
THAT'S THE ROOT OF THE PROB-LEM.
I'VE THOUGHT FOR A LONG TIME ABOUT WHAT LIGHT WOULD LOOK LIKE IF WE COULD SEE IT WHILE TRAVELING AT THE SAME SPEED OF LIGHT...
WHAT DO YOU GUYS THINK?
WE'D BE TRAVEL-ING AT THE SAME SPEED, SO...
THE LIGHT WOULD APPEAR STATIONARY, OF COURSE.
RULE OF ADDING VELOCITIES LIGHT SPEED C - SPACESHIP SPEED C = O
I THINK LIGHT WOULD CONTINUE TO APPEAR AS IF IT IS MOVING AS ALWAYS, EVEN IN THIS SITUATION.
REALLY?
RULE OF INVARIANCE IN LIGHT SPEED SPEED = C

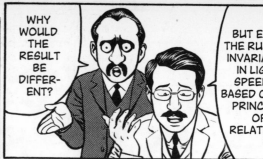

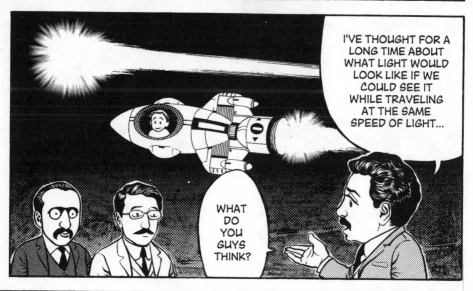

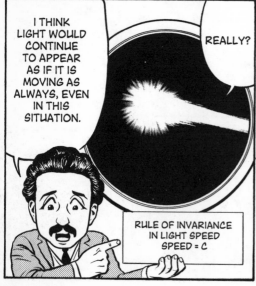

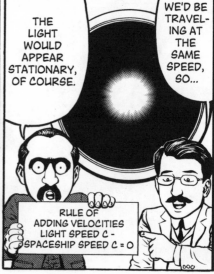

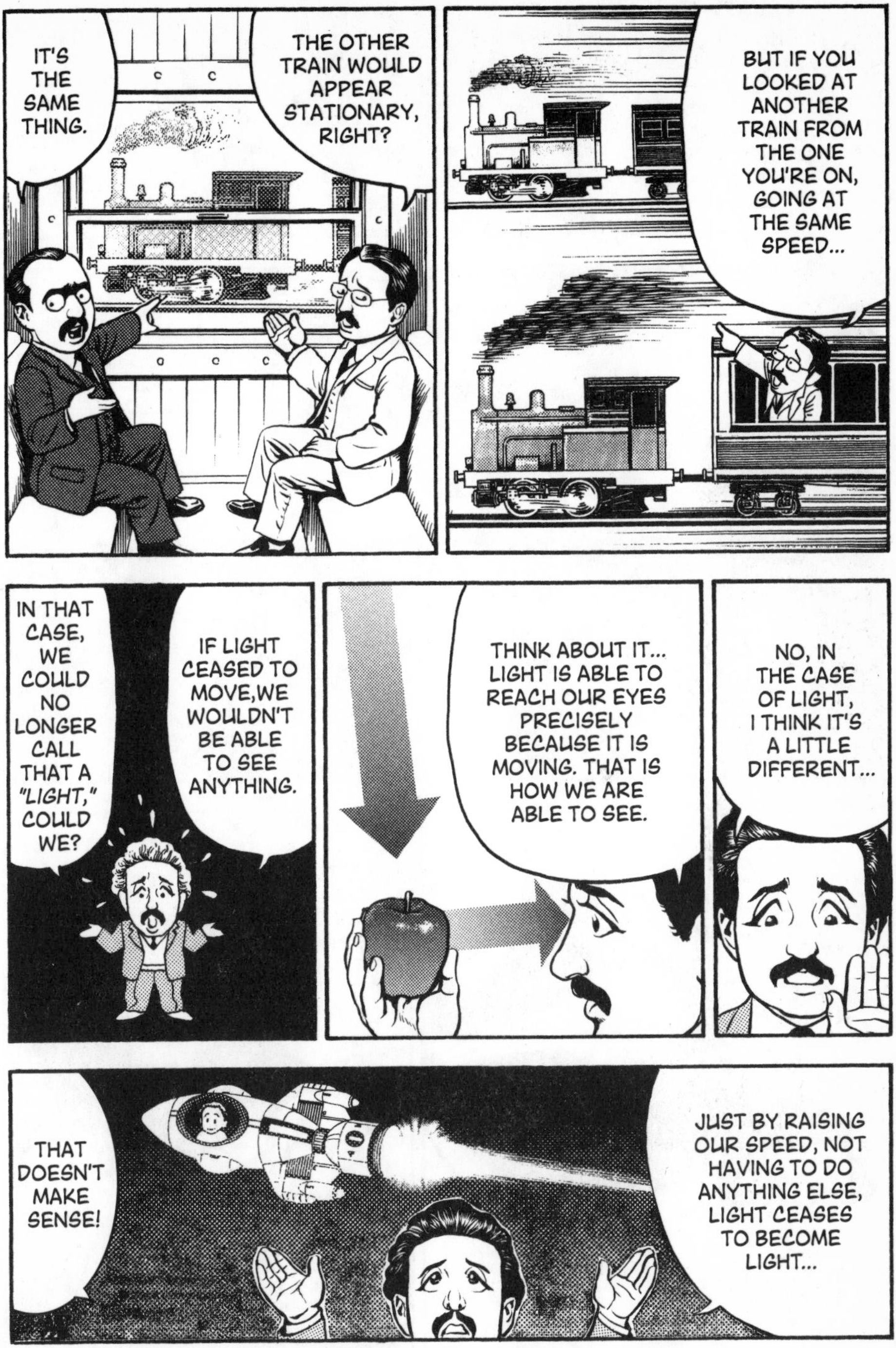
BUT IF YOU LOOKED AT ANOTHER TRAIN FROM THE ONE YOU'RE ON, GOING AT THE SAME SPEED...
THE OTHER TRAIN WOULD APPEAR STATIONARY, RIGHT?
IT'S THE SAME THING.
NO, IN THE CASE OF LIGHT, I THINK IT'S A LITTLE DIFFERENT...
THINK ABOUT IT... LIGHT IS ABLE TO REACH OUR EYES PRECISELY BECAUSE IT IS MOVING. THAT IS HOW WE ARE ABLE TO SEE.
IF LIGHT CEASED TO MOVE,WE WOULDN'T BE ABLE TO SEE ANYTHING.
IN THAT CASE, WE COULD NO LONGER CALL THAT A "LIGHT," COULD WE?
JUST BY RAISING OUR SPEED, NOT HAVING TO DO ANYTHING ELSE, LIGHT CEASES TO BECOME LIGHT...
THAT DOESN'T MAKE SENSE!

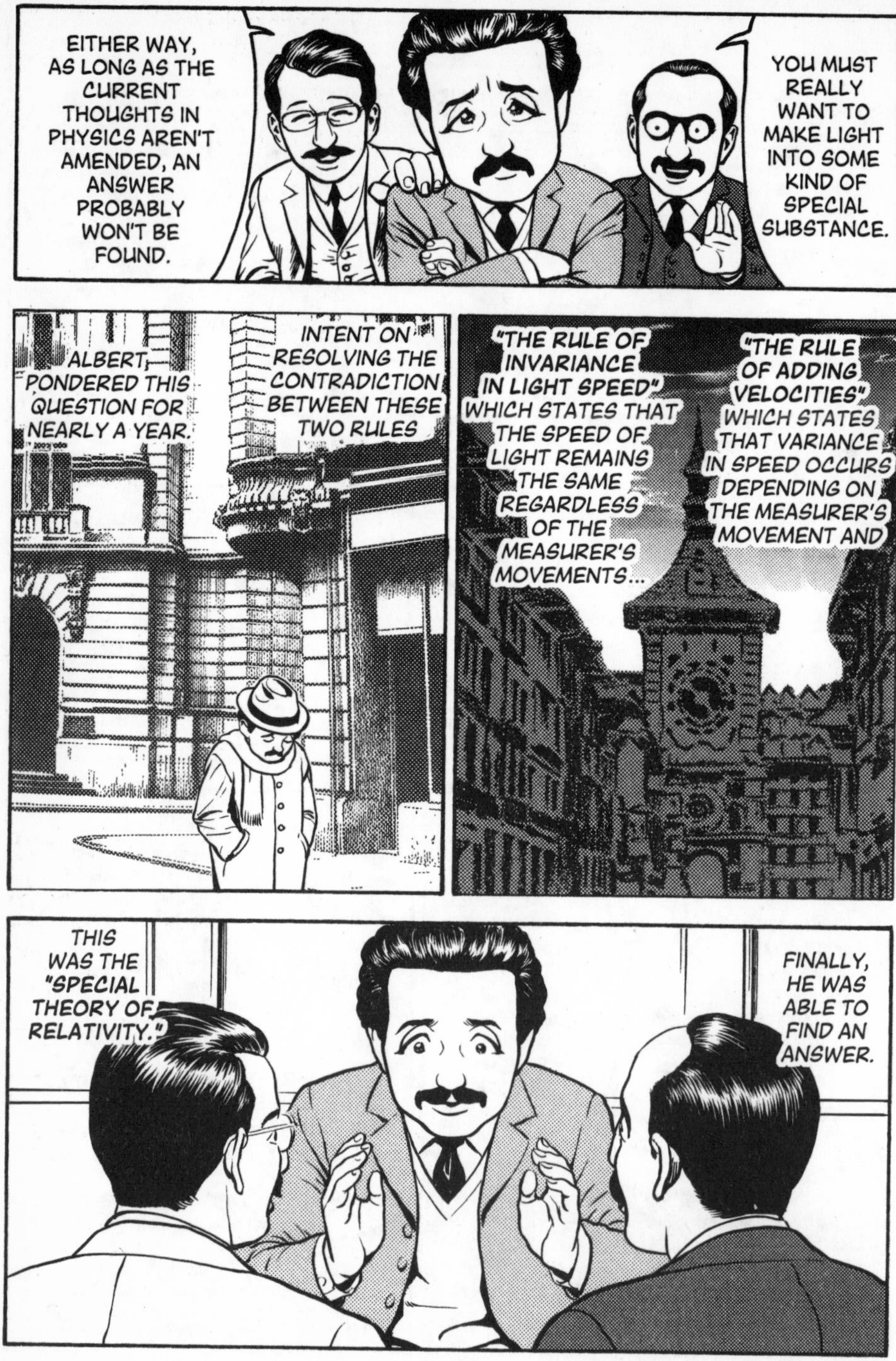
YOU MUST REALLY WANT TO MAKE LIGHT INTO SOME KIND OF SPECIAL SUBSTANCE.
EITHER WAY, AS LONG AS THE CURRENT THOUGHTS IN PHYSICS AREN'T AMENDED, AN ANSWER PROBABLY WON'T BE FOUND.
"THE RULE OF ADDING VELOCITIES" WHICH STATES THAT VARIANCE IN SPEED OCCURS DEPENDING ON THE MEASURER'S MOVEMENT AND
"THE RULE OF INVARIANCE IN LIGHT SPEED" WHICH STATES THAT THE SPEED OF LIGHT REMAINS THE SAME REGARDLESS OF THE MEASURER'S MOVEMENTS...
INTENT ON RESOLVING THE CONTRADICTION BETWEEN THESE TWO RULES
ALBERT, PONDERED THIS QUESTION FOR NEARLY A YEAR.
FINALLY, HE WAS ABLE TO FIND AN ANSWER.
THIS WAS THE "SPECIAL THEORY OF RELATIVITY."

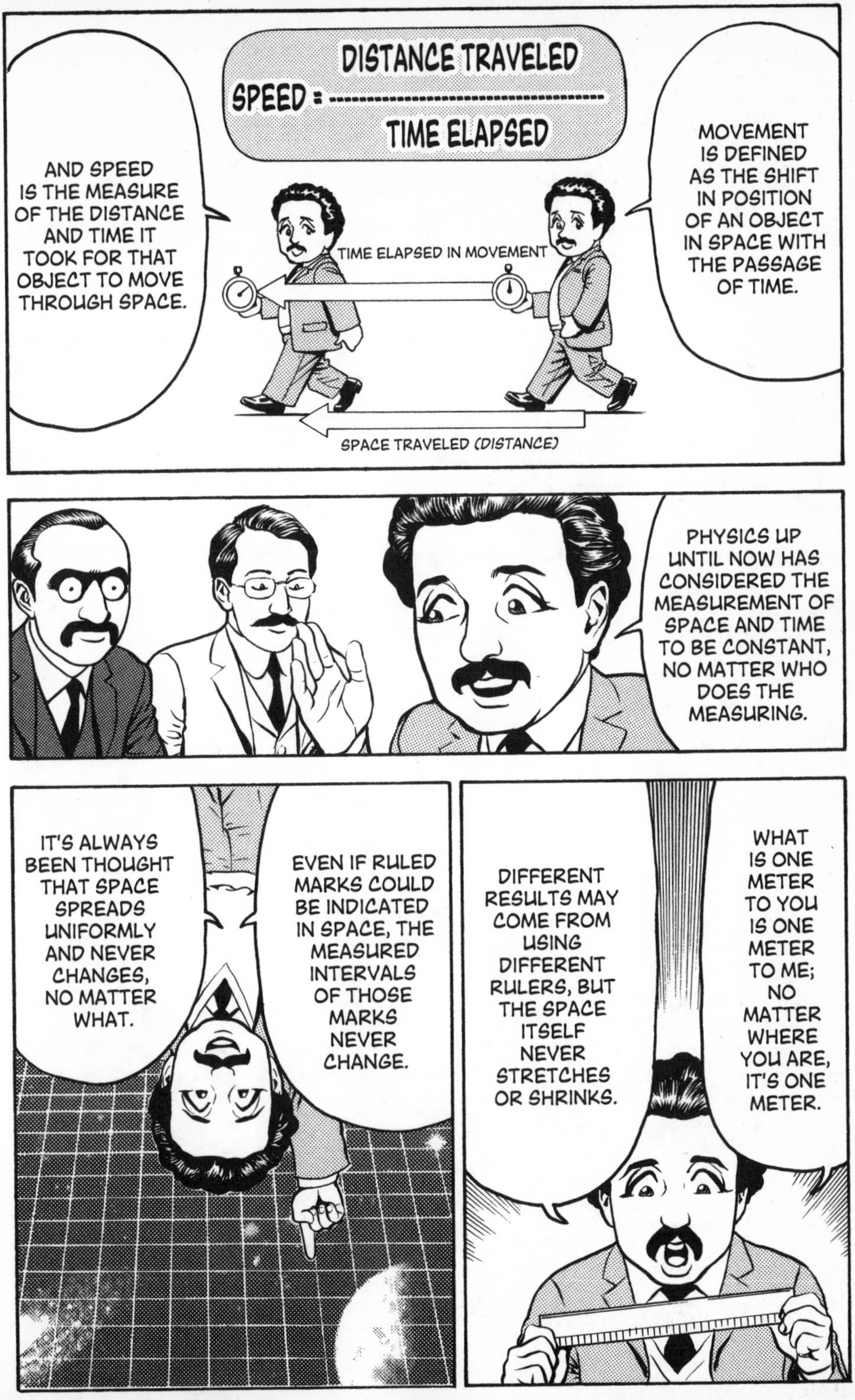
MOVEMENT IS DEFINED AS THE SHIFT IN POSITION OF AN OBJECT IN SPACE WITH THE PASSAGE OF TIME.
SPEED = DISTANCE TRAVELED / TIME ELAPSED
TIME ELAPSED IN MOVEMENT
AND SPEED IS THE MEASURE OF THE DISTANCE AND TIME IT TOOK FOR THAT OBJECT TO MOVE THROUGH SPACE.
SPACE TRAVELED (DISTANCE)
PHYSICS UP UNTIL NOW HAS CONSIDERED THE MEASUREMENT OF SPACE AND TIME TO BE CONSTANT, NO MATTER WHO DOES THE MEASURING.
WHAT IS ONE METER TO YOU IS ONE METER TO ME; NO MATTER WHERE YOU ARE, IT'S ONE METER.
DIFFERENT RESULTS MAY COME FROM USING DIFFERENT RULERS, BUT THE SPACE ITSELF NEVER STRETCHES OR SHRINKS.
EVEN IF RULED MARKS COULD BE INDICATED IN SPACE, THE MEASURED INTERVALS OF THOSE MARKS NEVER CHANGE.
IT'S ALWAYS BEEN THOUGHT THAT SPACE SPREADS UNIFORMLY AND NEVER CHANGES, NO MATTER WHAT.

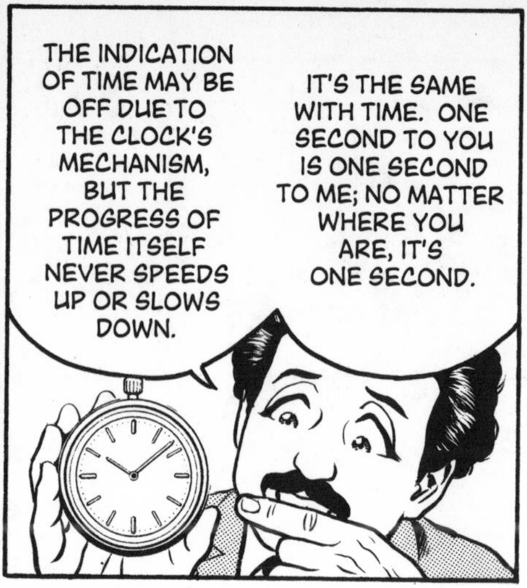
IT'S THE SAME WITH TIME. ONE SECOND TO YOU IS ONE SECOND TO ME; NO MATTER WHERE YOU ARE, IT'S ONE SECOND.
THE INDICATION OF TIME MAY BE OFF DUE TO THE CLOCK'S MECHANISM, BUT THE PROGRESS OF TIME ITSELF NEVER SPEEDS UP OR SLOWS DOWN.
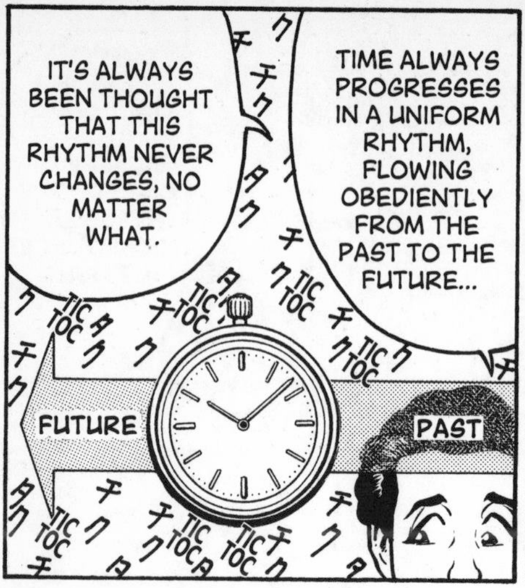
TIME ALWAYS PROGRESSES IN A UNIFORM RHYTHM, FLOWING OBEDIENTLY FROM THE PAST TO THE FUTURE...
IT'S ALWAYS BEEN THOUGHT THAT THIS RHYTHM NEVER CHANGES, NO MATTER WHAT.
TIC TOC
PAST
FUTURE
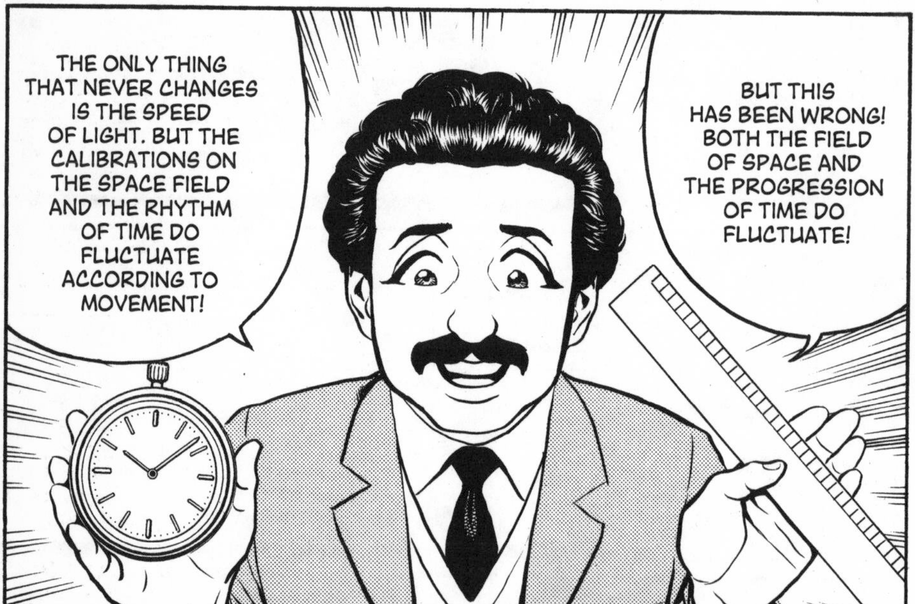
BUT THIS HAS BEEN WRONG! BOTH THE FIELD OF SPACE AND THE PROGRESSION OF TIME DO FLUCTUATE!
THE ONLY THING THAT NEVER CHANGES IS THE SPEED OF LIGHT. BUT THE CALIBRATIONS ON THE SPACE FIELD AND THE RHYTHM OF TIME DO FLUCTUATE ACCORDING TO MOVEMENT!
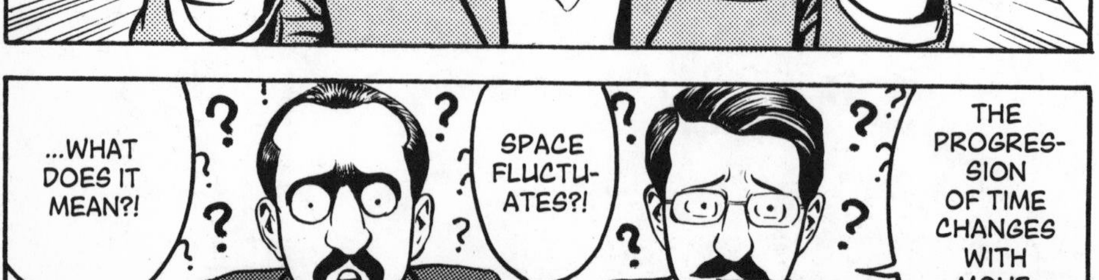
THE PROGRES-SION OF TIME CHANGES WITH MOVE-MENT?!
SPACE FLUCTU-ATES?!
...WHAT DOES IT MEAN?!

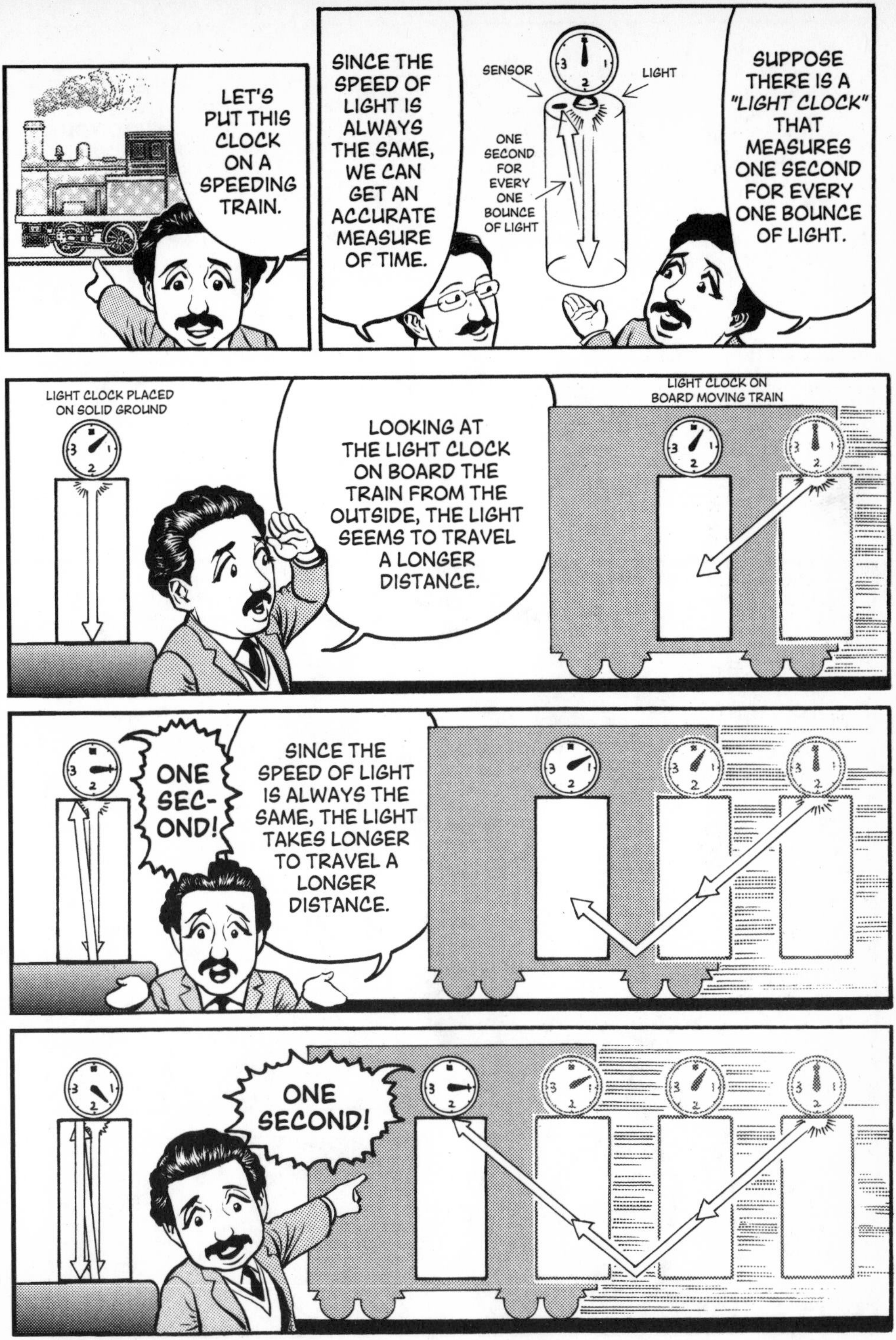
SUPPOSE THERE IS A "LIGHT CLOCK" THAT MEASURES ONE SECOND FOR EVERY ONE BOUNCE OF LIGHT.
LIGHT
SENSOR
ONE SECOND FOR EVERY ONE BOUNCE OF LIGHT
SINCE THE SPEED OF LIGHT IS ALWAYS THE SAME, WE CAN GET AN ACCURATE MEASURE OF TIME.
LET'S PUT THIS CLOCK ON A SPEEDING TRAIN.
LIGHT CLOCK ON BOARD MOVING TRAIN
LOOKING AT THE LIGHT CLOCK ON BOARD THE TRAIN FROM THE OUTSIDE, THE LIGHT SEEMS TO TRAVEL A LONGER DISTANCE.
LIGHT CLOCK PLACED ON SOLID GROUND
SINCE THE SPEED OF LIGHT IS ALWAYS THE SAME, THE LIGHT TAKES LONGER TO TRAVEL A LONGER DISTANCE.
ONE SEC-OND!
ONE SECOND!

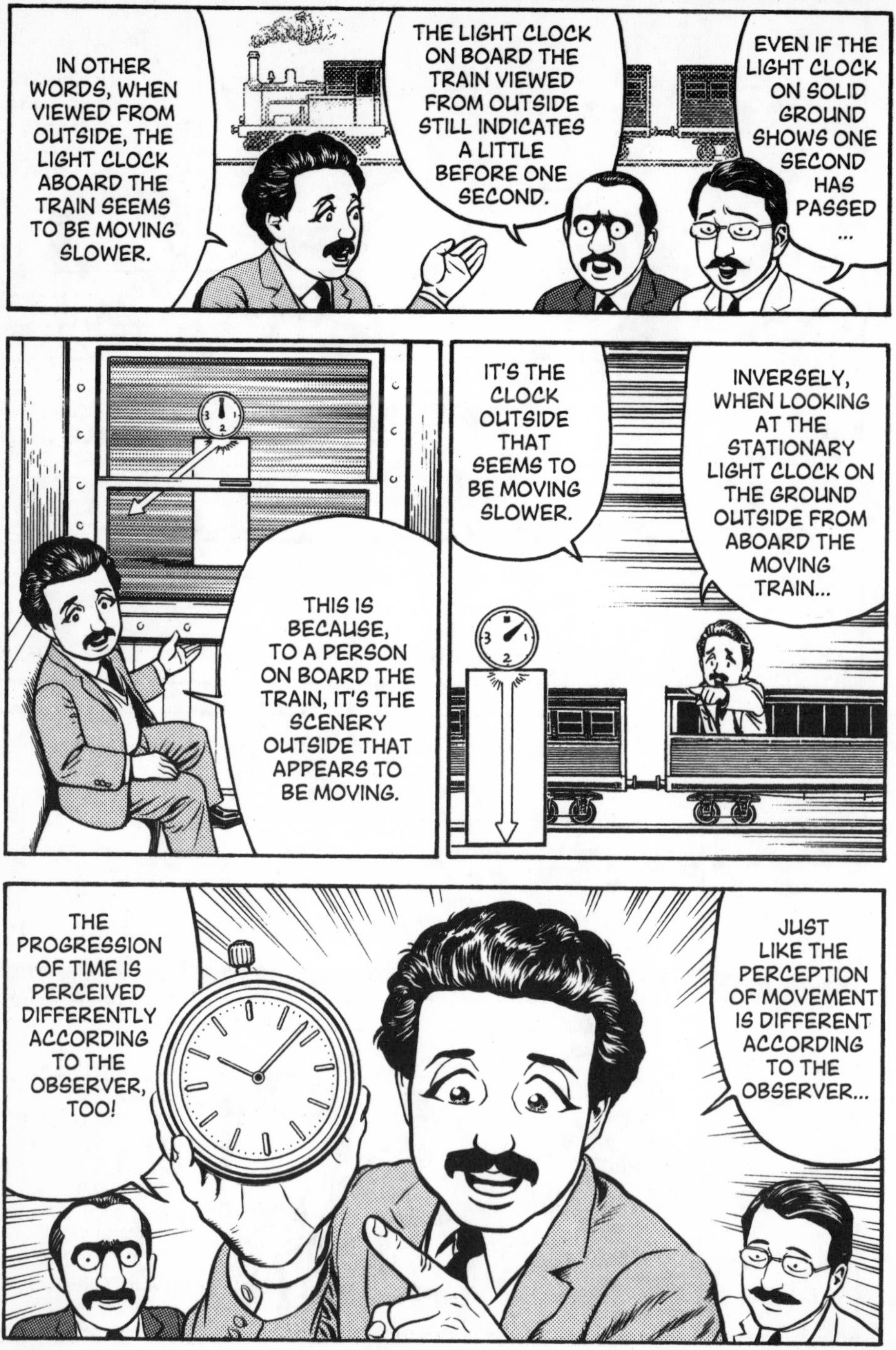

EVEN IF THE LIGHT CLOCK ON SOLID GROUND SHOWS ONE SECOND HAS PASSED ...
THE LIGHT CLOCK ON BOARD THE TRAIN VIEWED FROM OUTSIDE STILL INDICATES A LITTLE BEFORE ONE SECOND.
IN OTHER WORDS, WHEN VIEWED FROM OUTSIDE, THE LIGHT CLOCK ABOARD THE TRAIN SEEMS TO BE MOVING SLOWER.
INVERSELY, WHEN LOOKING AT THE STATIONARY LIGHT CLOCK ON THE GROUND OUTSIDE FROM ABOARD THE MOVING TRAIN...
IT'S THE CLOCK OUTSIDE THAT SEEMS TO BE MOVING SLOWER.
THIS IS BECAUSE, TO A PERSON ON BOARD THE TRAIN, IT'S THE SCENERY OUTSIDE THAT APPEARS TO BE MOVING.
JUST LIKE THE PERCEPTION OF MOVEMENT IS DIFFERENT ACCORDING TO THE OBSERVER...
THE PROGRESSION OF TIME IS PERCEIVED DIFFERENTLY ACCORDING TO THE OBSERVER, TOO!

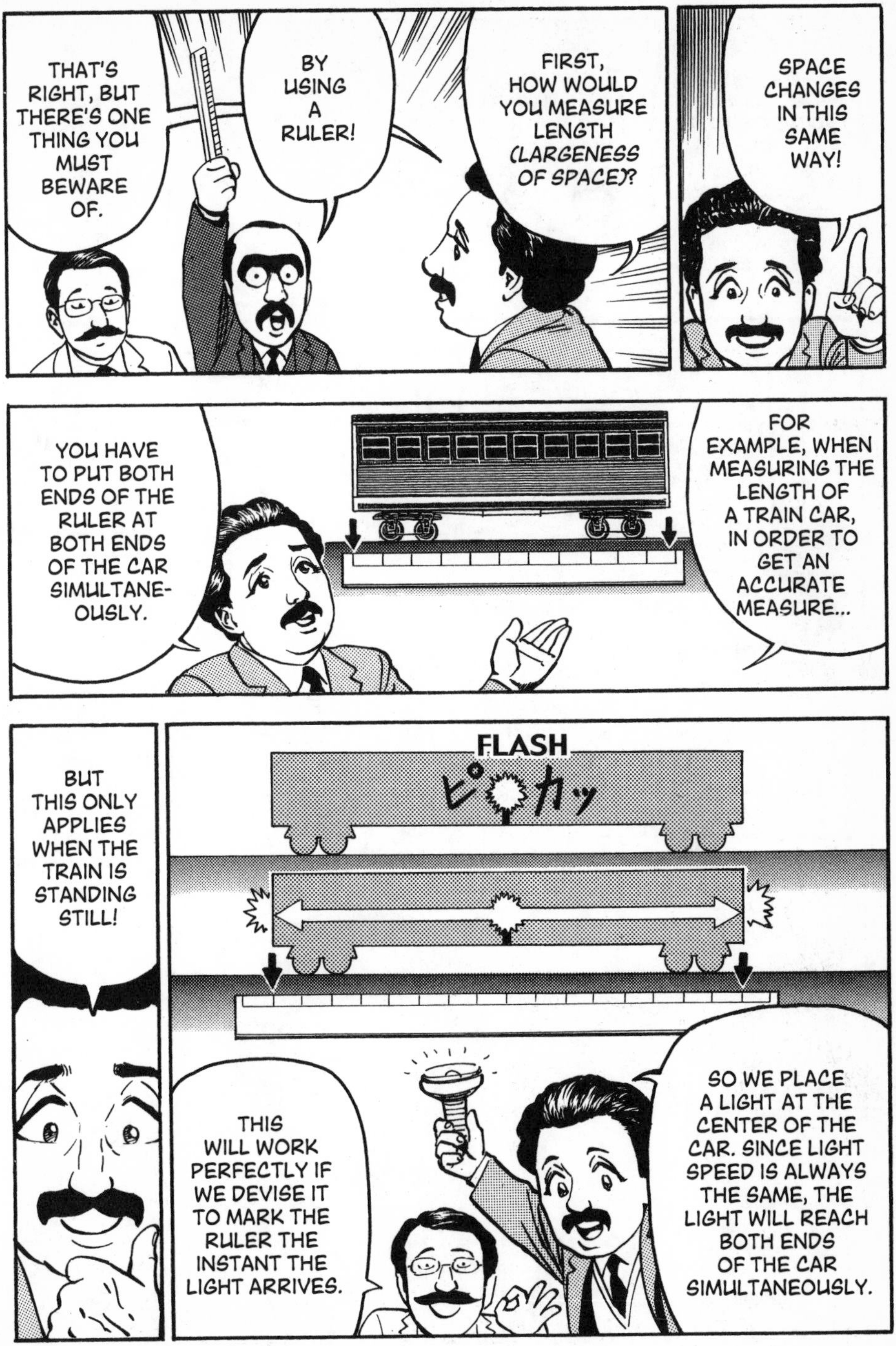
SPACE CHANGES IN THIS SAME WAY!
FIRST, HOW WOULD YOU MEASURE LENGTH (LARGENESS OF SPACE)?
BY USING A RULER!
THAT'S RIGHT, BUT THERE'S ONE THING YOU MUST BEWARE OF.
FOR EXAMPLE, WHEN MEASURING THE LENGTH OF A TRAIN CAR, IN ORDER TO GET AN ACCURATE MEASURE...
YOU HAVE TO PUT BOTH ENDS OF THE RULER AT BOTH ENDS OF THE CAR SIMULTANEOUSLY.
FLASH
ピカッ
SO WE PLACE A LIGHT AT THE CENTER OF THE CAR. SINCE LIGHT SPEED IS ALWAYS THE SAME, THE LIGHT WILL REACH BOTH ENDS OF THE CAR SIMULTANEOUSLY.
THIS WILL WORK PERFECTLY IF WE DEVISE IT TO MARK THE RULER THE INSTANT THE LIGHT ARRIVES.
BUT THIS ONLY APPLIES WHEN THE TRAIN IS STANDING STILL!

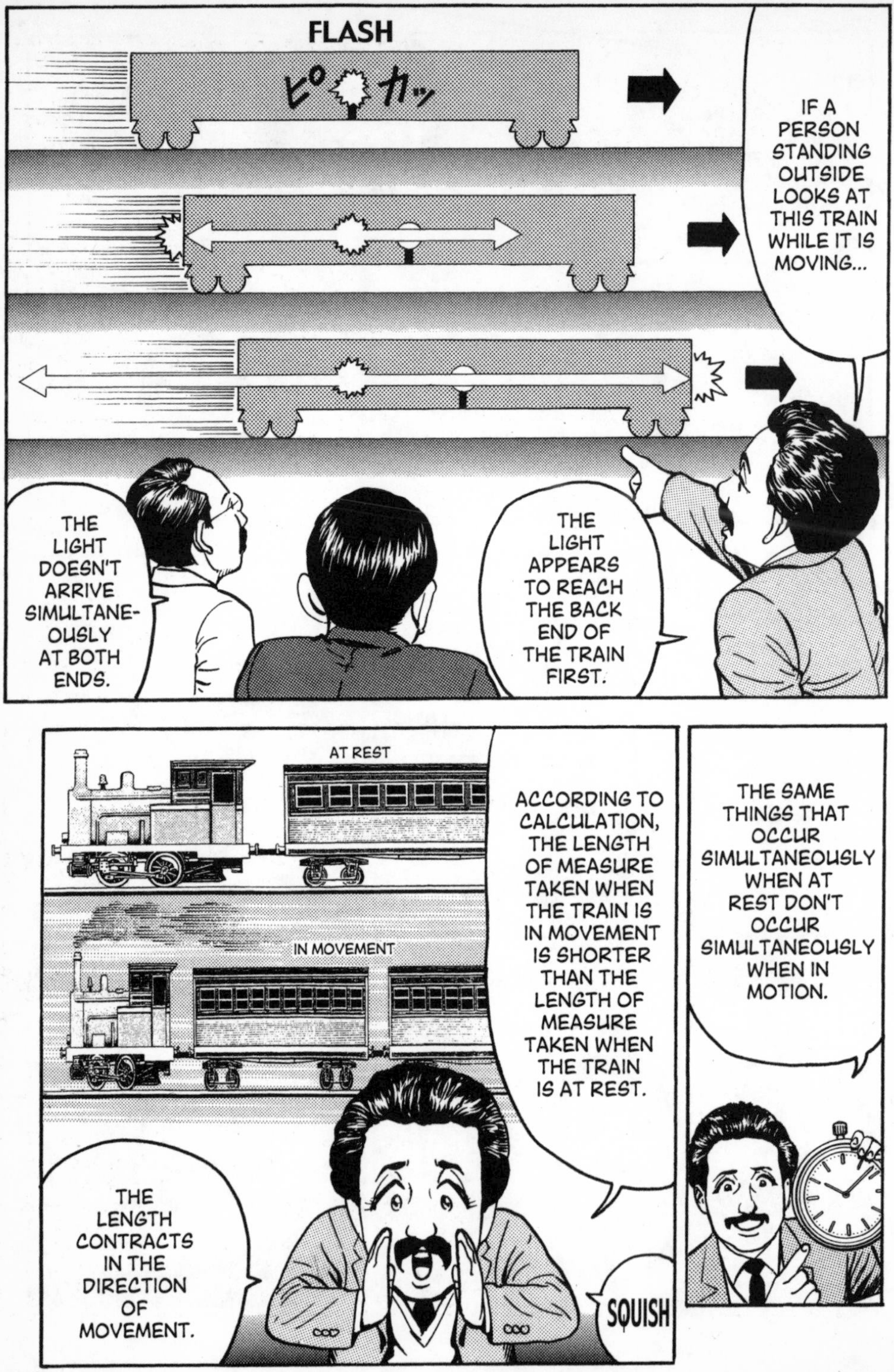

IF A PERSON STANDING OUTSIDE LOOKS AT THIS TRAIN WHILE IT IS MOVING...
FLASH
ピカッ
THE LIGHT APPEARS TO REACH THE BACK END OF THE TRAIN FIRST.
THE LIGHT DOESN'T ARRIVE SIMULTANEOUSLY AT BOTH ENDS.
THE SAME THINGS THAT OCCUR SIMULTANEOUSLY WHEN AT REST DON'T OCCUR SIMULTANEOUSLY WHEN IN MOTION.
ACCORDING TO CALCULATION, THE LENGTH OF MEASURE TAKEN WHEN THE TRAIN IS IN MOVEMENT IS SHORTER THAN THE LENGTH OF MEASURE TAKEN WHEN THE TRAIN IS AT REST.
AT REST
IN MOVEMENT
SQUISH
THE LENGTH CONTRACTS IN THE DIRECTION OF MOVEMENT.

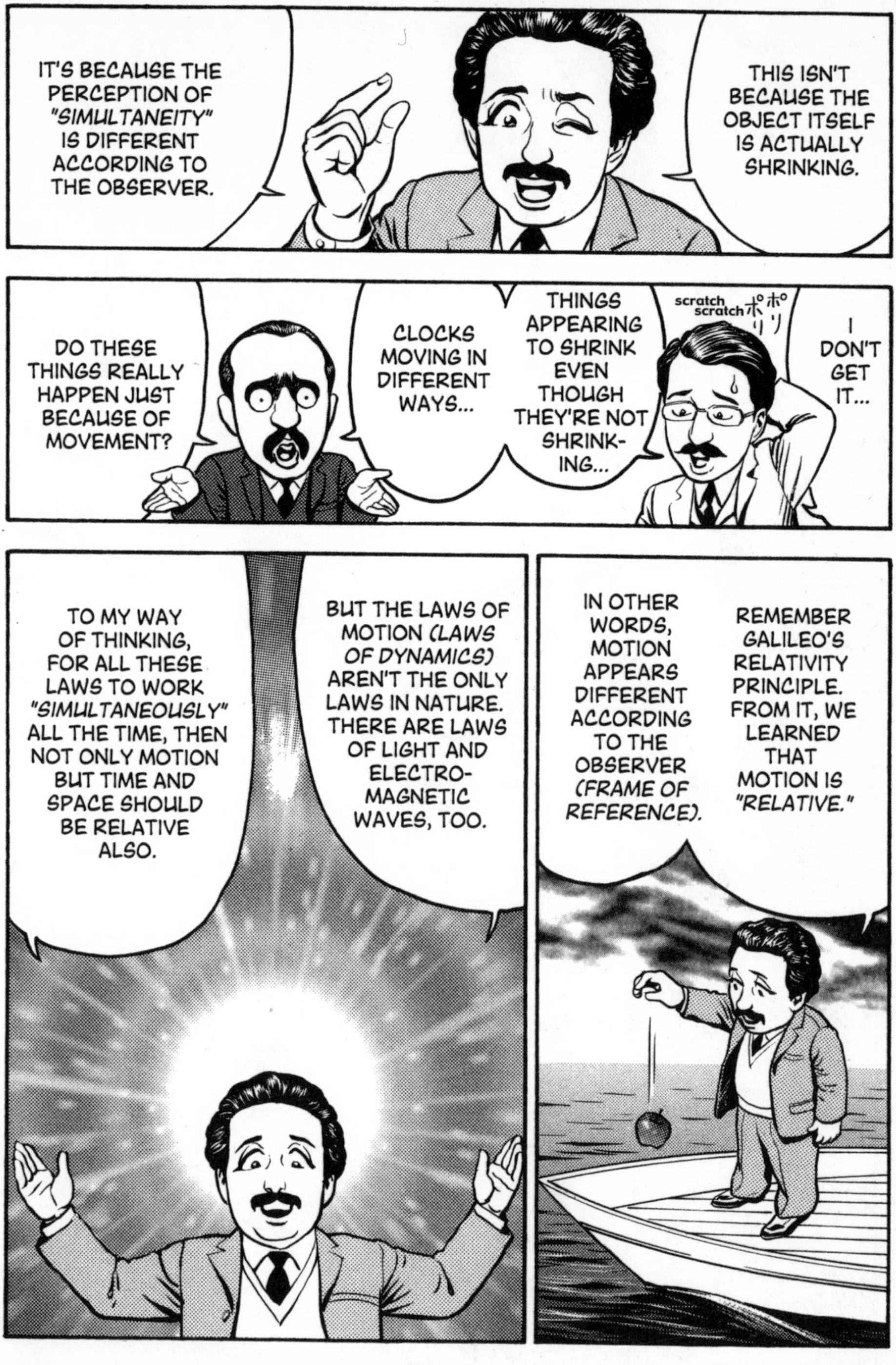
THIS ISN'T BECAUSE THE OBJECT ITSELF IS ACTUALLY SHRINKING.
IT'S BECAUSE THE PERCEPTION OF "SIMULTANEITY" IS DIFFERENT ACCORDING TO THE OBSERVER.
I DON'T GET IT...
scratch scratch ポリポリ
THINGS APPEARING TO SHRINK EVEN THOUGH THEY'RE NOT SHRINK-ING...
CLOCKS MOVING IN DIFFERENT WAYS...
DO THESE THINGS REALLY HAPPEN JUST BECAUSE OF MOVEMENT?
REMEMBER GALILEO'S RELATIVITY PRINCIPLE. FROM IT, WE LEARNED THAT MOTION IS "RELATIVE."
IN OTHER WORDS, MOTION APPEARS DIFFERENT ACCORDING TO THE OBSERVER (FRAME OF REFERENCE).
BUT THE LAWS OF MOTION (LAWS OF DYNAMICS) AREN'T THE ONLY LAWS IN NATURE. THERE ARE LAWS OF LIGHT AND ELECTRO-MAGNETIC WAVES, TOO.
TO MY WAY OF THINKING, FOR ALL THESE LAWS TO WORK "SIMULTANEOUSLY" ALL THE TIME, THEN NOT ONLY MOTION BUT TIME AND SPACE SHOULD BE RELATIVE ALSO.

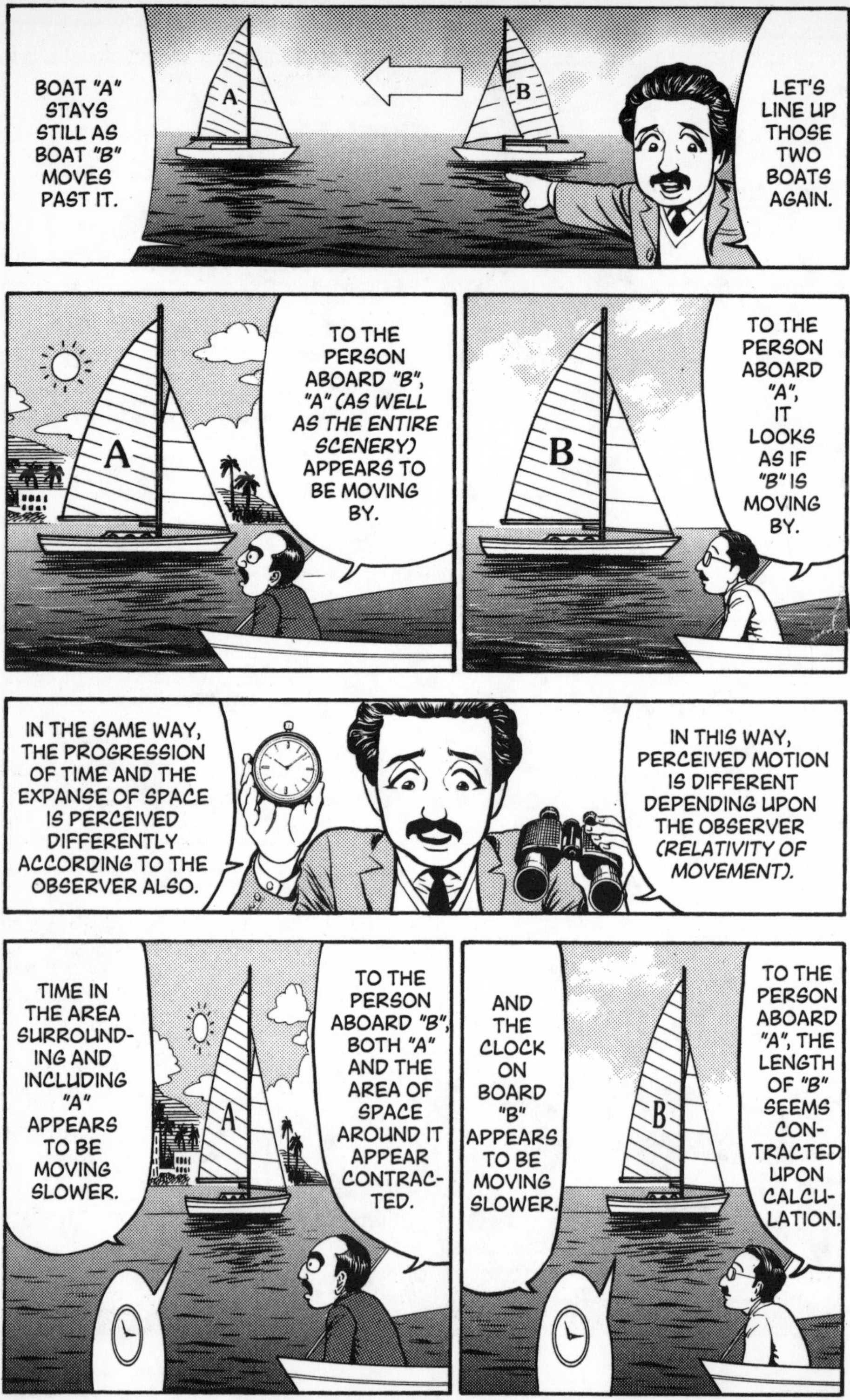
LET'S LINE UP THOSE TWO BOATS AGAIN.
BOAT "A" STAYS STILL AS BOAT "B" MOVES PAST IT.
TO THE PERSON ABOARD "A", IT LOOKS AS IF "B" IS MOVING BY.
TO THE PERSON ABOARD "B", "A" (AS WELL AS THE ENTIRE SCENERY) APPEARS TO BE MOVING BY.
IN THIS WAY, PERCEIVED MOTION IS DIFFERENT DEPENDING UPON THE OBSERVER (RELATIVITY OF MOVEMENT).
IN THE SAME WAY, THE PROGRESSION OF TIME AND THE EXPANSE OF SPACE IS PERCEIVED DIFFERENTLY ACCORDING TO THE OBSERVER ALSO.
TO THE PERSON ABOARD "A", THE LENGTH OF "B" SEEMS CONTRACTED UPON CALCULATION.
AND THE CLOCK ON BOARD "B" APPEARS TO BE MOVING SLOWER.
TO THE PERSON ABOARD "B", BOTH "A" AND THE AREA OF SPACE AROUND IT APPEAR CONTRACTED.
TIME IN THE AREA SURROUNDING AND INCLUDING "A" APPEARS TO BE MOVING SLOWER.

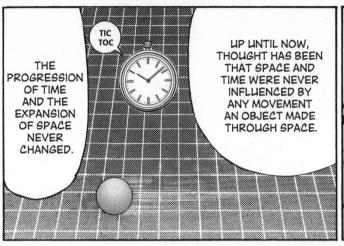

I'LL REPEAT.
UP UNTIL NOW, THOUGHT HAS BEEN THAT SPACE AND TIME WERE NEVER INFLUENCED BY ANY MOVEMENT AN OBJECT MADE THROUGH SPACE.
TIC TOC
THE PROGRESSION OF TIME AND THE EXPANSION OF SPACE NEVER CHANGED.
BUT THAT'S NOT THE CASE.
TIC
TOC
THE PROGRESSION OF TIME AND THE EXPANSION OF SPACE *DO* CHANGE ACCORDING TO THE MOVEMENT OF AN OBJECT!
I SAY *"CHANGE"* BUT IT'S NOT AS IF THEY CHANGE RANDOMLY. THERE IS ONE RULE.
THAT IS TO ALWAYS KEEP THE SPEED OF LIGHT THE SAME!
RULE OF INVARIANCE IN LIGHT SPEED

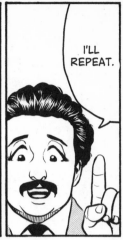

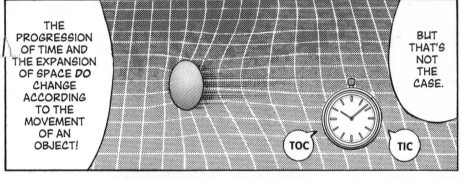

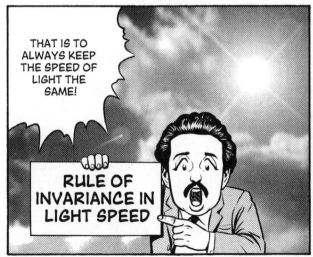

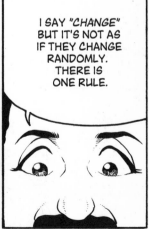

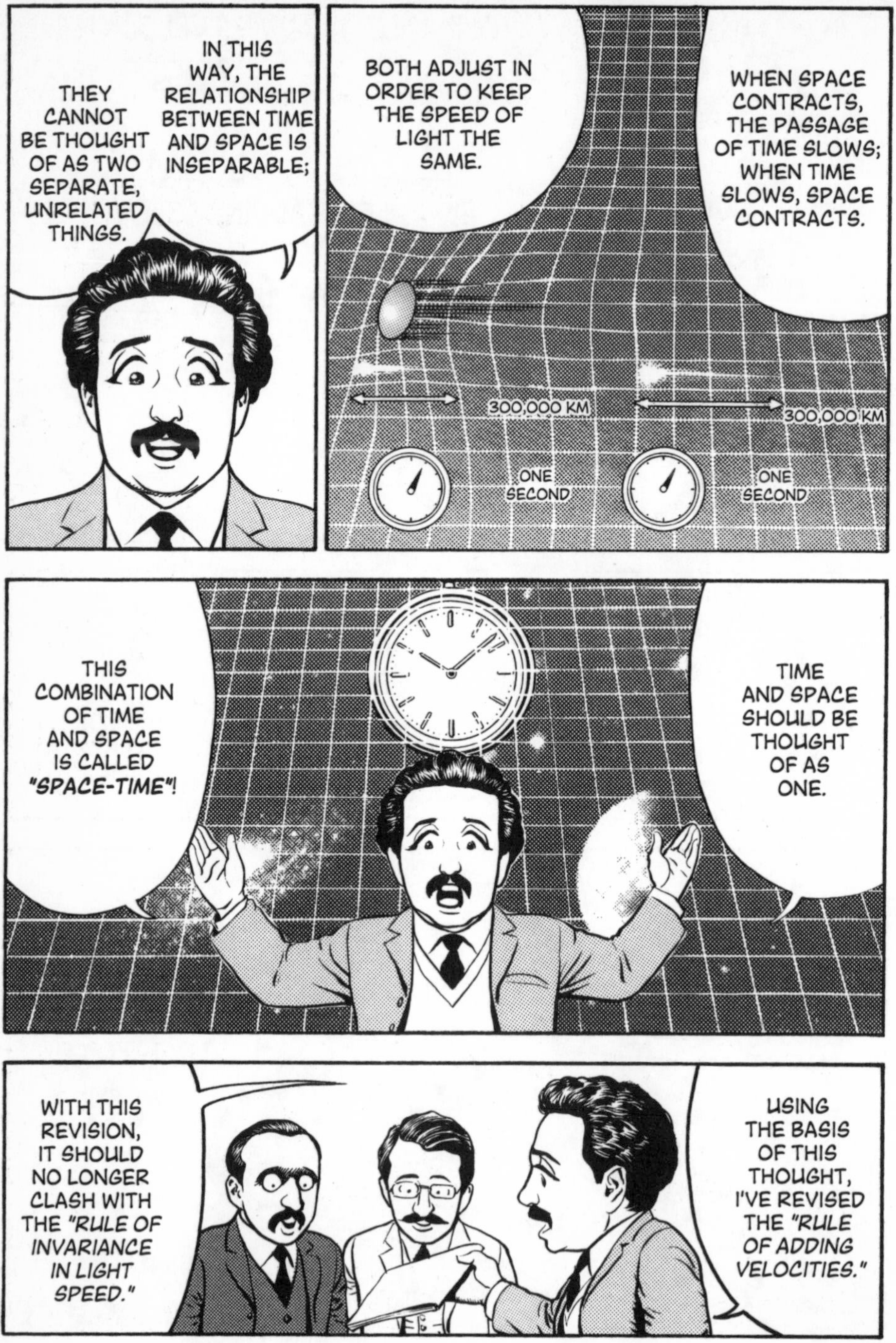
WHEN SPACE CONTRACTS, THE PASSAGE OF TIME SLOWS; WHEN TIME SLOWS, SPACE CONTRACTS.
BOTH ADJUST IN ORDER TO KEEP THE SPEED OF LIGHT THE SAME.
300,000 KM
ONE SECOND
300,000 KM
ONE SECOND
IN THIS WAY, THE RELATIONSHIP BETWEEN TIME AND SPACE IS INSEPARABLE;
THEY CANNOT BE THOUGHT OF AS TWO SEPARATE, UNRELATED THINGS.
TIME AND SPACE SHOULD BE THOUGHT OF AS ONE.
THIS COMBINATION OF TIME AND SPACE IS CALLED ***"SPACE-TIME"***!
USING THE BASIS OF THIS THOUGHT, I'VE REVISED THE *"RULE OF ADDING VELOCITIES."*
WITH THIS REVISION, IT SHOULD NO LONGER CLASH WITH THE *"RULE OF INVARIANCE IN LIGHT SPEED."*

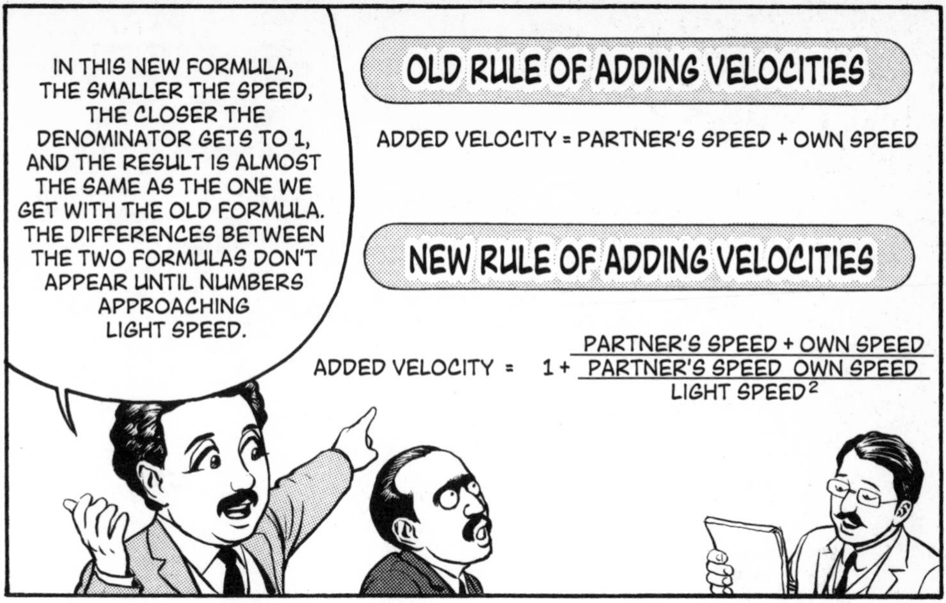
OLD RULE OF ADDING VELOCITIES
ADDED VELOCITY = PARTNER'S SPEED + OWN SPEED
NEW RULE OF ADDING VELOCITIES
PARTNER'S SPEED + OWN SPEED
ADDED VELOCITY = 1 + PARTNER'S SPEED OWN SPEED
LIGHT SPEED²
IN THIS NEW FORMULA, THE SMALLER THE SPEED, THE CLOSER THE DENOMINATOR GETS TO 1, AND THE RESULT IS ALMOST THE SAME AS THE ONE WE GET WITH THE OLD FORMULA. THE DIFFERENCES BETWEEN THE TWO FORMULAS DON'T APPEAR UNTIL NUMBERS APPROACHING LIGHT SPEED.

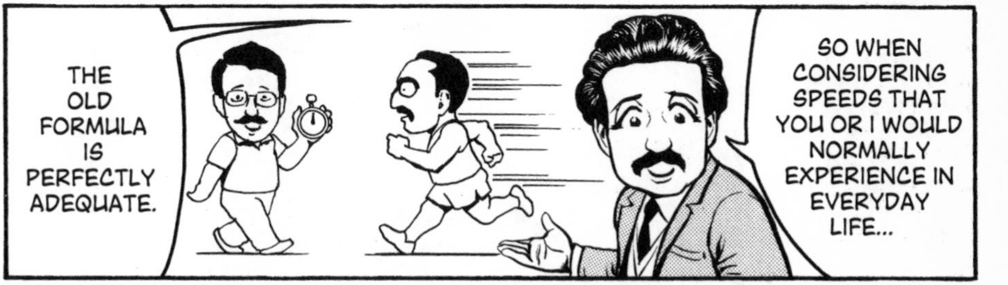
SO WHEN CONSIDERING SPEEDS THAT YOU OR I WOULD NORMALLY EXPERIENCE IN EVERYDAY LIFE...
THE OLD FORMULA IS PERFECTLY ADEQUATE.

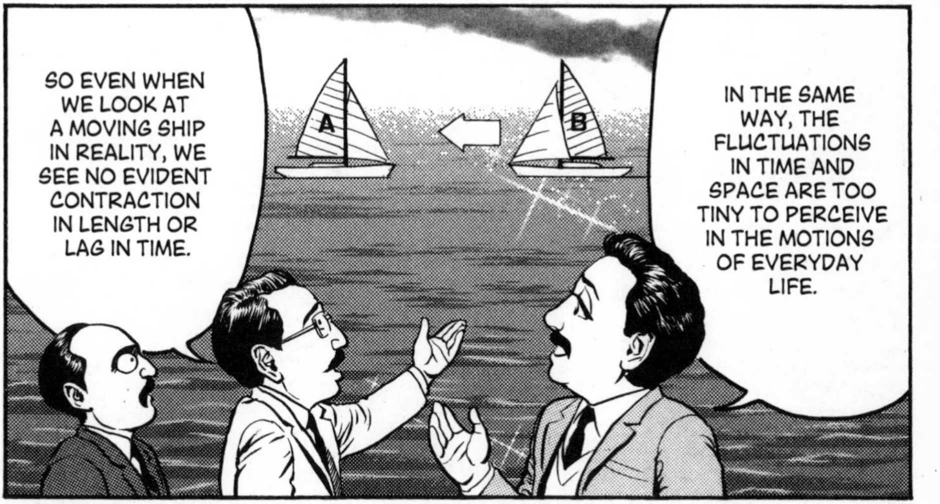
IN THE SAME WAY, THE FLUCTUATIONS IN TIME AND SPACE ARE TOO TINY TO PERCEIVE IN THE MOTIONS OF EVERYDAY LIFE.
B
A
SO EVEN WHEN WE LOOK AT A MOVING SHIP IN REALITY, WE SEE NO EVIDENT CONTRACTION IN LENGTH OR LAG IN TIME.

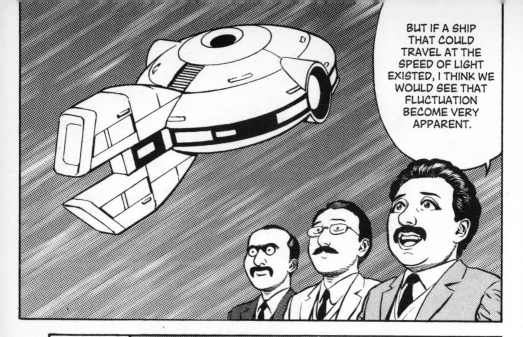

BUT IF A SHIP THAT COULD TRAVEL AT THE SPEED OF LIGHT EXISTED, I THINK WE WOULD SEE THAT FLUCTUATION BECOME VERY APPARENT.
TIME INSIDE THE SHIP WOULD SLOW, AND THE LENGTH OF THE SHIP WOULD APPEAR CONTRACTED.
AND, UPON CALCULATION, WE WOULD SEE THAT THE MASS (WEIGHT) HAS ALSO INCREASED.
THE CLOSER THE SHIP'S SPEED GETS TO THE SPEED OF LIGHT, THE SLOWER THE PROGRESSION OF TIME, AND THE MORE CONTRACTED AND HEAVIER THE SHIP.
ACCORDING TO CALCULATION, WHEN THE SHIP REACHES THE SPEED OF LIGHT, TIME WOULD STOP, THE LENGTH OF THE SHIP WOULD EQUAL ZERO, AND THE MASS WOULD BE INFINITE!
BUT IN REALITY, NO SUCH SITUATION IS POSSIBLE.

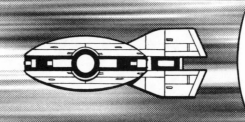

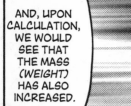

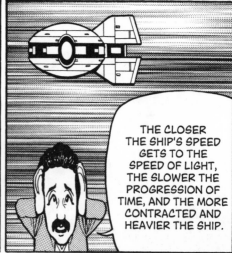

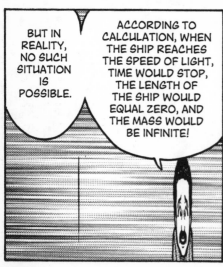

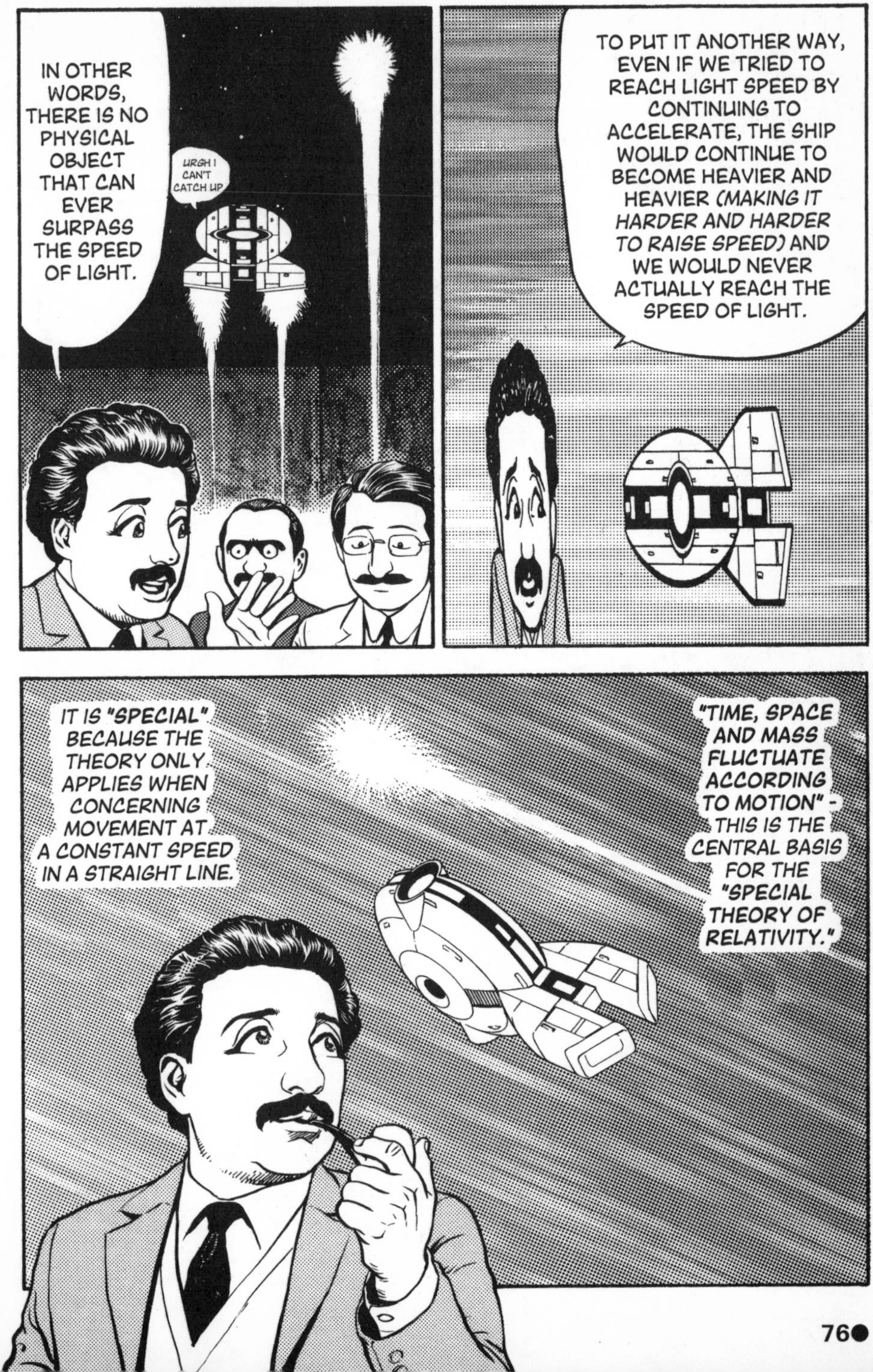
TO PUT IT ANOTHER WAY, EVEN IF WE TRIED TO REACH LIGHT SPEED BY CONTINUING TO ACCELERATE, THE SHIP WOULD CONTINUE TO BECOME HEAVIER AND HEAVIER (MAKING IT HARDER AND HARDER TO RAISE SPEED) AND WE WOULD NEVER ACTUALLY REACH THE SPEED OF LIGHT.
IN OTHER WORDS, THERE IS NO PHYSICAL OBJECT THAT CAN EVER SURPASS THE SPEED OF LIGHT.
URGH I CAN'T CATCH UP
"TIME, SPACE AND MASS FLUCTUATE ACCORDING TO MOTION" - THIS IS THE CENTRAL BASIS FOR THE "SPECIAL THEORY OF RELATIVITY."
IT IS "SPECIAL" BECAUSE THE THEORY ONLY APPLIES WHEN CONCERNING MOVEMENT AT A CONSTANT SPEED IN A STRAIGHT LINE.

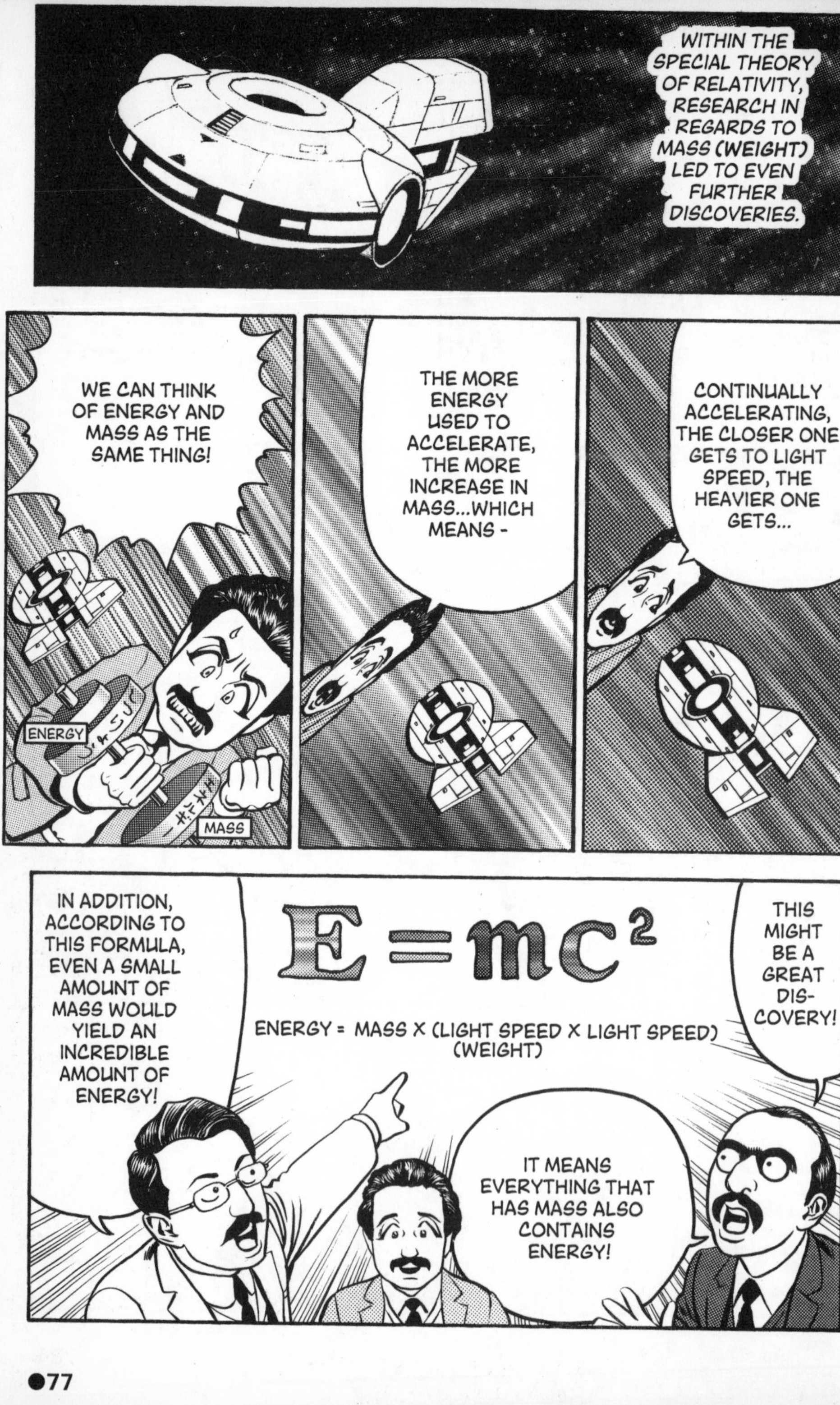

WITHIN THE SPECIAL THEORY OF RELATIVITY, RESEARCH IN REGARDS TO MASS (WEIGHT) LED TO EVEN FURTHER DISCOVERIES.
WE CAN THINK OF ENERGY AND MASS AS THE SAME THING!
ENERGY
MASS
THE MORE ENERGY USED TO ACCELERATE, THE MORE INCREASE IN MASS...WHICH MEANS -
CONTINUALLY ACCELERATING, THE CLOSER ONE GETS TO LIGHT SPEED, THE HEAVIER ONE GETS...
IN ADDITION, ACCORDING TO THIS FORMULA, EVEN A SMALL AMOUNT OF MASS WOULD YIELD AN INCREDIBLE AMOUNT OF ENERGY!
E = mc²
ENERGY = MASS X (LIGHT SPEED X LIGHT SPEED)
(WEIGHT)
IT MEANS EVERYTHING THAT HAS MASS ALSO CONTAINS ENERGY!
THIS MIGHT BE A GREAT DIS-COVERY!

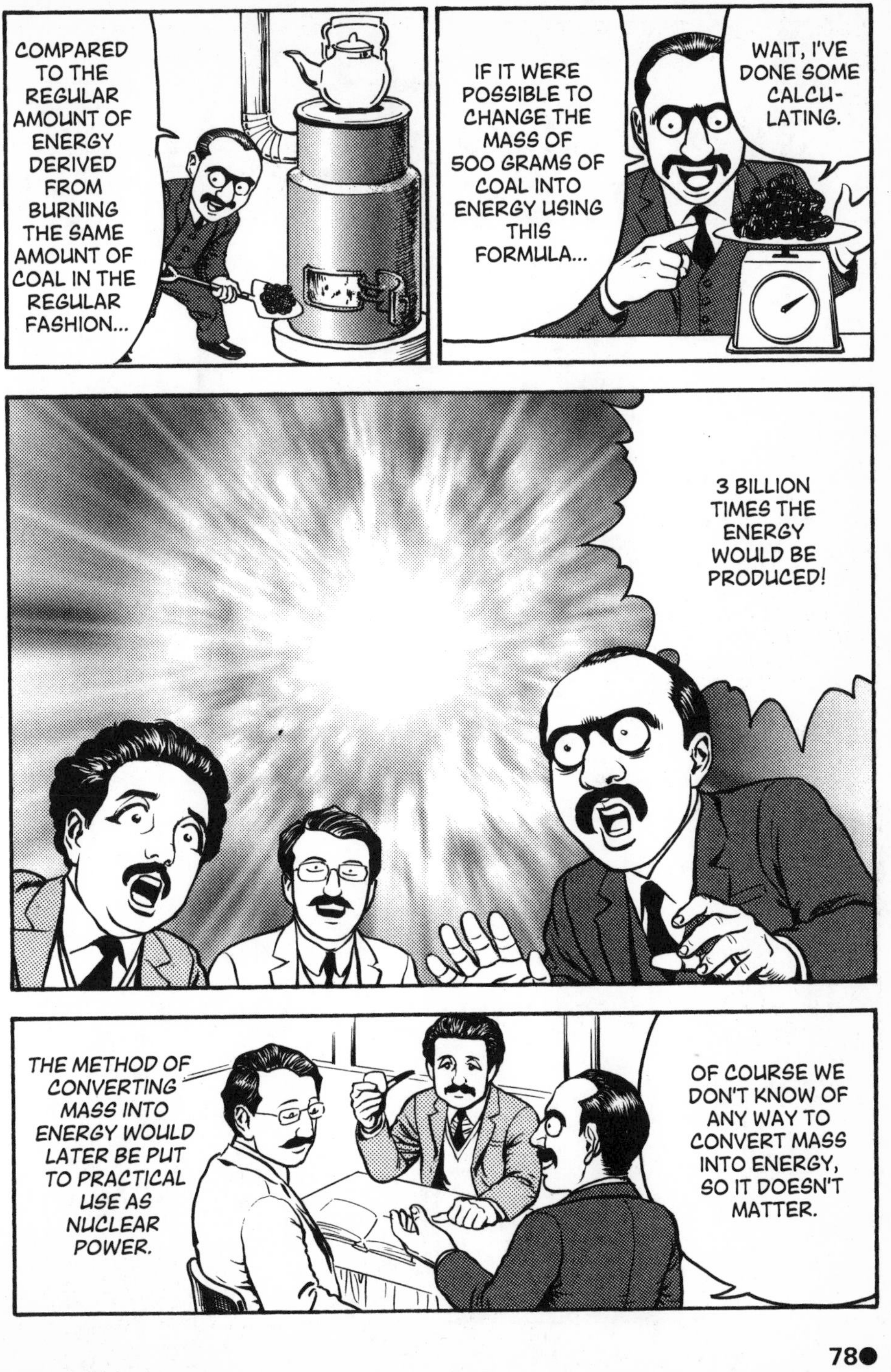
WAIT, I'VE DONE SOME CALCU-LATING.
IF IT WERE POSSIBLE TO CHANGE THE MASS OF 500 GRAMS OF COAL INTO ENERGY USING THIS FORMULA...
COMPARED TO THE REGULAR AMOUNT OF ENERGY DERIVED FROM BURNING THE SAME AMOUNT OF COAL IN THE REGULAR FASHION...
3 BILLION TIMES THE ENERGY WOULD BE PRODUCED!
OF COURSE WE DON'T KNOW OF ANY WAY TO CONVERT MASS INTO ENERGY, SO IT DOESN'T MATTER.
THE METHOD OF CONVERTING MASS INTO ENERGY WOULD LATER BE PUT TO PRACTICAL USE AS NUCLEAR POWER.

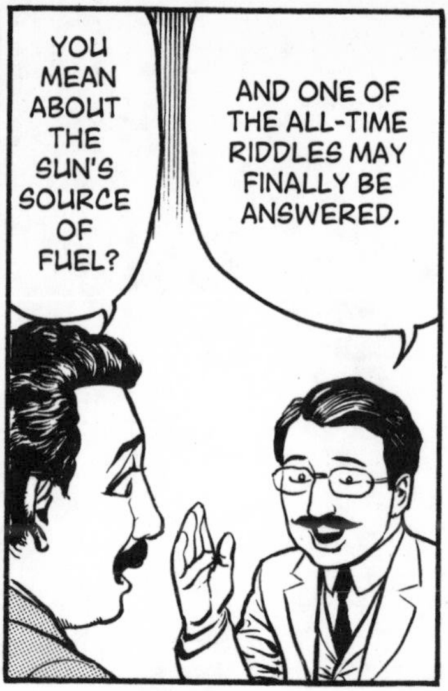
AND ONE OF THE ALL-TIME RIDDLES MAY FINALLY BE ANSWERED.
YOU MEAN ABOUT THE SUN'S SOURCE OF FUEL?
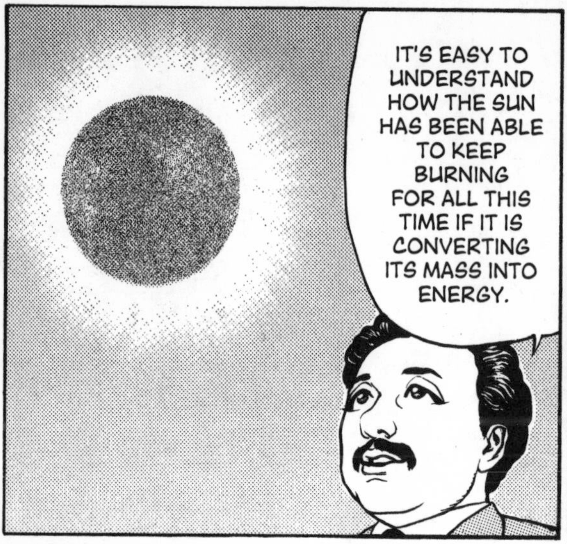
IT'S EASY TO UNDERSTAND HOW THE SUN HAS BEEN ABLE TO KEEP BURNING FOR ALL THIS TIME IF IT IS CONVERTING ITS MASS INTO ENERGY.
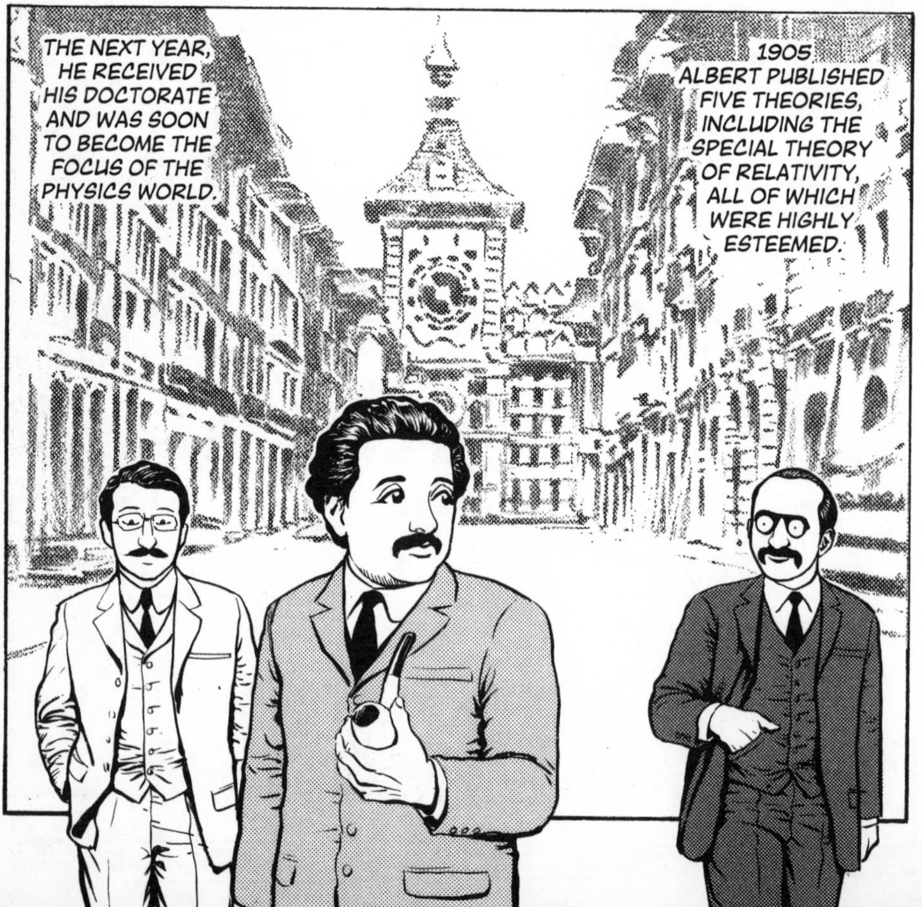
1905 ALBERT PUBLISHED FIVE THEORIES, INCLUDING THE SPECIAL THEORY OF RELATIVITY, ALL OF WHICH WERE HIGHLY ESTEEMED.
THE NEXT YEAR, HE RECEIVED HIS DOCTORATE AND WAS SOON TO BECOME THE FOCUS OF THE PHYSICS WORLD.

CHAPTER 4
THE NEW THEORY PROVEN

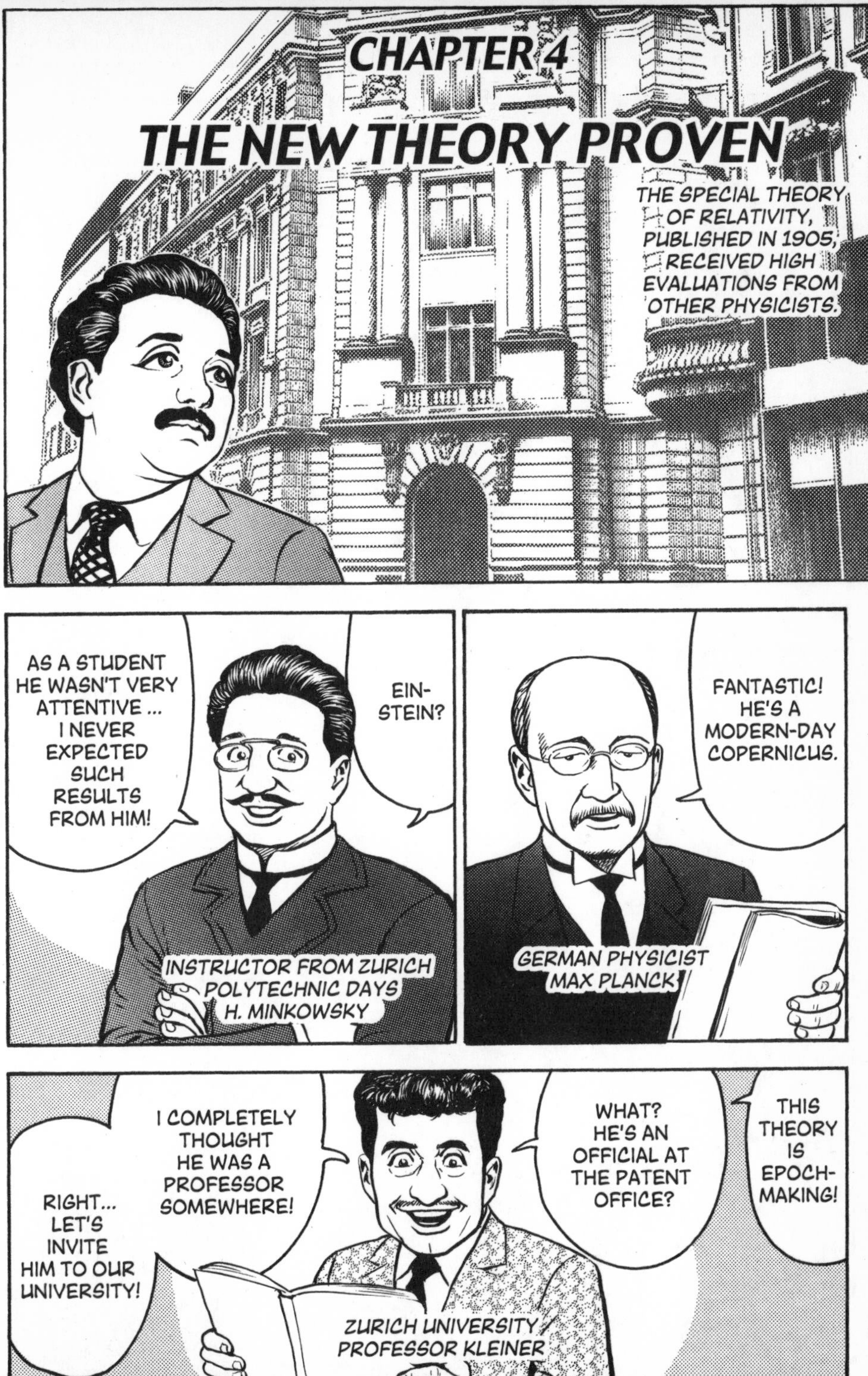
THE SPECIAL THEORY OF RELATIVITY, PUBLISHED IN 1905, RECEIVED HIGH EVALUATIONS FROM OTHER PHYSICISTS.
FANTASTIC! HE'S A MODERN-DAY COPERNICUS.
GERMAN PHYSICIST MAX PLANCK
EIN-STEIN?
AS A STUDENT HE WASN'T VERY ATTENTIVE ... I NEVER EXPECTED SUCH RESULTS FROM HIM!
INSTRUCTOR FROM ZURICH POLYTECHNIC DAYS H. MINKOWSKY
THIS THEORY IS EPOCH-MAKING!
WHAT? HE'S AN OFFICIAL AT THE PATENT OFFICE?
I COMPLETELY THOUGHT HE WAS A PROFESSOR SOMEWHERE!
RIGHT... LET'S INVITE HIM TO OUR UNIVERSITY!
ZURICH UNIVERSITY PROFESSOR KLEINER

COPERNICUS (1473-1543) POLISH ASTRONOMER AND PRIEST. OVERTURNED THE CHRISTIANITY-BASED THEORY OF THE UNIVERSE HED AT THE TIME BY PROCLAIMING THE EARTH REVOLVED AROUND THE SUN,THEREBY ESTABLISHING THE PRESENT-DAY VIEW OF THE UNIVERSE.

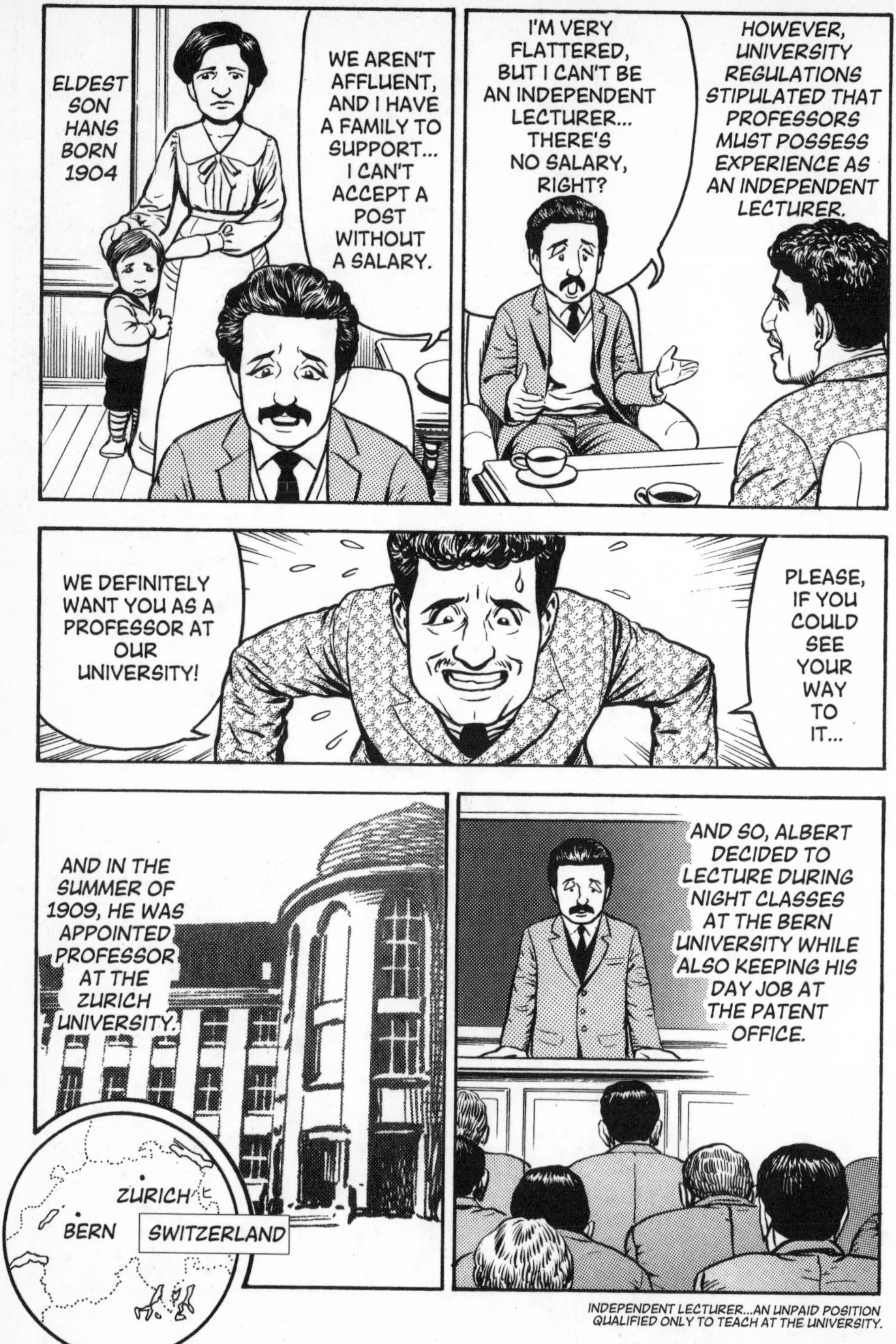
HOWEVER, UNIVERSITY REGULATIONS STIPULATED THAT PROFESSORS MUST POSSESS EXPERIENCE AS AN INDEPENDENT LECTURER.
I'M VERY FLATTERED, BUT I CAN'T BE AN INDEPENDENT LECTURER... THERE'S NO SALARY, RIGHT?
WE AREN'T AFFLUENT, AND I HAVE A FAMILY TO SUPPORT... I CAN'T ACCEPT A POST WITHOUT A SALARY.
ELDEST SON HANS BORN 1904
PLEASE, IF YOU COULD SEE YOUR WAY TO IT...
WE DEFINITELY WANT YOU AS A PROFESSOR AT OUR UNIVERSITY!
AND SO, ALBERT DECIDED TO LECTURE DURING NIGHT CLASSES AT THE BERN UNIVERSITY WHILE ALSO KEEPING HIS DAY JOB AT THE PATENT OFFICE.
AND IN THE SUMMER OF 1909, HE WAS APPOINTED PROFESSOR AT THE ZURICH UNIVERSITY.
ZURICH
BERN
SWITZERLAND

INDEPENDENT LECTURER...AN UNPAID POSITION QUALIFIED ONLY TO TEACH AT THE UNIVERSITY.

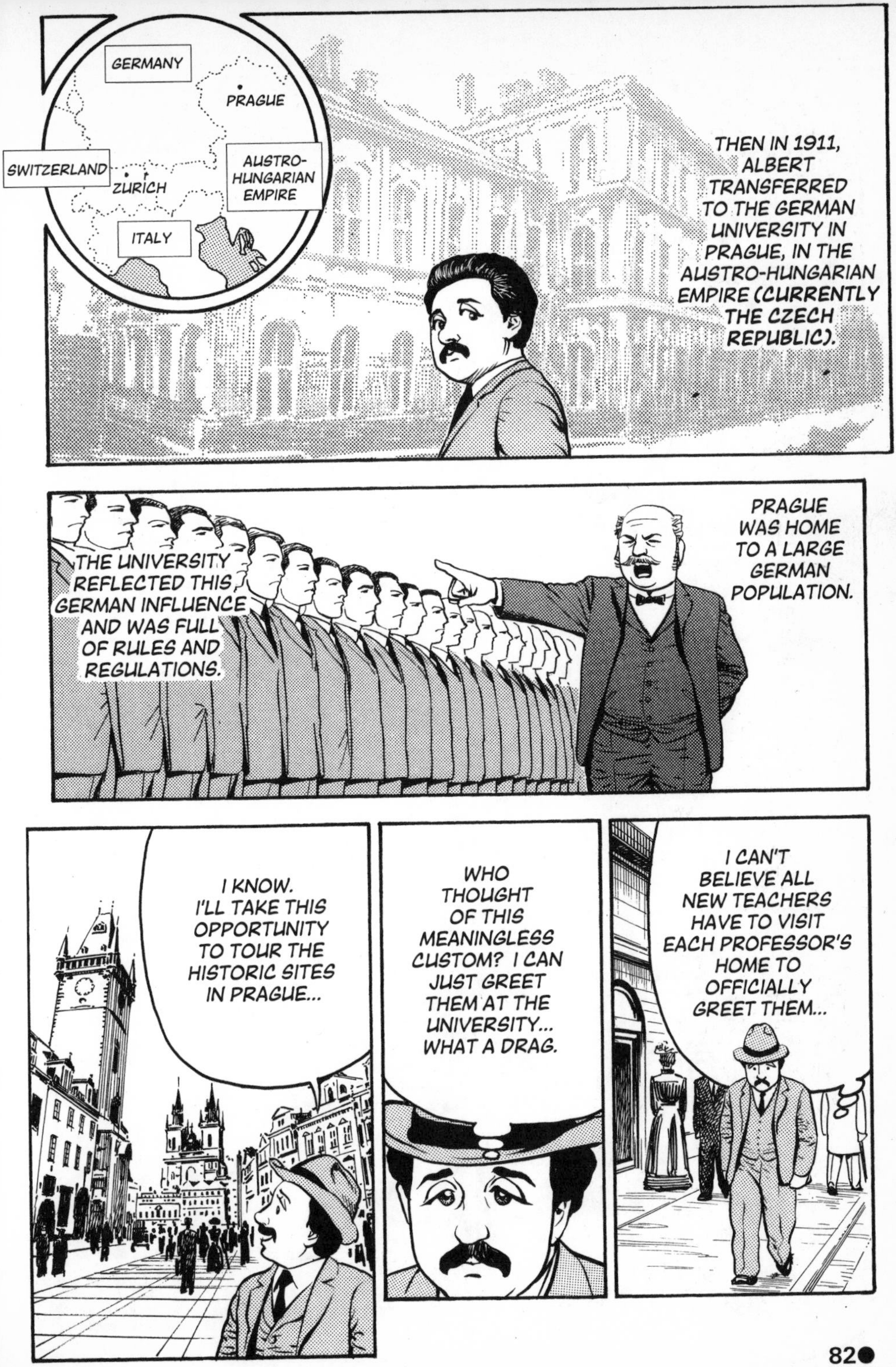
THEN IN 1911, ALBERT TRANSFERRED TO THE GERMAN UNIVERSITY IN PRAGUE, IN THE AUSTRO-HUNGARIAN EMPIRE (CURRENTLY THE CZECH REPUBLIC).
GERMANY
PRAGUE
SWITZERLAND
ZURICH
AUSTRO-HUNGARIAN EMPIRE
ITALY
PRAGUE WAS HOME TO A LARGE GERMAN POPULATION.
THE UNIVERSITY REFLECTED THIS GERMAN INFLUENCE AND WAS FULL OF RULES AND REGULATIONS.
I CAN'T BELIEVE ALL NEW TEACHERS HAVE TO VISIT EACH PROFESSOR'S HOME TO OFFICIALLY GREET THEM...
WHO THOUGHT OF THIS MEANINGLESS CUSTOM? I CAN JUST GREET THEM AT THE UNIVERSITY... WHAT A DRAG.
I KNOW. I'LL TAKE THIS OPPORTUNITY TO TOUR THE HISTORIC SITES IN PRAGUE...

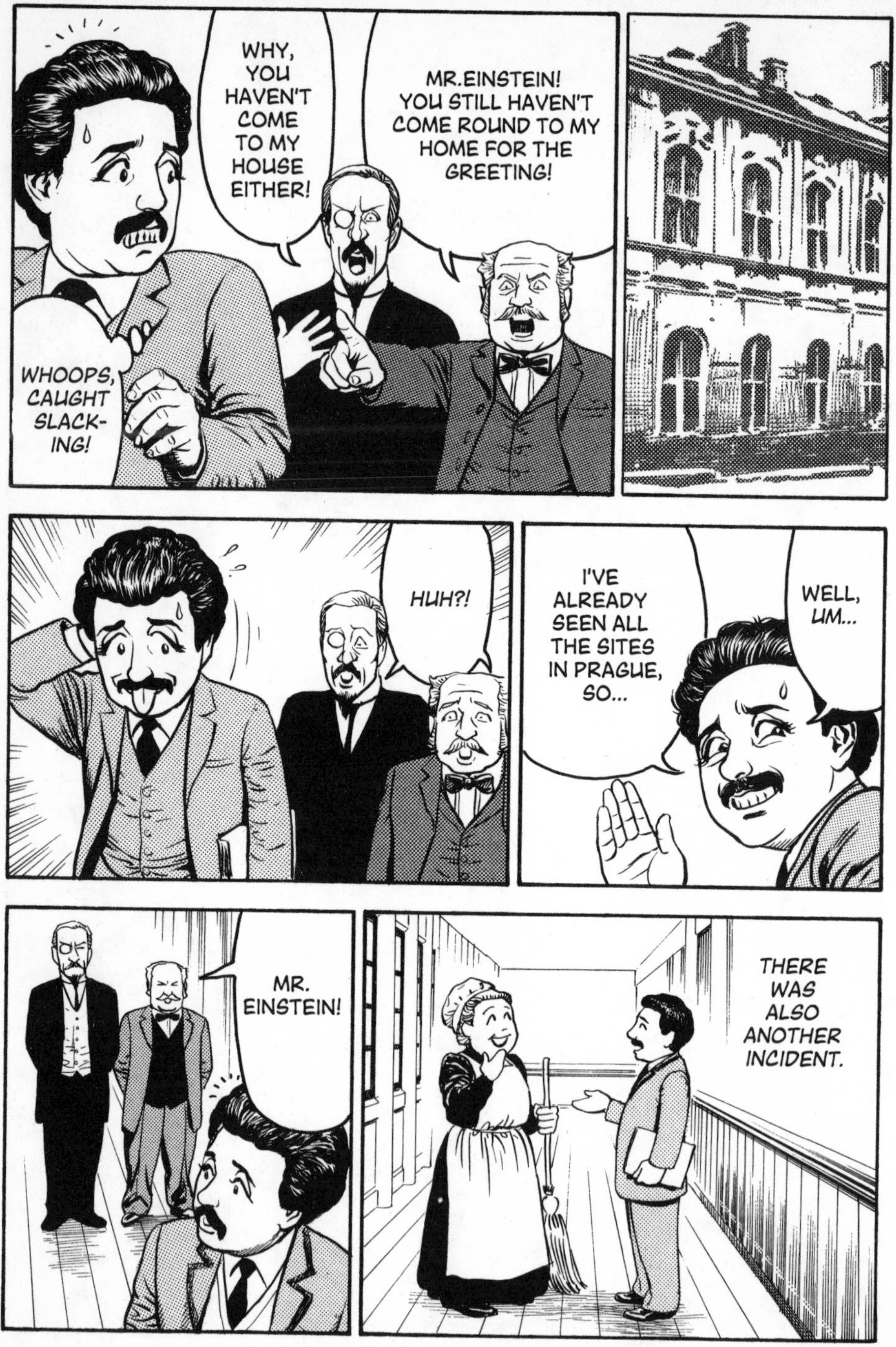
MR.EINSTEIN! YOU STILL HAVEN'T COME ROUND TO MY HOME FOR THE GREETING!
WHY, YOU HAVEN'T COME TO MY HOUSE EITHER!
WHOOPS, CAUGHT SLACKING!
WELL, UM...
I'VE ALREADY SEEN ALL THE SITES IN PRAGUE, SO...
HUH?!
THERE WAS ALSO ANOTHER INCIDENT.
MR. EINSTEIN!

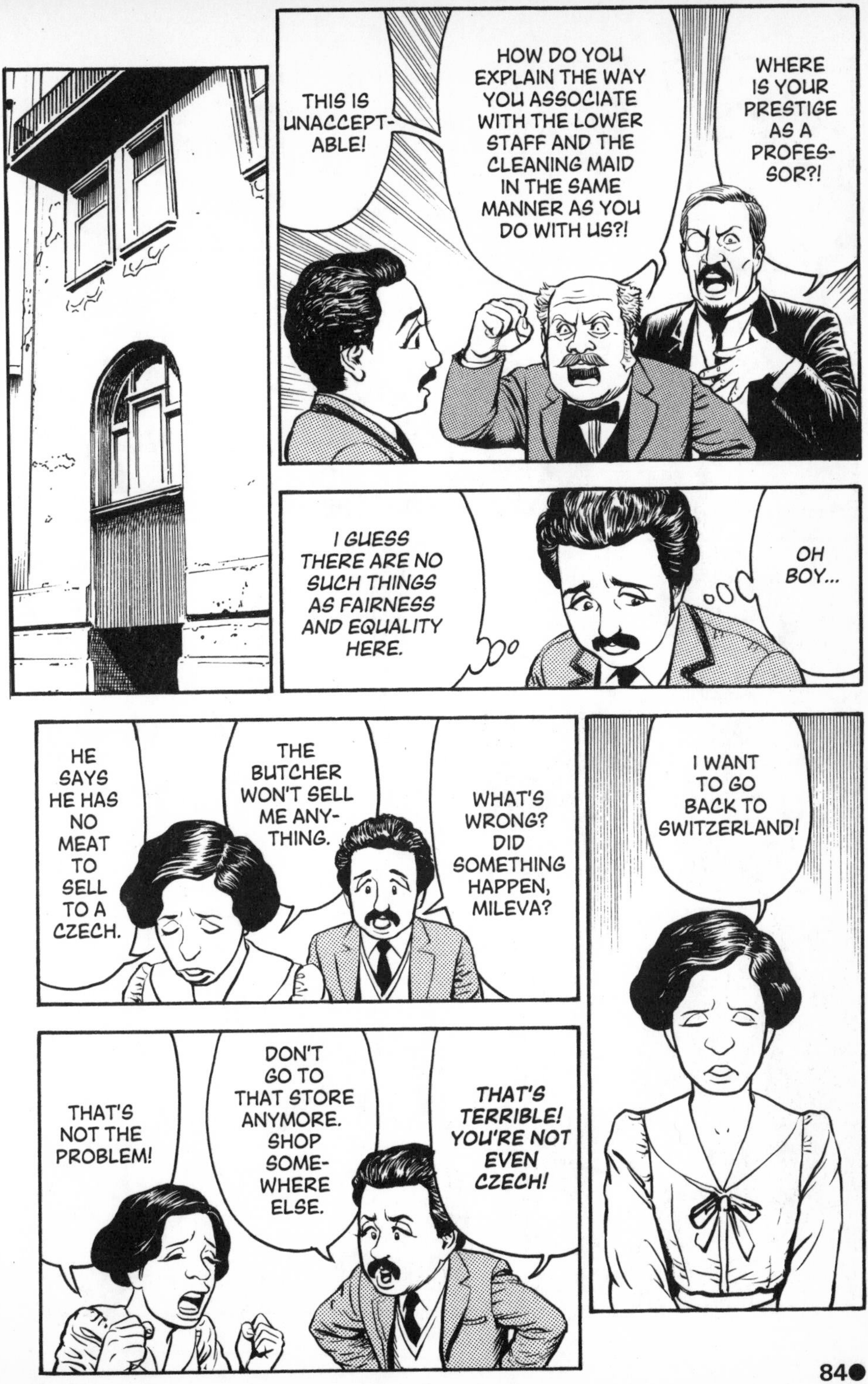

WHERE IS YOUR PRESTIGE AS A PROFESSOR?!
HOW DO YOU EXPLAIN THE WAY YOU ASSOCIATE WITH THE LOWER STAFF AND THE CLEANING MAID IN THE SAME MANNER AS YOU DO WITH US?!
THIS IS UNACCEPTABLE!
OH BOY...
I GUESS THERE ARE NO SUCH THINGS AS FAIRNESS AND EQUALITY HERE.
I WANT TO GO BACK TO SWITZERLAND!
WHAT'S WRONG? DID SOMETHING HAPPEN, MILEVA?
THE BUTCHER WON'T SELL ME ANYTHING.
HE SAYS HE HAS NO MEAT TO SELL TO A CZECH.
THAT'S TERRIBLE! YOU'RE NOT EVEN CZECH!
DON'T GO TO THAT STORE ANYMORE. SHOP SOMEWHERE ELSE.
THAT'S NOT THE PROBLEM!

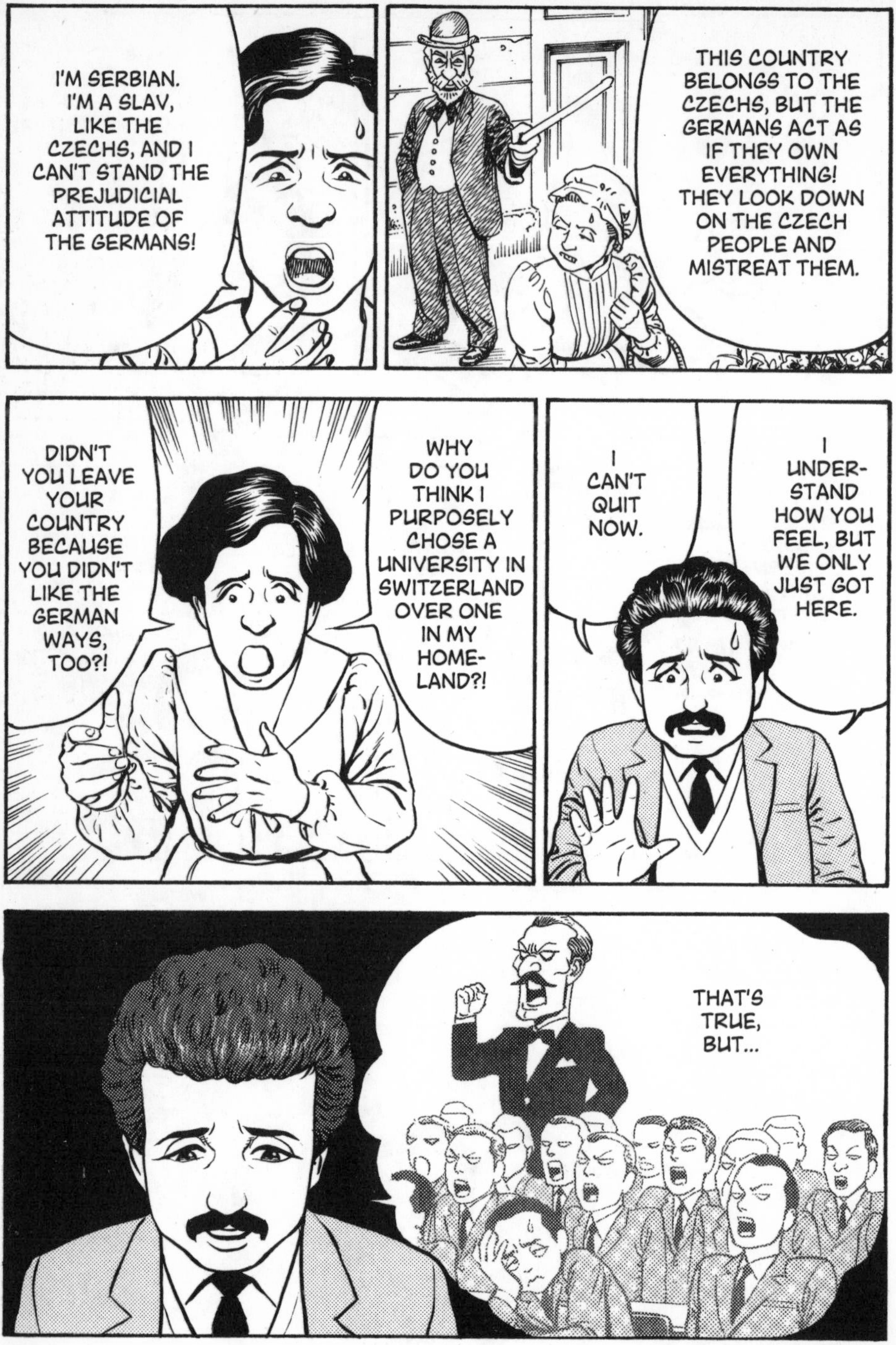
THIS COUNTRY BELONGS TO THE CZECHS, BUT THE GERMANS ACT AS IF THEY OWN EVERYTHING! THEY LOOK DOWN ON THE CZECH PEOPLE AND MISTREAT THEM.
I'M SERBIAN. I'M A SLAV, LIKE THE CZECHS, AND I CAN'T STAND THE PREJUDICIAL ATTITUDE OF THE GERMANS!
I UNDERSTAND HOW YOU FEEL, BUT WE ONLY JUST GOT HERE.
I CAN'T QUIT NOW.
WHY DO YOU THINK I PURPOSELY CHOSE A UNIVERSITY IN SWITZERLAND OVER ONE IN MY HOMELAND?!
DIDN'T YOU LEAVE YOUR COUNTRY BECAUSE YOU DIDN'T LIKE THE GERMAN WAYS, TOO?!
THAT'S TRUE, BUT...

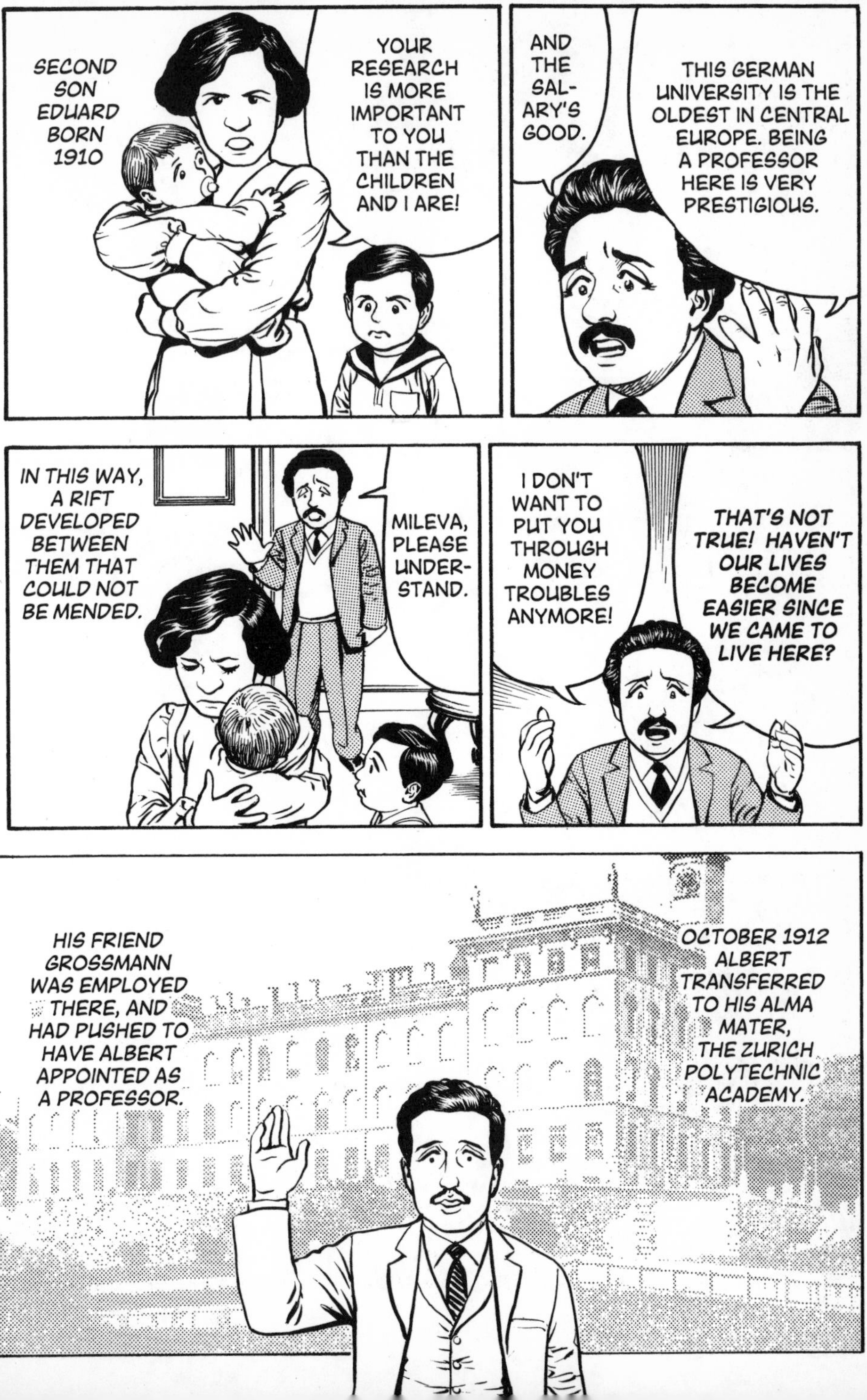
THIS GERMAN UNIVERSITY IS THE OLDEST IN CENTRAL EUROPE. BEING A PROFESSOR HERE IS VERY PRESTIGIOUS.
AND THE SAL-ARY'S GOOD.
YOUR RESEARCH IS MORE IMPORTANT TO YOU THAN THE CHILDREN AND I ARE!
SECOND SON EDUARD BORN 1910
THAT'S NOT TRUE! HAVEN'T OUR LIVES BECOME EASIER SINCE WE CAME TO LIVE HERE?
I DON'T WANT TO PUT YOU THROUGH MONEY TROUBLES ANYMORE!
MILEVA, PLEASE UNDER-STAND.
IN THIS WAY, A RIFT DEVELOPED BETWEEN THEM THAT COULD NOT BE MENDED.
OCTOBER 1912 ALBERT TRANSFERRED TO HIS ALMA MATER, THE ZURICH POLYTECHNIC ACADEMY.
HIS FRIEND GROSSMANN WAS EMPLOYED THERE, AND HAD PUSHED TO HAVE ALBERT APPOINTED AS A PROFESSOR.

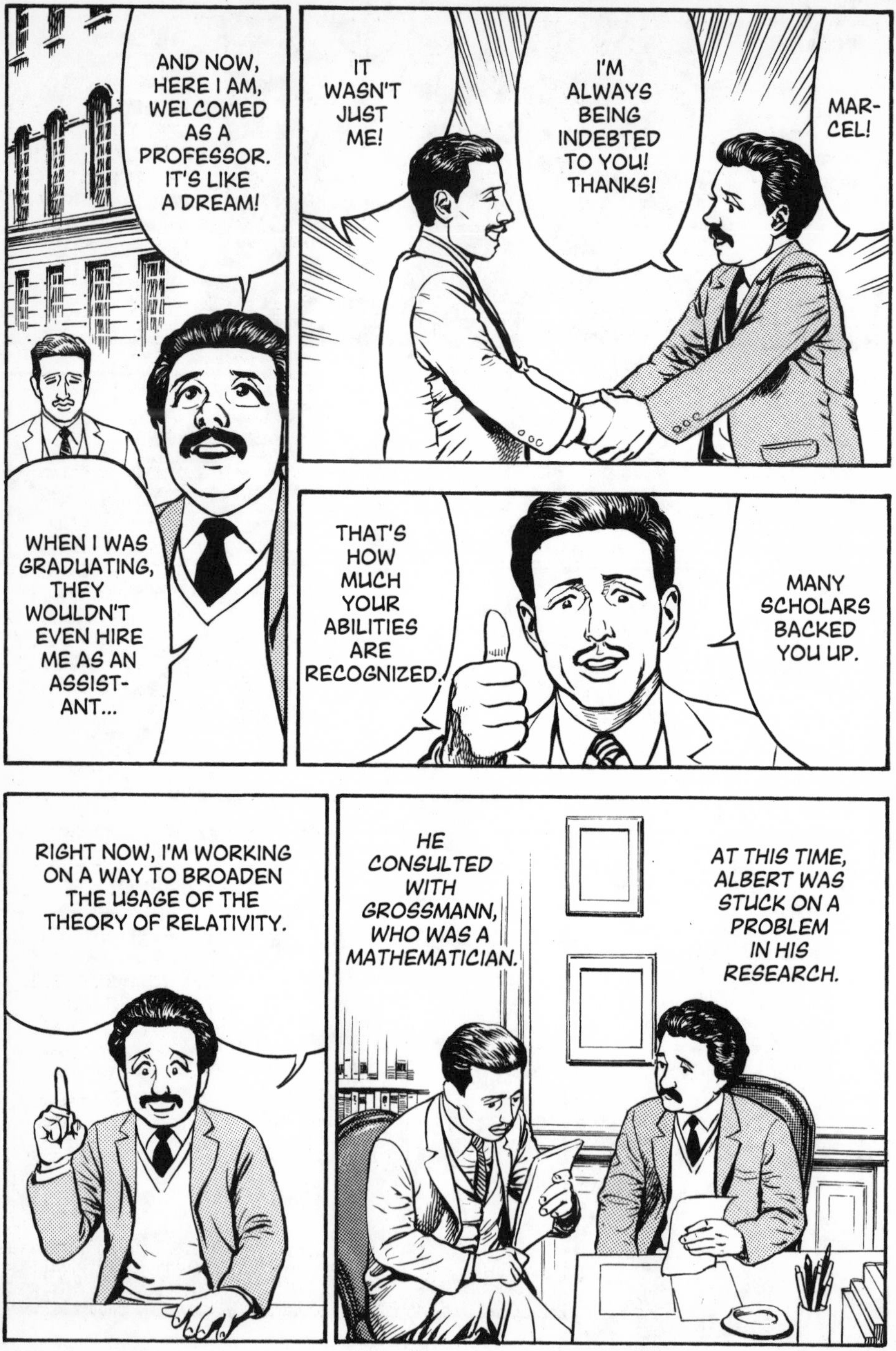
MAR-CEL!
I'M ALWAYS BEING INDEBTED TO YOU! THANKS!
IT WASN'T JUST ME!
MANY SCHOLARS BACKED YOU UP.
THAT'S HOW MUCH YOUR ABILITIES ARE RECOGNIZED.
AND NOW, HERE I AM, WELCOMED AS A PROFESSOR. IT'S LIKE A DREAM!
WHEN I WAS GRADUATING, THEY WOULDN'T EVEN HIRE ME AS AN ASSIST-ANT...
AT THIS TIME, ALBERT WAS STUCK ON A PROBLEM IN HIS RESEARCH.
HE CONSULTED WITH GROSSMANN, WHO WAS A MATHEMATICIAN.
RIGHT NOW, I'M WORKING ON A WAY TO BROADEN THE USAGE OF THE THEORY OF RELATIVITY.

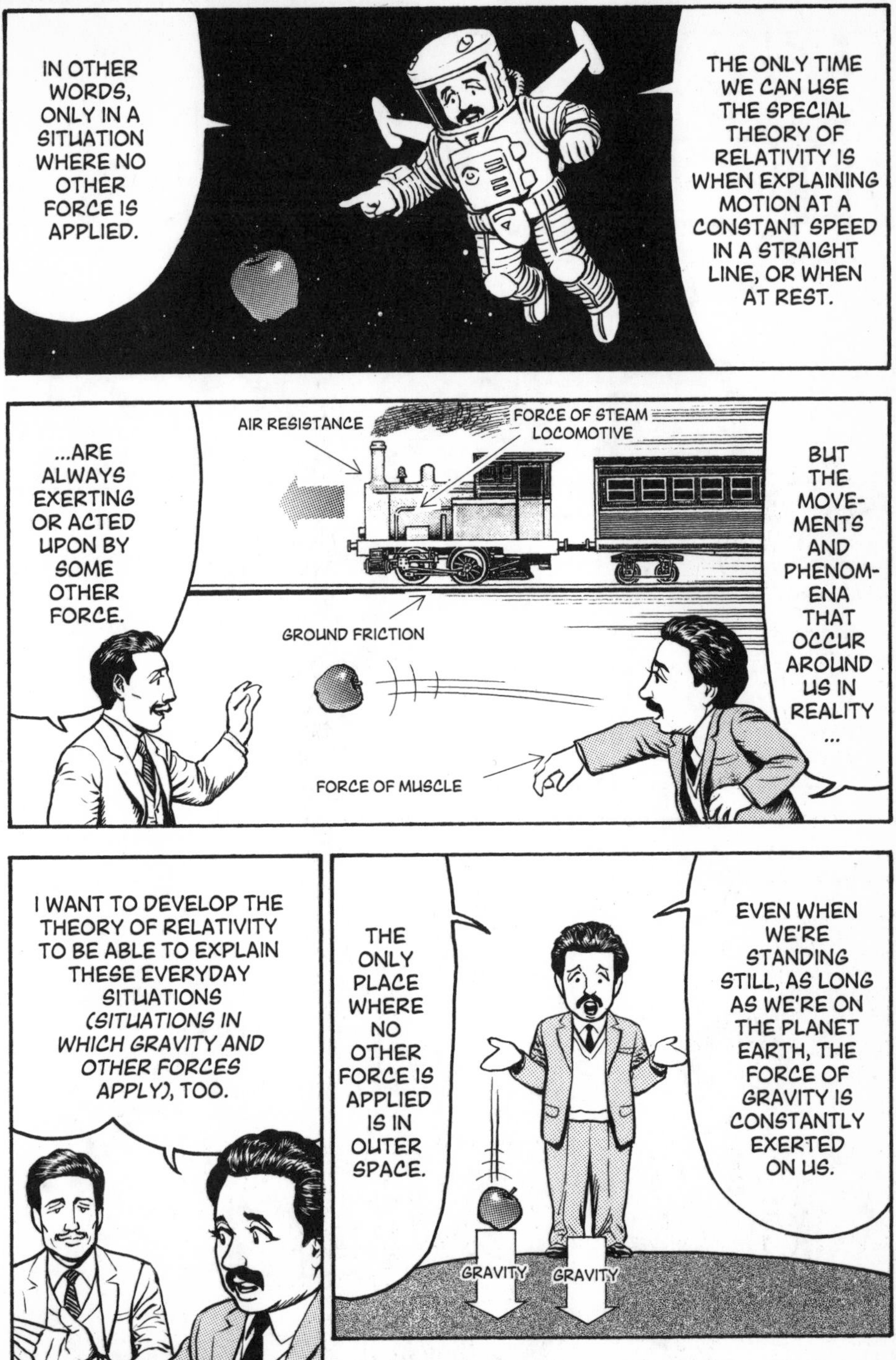
THE ONLY TIME WE CAN USE THE SPECIAL THEORY OF RELATIVITY IS WHEN EXPLAINING MOTION AT A CONSTANT SPEED IN A STRAIGHT LINE, OR WHEN AT REST.
IN OTHER WORDS, ONLY IN A SITUATION WHERE NO OTHER FORCE IS APPLIED.
BUT THE MOVEMENTS AND PHENOMENA THAT OCCUR AROUND US IN REALITY ...
...ARE ALWAYS EXERTING OR ACTED UPON BY SOME OTHER FORCE.
AIR RESISTANCE
FORCE OF STEAM LOCOMOTIVE
GROUND FRICTION
FORCE OF MUSCLE
EVEN WHEN WE'RE STANDING STILL, AS LONG AS WE'RE ON THE PLANET EARTH, THE FORCE OF GRAVITY IS CONSTANTLY EXERTED ON US.
THE ONLY PLACE WHERE NO OTHER FORCE IS APPLIED IS IN OUTER SPACE.
GRAVITY
GRAVITY
I WANT TO DEVELOP THE THEORY OF RELATIVITY TO BE ABLE TO EXPLAIN THESE EVERYDAY SITUATIONS *(SITUATIONS IN WHICH GRAVITY AND OTHER FORCES APPLY)*, TOO.

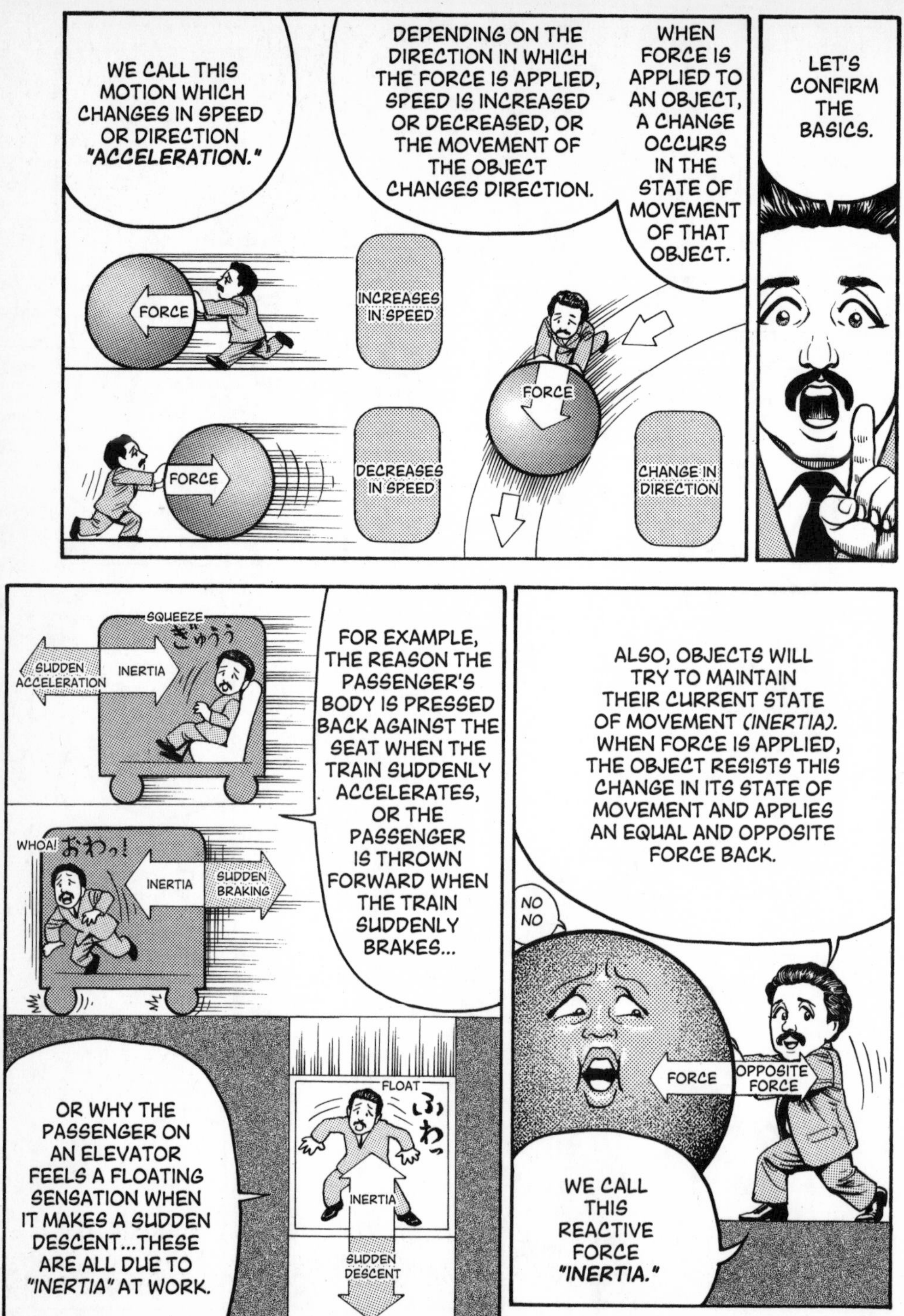
LET'S CONFIRM THE BASICS.
WHEN FORCE IS APPLIED TO AN OBJECT, A CHANGE OCCURS IN THE STATE OF MOVEMENT OF THAT OBJECT.
DEPENDING ON THE DIRECTION IN WHICH THE FORCE IS APPLIED, SPEED IS INCREASED OR DECREASED, OR THE MOVEMENT OF THE OBJECT CHANGES DIRECTION.
WE CALL THIS MOTION WHICH CHANGES IN SPEED OR DIRECTION "ACCELERATION."
FORCE
CHANGE IN DIRECTION
FORCE
INCREASES IN SPEED
FORCE
DECREASES IN SPEED
FORCE
ALSO, OBJECTS WILL TRY TO MAINTAIN THEIR CURRENT STATE OF MOVEMENT (INERTIA). WHEN FORCE IS APPLIED, THE OBJECT RESISTS THIS CHANGE IN ITS STATE OF MOVEMENT AND APPLIES AN EQUAL AND OPPOSITE FORCE BACK.
NO NO
OPPOSITE FORCE
FORCE
WE CALL THIS REACTIVE FORCE "INERTIA."
FOR EXAMPLE, THE REASON THE PASSENGER'S BODY IS PRESSED BACK AGAINST THE SEAT WHEN THE TRAIN SUDDENLY ACCELERATES, OR THE PASSENGER IS THROWN FORWARD WHEN THE TRAIN SUDDENLY BRAKES...
SQUEEZE ぎゅうう
INERTIA
SUDDEN ACCELERATION
WHOA! おわっ!
SUDDEN BRAKING
INERTIA
FLOAT ふわっ
INERTIA
SUDDEN DESCENT
OR WHY THE PASSENGER ON AN ELEVATOR FEELS A FLOATING SENSATION WHEN IT MAKES A SUDDEN DESCENT...THESE ARE ALL DUE TO "INERTIA" AT WORK.

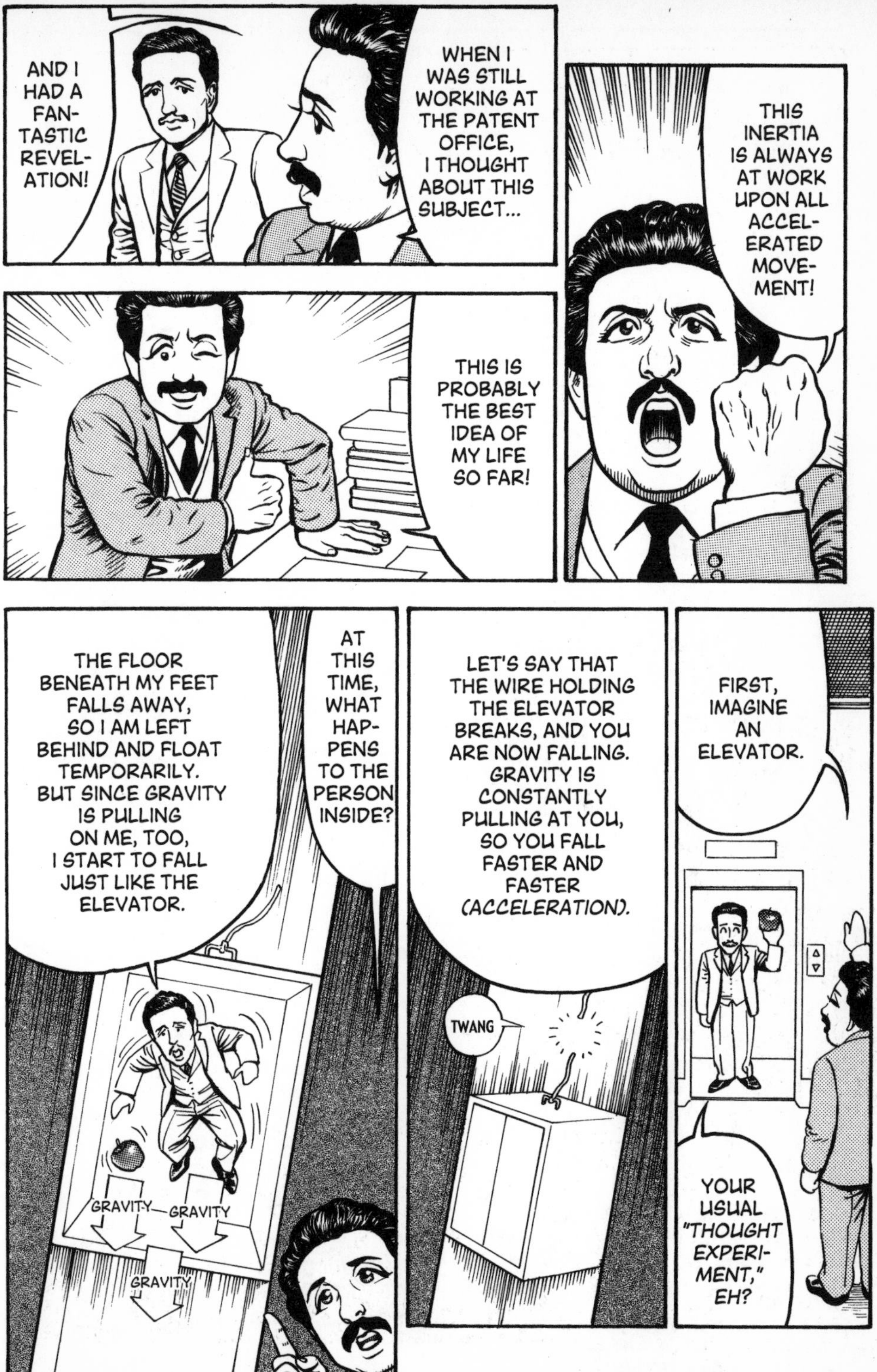
THIS INERTIA IS ALWAYS AT WORK UPON ALL ACCELERATED MOVEMENT!
WHEN I WAS STILL WORKING AT THE PATENT OFFICE, I THOUGHT ABOUT THIS SUBJECT...
AND I HAD A FANTASTIC REVELATION!
THIS IS PROBABLY THE BEST IDEA OF MY LIFE SO FAR!
FIRST, IMAGINE AN ELEVATOR.
YOUR USUAL "THOUGHT EXPERIMENT," EH?
LET'S SAY THAT THE WIRE HOLDING THE ELEVATOR BREAKS, AND YOU ARE NOW FALLING. GRAVITY IS CONSTANTLY PULLING AT YOU, SO YOU FALL FASTER AND FASTER (ACCELERATION).
TWANG
AT THIS TIME, WHAT HAPPENS TO THE PERSON INSIDE?
THE FLOOR BENEATH MY FEET FALLS AWAY, SO I AM LEFT BEHIND AND FLOAT TEMPORARILY. BUT SINCE GRAVITY IS PULLING ON ME, TOO, I START TO FALL JUST LIKE THE ELEVATOR.
GRAVITY
GRAVITY
GRAVITY

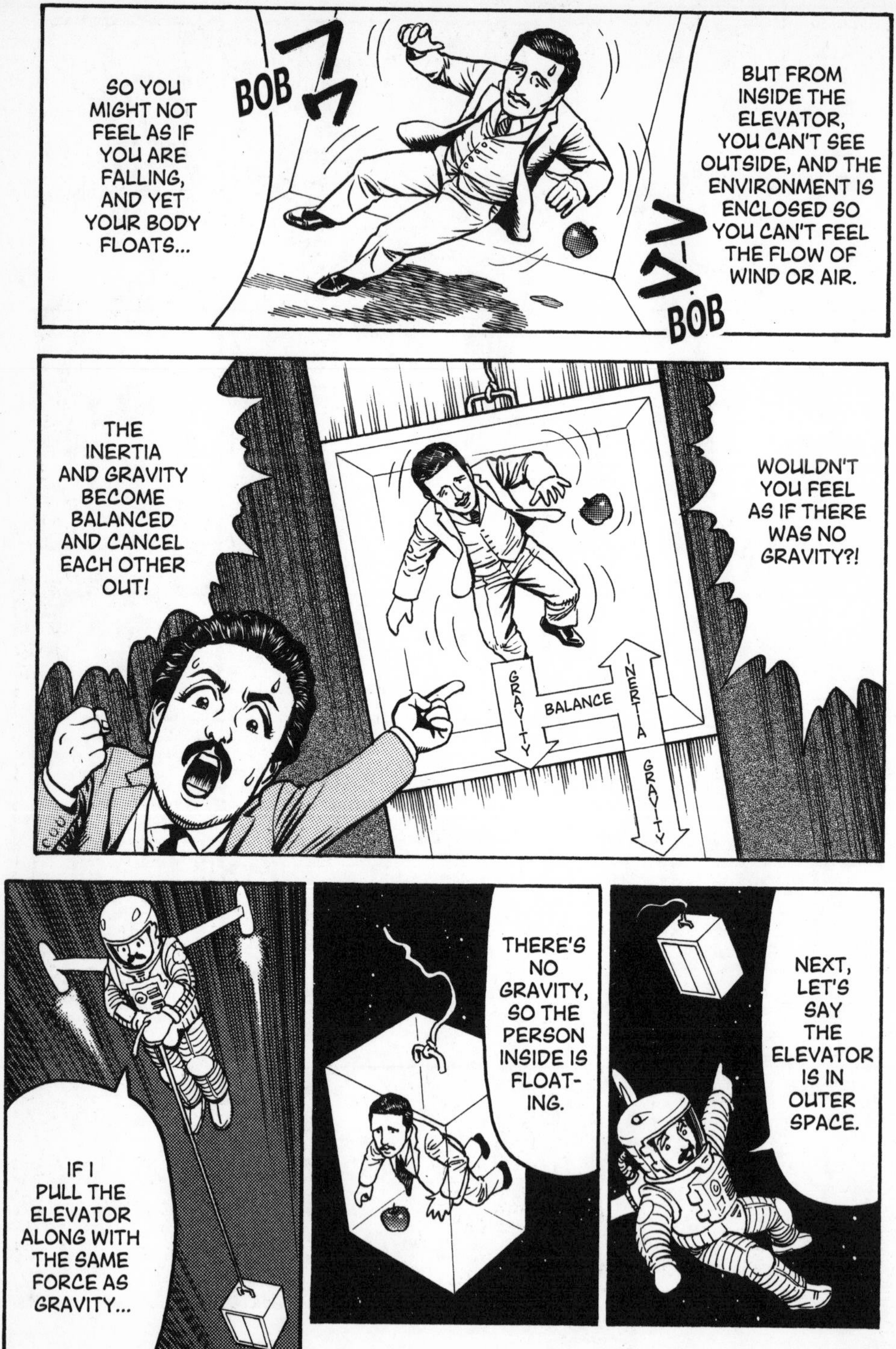
BUT FROM INSIDE THE ELEVATOR, YOU CAN'T SEE OUTSIDE, AND THE ENVIRONMENT IS ENCLOSED SO YOU CAN'T FEEL THE FLOW OF WIND OR AIR.
BOB
BOB
SO YOU MIGHT NOT FEEL AS IF YOU ARE FALLING, AND YET YOUR BODY FLOATS...
WOULDN'T YOU FEEL AS IF THERE WAS NO GRAVITY?!
INERTIA
GRAVITY
BALANCE
GRAVITY
THE INERTIA AND GRAVITY BECOME BALANCED AND CANCEL EACH OTHER OUT!
NEXT, LET'S SAY THE ELEVATOR IS IN OUTER SPACE.
THERE'S NO GRAVITY, SO THE PERSON INSIDE IS FLOAT-ING.
IF I PULL THE ELEVATOR ALONG WITH THE SAME FORCE AS GRAVITY...

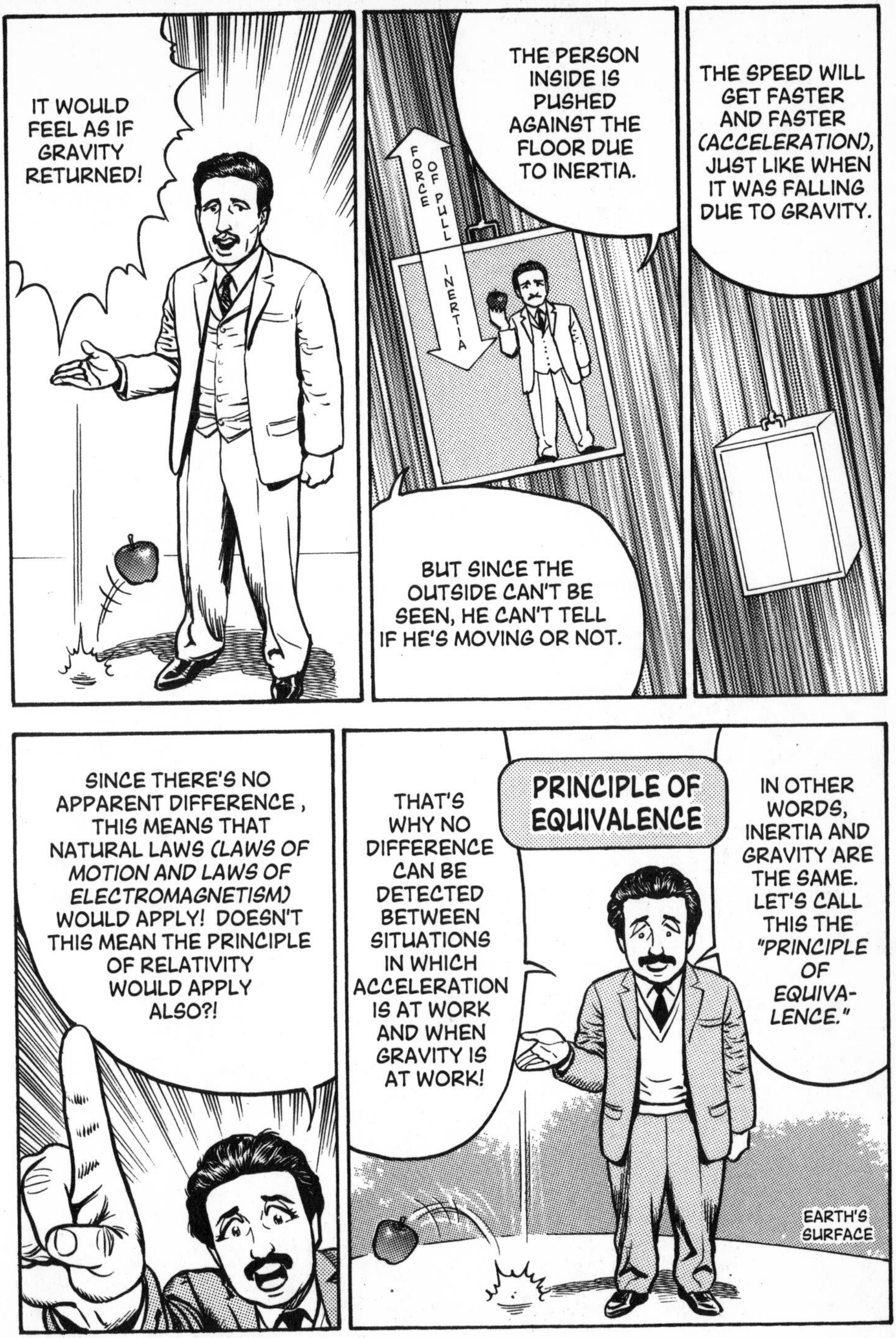
THE SPEED WILL GET FASTER AND FASTER (ACCELERATION), JUST LIKE WHEN IT WAS FALLING DUE TO GRAVITY.
THE PERSON INSIDE IS PUSHED AGAINST THE FLOOR DUE TO INERTIA.
FORCE OF PULL
INERTIA
BUT SINCE THE OUTSIDE CAN'T BE SEEN, HE CAN'T TELL IF HE'S MOVING OR NOT.
IT WOULD FEEL AS IF GRAVITY RETURNED!
IN OTHER WORDS, INERTIA AND GRAVITY ARE THE SAME. LET'S CALL THIS THE "PRINCIPLE OF EQUIVA-LENCE."
PRINCIPLE OF EQUIVALENCE
THAT'S WHY NO DIFFERENCE CAN BE DETECTED BETWEEN SITUATIONS IN WHICH ACCELERATION IS AT WORK AND WHEN GRAVITY IS AT WORK!
EARTH'S SURFACE
SINCE THERE'S NO APPARENT DIFFERENCE , THIS MEANS THAT NATURAL LAWS (LAWS OF MOTION AND LAWS OF ELECTROMAGNETISM) WOULD APPLY! DOESN'T THIS MEAN THE PRINCIPLE OF RELATIVITY WOULD APPLY ALSO?!

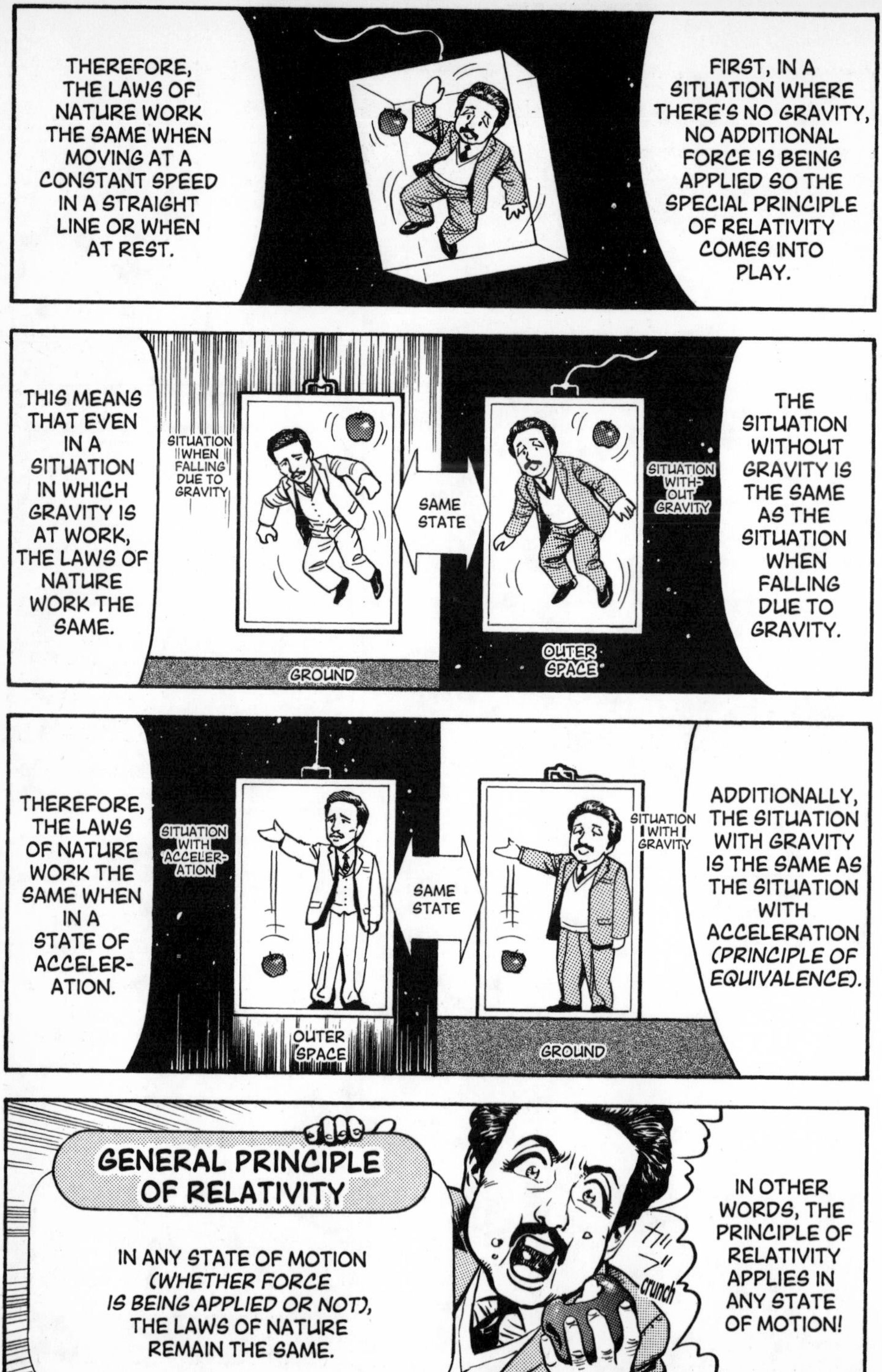
FIRST, IN A SITUATION WHERE THERE'S NO GRAVITY, NO ADDITIONAL FORCE IS BEING APPLIED SO THE SPECIAL PRINCIPLE OF RELATIVITY COMES INTO PLAY.
THEREFORE, THE LAWS OF NATURE WORK THE SAME WHEN MOVING AT A CONSTANT SPEED IN A STRAIGHT LINE OR WHEN AT REST.
THE SITUATION WITHOUT GRAVITY IS THE SAME AS THE SITUATION WHEN FALLING DUE TO GRAVITY.
SITUATION WITHOUT GRAVITY
OUTER SPACE
SAME STATE
SITUATION WHEN FALLING DUE TO GRAVITY
GROUND
THIS MEANS THAT EVEN IN A SITUATION IN WHICH GRAVITY IS AT WORK, THE LAWS OF NATURE WORK THE SAME.
ADDITIONALLY, THE SITUATION WITH GRAVITY IS THE SAME AS THE SITUATION WITH ACCELERATION (PRINCIPLE OF EQUIVALENCE).
SITUATION WITH GRAVITY
GROUND
SAME STATE
SITUATION WITH ACCELERATION
OUTER SPACE
THEREFORE, THE LAWS OF NATURE WORK THE SAME WHEN IN A STATE OF ACCELERATION.
IN OTHER WORDS, THE PRINCIPLE OF RELATIVITY APPLIES IN ANY STATE OF MOTION!
crunch
GENERAL PRINCIPLE OF RELATIVITY
IN ANY STATE OF MOTION (WHETHER FORCE IS BEING APPLIED OR NOT), THE LAWS OF NATURE REMAIN THE SAME.

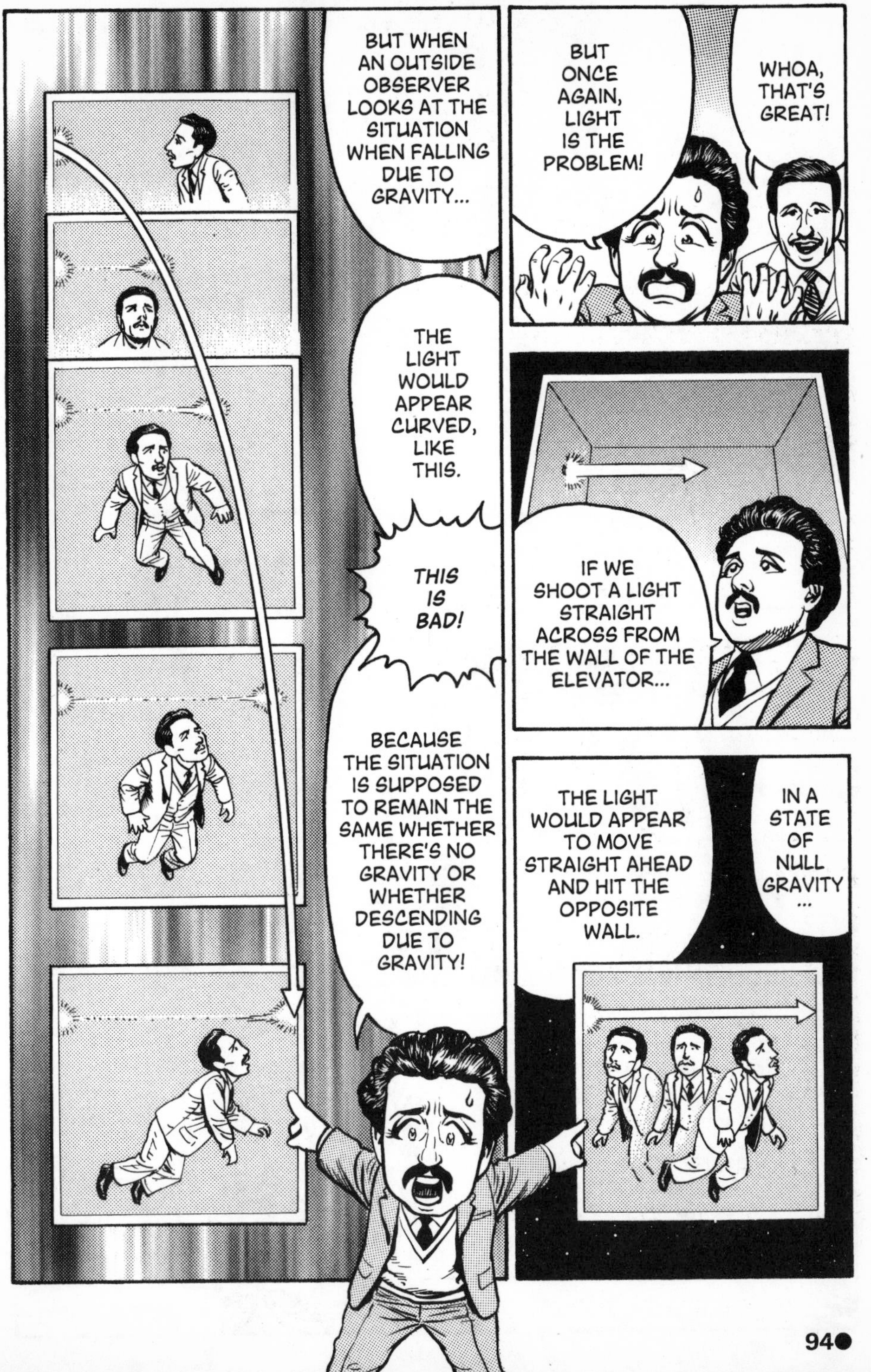

WHOA, THAT'S GREAT!
BUT ONCE AGAIN, LIGHT IS THE PROBLEM!
IF WE SHOOT A LIGHT STRAIGHT ACROSS FROM THE WALL OF THE ELEVATOR...
IN A STATE OF NULL GRAVITY...
THE LIGHT WOULD APPEAR TO MOVE STRAIGHT AHEAD AND HIT THE OPPOSITE WALL.
BUT WHEN AN OUTSIDE OBSERVER LOOKS AT THE SITUATION WHEN FALLING DUE TO GRAVITY...
THE LIGHT WOULD APPEAR CURVED, LIKE THIS.
THIS IS BAD!
BECAUSE THE SITUATION IS SUPPOSED TO REMAIN THE SAME WHETHER THERE'S NO GRAVITY OR WHETHER DESCENDING DUE TO GRAVITY!

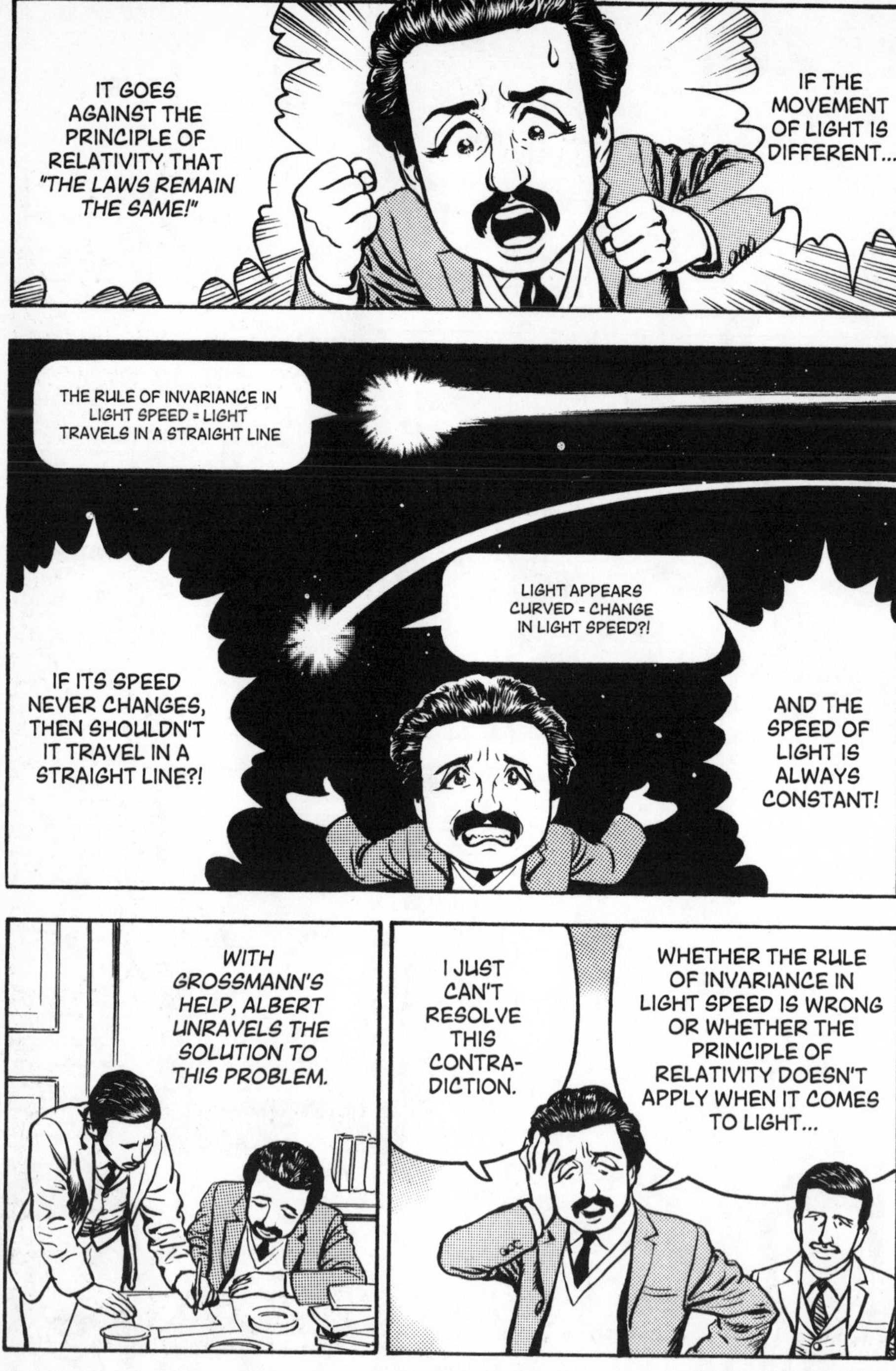
IF THE MOVEMENT OF LIGHT IS DIFFERENT...
IT GOES AGAINST THE PRINCIPLE OF RELATIVITY THAT "THE LAWS REMAIN THE SAME!"
THE RULE OF INVARIANCE IN LIGHT SPEED = LIGHT TRAVELS IN A STRAIGHT LINE
LIGHT APPEARS CURVED = CHANGE IN LIGHT SPEED?!
AND THE SPEED OF LIGHT IS ALWAYS CONSTANT!
IF ITS SPEED NEVER CHANGES, THEN SHOULDN'T IT TRAVEL IN A STRAIGHT LINE?!
WHETHER THE RULE OF INVARIANCE IN LIGHT SPEED IS WRONG OR WHETHER THE PRINCIPLE OF RELATIVITY DOESN'T APPLY WHEN IT COMES TO LIGHT...
I JUST CAN'T RESOLVE THIS CONTRA-DICTION.
WITH GROSSMANN'S HELP, ALBERT UNRAVELS THE SOLUTION TO THIS PROBLEM.

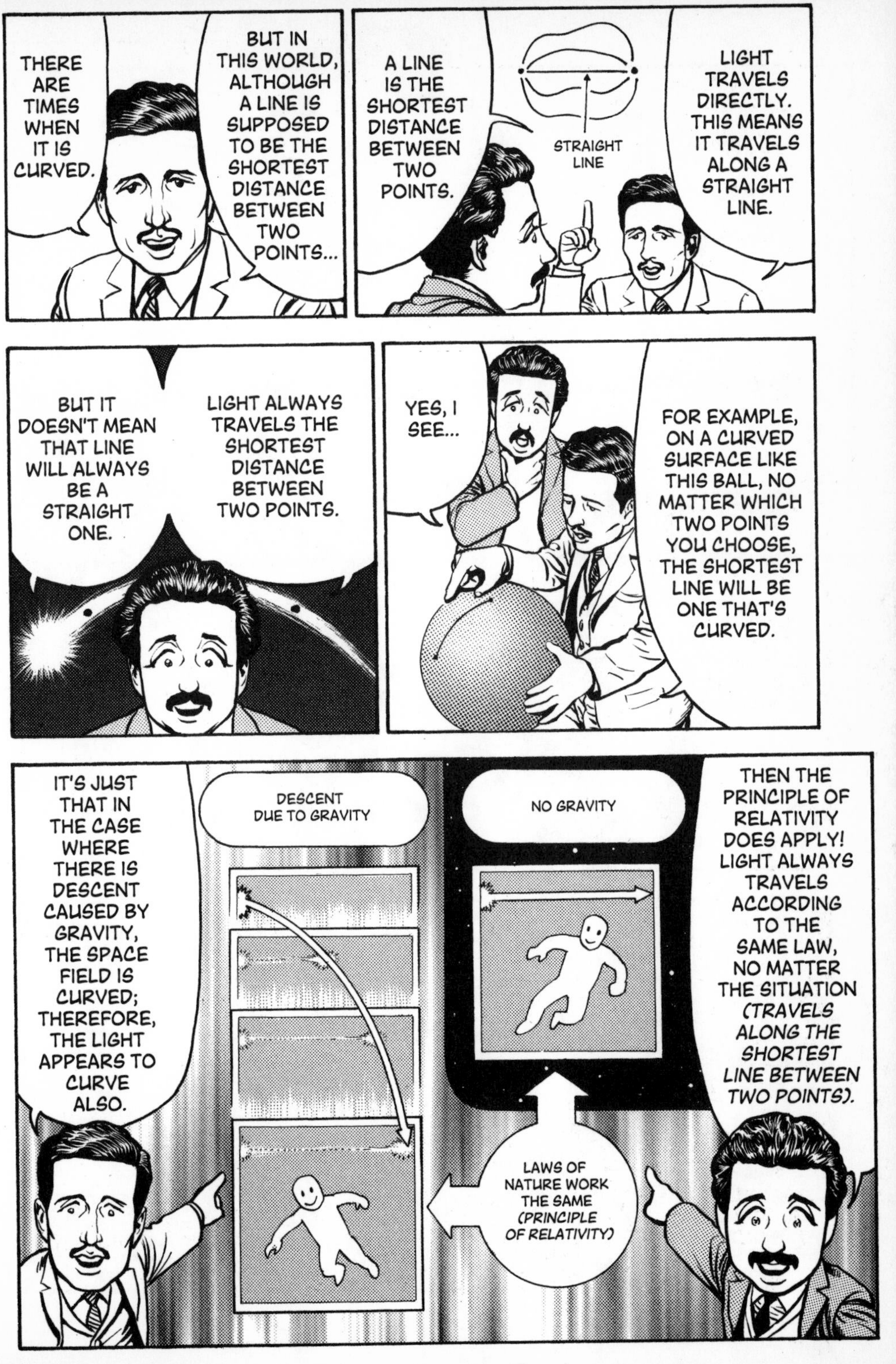
LIGHT TRAVELS DIRECTLY. THIS MEANS IT TRAVELS ALONG A STRAIGHT LINE.
STRAIGHT LINE
A LINE IS THE SHORTEST DISTANCE BETWEEN TWO POINTS.
BUT IN THIS WORLD, ALTHOUGH A LINE IS SUPPOSED TO BE THE SHORTEST DISTANCE BETWEEN TWO POINTS...
THERE ARE TIMES WHEN IT IS CURVED.
FOR EXAMPLE, ON A CURVED SURFACE LIKE THIS BALL, NO MATTER WHICH TWO POINTS YOU CHOOSE, THE SHORTEST LINE WILL BE ONE THAT'S CURVED.
YES, I SEE...
LIGHT ALWAYS TRAVELS THE SHORTEST DISTANCE BETWEEN TWO POINTS.
BUT IT DOESN'T MEAN THAT LINE WILL ALWAYS BE A STRAIGHT ONE.
THEN THE PRINCIPLE OF RELATIVITY DOES APPLY! LIGHT ALWAYS TRAVELS ACCORDING TO THE SAME LAW, NO MATTER THE SITUATION (TRAVELS ALONG THE SHORTEST LINE BETWEEN TWO POINTS).
NO GRAVITY
LAWS OF NATURE WORK THE SAME (PRINCIPLE OF RELATIVITY)
DESCENT DUE TO GRAVITY
IT'S JUST THAT IN THE CASE WHERE THERE IS DESCENT CAUSED BY GRAVITY, THE SPACE FIELD IS CURVED; THEREFORE, THE LIGHT APPEARS TO CURVE ALSO.

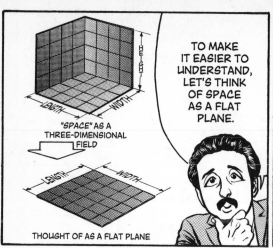

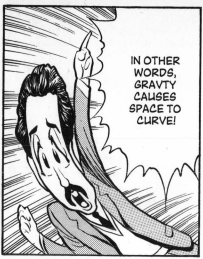

IN OTHER WORDS, GRAVTY CAUSES SPACE TO CURVE!
TO MAKE IT EASIER TO UNDERSTAND, LET'S THINK OF SPACE AS A FLAT PLANE.
HEIGHT
WIDTH
LENGTH
"SPACE" AS A THREE-DIMENSIONAL FIELD
WIDTH
LENGTH
THOUGHT OF AS A FLAT PLANE
MAYBE A CURVED SPACE FIELD LOOKS LIKE THIS.
GRAVITY
THAT MEANS THE RULE OF INVARIANCE IN LIGHT SPEED ONLY APPLIES WHEN THERE IS NO GRAVITY.
BUT LOOKING AT LIGHT WHILE ON EARTH'S SURFACE, THE LIGHT DOESN'T APPEAR CURVED.
THAT'S PROBABLY BECAUSE THE EARTH'S FORCE OF GRAVITY IS TOO SMALL.
THE FASTER THE ACCELER-ATION DURING DESCENT, AND ACCORD-INGLY, THE LARGER THE MASS...
ACCELERATION DUE TO GRAVITY
THE BIGGER THE CURVATURE OF LIGHT SHOULD APPEAR!

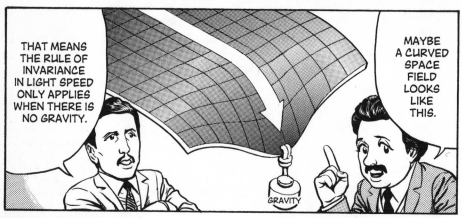

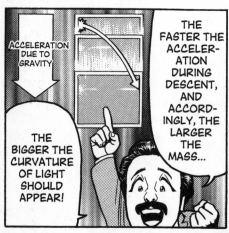

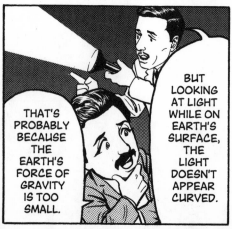

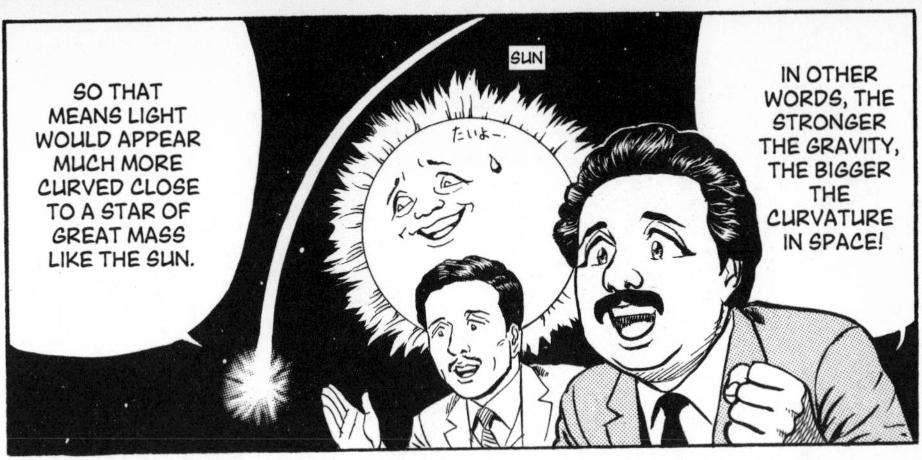
IN OTHER WORDS, THE STRONGER THE GRAVITY, THE BIGGER THE CURVATURE IN SPACE!
SUN
たいよー
SO THAT MEANS LIGHT WOULD APPEAR MUCH MORE CURVED CLOSE TO A STAR OF GREAT MASS LIKE THE SUN.
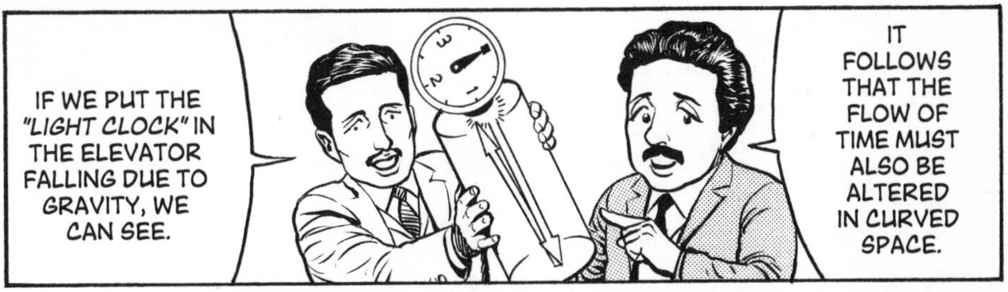
IT FOLLOWS THAT THE FLOW OF TIME MUST ALSO BE ALTERED IN CURVED SPACE.
IF WE PUT THE *"LIGHT CLOCK"* IN THE ELEVATOR FALLING DUE TO GRAVITY, WE CAN SEE.
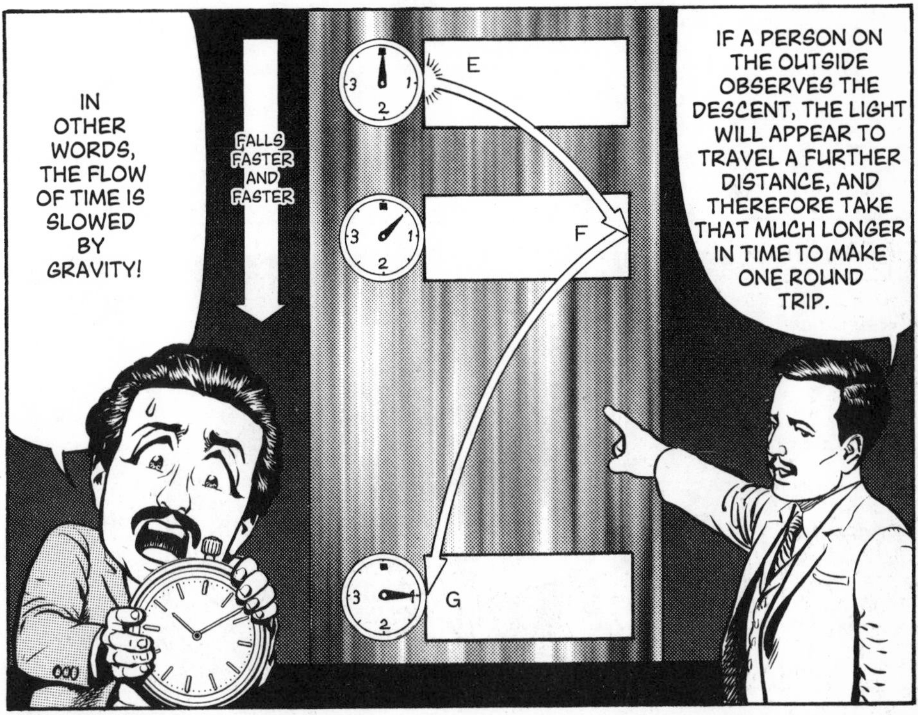
IF A PERSON ON THE OUTSIDE OBSERVES THE DESCENT, THE LIGHT WILL APPEAR TO TRAVEL A FURTHER DISTANCE, AND THEREFORE TAKE THAT MUCH LONGER IN TIME TO MAKE ONE ROUND TRIP.
E
F
G
FALLS FASTER AND FASTER
IN OTHER WORDS, THE FLOW OF TIME IS SLOWED BY GRAVITY!

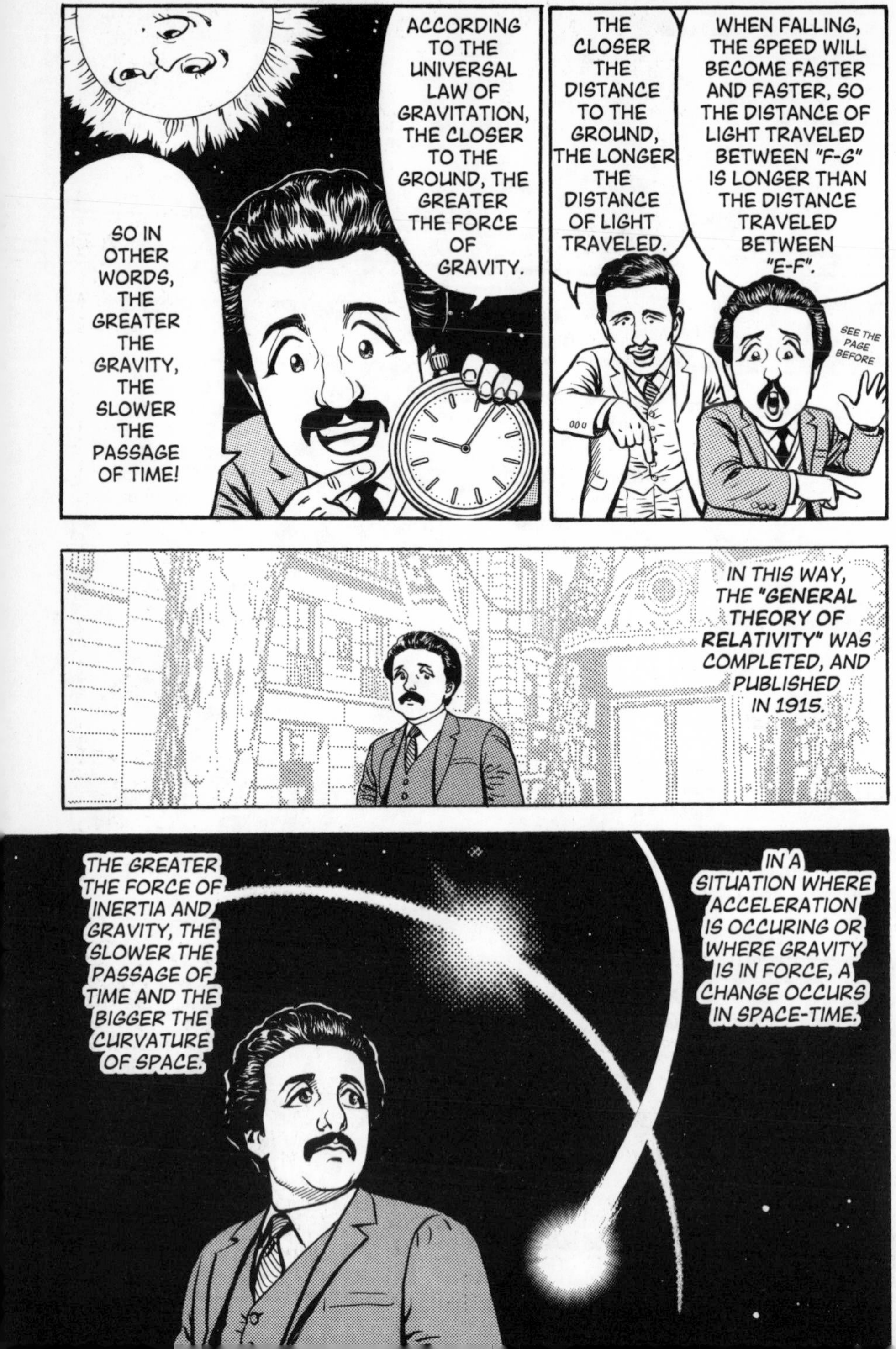
WHEN FALLING, THE SPEED WILL BECOME FASTER AND FASTER, SO THE DISTANCE OF LIGHT TRAVELED BETWEEN "F-G" IS LONGER THAN THE DISTANCE TRAVELED BETWEEN "E-F".
THE CLOSER THE DISTANCE TO THE GROUND, THE LONGER THE DISTANCE OF LIGHT TRAVELED.
SEE THE PAGE BEFORE
ACCORDING TO THE UNIVERSAL LAW OF GRAVITATION, THE CLOSER TO THE GROUND, THE GREATER THE FORCE OF GRAVITY.
SO IN OTHER WORDS, THE GREATER THE GRAVITY, THE SLOWER THE PASSAGE OF TIME!
IN THIS WAY, THE "GENERAL THEORY OF RELATIVITY" WAS COMPLETED, AND PUBLISHED IN 1915.
IN A SITUATION WHERE ACCELERATION IS OCCURING OR WHERE GRAVITY IS IN FORCE, A CHANGE OCCURS IN SPACE-TIME.
THE GREATER THE FORCE OF INERTIA AND GRAVITY, THE SLOWER THE PASSAGE OF TIME AND THE BIGGER THE CURVATURE OF SPACE.

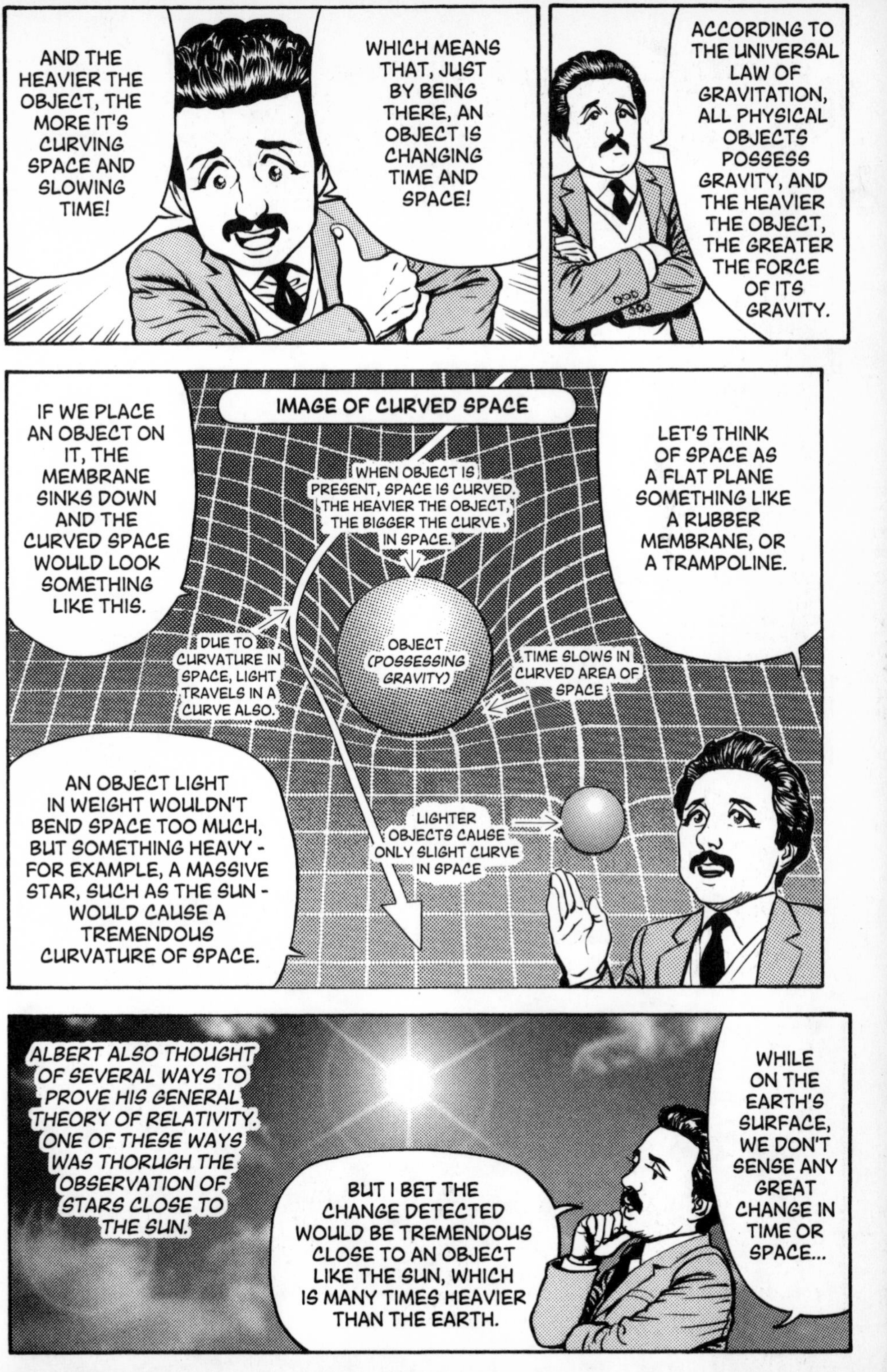
ACCORDING TO THE UNIVERSAL LAW OF GRAVITATION, ALL PHYSICAL OBJECTS POSSESS GRAVITY, AND THE HEAVIER THE OBJECT, THE GREATER THE FORCE OF ITS GRAVITY.
WHICH MEANS THAT, JUST BY BEING THERE, AN OBJECT IS CHANGING TIME AND SPACE!
AND THE HEAVIER THE OBJECT, THE MORE IT'S CURVING SPACE AND SLOWING TIME!
LET'S THINK OF SPACE AS A FLAT PLANE SOMETHING LIKE A RUBBER MEMBRANE, OR A TRAMPOLINE.
IMAGE OF CURVED SPACE
IF WE PLACE AN OBJECT ON IT, THE MEMBRANE SINKS DOWN AND THE CURVED SPACE WOULD LOOK SOMETHING LIKE THIS.
WHEN OBJECT IS PRESENT, SPACE IS CURVED. THE HEAVIER THE OBJECT, THE BIGGER THE CURVE IN SPACE.
OBJECT (POSSESSING GRAVITY)
TIME SLOWS IN CURVED AREA OF SPACE
DUE TO CURVATURE IN SPACE, LIGHT TRAVELS IN A CURVE ALSO.
LIGHTER OBJECTS CAUSE ONLY SLIGHT CURVE IN SPACE
AN OBJECT LIGHT IN WEIGHT WOULDN'T BEND SPACE TOO MUCH, BUT SOMETHING HEAVY - FOR EXAMPLE, A MASSIVE STAR, SUCH AS THE SUN - WOULD CAUSE A TREMENDOUS CURVATURE OF SPACE.
WHILE ON THE EARTH'S SURFACE, WE DON'T SENSE ANY GREAT CHANGE IN TIME OR SPACE...
BUT I BET THE CHANGE DETECTED WOULD BE TREMENDOUS CLOSE TO AN OBJECT LIKE THE SUN, WHICH IS MANY TIMES HEAVIER THAN THE EARTH.
ALBERT ALSO THOUGHT OF SEVERAL WAYS TO PROVE HIS GENERAL THEORY OF RELATIVITY. ONE OF THESE WAYS WAS THORUGH THE OBSERVATION OF STARS CLOSE TO THE SUN.

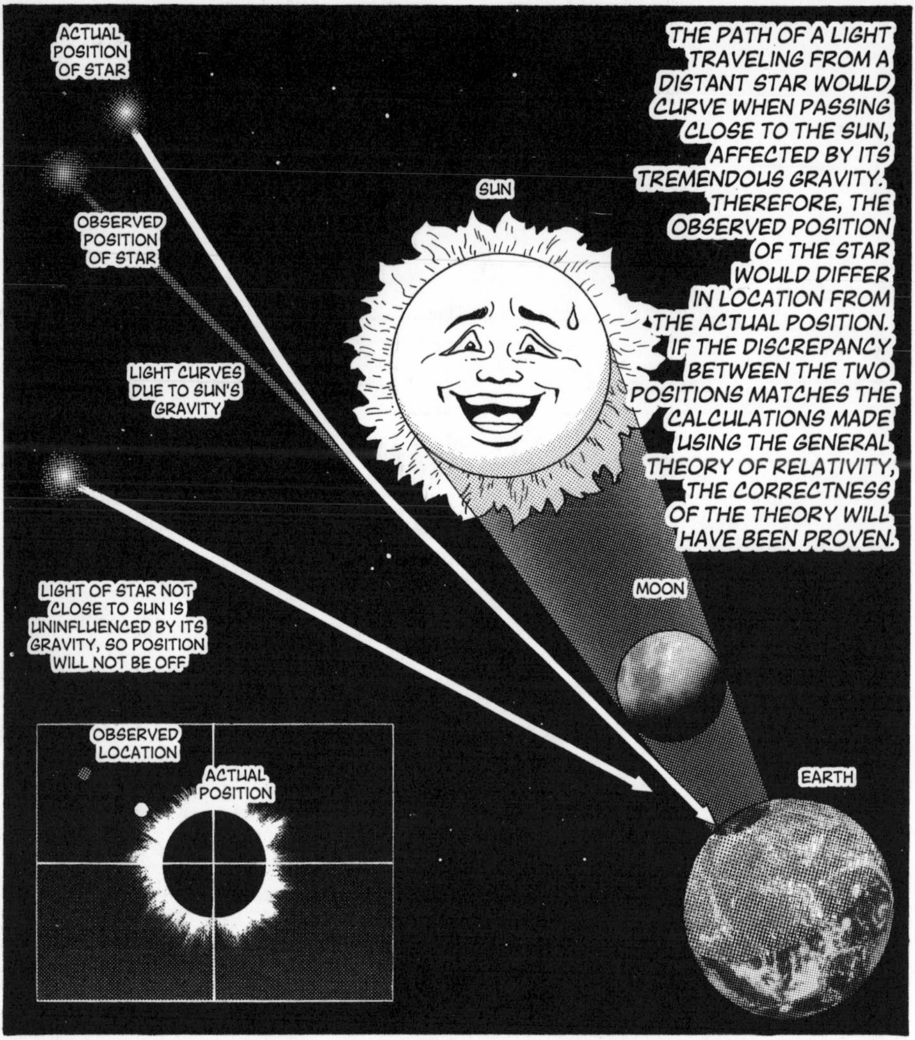
THE PATH OF A LIGHT TRAVELING FROM A DISTANT STAR WOULD CURVE WHEN PASSING CLOSE TO THE SUN, AFFECTED BY ITS TREMENDOUS GRAVITY. THEREFORE, THE OBSERVED POSITION OF THE STAR WOULD DIFFER IN LOCATION FROM THE ACTUAL POSITION. IF THE DISCREPANCY BETWEEN THE TWO POSITIONS MATCHES THE CALCULATIONS MADE USING THE GENERAL THEORY OF RELATIVITY, THE CORRECTNESS OF THE THEORY WILL HAVE BEEN PROVEN.
SUN
ACTUAL POSITION OF STAR
OBSERVED POSITION OF STAR
LIGHT CURVES DUE TO SUN'S GRAVITY
MOON
LIGHT OF STAR NOT CLOSE TO SUN IS UNINFLUENCED BY ITS GRAVITY, SO POSITION WILL NOT BE OFF
EARTH
OBSERVED LOCATION
ACTUAL POSITION

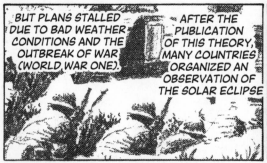

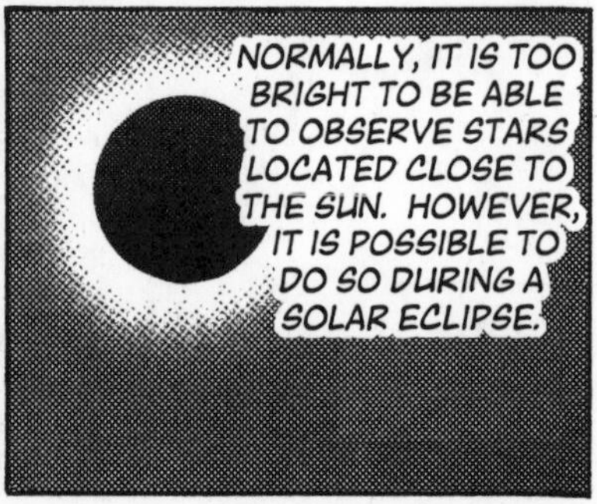
NORMALLY, IT IS TOO BRIGHT TO BE ABLE TO OBSERVE STARS LOCATED CLOSE TO THE SUN. HOWEVER, IT IS POSSIBLE TO DO SO DURING A SOLAR ECLIPSE.

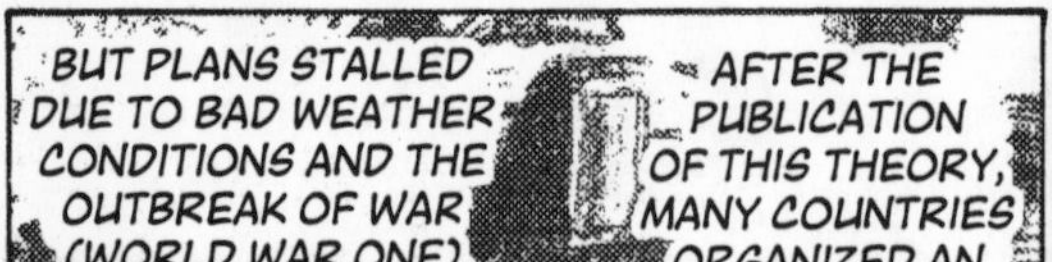
AFTER THE PUBLICATION OF THIS THEORY, MANY COUNTRIES ORGANIZED AN OBSERVATION OF THE SOLAR ECLIPSE
BUT PLANS STALLED DUE TO BAD WEATHER CONDITIONS AND THE OUTBREAK OF WAR (WORLD WAR ONE).

WORLD WAR ONE...CENTERED IN EUROPE, THE GREAT WAR WHICH BEGAN IN JUNE OF 1914 WITH THE OCCURRENCE OF THE SARAJEVO INCIDENT.

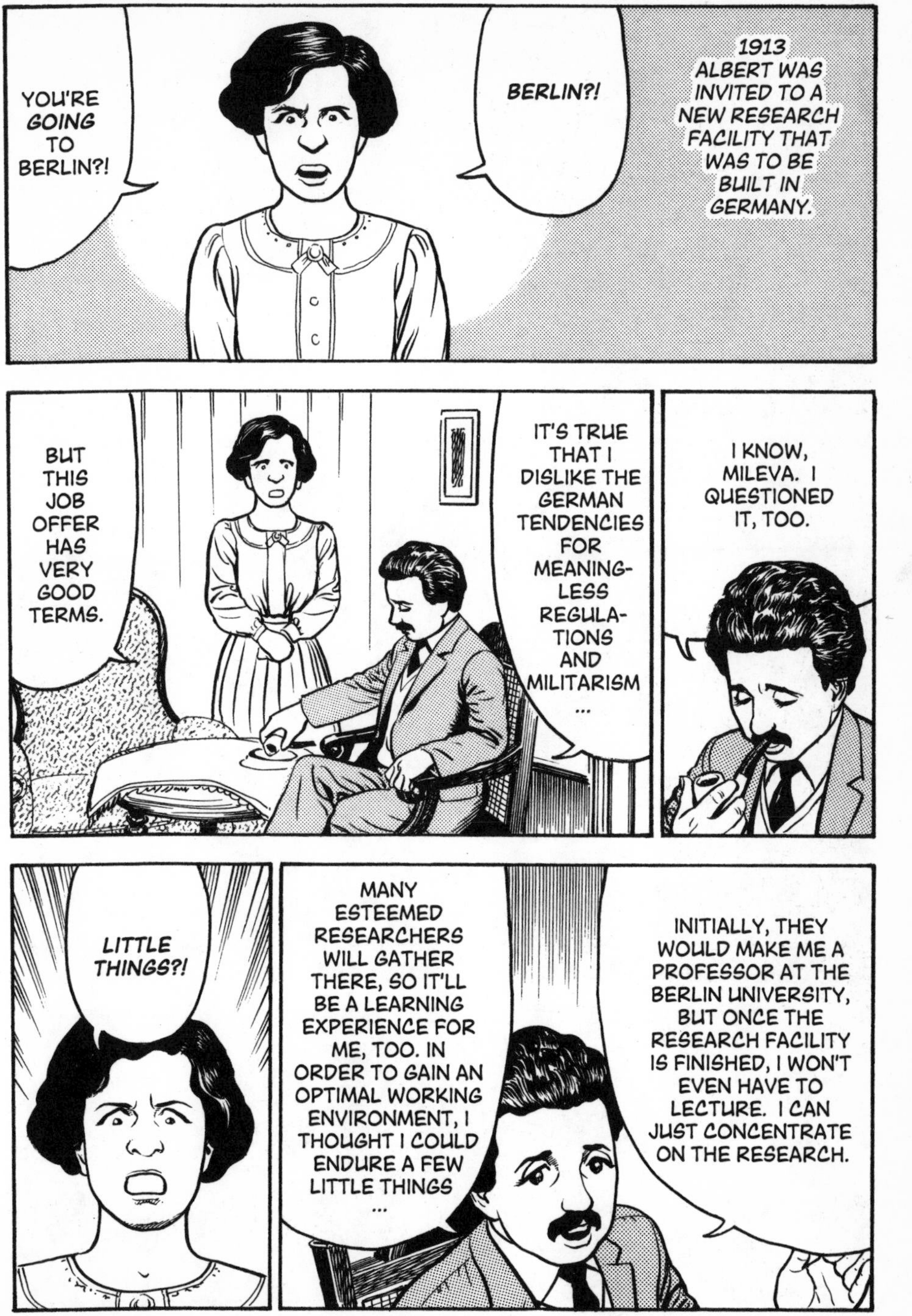
1913 ALBERT WAS INVITED TO A NEW RESEARCH FACILITY THAT WAS TO BE BUILT IN GERMANY.
BERLIN?!
YOU'RE GOING TO BERLIN?!
I KNOW, MILEVA. I QUESTIONED IT, TOO.
IT'S TRUE THAT I DISLIKE THE GERMAN TENDENCIES FOR MEANING-LESS REGULA-TIONS AND MILITARISM ...
BUT THIS JOB OFFER HAS VERY GOOD TERMS.
INITIALLY, THEY WOULD MAKE ME A PROFESSOR AT THE BERLIN UNIVERSITY, BUT ONCE THE RESEARCH FACILITY IS FINISHED, I WON'T EVEN HAVE TO LECTURE. I CAN JUST CONCENTRATE ON THE RESEARCH.
MANY ESTEEMED RESEARCHERS WILL GATHER THERE, SO IT'LL BE A LEARNING EXPERIENCE FOR ME, TOO. IN ORDER TO GAIN AN OPTIMAL WORKING ENVIRONMENT, I THOUGHT I COULD ENDURE A FEW LITTLE THINGS ...
LITTLE THINGS?!

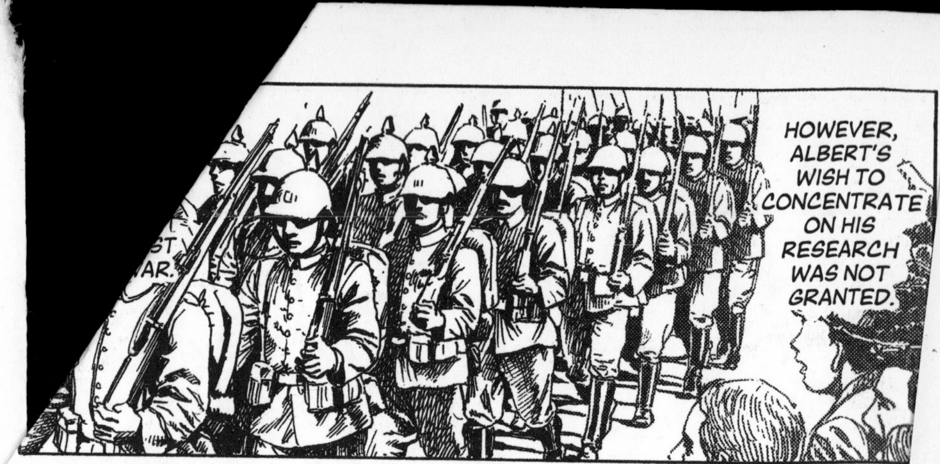
HOWEVER, ALBERT'S WISH TO CONCENTRATE ON HIS RESEARCH WAS NOT GRANTED.

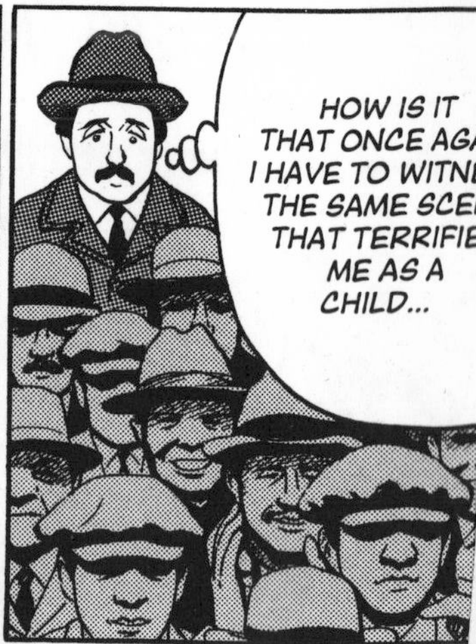
HOW IS IT THAT ONCE AGAI I HAVE TO WITNES THE SAME SCEN THAT TERRIFIED ME AS A CHILD...

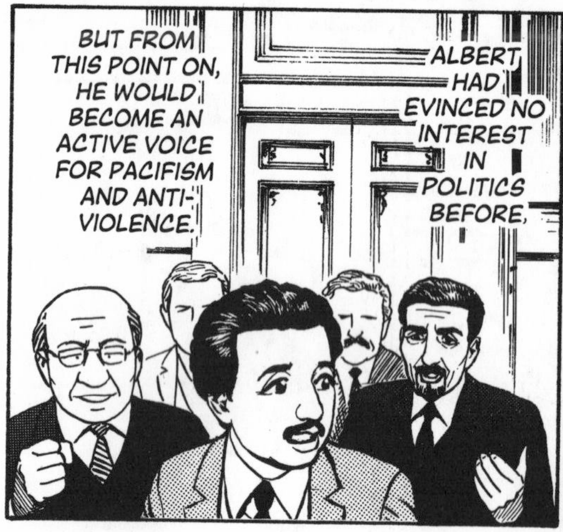
ALBERT HAD EVINCED NO INTEREST IN POLITICS BEFORE,
BUT FROM THIS POINT ON, HE WOULD BECOME AN ACTIVE VOICE FOR PACIFISM AND ANTI-VIOLENCE.

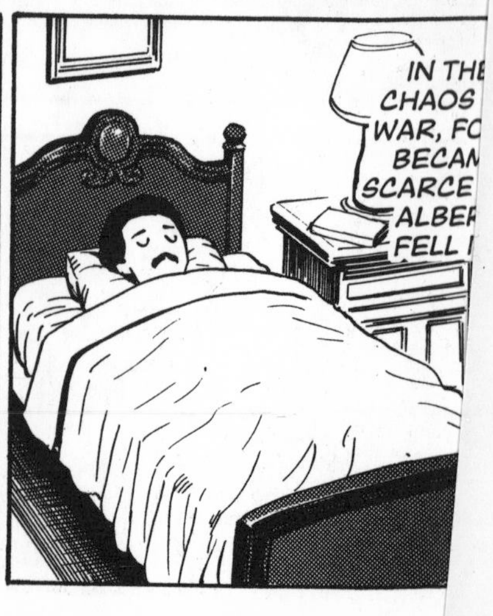
IN THE CHAOS WAR, FO BECAM SCARCE ALBER FELL I

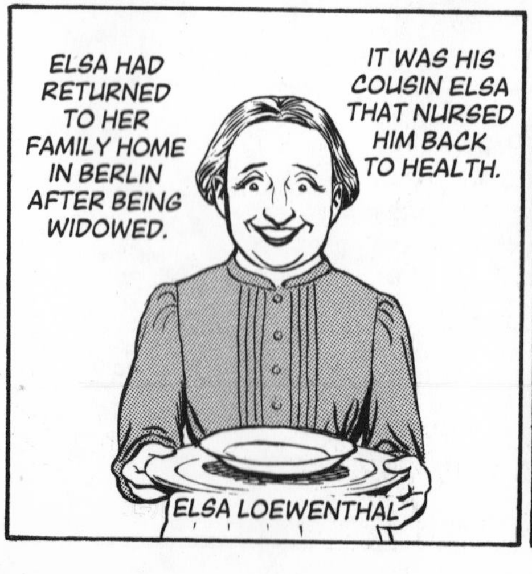
IT WAS HIS COUSIN ELSA THAT NURSED HIM BACK TO HEALTH.
ELSA HAD RETURNED TO HER FAMILY HOME IN BERLIN AFTER BEING WIDOWED.
ELSA LOEWENTHAL

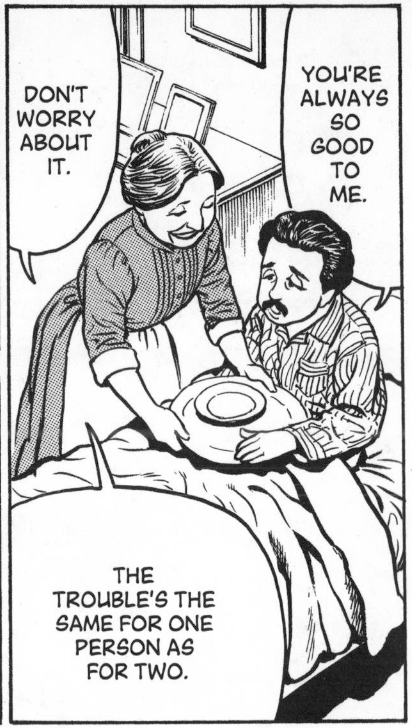
YOU'RE ALWAYS SO GOOD TO ME.
DON'T WORRY ABOUT IT.
THE TROUBLE'S THE SAME FOR ONE PERSON AS FOR TWO.

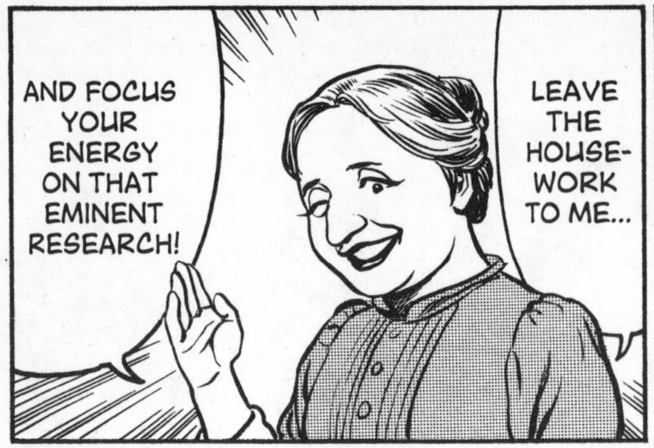
LEAVE THE HOUSE-WORK TO ME...
AND FOCUS YOUR ENERGY ON THAT EMINENT RESEARCH!

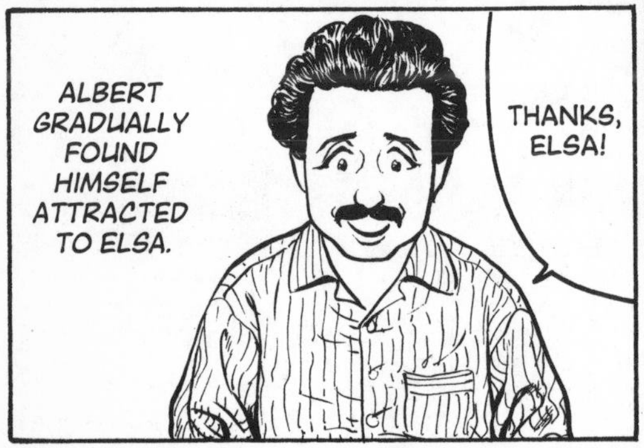
THANKS, ELSA!
ALBERT GRADUALLY FOUND HIMSELF ATTRACTED TO ELSA.

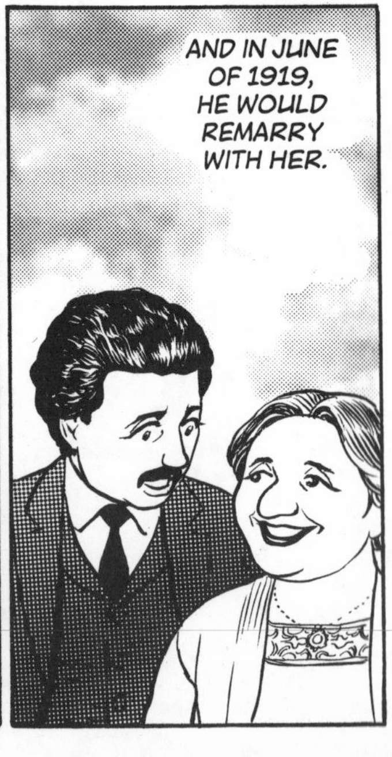
AND IN JUNE OF 1919, HE WOULD REMARRY WITH HER.

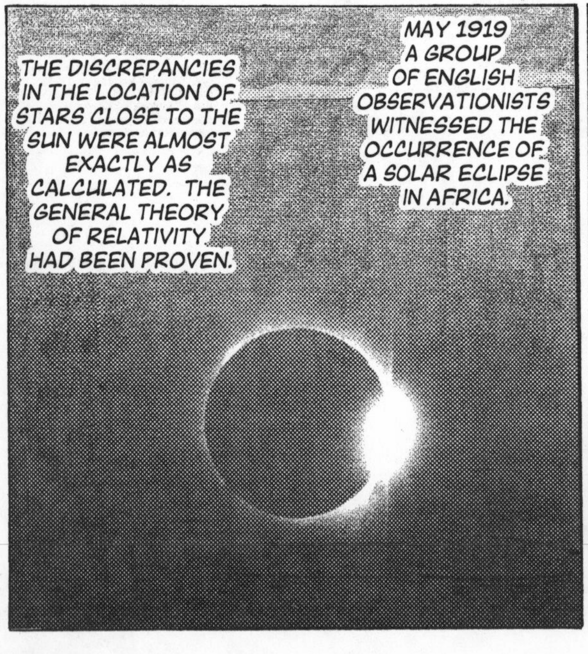
MAY 1919 A GROUP OF ENGLISH OBSERVATIONISTS WITNESSED THE OCCURRENCE OF A SOLAR ECLIPSE IN AFRICA.
THE DISCREPANCIES IN THE LOCATION OF STARS CLOSE TO THE SUN WERE ALMOST EXACTLY AS CALCULATED. THE GENERAL THEORY OF RELATIVITY HAD BEEN PROVEN.

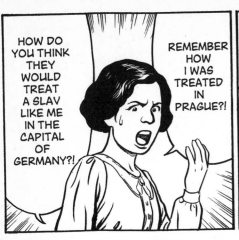
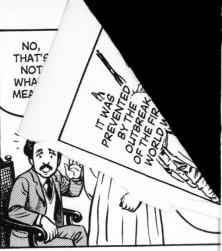
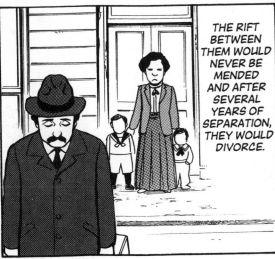
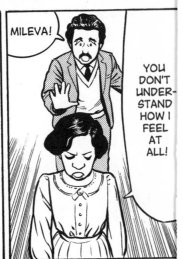
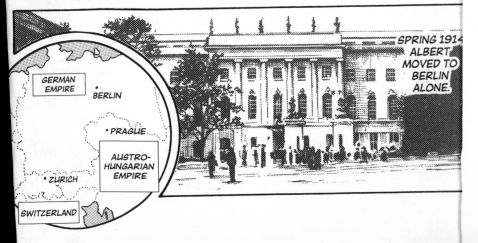
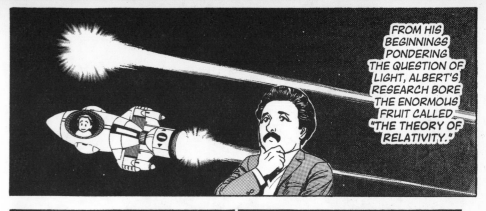
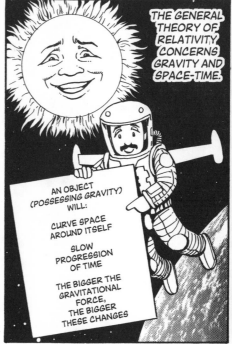
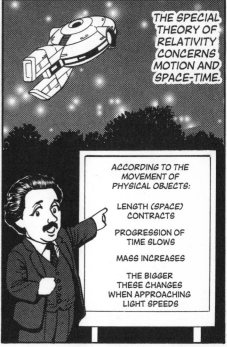
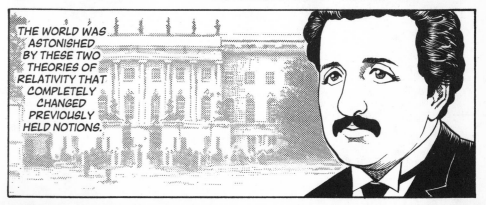

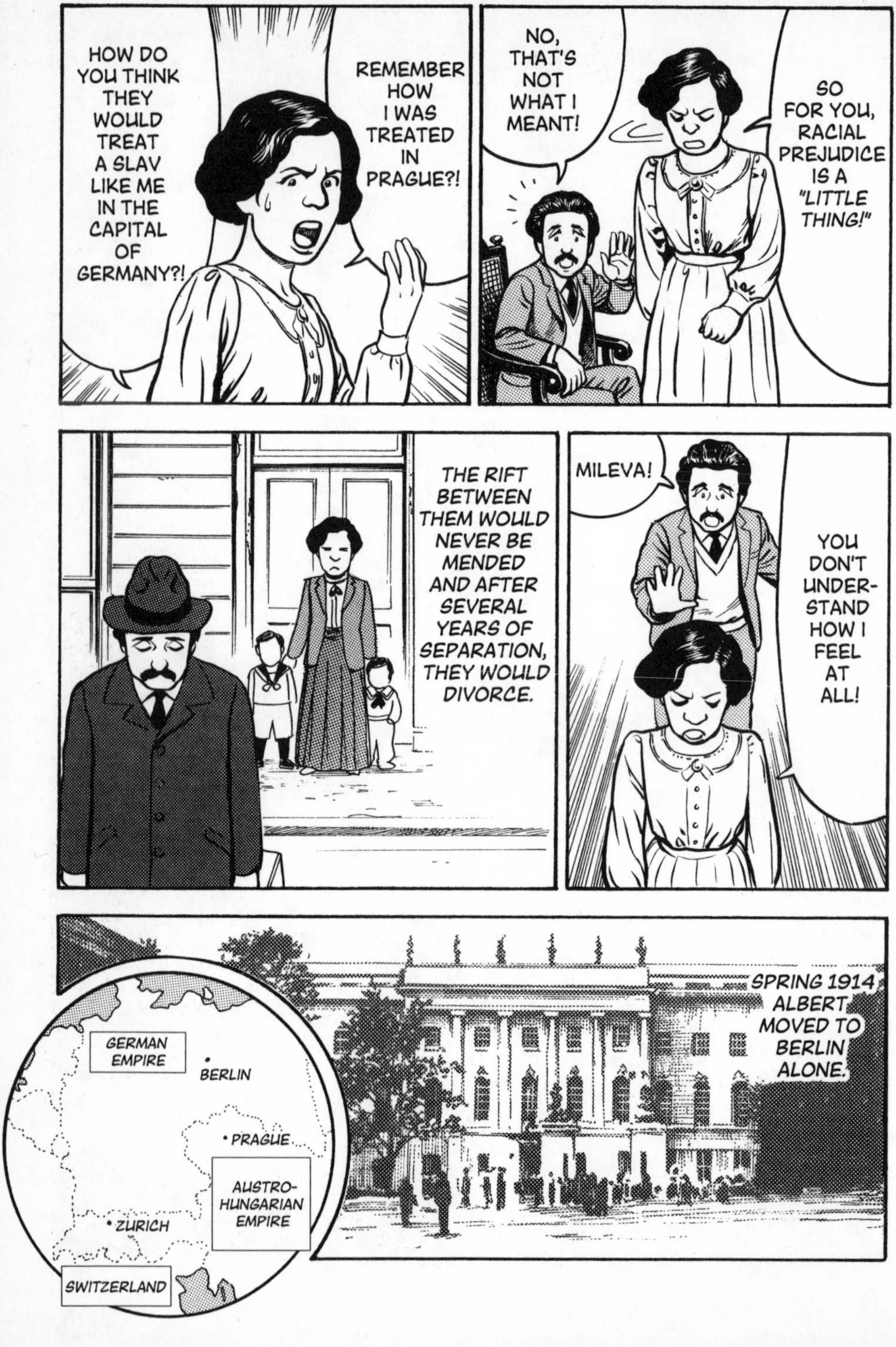
SO FOR YOU, RACIAL PREJUDICE IS A "LITTLE THING!"
NO, THAT'S NOT WHAT I MEANT!
REMEMBER HOW I WAS TREATED IN PRAGUE?!
HOW DO YOU THINK THEY WOULD TREAT A SLAV LIKE ME IN THE CAPITAL OF GERMANY?!
YOU DON'T UNDER-STAND HOW I FEEL AT ALL!
MILEVA!
THE RIFT BETWEEN THEM WOULD NEVER BE MENDED AND AFTER SEVERAL YEARS OF SEPARATION, THEY WOULD DIVORCE.
SPRING 1914 ALBERT MOVED TO BERLIN ALONE.
GERMAN EMPIRE
BERLIN
PRAGUE
AUSTRO-HUNGARIAN EMPIRE
ZURICH
SWITZERLAND

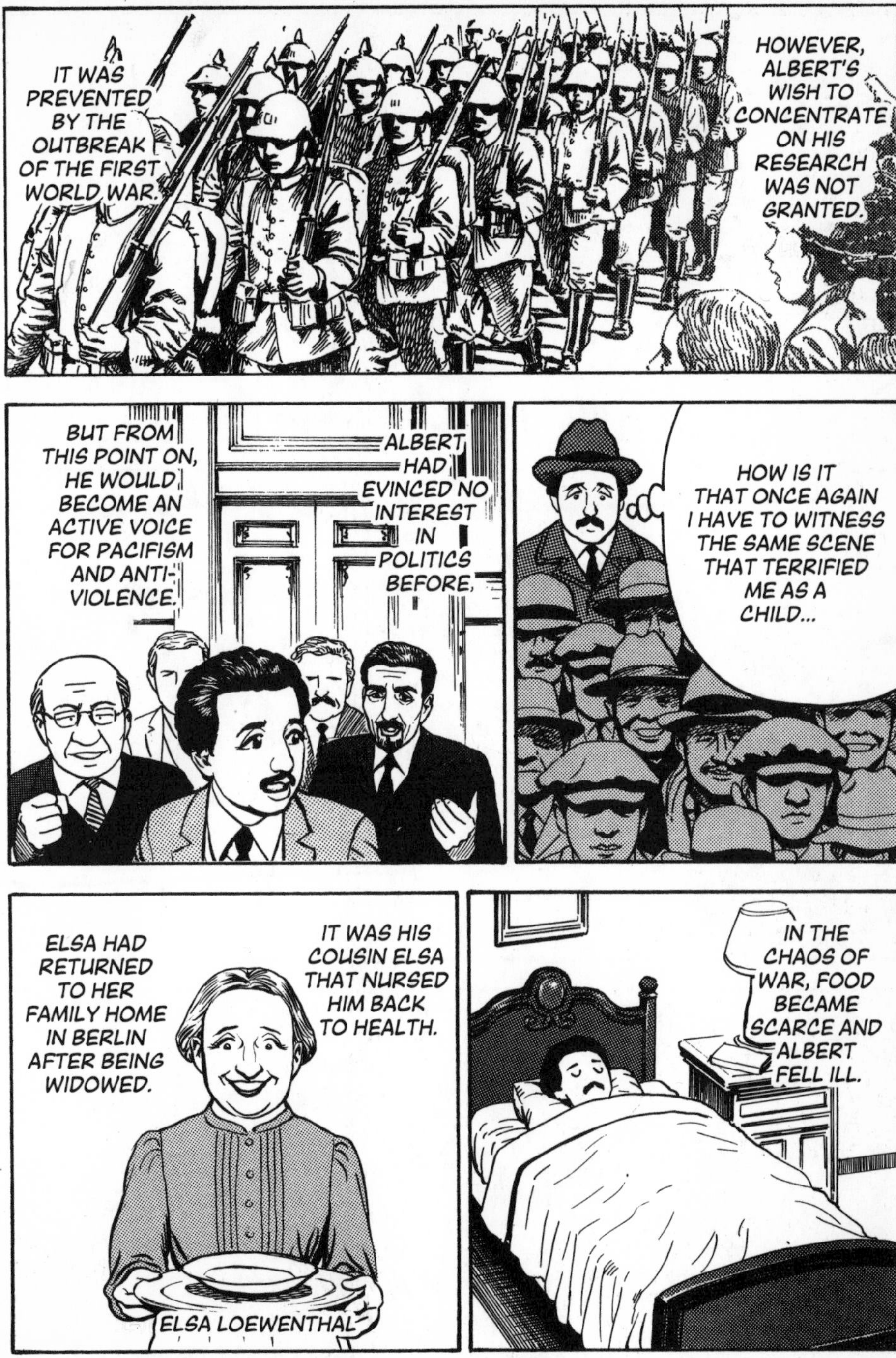
HOWEVER, ALBERT'S WISH TO CONCENTRATE ON HIS RESEARCH WAS NOT GRANTED.
IT WAS PREVENTED BY THE OUTBREAK OF THE FIRST WORLD WAR.
HOW IS IT THAT ONCE AGAIN I HAVE TO WITNESS THE SAME SCENE THAT TERRIFIED ME AS A CHILD...
ALBERT HAD EVINCED NO INTEREST IN POLITICS BEFORE,
BUT FROM THIS POINT ON, HE WOULD BECOME AN ACTIVE VOICE FOR PACIFISM AND ANTI-VIOLENCE.
IN THE CHAOS OF WAR, FOOD BECAME SCARCE AND ALBERT FELL ILL.
IT WAS HIS COUSIN ELSA THAT NURSED HIM BACK TO HEALTH.
ELSA HAD RETURNED TO HER FAMILY HOME IN BERLIN AFTER BEING WIDOWED.
ELSA LOEWENTHAL

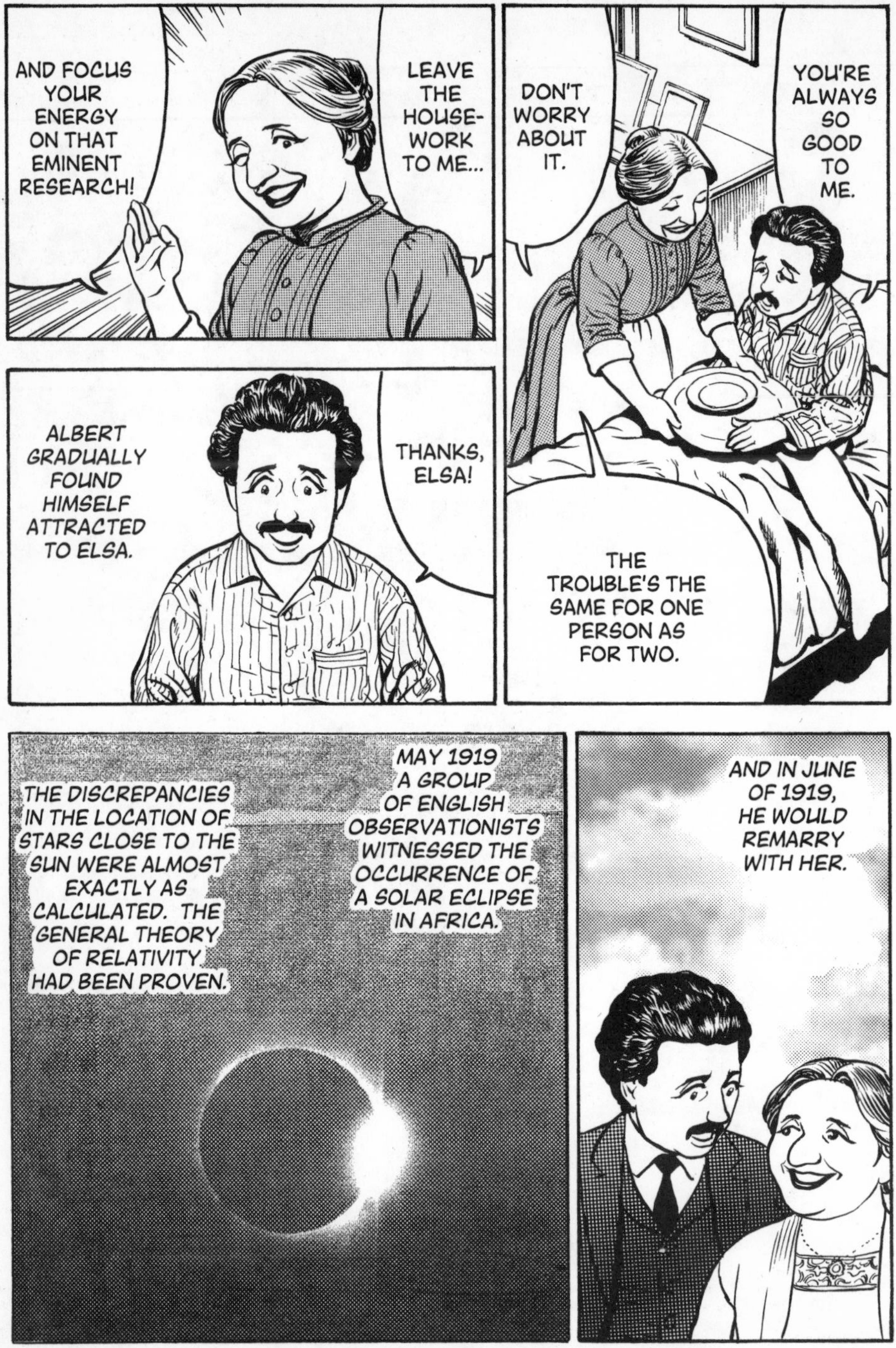
YOU'RE ALWAYS SO GOOD TO ME.
DON'T WORRY ABOUT IT.
THE TROUBLE'S THE SAME FOR ONE PERSON AS FOR TWO.
LEAVE THE HOUSE-WORK TO ME...
AND FOCUS YOUR ENERGY ON THAT EMINENT RESEARCH!
THANKS, ELSA!
ALBERT GRADUALLY FOUND HIMSELF ATTRACTED TO ELSA.
AND IN JUNE OF 1919, HE WOULD REMARRY WITH HER.
MAY 1919 A GROUP OF ENGLISH OBSERVATIONISTS WITNESSED THE OCCURRENCE OF A SOLAR ECLIPSE IN AFRICA.
THE DISCREPANCIES IN THE LOCATION OF STARS CLOSE TO THE SUN WERE ALMOST EXACTLY AS CALCULATED. THE GENERAL THEORY OF RELATIVITY HAD BEEN PROVEN.

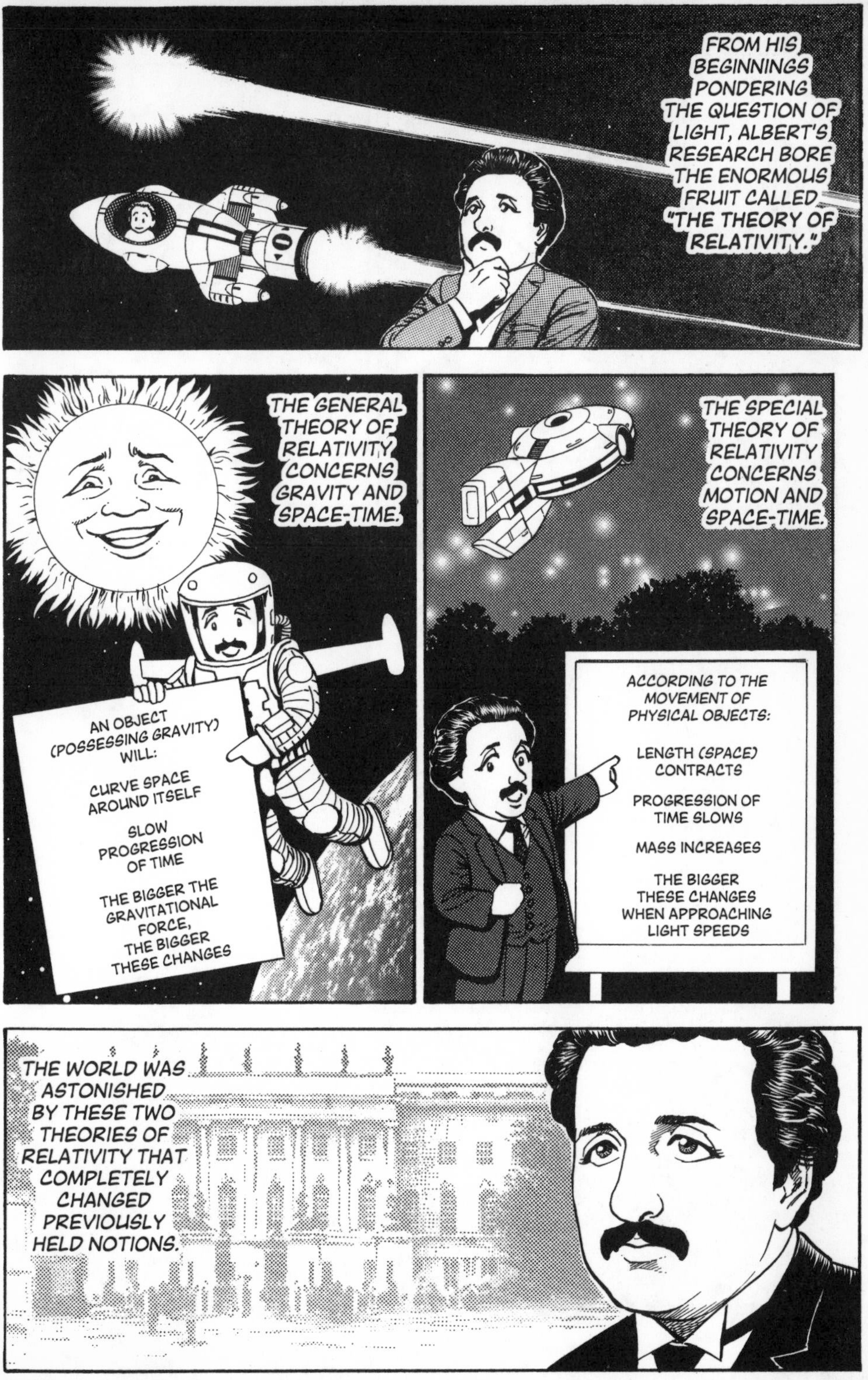
FROM HIS BEGINNINGS PONDERING THE QUESTION OF LIGHT, ALBERT'S RESEARCH BORE THE ENORMOUS FRUIT CALLED "THE THEORY OF RELATIVITY."
THE SPECIAL THEORY OF RELATIVITY CONCERNS MOTION AND SPACE-TIME.
ACCORDING TO THE MOVEMENT OF PHYSICAL OBJECTS:
LENGTH (SPACE) CONTRACTS
PROGRESSION OF TIME SLOWS
MASS INCREASES
THE BIGGER THESE CHANGES WHEN APPROACHING LIGHT SPEEDS
THE GENERAL THEORY OF RELATIVITY CONCERNS GRAVITY AND SPACE-TIME.
AN OBJECT (POSSESSING GRAVITY) WILL:
CURVE SPACE AROUND ITSELF
SLOW PROGRESSION OF TIME
THE BIGGER THE GRAVITATIONAL FORCE, THE BIGGER THESE CHANGES
THE WORLD WAS ASTONISHED BY THESE TWO THEORIES OF RELATIVITY THAT COMPLETELY CHANGED PREVIOUSLY HELD NOTIONS.

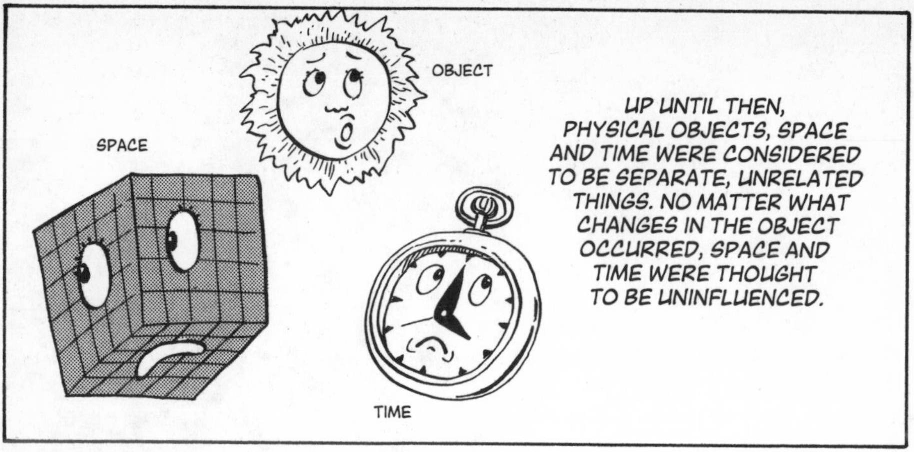
OBJECT
SPACE
TIME
UP UNTIL THEN, PHYSICAL OBJECTS, SPACE AND TIME WERE CONSIDERED TO BE SEPARATE, UNRELATED THINGS. NO MATTER WHAT CHANGES IN THE OBJECT OCCURRED, SPACE AND TIME WERE THOUGHT TO BE UNINFLUENCED.

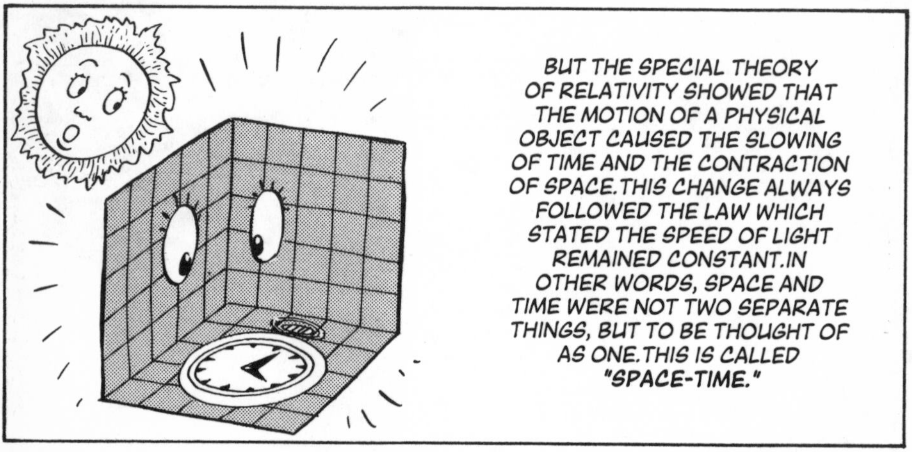
BUT THE SPECIAL THEORY OF RELATIVITY SHOWED THAT THE MOTION OF A PHYSICAL OBJECT CAUSED THE SLOWING OF TIME AND THE CONTRACTION OF SPACE.THIS CHANGE ALWAYS FOLLOWED THE LAW WHICH STATED THE SPEED OF LIGHT REMAINED CONSTANT.IN OTHER WORDS, SPACE AND TIME WERE NOT TWO SEPARATE THINGS, BUT TO BE THOUGHT OF AS ONE.THIS IS CALLED "SPACE-TIME."

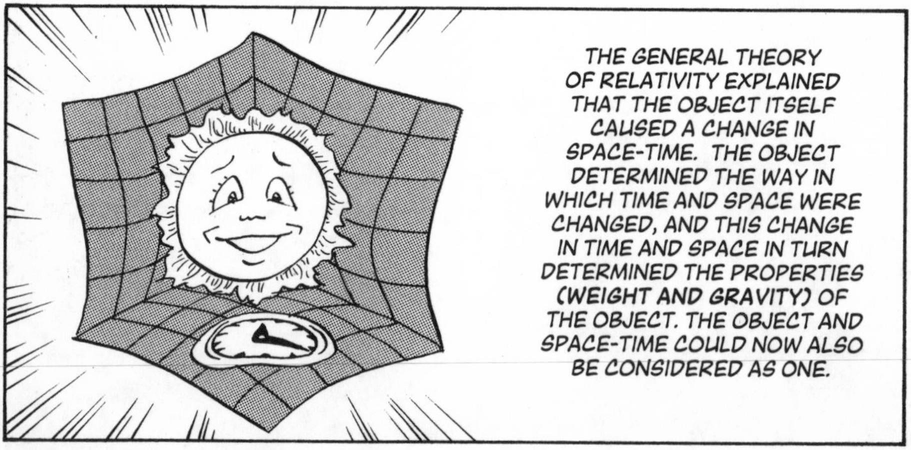
THE GENERAL THEORY OF RELATIVITY EXPLAINED THAT THE OBJECT ITSELF CAUSED A CHANGE IN SPACE-TIME. THE OBJECT DETERMINED THE WAY IN WHICH TIME AND SPACE WERE CHANGED, AND THIS CHANGE IN TIME AND SPACE IN TURN DETERMINED THE PROPERTIES (WEIGHT AND GRAVITY) OF THE OBJECT. THE OBJECT AND SPACE-TIME COULD NOW ALSO BE CONSIDERED AS ONE.

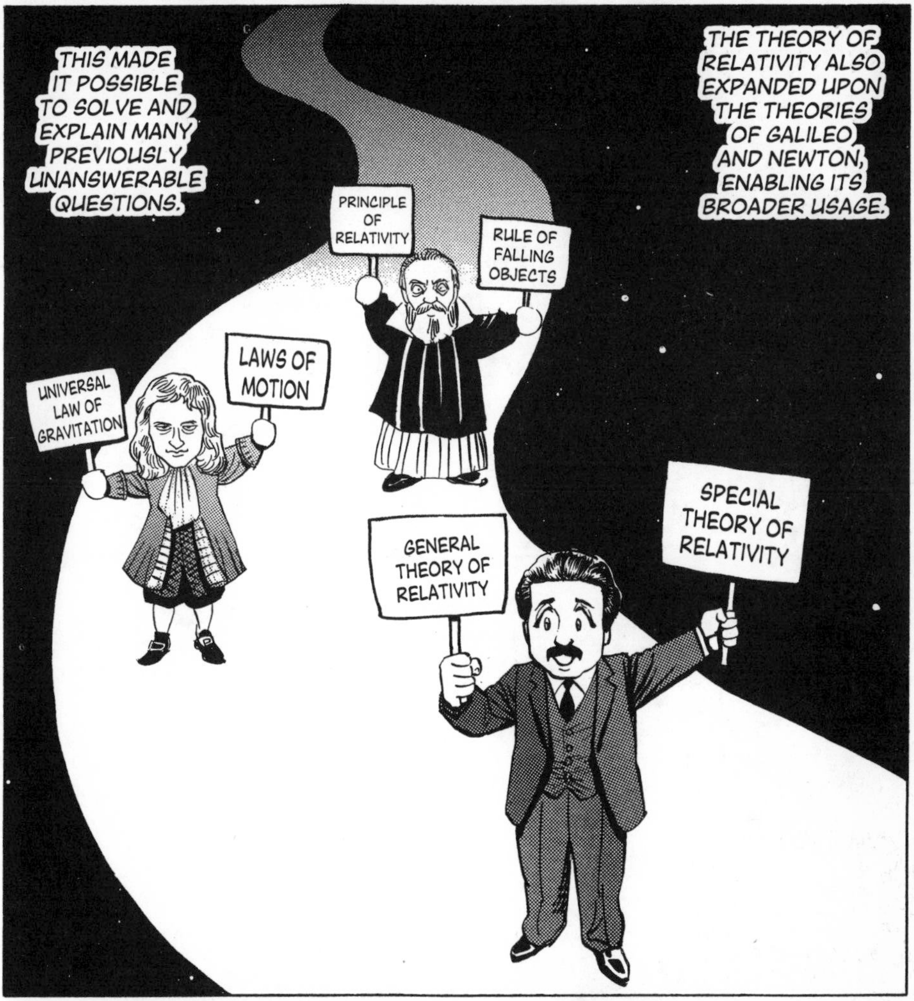
THE THEORY OF RELATIVITY ALSO EXPANDED UPON THE THEORIES OF GALILEO AND NEWTON, ENABLING ITS BROADER USAGE.
THIS MADE IT POSSIBLE TO SOLVE AND EXPLAIN MANY PREVIOUSLY UNANSWERABLE QUESTIONS.
RULE OF FALLING OBJECTS
PRINCIPLE OF RELATIVITY
LAWS OF MOTION
UNIVERSAL LAW OF GRAVITATION
SPECIAL THEORY OF RELATIVITY
GENERAL THEORY OF RELATIVITY

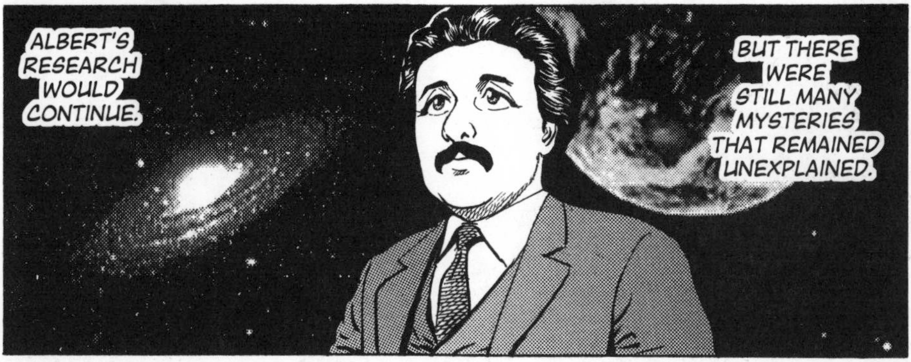
BUT THERE WERE STILL MANY MYSTERIES THAT REMAINED UNEXPLAINED.
ALBERT'S RESEARCH WOULD CONTINUE.

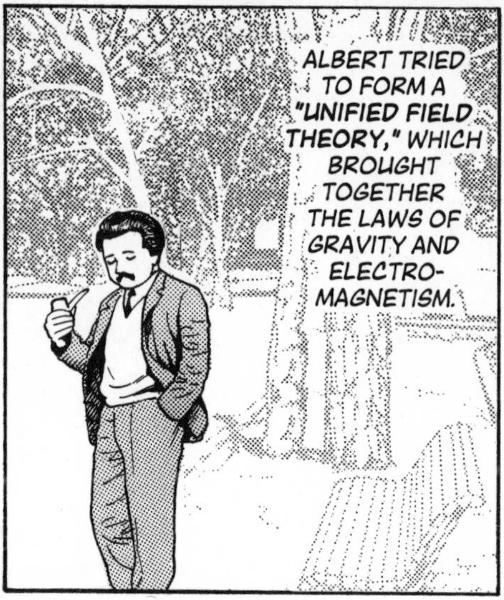
ALBERT TRIED TO FORM A "UNIFIED FIELD THEORY," WHICH BROUGHT TOGETHER THE LAWS OF GRAVITY AND ELECTRO-MAGNETISM.

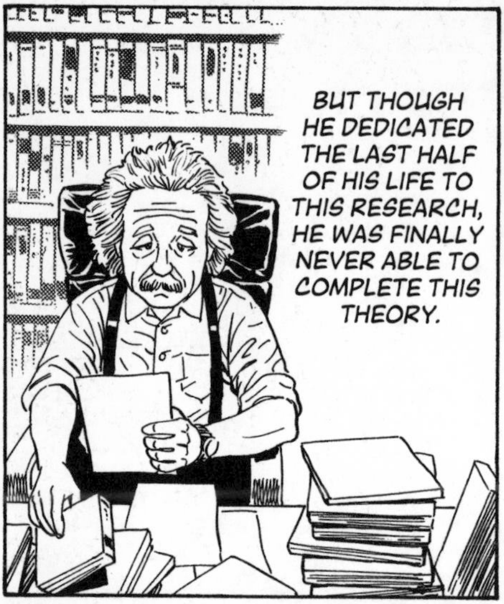
BUT THOUGH HE DEDICATED THE LAST HALF OF HIS LIFE TO THIS RESEARCH, HE WAS FINALLY NEVER ABLE TO COMPLETE THIS THEORY.

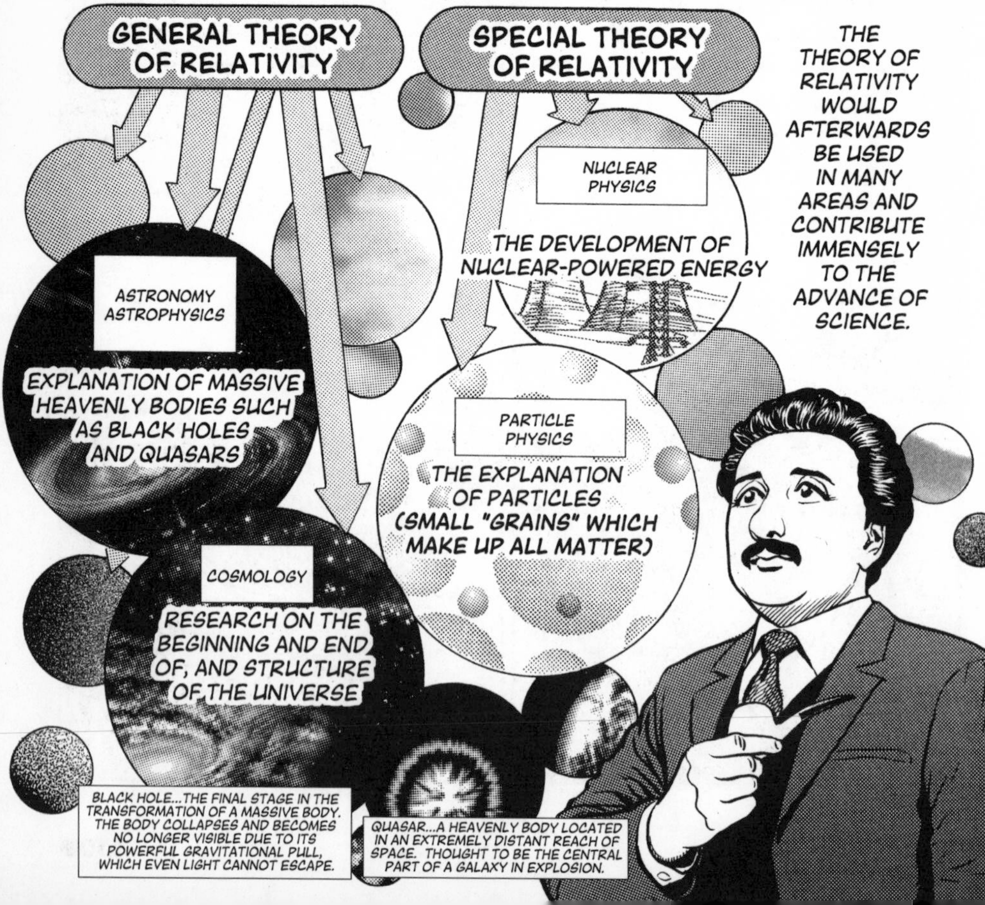
THE THEORY OF RELATIVITY WOULD AFTERWARDS BE USED IN MANY AREAS AND CONTRIBUTE IMMENSELY TO THE ADVANCE OF SCIENCE.
SPECIAL THEORY OF RELATIVITY
GENERAL THEORY OF RELATIVITY
NUCLEAR PHYSICS
THE DEVELOPMENT OF NUCLEAR-POWERED ENERGY
PARTICLE PHYSICS
THE EXPLANATION OF PARTICLES (SMALL "GRAINS" WHICH MAKE UP ALL MATTER)
ASTRONOMY ASTROPHYSICS
EXPLANATION OF MASSIVE HEAVENLY BODIES SUCH AS BLACK HOLES AND QUASARS
COSMOLOGY
RESEARCH ON THE BEGINNING AND END OF, AND STRUCTURE OF THE UNIVERSE
QUASAR...A HEAVENLY BODY LOCATED IN AN EXTREMELY DISTANT REACH OF SPACE. THOUGHT TO BE THE CENTRAL PART OF A GALAXY IN EXPLOSION.
BLACK HOLE...THE FINAL STAGE IN THE TRANSFORMATION OF A MASSIVE BODY. THE BODY COLLAPSES AND BECOMES NO LONGER VISIBLE DUE TO ITS POWERFUL GRAVITATIONAL PULL, WHICH EVEN LIGHT CANNOT ESCAPE.

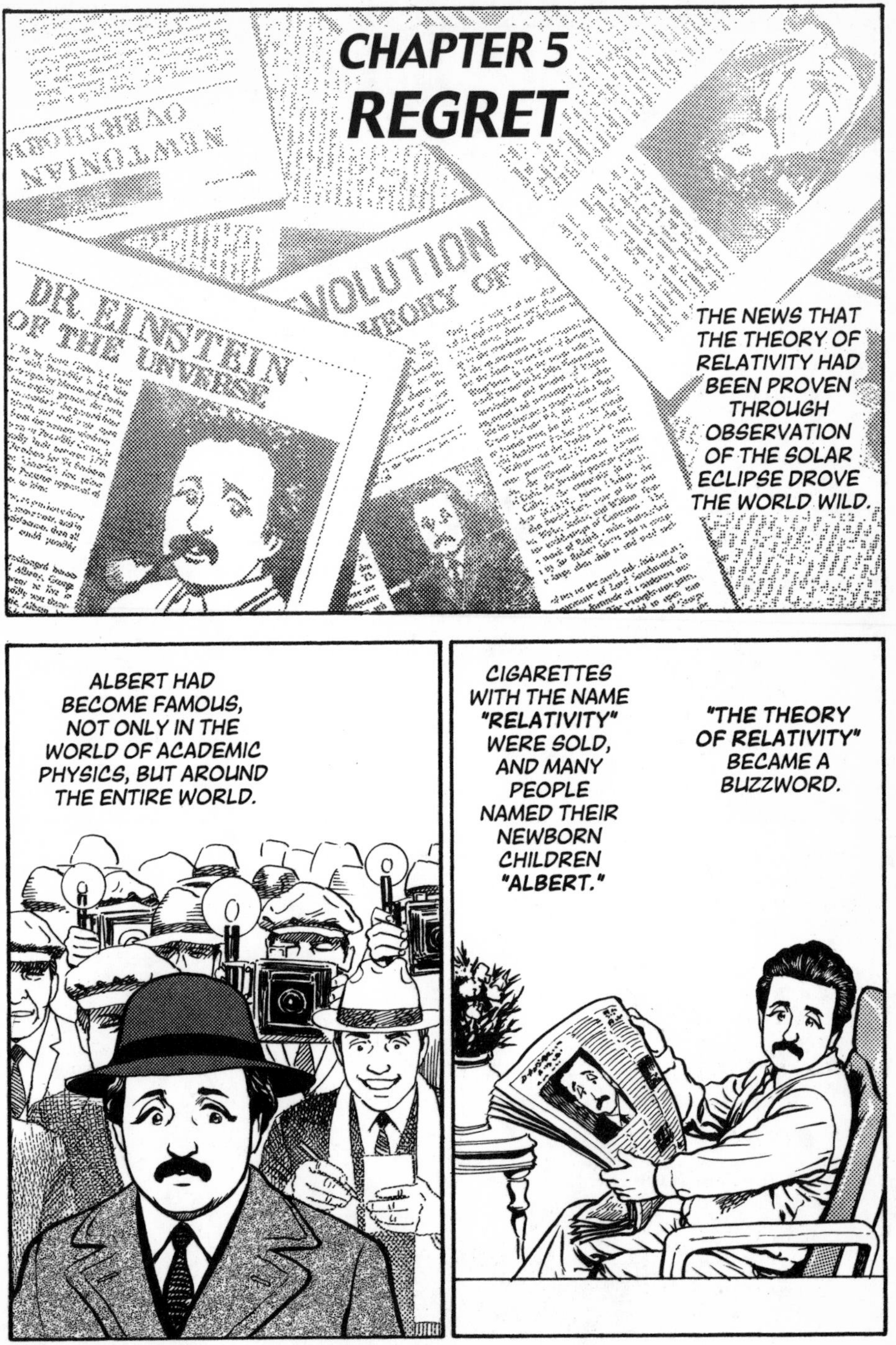
CHAPTER 5
REGRET
DR. EINSTEIN
OF THE UNIVERSE
THE NEWS THAT THE THEORY OF RELATIVITY HAD BEEN PROVEN THROUGH OBSERVATION OF THE SOLAR ECLIPSE DROVE THE WORLD WILD.
"THE THEORY OF RELATIVITY" BECAME A BUZZWORD.
CIGARETTES WITH THE NAME "RELATIVITY" WERE SOLD, AND MANY PEOPLE NAMED THEIR NEWBORN CHILDREN "ALBERT."
ALBERT HAD BECOME FAMOUS, NOT ONLY IN THE WORLD OF ACADEMIC PHYSICS, BUT AROUND THE ENTIRE WORLD.

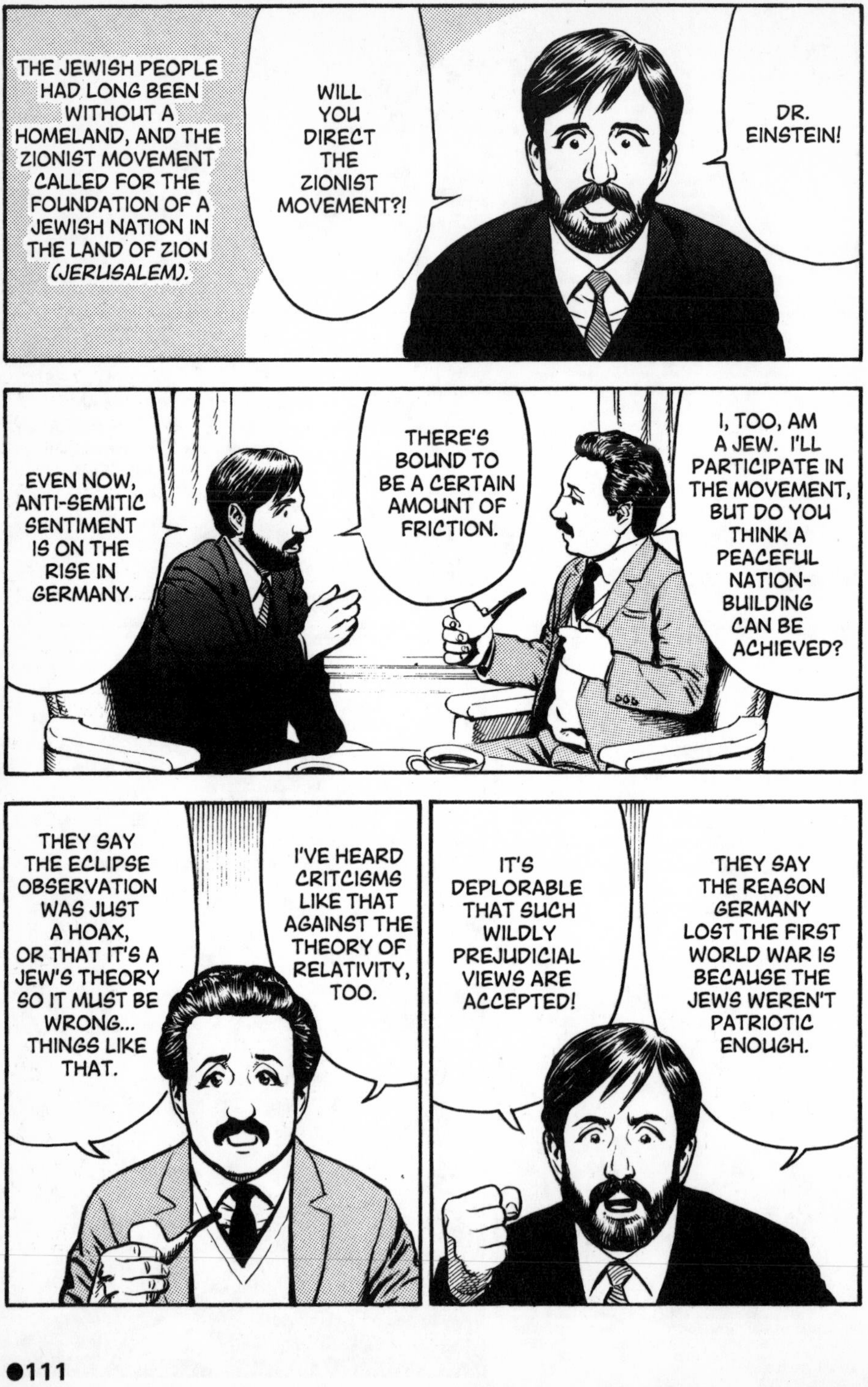
DR. EINSTEIN!
WILL YOU DIRECT THE ZIONIST MOVEMENT?!
THE JEWISH PEOPLE HAD LONG BEEN WITHOUT A HOMELAND, AND THE ZIONIST MOVEMENT CALLED FOR THE FOUNDATION OF A JEWISH NATION IN THE LAND OF ZION (JERUSALEM).
I, TOO, AM A JEW. I'LL PARTICIPATE IN THE MOVEMENT, BUT DO YOU THINK A PEACEFUL NATION-BUILDING CAN BE ACHIEVED?
THERE'S BOUND TO BE A CERTAIN AMOUNT OF FRICTION.
EVEN NOW, ANTI-SEMITIC SENTIMENT IS ON THE RISE IN GERMANY.
THEY SAY THE REASON GERMANY LOST THE FIRST WORLD WAR IS BECAUSE THE JEWS WEREN'T PATRIOTIC ENOUGH.
IT'S DEPLORABLE THAT SUCH WILDLY PREJUDICIAL VIEWS ARE ACCEPTED!
I'VE HEARD CRITCISMS LIKE THAT AGAINST THE THEORY OF RELATIVITY, TOO.
THEY SAY THE ECLIPSE OBSERVATION WAS JUST A HOAX, OR THAT IT'S A JEW'S THEORY SO IT MUST BE WRONG... THINGS LIKE THAT.

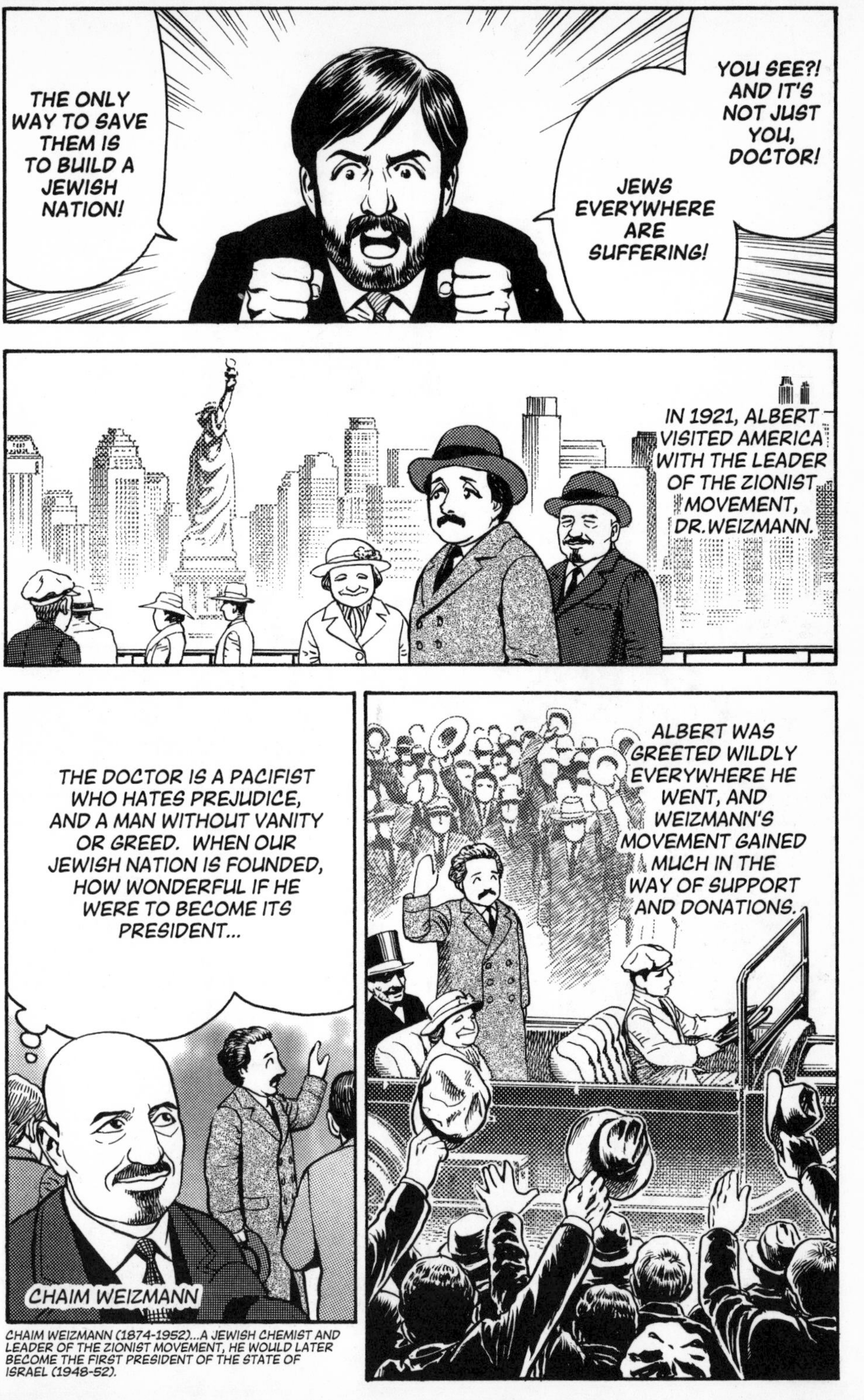

YOU SEE?! AND IT'S NOT JUST YOU, DOCTOR!
JEWS EVERYWHERE ARE SUFFERING!
THE ONLY WAY TO SAVE THEM IS TO BUILD A JEWISH NATION!
IN 1921, ALBERT VISITED AMERICA WITH THE LEADER OF THE ZIONIST MOVEMENT, DR.WEIZMANN.
ALBERT WAS GREETED WILDLY EVERYWHERE HE WENT, AND WEIZMANN'S MOVEMENT GAINED MUCH IN THE WAY OF SUPPORT AND DONATIONS.
THE DOCTOR IS A PACIFIST WHO HATES PREJUDICE, AND A MAN WITHOUT VANITY OR GREED. WHEN OUR JEWISH NATION IS FOUNDED, HOW WONDERFUL IF HE WERE TO BECOME ITS PRESIDENT...
CHAIM WEIZMANN

CHAIM WEIZMANN (1874-1952)...A JEWISH CHEMIST AND LEADER OF THE ZIONIST MOVEMENT, HE WOULD LATER BECOME THE FIRST PRESIDENT OF THE STATE OF ISRAEL (1948-52).

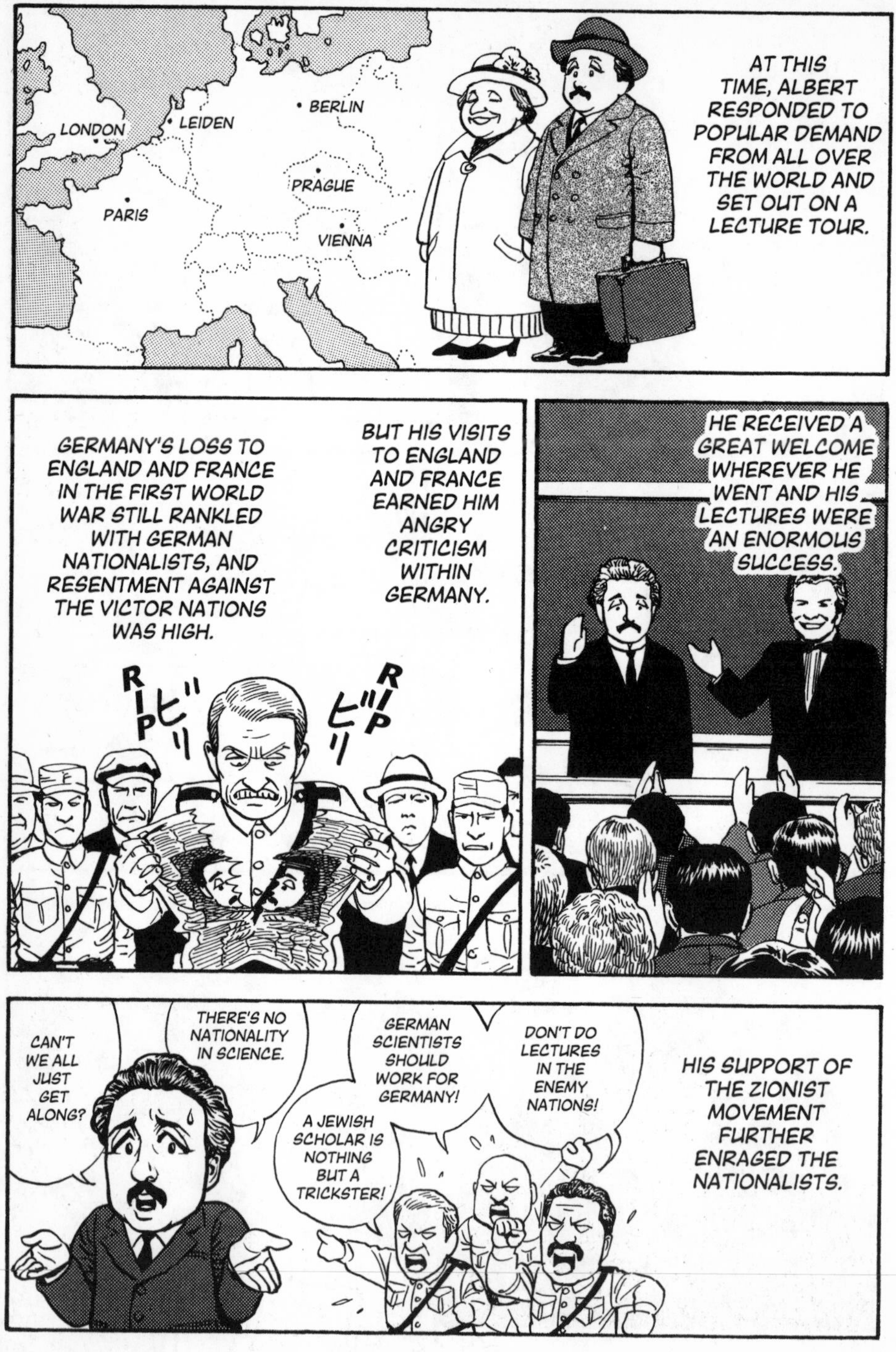
AT THIS TIME, ALBERT RESPONDED TO POPULAR DEMAND FROM ALL OVER THE WORLD AND SET OUT ON A LECTURE TOUR.
BERLIN
LEIDEN
LONDON
PRAGUE
PARIS
VIENNA
HE RECEIVED A GREAT WELCOME WHEREVER HE WENT AND HIS LECTURES WERE AN ENORMOUS SUCCESS.
BUT HIS VISITS TO ENGLAND AND FRANCE EARNED HIM ANGRY CRITICISM WITHIN GERMANY.
GERMANY'S LOSS TO ENGLAND AND FRANCE IN THE FIRST WORLD WAR STILL RANKLED WITH GERMAN NATIONALISTS, AND RESENTMENT AGAINST THE VICTOR NATIONS WAS HIGH.
RIP ビリ
RIP ビリ
HIS SUPPORT OF THE ZIONIST MOVEMENT FURTHER ENRAGED THE NATIONALISTS.
DON'T DO LECTURES IN THE ENEMY NATIONS!
GERMAN SCIENTISTS SHOULD WORK FOR GERMANY!
A JEWISH SCHOLAR IS NOTHING BUT A TRICKSTER!
THERE'S NO NATIONALITY IN SCIENCE.
CAN'T WE ALL JUST GET ALONG?

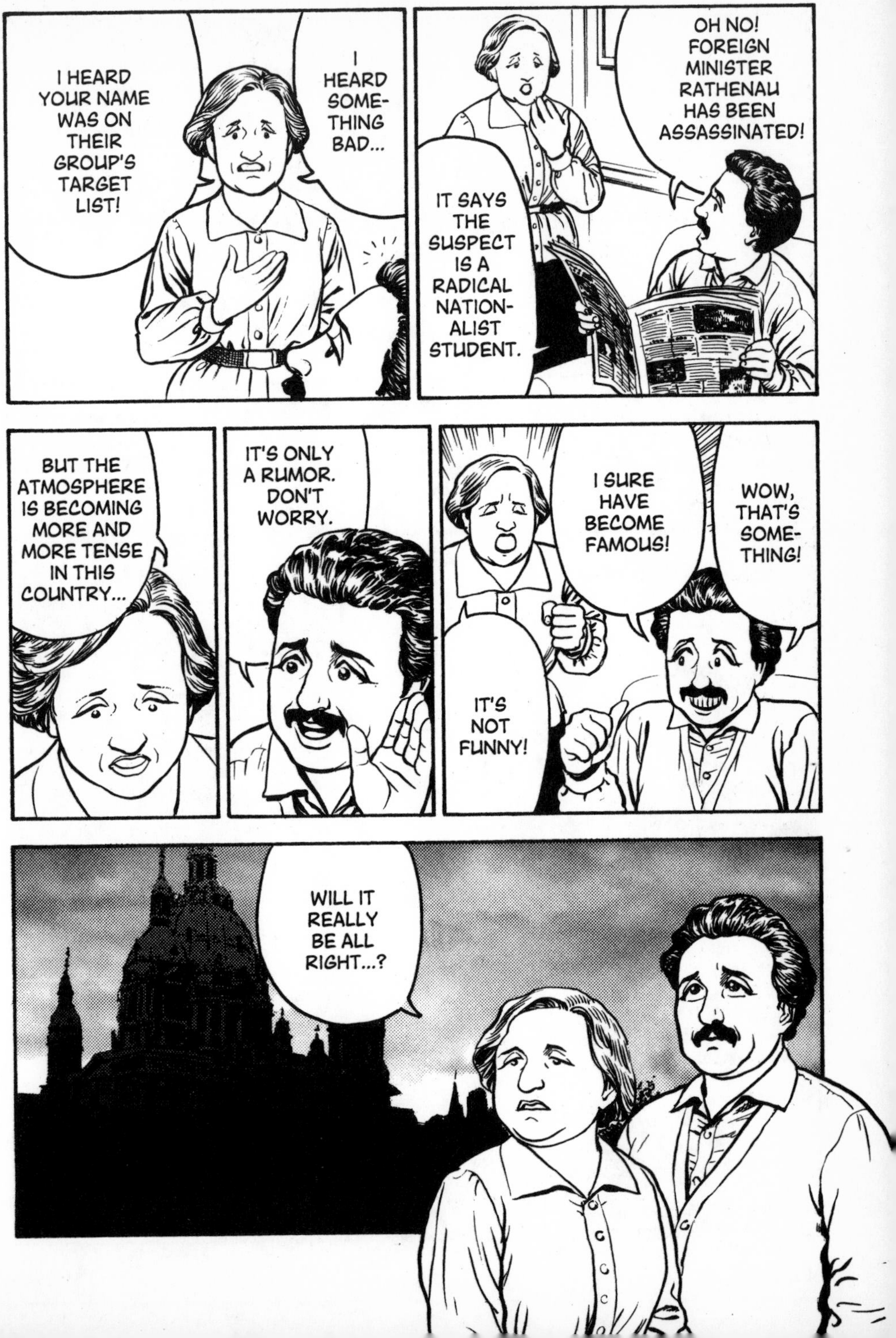

OH NO! FOREIGN MINISTER RATHENAU HAS BEEN ASSASSINATED!
IT SAYS THE SUSPECT IS A RADICAL NATIONALIST STUDENT.
I HEARD SOMETHING BAD...
I HEARD YOUR NAME WAS ON THEIR GROUP'S TARGET LIST!
WOW, THAT'S SOMETHING!
I SURE HAVE BECOME FAMOUS!
IT'S NOT FUNNY!
IT'S ONLY A RUMOR. DON'T WORRY.
BUT THE ATMOSPHERE IS BECOMING MORE AND MORE TENSE IN THIS COUNTRY...
WILL IT REALLY BE ALL RIGHT...?

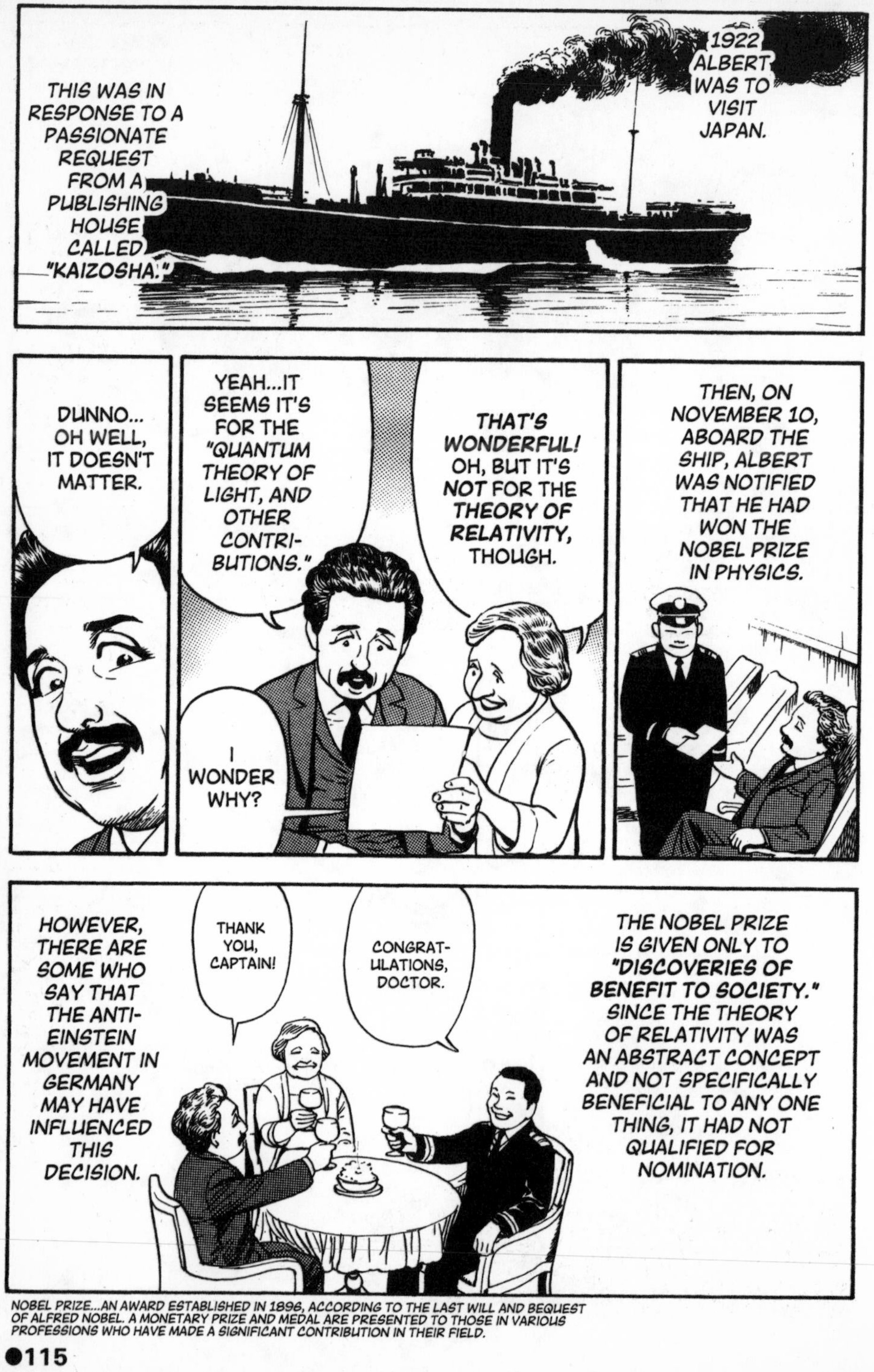

1922 ALBERT WAS TO VISIT JAPAN.
THIS WAS IN RESPONSE TO A PASSIONATE REQUEST FROM A PUBLISHING HOUSE CALLED "KAIZOSHA."
THEN, ON NOVEMBER 10, ABOARD THE SHIP, ALBERT WAS NOTIFIED THAT HE HAD WON THE NOBEL PRIZE IN PHYSICS.
THAT'S WONDERFUL! OH, BUT IT'S NOT FOR THE THEORY OF RELATIVITY, THOUGH.
YEAH...IT SEEMS IT'S FOR THE "QUANTUM THEORY OF LIGHT, AND OTHER CONTRIBUTIONS."
I WONDER WHY?
DUNNO... OH WELL, IT DOESN'T MATTER.
THE NOBEL PRIZE IS GIVEN ONLY TO "DISCOVERIES OF BENEFIT TO SOCIETY." SINCE THE THEORY OF RELATIVITY WAS AN ABSTRACT CONCEPT AND NOT SPECIFICALLY BENEFICIAL TO ANY ONE THING, IT HAD NOT QUALIFIED FOR NOMINATION.
CONGRATULATIONS, DOCTOR.
THANK YOU, CAPTAIN!
HOWEVER, THERE ARE SOME WHO SAY THAT THE ANTI-EINSTEIN MOVEMENT IN GERMANY MAY HAVE INFLUENCED THIS DECISION.

NOBEL PRIZE...AN AWARD ESTABLISHED IN 1896, ACCORDING TO THE LAST WILL AND BEQUEST OF ALFRED NOBEL. A MONETARY PRIZE AND MEDAL ARE PRESENTED TO THOSE IN VARIOUS PROFESSIONS WHO HAVE MADE A SIGNIFICANT CONTRIBUTION IN THEIR FIELD.

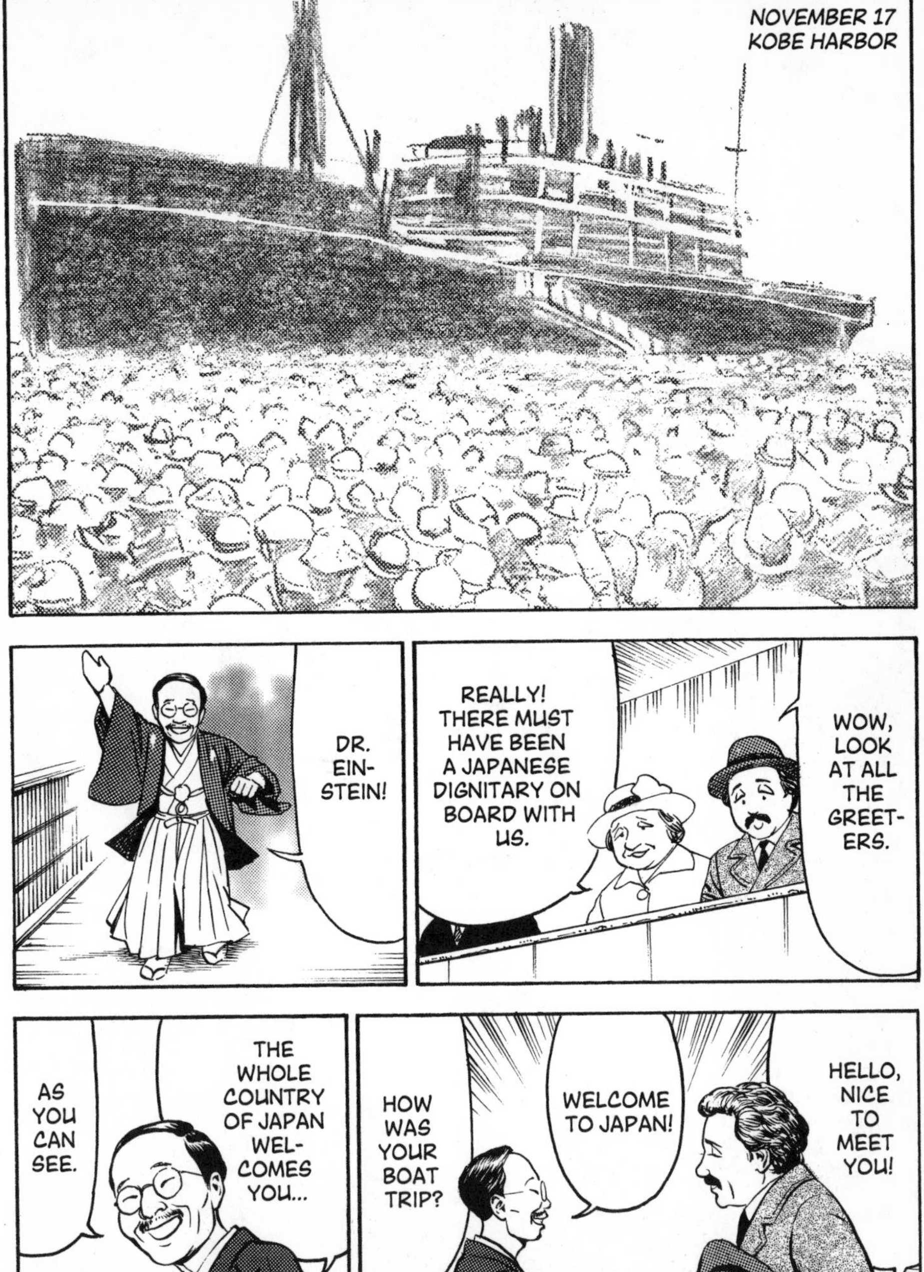
NOVEMBER 17
KOBE HARBOR
WOW, LOOK AT ALL THE GREETERS.
REALLY! THERE MUST HAVE BEEN A JAPANESE DIGNITARY ON BOARD WITH US.
DR. EINSTEIN!
HELLO, NICE TO MEET YOU!
WELCOME TO JAPAN!
HOW WAS YOUR BOAT TRIP?
THE WHOLE COUNTRY OF JAPAN WELCOMES YOU...
AS YOU CAN SEE.

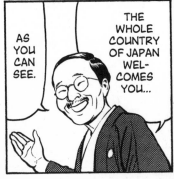

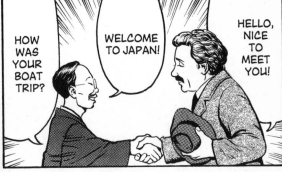

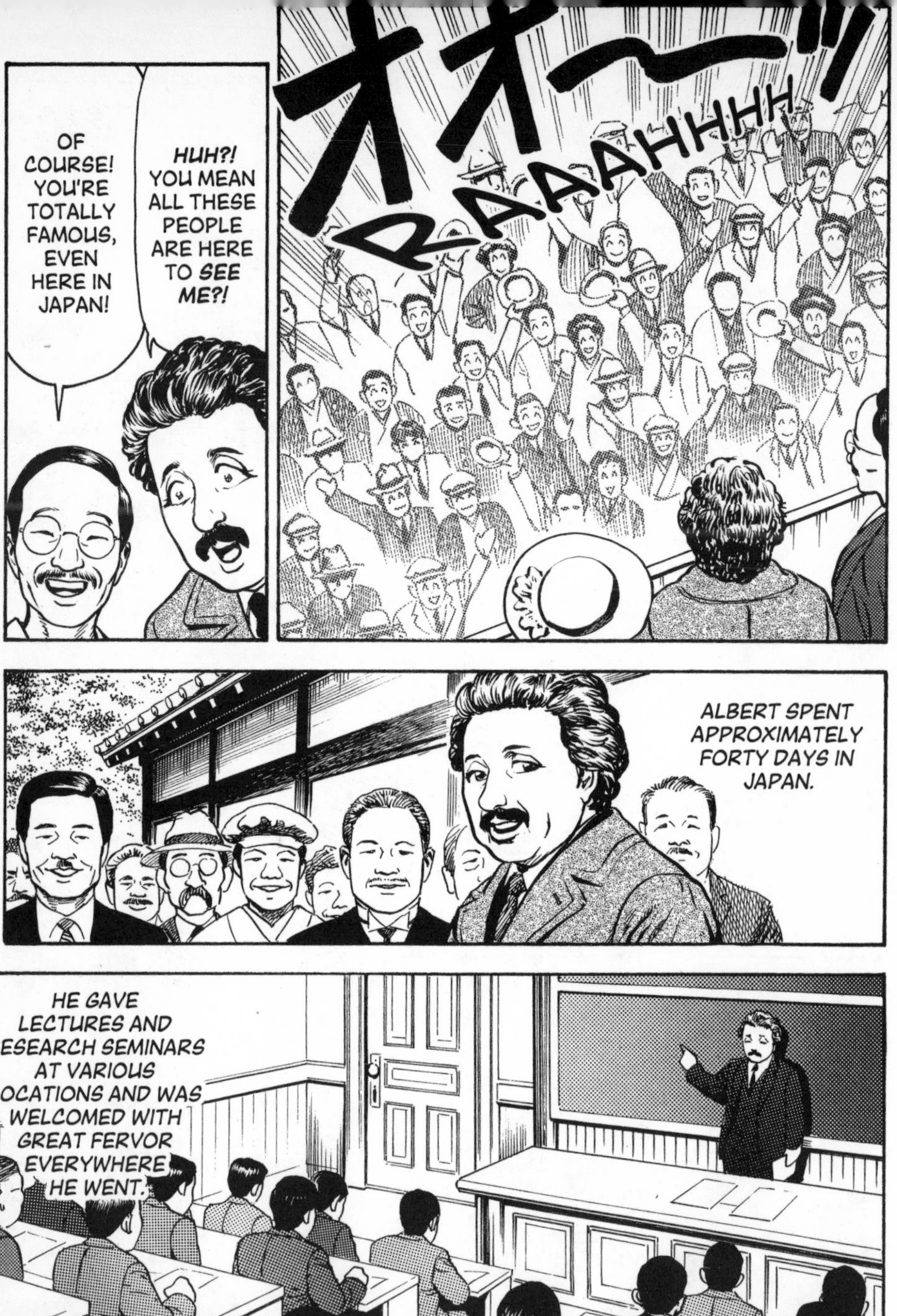
オオ〜〜ッ
RAAAHHHH
HUH?! YOU MEAN ALL THESE PEOPLE ARE HERE TO SEE ME?!
OF COURSE! YOU'RE TOTALLY FAMOUS, EVEN HERE IN JAPAN!
ALBERT SPENT APPROXIMATELY FORTY DAYS IN JAPAN.
HE GAVE LECTURES AND RESEARCH SEMINARS AT VARIOUS LOCATIONS AND WAS WELCOMED WITH GREAT FERVOR EVERYWHERE HE WENT.

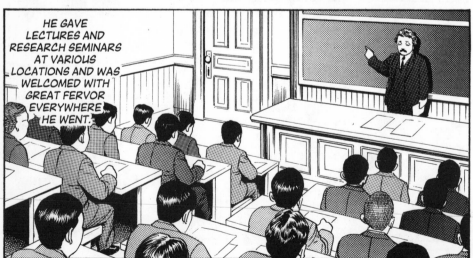

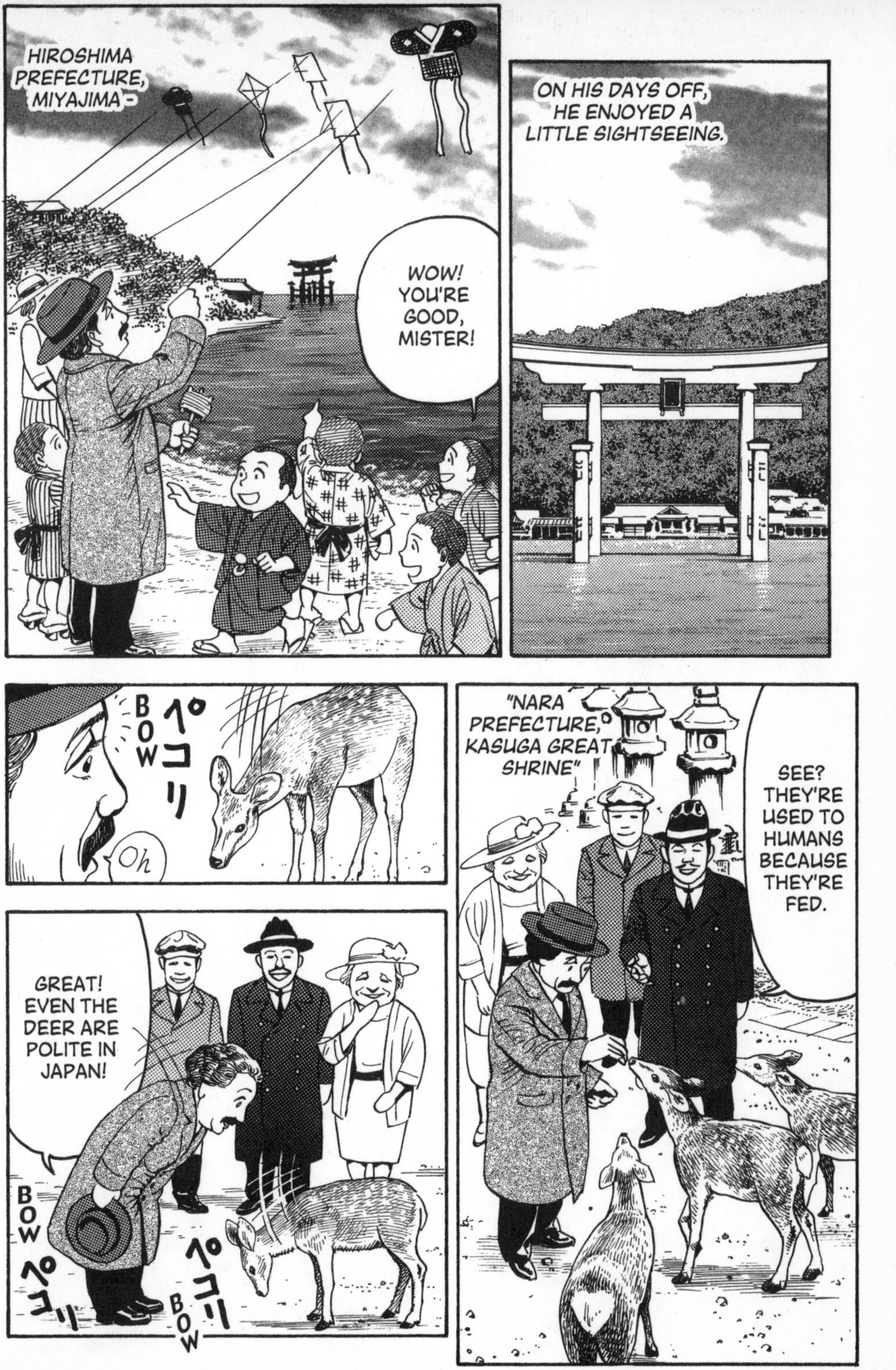
ON HIS DAYS OFF, HE ENJOYED A LITTLE SIGHTSEEING.
HIROSHIMA PREFECTURE, MIYAJIMA -
WOW! YOU'RE GOOD, MISTER!
"NARA PREFECTURE, KASUGA GREAT SHRINE"
SEE? THEY'RE USED TO HUMANS BECAUSE THEY'RE FED.
BOW
ペコリ
Oh
GREAT! EVEN THE DEER ARE POLITE IN JAPAN!
BOW
ペコリ
BOW
ペコリ

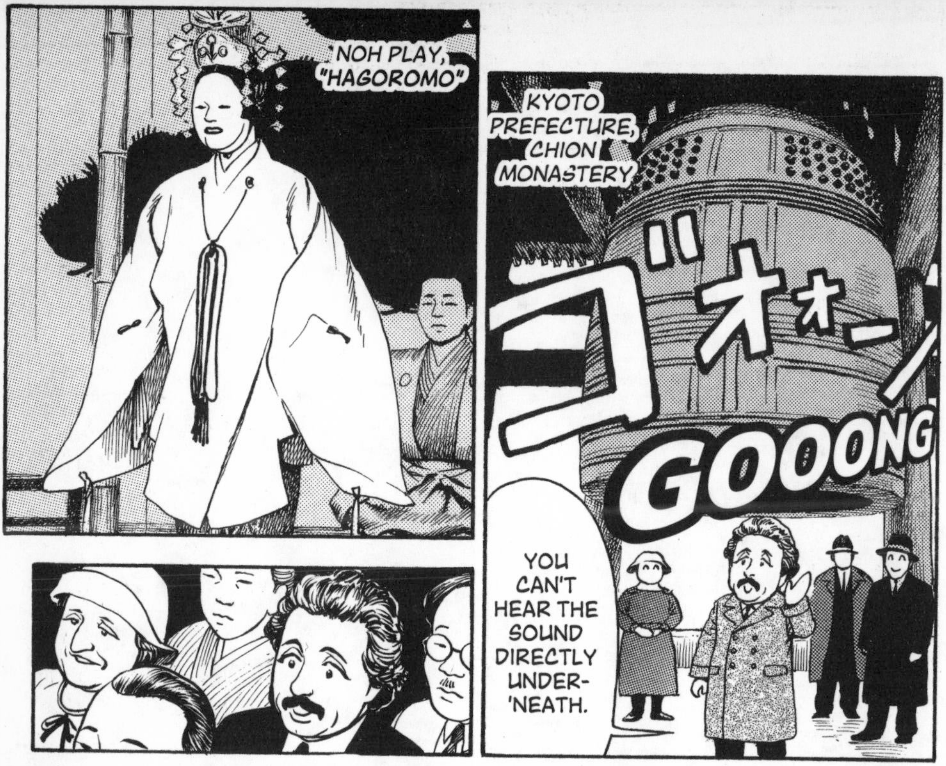
KYOTO PREFECTURE, CHION MONASTERY
ゴォーン
GOOOONG
YOU CAN'T HEAR THE SOUND DIRECTLY UNDER-'NEATH.
NOH PLAY, "HAGOROMO"

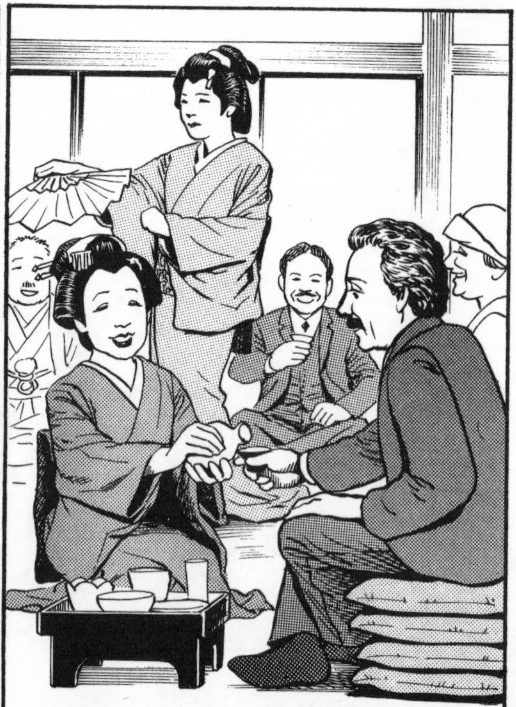

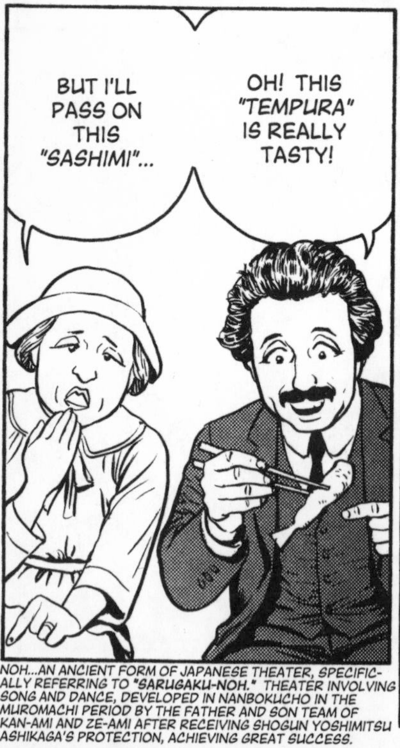
OH! THIS "TEMPURA" IS REALLY TASTY!
BUT I'LL PASS ON THIS "SASHIMI"...

NOH...AN ANCIENT FORM OF JAPANESE THEATER, SPECIFICALLY REFERRING TO "SARUGAKU-NOH." THEATER INVOLVING SONG AND DANCE, DEVELOPED IN NANBOKUCHO IN THE MUROMACHI PERIOD BY THE FATHER AND SON TEAM OF KAN-AMI AND ZE-AMI AFTER RECEIVING SHOGUN YOSHIMITSU ASHIKAGA'S PROTECTION, ACHIEVING GREAT SUCCESS.

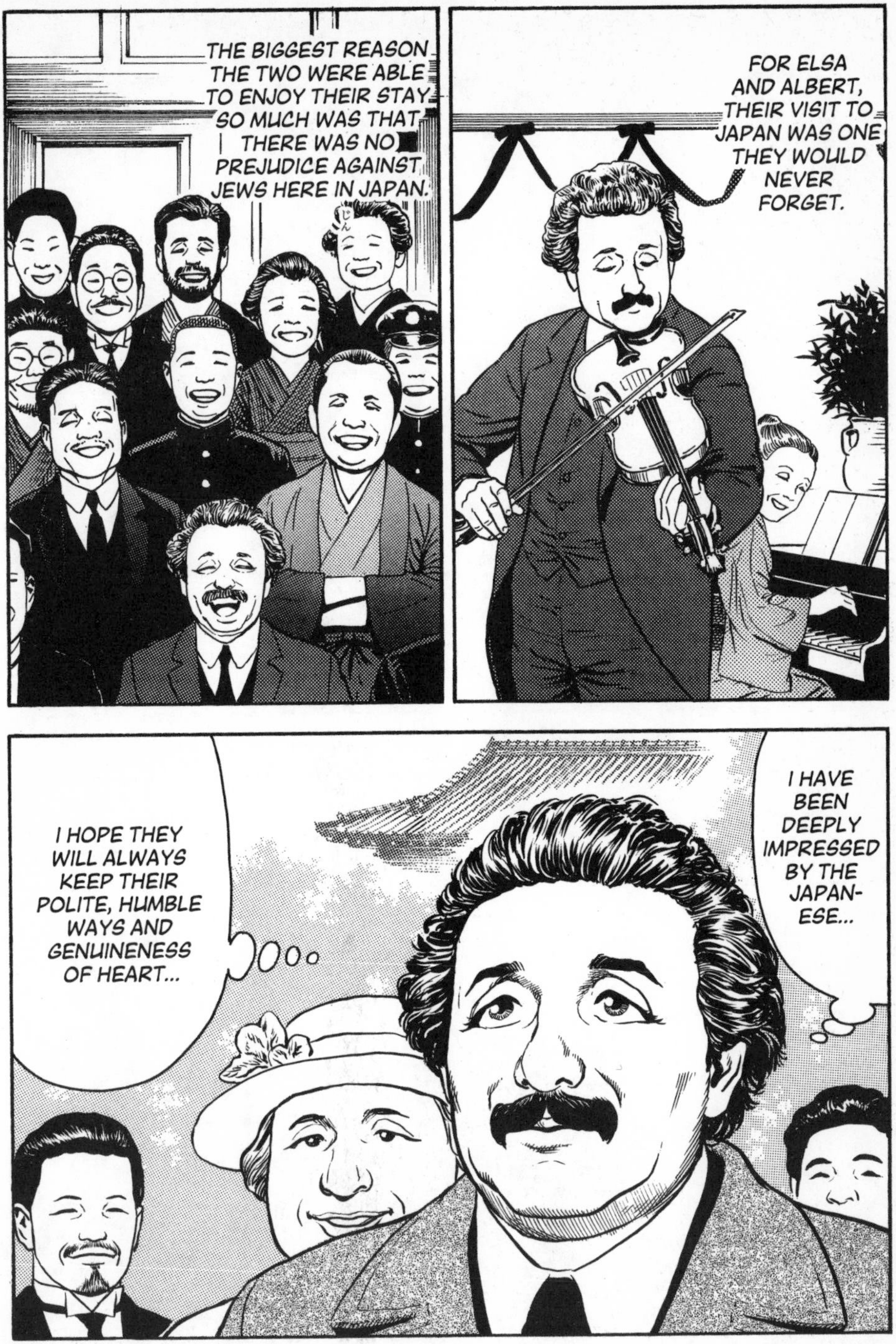
FOR ELSA AND ALBERT, THEIR VISIT TO JAPAN WAS ONE THEY WOULD NEVER FORGET.
THE BIGGEST REASON THE TWO WERE ABLE TO ENJOY THEIR STAY SO MUCH WAS THAT THERE WAS NO PREJUDICE AGAINST JEWS HERE IN JAPAN.
I HAVE BEEN DEEPLY IMPRESSED BY THE JAPAN-ESE...
I HOPE THEY WILL ALWAYS KEEP THEIR POLITE, HUMBLE WAYS AND GENUINENESS OF HEART...

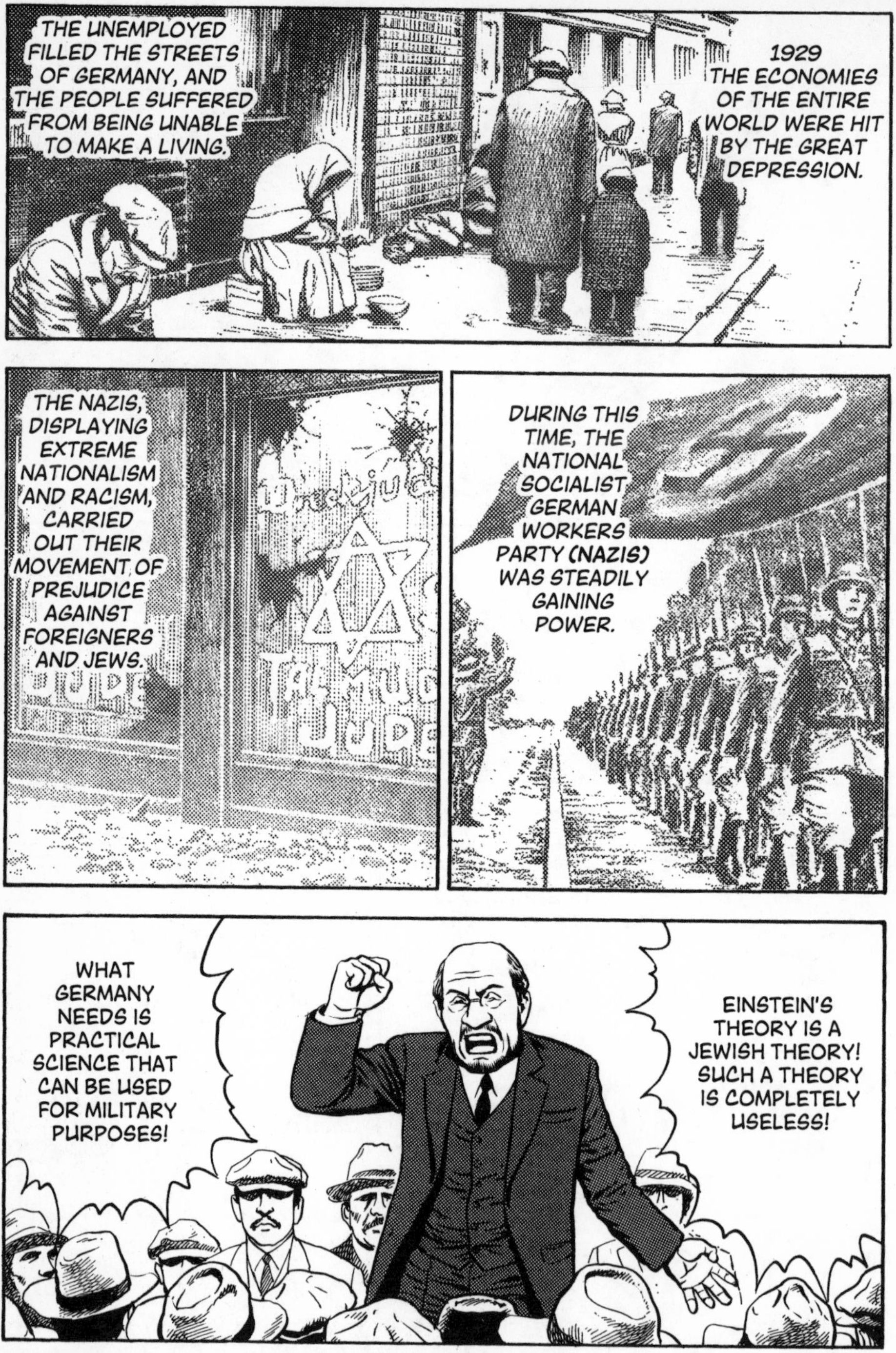
1929
THE ECONOMIES OF THE ENTIRE WORLD WERE HIT BY THE GREAT DEPRESSION.
THE UNEMPLOYED FILLED THE STREETS OF GERMANY, AND THE PEOPLE SUFFERED FROM BEING UNABLE TO MAKE A LIVING.
DURING THIS TIME, THE NATIONAL SOCIALIST GERMAN WORKERS PARTY (NAZIS) WAS STEADILY GAINING POWER.
THE NAZIS, DISPLAYING EXTREME NATIONALISM AND RACISM, CARRIED OUT THEIR MOVEMENT OF PREJUDICE AGAINST FOREIGNERS AND JEWS.
EINSTEIN'S THEORY IS A JEWISH THEORY! SUCH A THEORY IS COMPLETELY USELESS!
WHAT GERMANY NEEDS IS PRACTICAL SCIENCE THAT CAN BE USED FOR MILITARY PURPOSES!

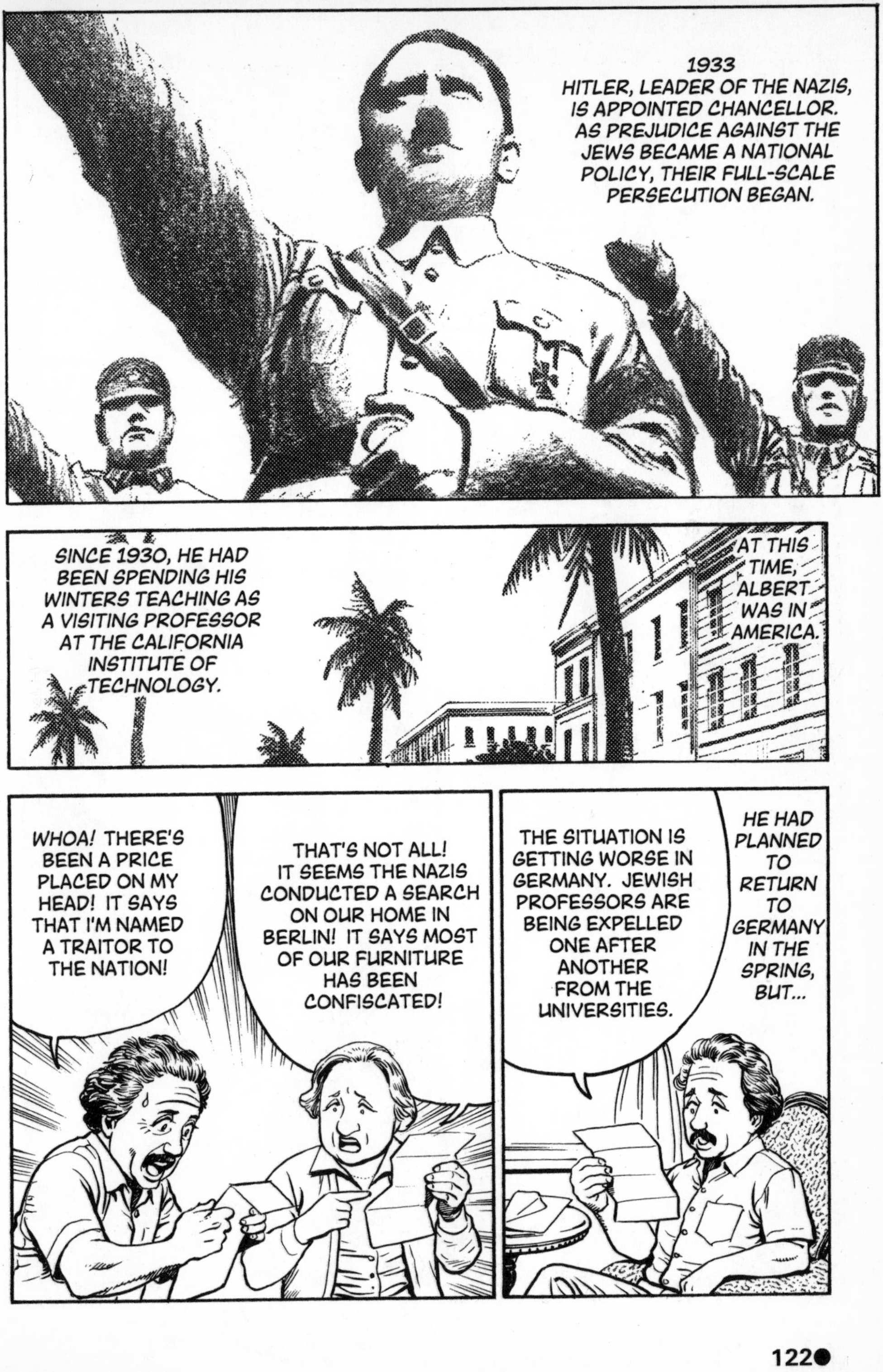
1933
HITLER, LEADER OF THE NAZIS, IS APPOINTED CHANCELLOR. AS PREJUDICE AGAINST THE JEWS BECAME A NATIONAL POLICY, THEIR FULL-SCALE PERSECUTION BEGAN.
AT THIS TIME, ALBERT WAS IN AMERICA.
SINCE 1930, HE HAD BEEN SPENDING HIS WINTERS TEACHING AS A VISITING PROFESSOR AT THE CALIFORNIA INSTITUTE OF TECHNOLOGY.
HE HAD PLANNED TO RETURN TO GERMANY IN THE SPRING, BUT...
THE SITUATION IS GETTING WORSE IN GERMANY. JEWISH PROFESSORS ARE BEING EXPELLED ONE AFTER ANOTHER FROM THE UNIVERSITIES.
WHOA! THERE'S BEEN A PRICE PLACED ON MY HEAD! IT SAYS THAT I'M NAMED A TRAITOR TO THE NATION!
THAT'S NOT ALL! IT SEEMS THE NAZIS CONDUCTED A SEARCH ON OUR HOME IN BERLIN! IT SAYS MOST OF OUR FURNITURE HAS BEEN CONFISCATED!

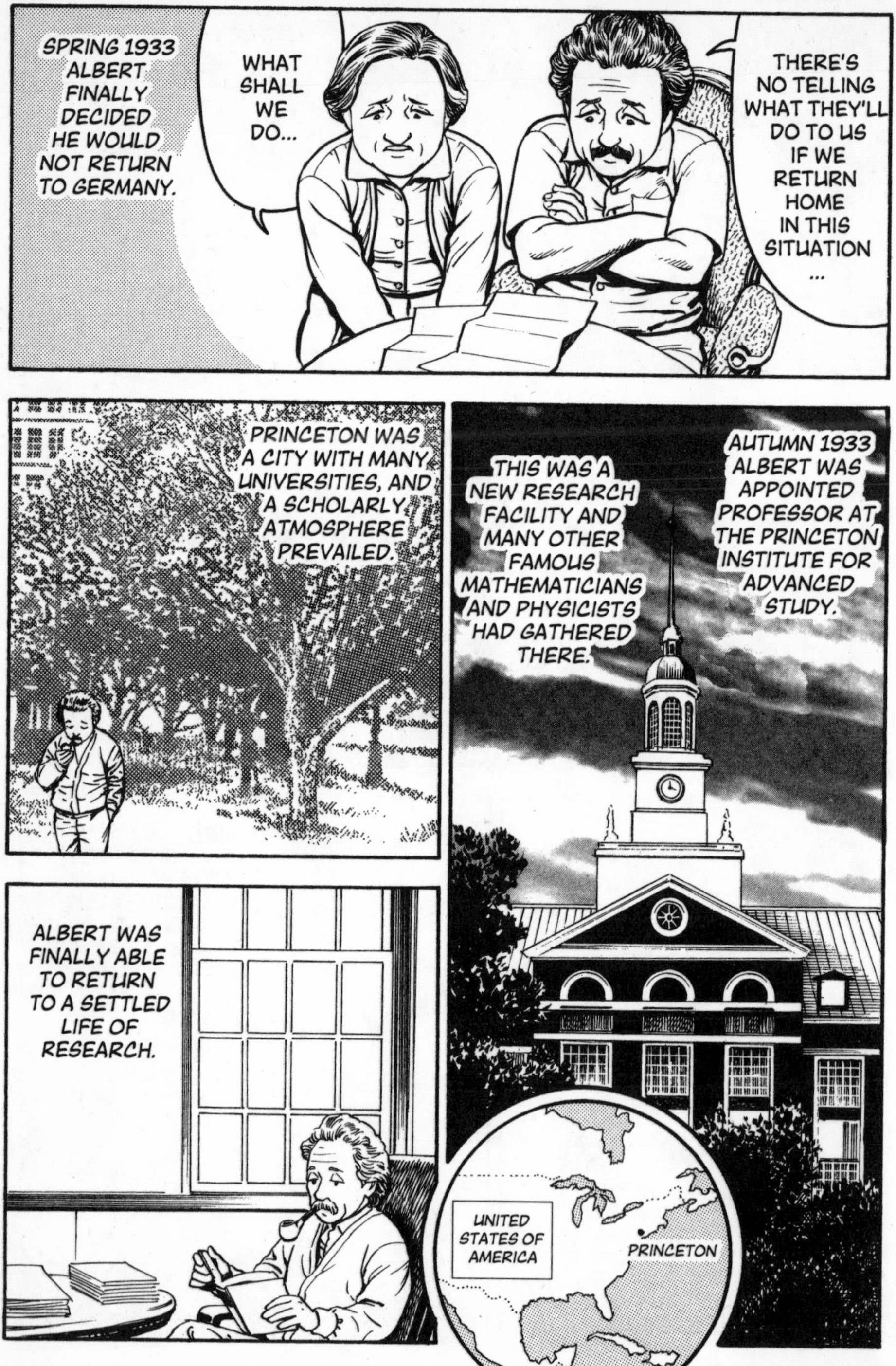
THERE'S NO TELLING WHAT THEY'LL DO TO US IF WE RETURN HOME IN THIS SITUATION ...
WHAT SHALL WE DO...
SPRING 1933 ALBERT FINALLY DECIDED HE WOULD NOT RETURN TO GERMANY.
AUTUMN 1933 ALBERT WAS APPOINTED PROFESSOR AT THE PRINCETON INSTITUTE FOR ADVANCED STUDY.
THIS WAS A NEW RESEARCH FACILITY AND MANY OTHER FAMOUS MATHEMATICIANS AND PHYSICISTS HAD GATHERED THERE.
PRINCETON
UNITED STATES OF AMERICA
PRINCETON WAS A CITY WITH MANY UNIVERSITIES, AND A SCHOLARLY ATMOSPHERE PREVAILED.
ALBERT WAS FINALLY ABLE TO RETURN TO A SETTLED LIFE OF RESEARCH.

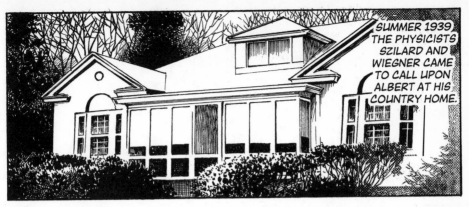

SUMMER 1939 THE PHYSICISTS SZILARD AND WIEGNER CAME TO CALL UPON ALBERT AT HIS COUNTRY HOME.
DR.EINSTEIN, WE'VE COME TO YOU WITH A VERY URGENT REQUEST.
SZILARD
DOCTOR, ARE YOU AWARE OF THE NUCLEAR FISSION EXPERIMENT THAT OCCURRED...
IN GERMANY, LAST YEAR?
WIEGNER
NO, I HAVEN'T HEARD.
WHEN URANIUM 235 WAS STRUCK BY A NEUTRON, THE ATOMIC NUCLEUS SPLIT INTO THREE - BARIUM, KRYPTON, AND NEUTRON - ALONG WITH ELECTROMAGNETIC WAVES.
NEUTRON
URANIUM 235
KRYPTON
BARIUM
GAMMA RAY
(ENERGY)
BARIUM
KRYPTON
URANIUM 235
AFTER FISSION
BEFORE FISSION
AND WHAT WAS LEFT AFTER THE FISSION WAS LIGHTER THAN THE SAME COMPONENTS BEFORE THE FISSION.

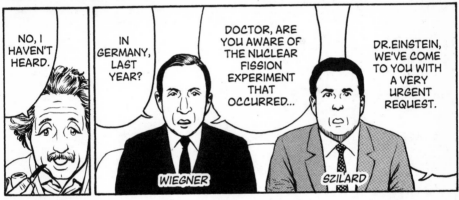

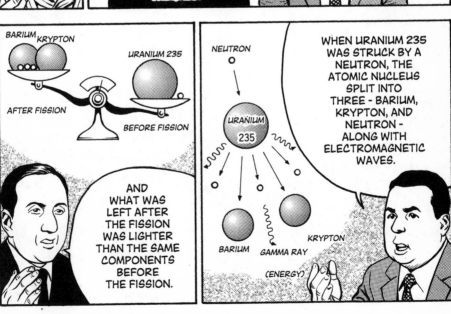

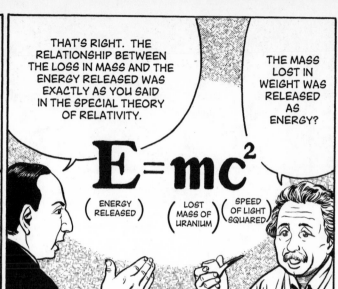

THE MASS LOST IN WEIGHT WAS RELEASED AS ENERGY?
THAT'S RIGHT. THE RELATIONSHIP BETWEEN THE LOSS IN MASS AND THE ENERGY RELEASED WAS EXACTLY AS YOU SAID IN THE SPECIAL THEORY OF RELATIVITY.
$E=mc^2$
(ENERGY RELEASED)
(LOST MASS OF URANIUM)
(SPEED OF LIGHT SQUARED)
IF THAT WERE ALL, THIS WOULD BE GOOD NEWS - THE CORRECTNESS OF THE THEORY OF RELATIVITY HAS BEEN PROVEN BY EXPERIMENT. THE PROBLEM IS THAT THERE'S MORE.
IF THERE IS ANY URANIUM 235 NEAR THE NEUTRONS CREATED BY THE FIRST SPLIT, THEN THAT URANIUM 235 WOULD SPLIT, ALSO.
AND THE NEUTRONS CREATED FROM THAT SPLIT WOULD CAUSE FURTHER SPLITTING, AND A CHAIN REACTION WOULD OCCUR.
IF THIS CHAIN REACTION WERE MADE TO OCCUR SUDDENLY, A TREMENDOUS AMOUNT OF ENERGY WOULD BE RELEASED!
COULD THIS NOT BE USED FOR THE CREATION OF A WEAPON OF MASS DESTRUCTION?!

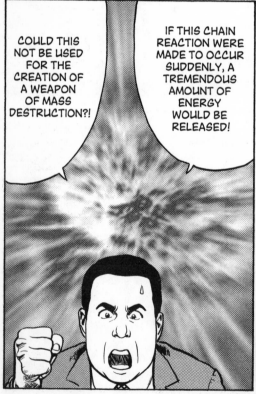

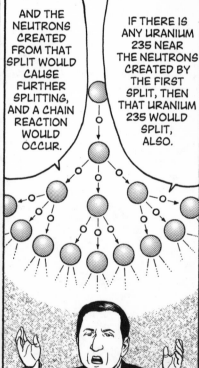

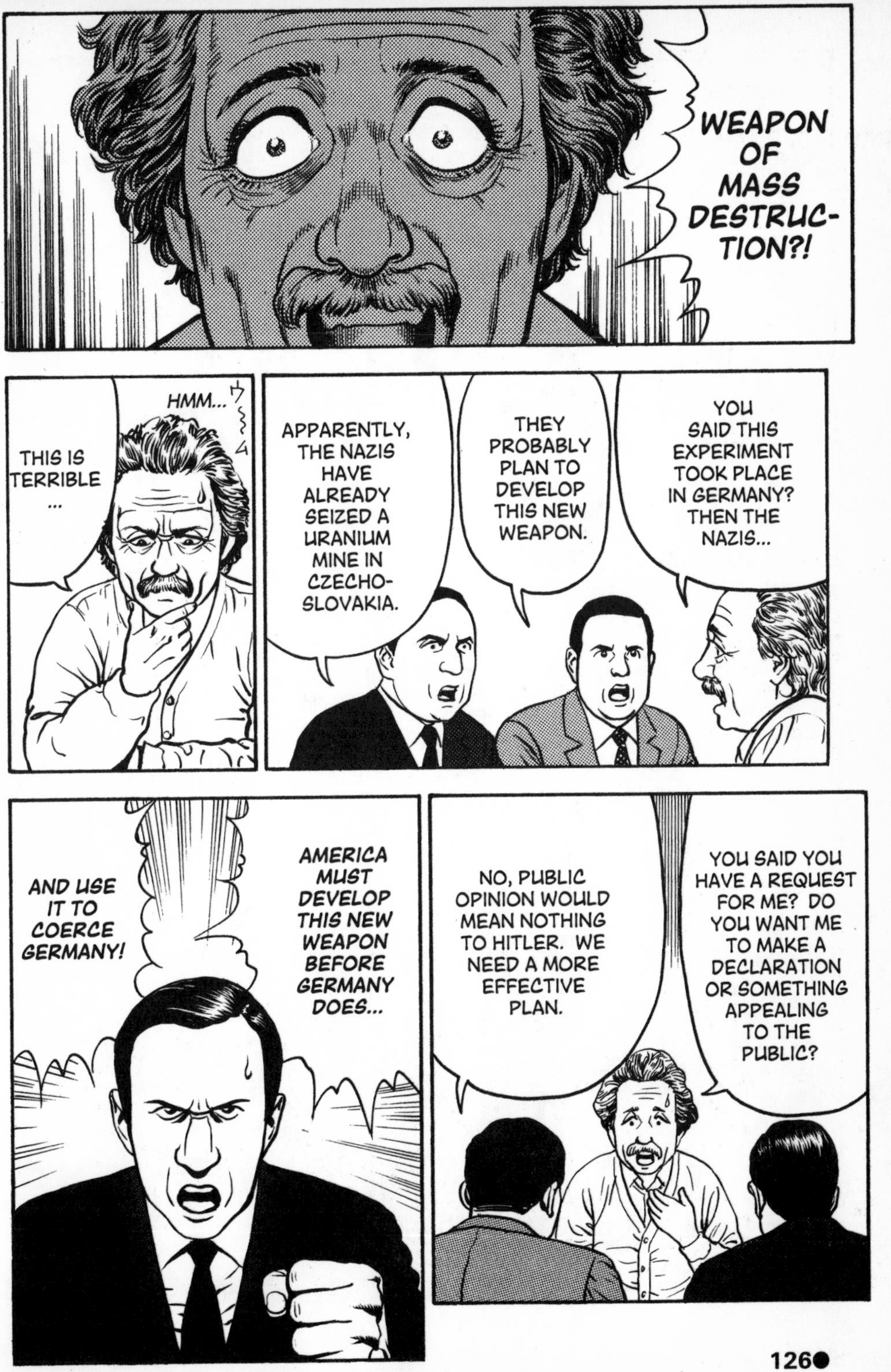
WEAPON OF MASS DESTRUC-TION?!
YOU SAID THIS EXPERIMENT TOOK PLACE IN GERMANY? THEN THE NAZIS...
THEY PROBABLY PLAN TO DEVELOP THIS NEW WEAPON.
APPARENTLY, THE NAZIS HAVE ALREADY SEIZED A URANIUM MINE IN CZECHO-SLOVAKIA.
HMM...
THIS IS TERRIBLE ...
YOU SAID YOU HAVE A REQUEST FOR ME? DO YOU WANT ME TO MAKE A DECLARATION OR SOMETHING APPEALING TO THE PUBLIC?
NO, PUBLIC OPINION WOULD MEAN NOTHING TO HITLER. WE NEED A MORE EFFECTIVE PLAN.
AMERICA MUST DEVELOP THIS NEW WEAPON BEFORE GERMANY DOES...
AND USE IT TO COERCE GERMANY!

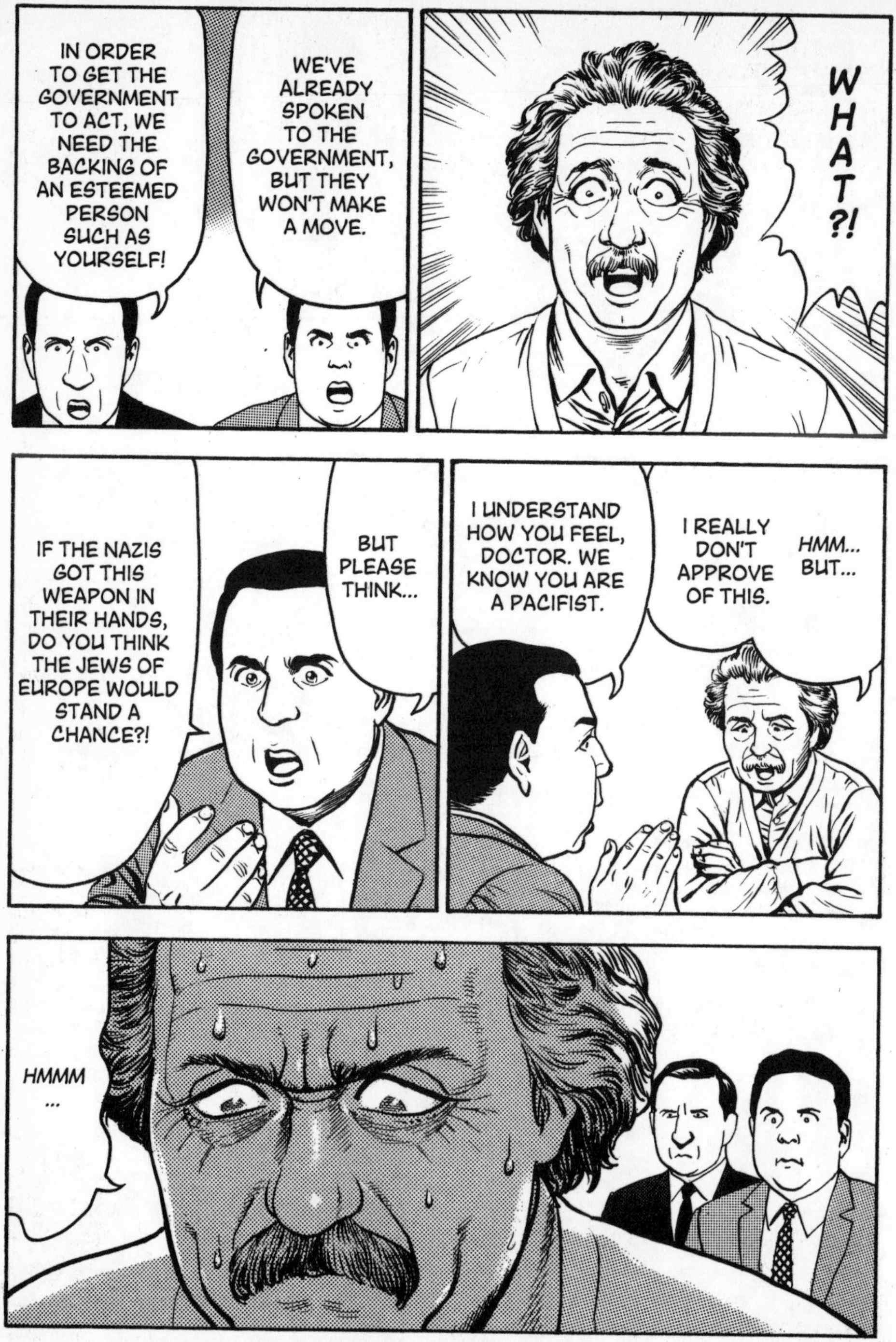
WHAT?!
WE'VE ALREADY SPOKEN TO THE GOVERNMENT, BUT THEY WON'T MAKE A MOVE.
IN ORDER TO GET THE GOVERNMENT TO ACT, WE NEED THE BACKING OF AN ESTEEMED PERSON SUCH AS YOURSELF!
HMM... BUT...
I REALLY DON'T APPROVE OF THIS.
I UNDERSTAND HOW YOU FEEL, DOCTOR. WE KNOW YOU ARE A PACIFIST.
BUT PLEASE THINK...
IF THE NAZIS GOT THIS WEAPON IN THEIR HANDS, DO YOU THINK THE JEWS OF EUROPE WOULD STAND A CHANCE?!
HMMM ...

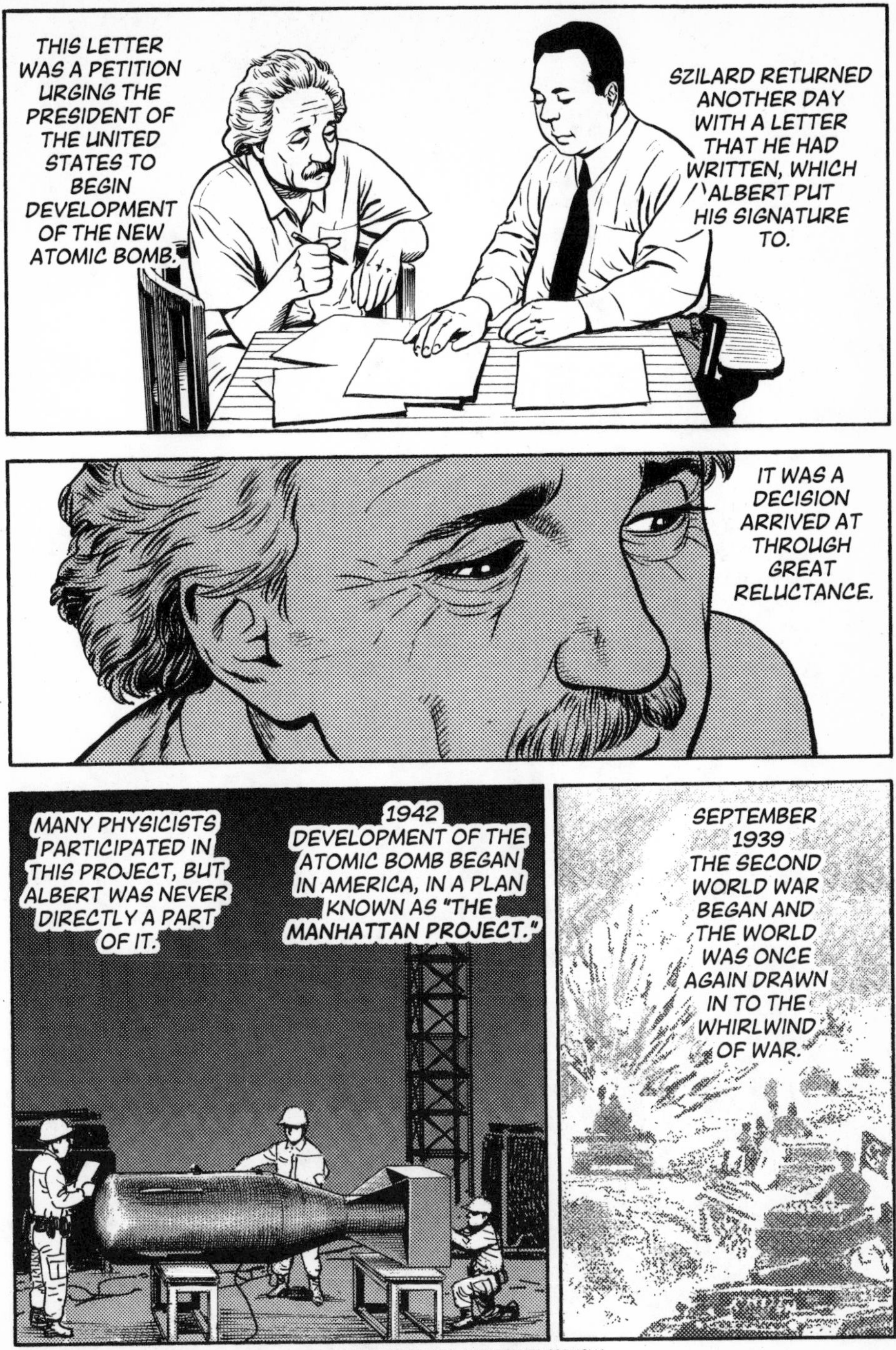
SZILARD RETURNED ANOTHER DAY WITH A LETTER THAT HE HAD WRITTEN, WHICH ALBERT PUT HIS SIGNATURE TO.
THIS LETTER WAS A PETITION URGING THE PRESIDENT OF THE UNITED STATES TO BEGIN DEVELOPMENT OF THE NEW ATOMIC BOMB.
IT WAS A DECISION ARRIVED AT THROUGH GREAT RELUCTANCE.
SEPTEMBER 1939 THE SECOND WORLD WAR BEGAN AND THE WORLD WAS ONCE AGAIN DRAWN IN TO THE WHIRLWIND OF WAR.
1942 DEVELOPMENT OF THE ATOMIC BOMB BEGAN IN AMERICA, IN A PLAN KNOWN AS "THE MANHATTAN PROJECT."
MANY PHYSICISTS PARTICIPATED IN THIS PROJECT, BUT ALBERT WAS NEVER DIRECTLY A PART OF IT.

ATOMIC BOMB...A BOMB THAT RELEASES A MASSIVE AMOUNT OF ENERGY INSTANTANEOUSLY, CAUSED BY THE CHAIN REACTION OF NUCLEAR FISSION. DESTROYS THROUGH RADIATION POISONING, FIRES AND BURNS DUE TO HEAT RADIATION, AND SHOCKWAVE.

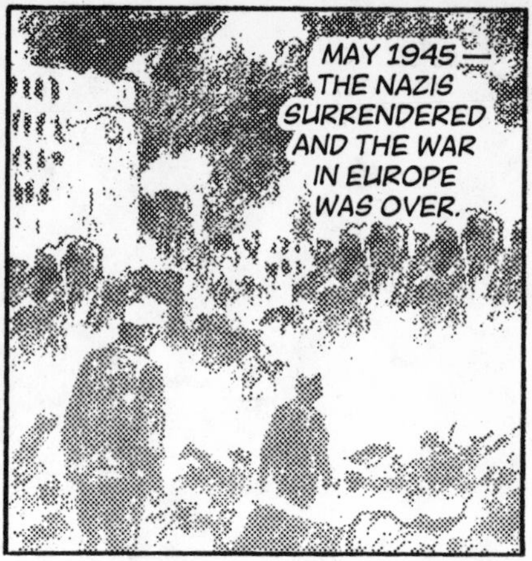
MAY 1945 — THE NAZIS SURRENDERED AND THE WAR IN EUROPE WAS OVER.

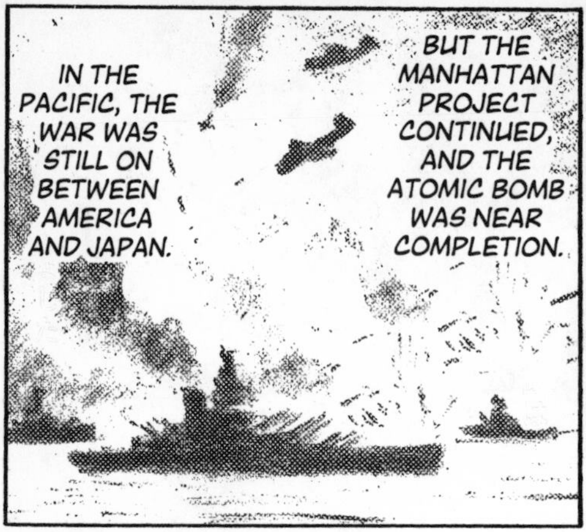
BUT THE MANHATTAN PROJECT CONTINUED, AND THE ATOMIC BOMB WAS NEAR COMPLETION.
IN THE PACIFIC, THE WAR WAS STILL ON BETWEEN AMERICA AND JAPAN.

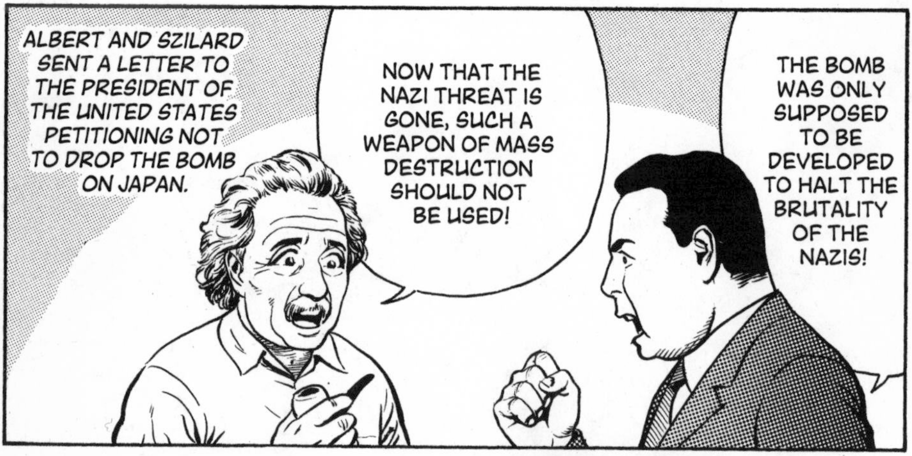
THE BOMB WAS ONLY SUPPOSED TO BE DEVELOPED TO HALT THE BRUTALITY OF THE NAZIS!
NOW THAT THE NAZI THREAT IS GONE, SUCH A WEAPON OF MASS DESTRUCTION SHOULD NOT BE USED!
ALBERT AND SZILARD SENT A LETTER TO THE PRESIDENT OF THE UNITED STATES PETITIONING NOT TO DROP THE BOMB ON JAPAN.

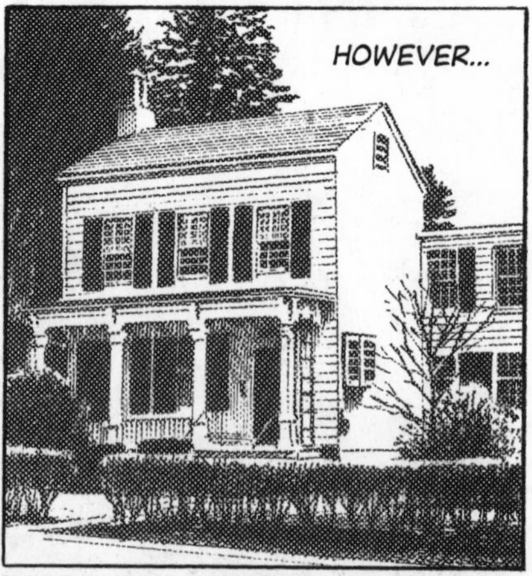
HOWEVER...

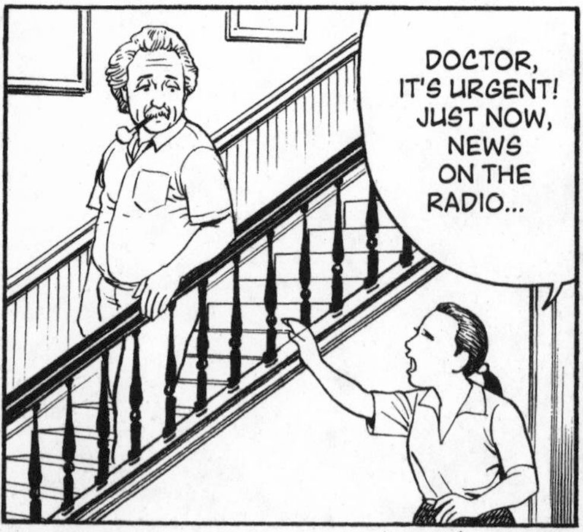
DOCTOR, IT'S URGENT! JUST NOW, NEWS ON THE RADIO...

↑ SECRETARY

WORLD WAR TWO...AFTER THE GREAT DEPRESSION, THE WORLD WAR THAT WAS TRIGGERED BY THE GERMAN INVASION OF POLAND IN 1939.

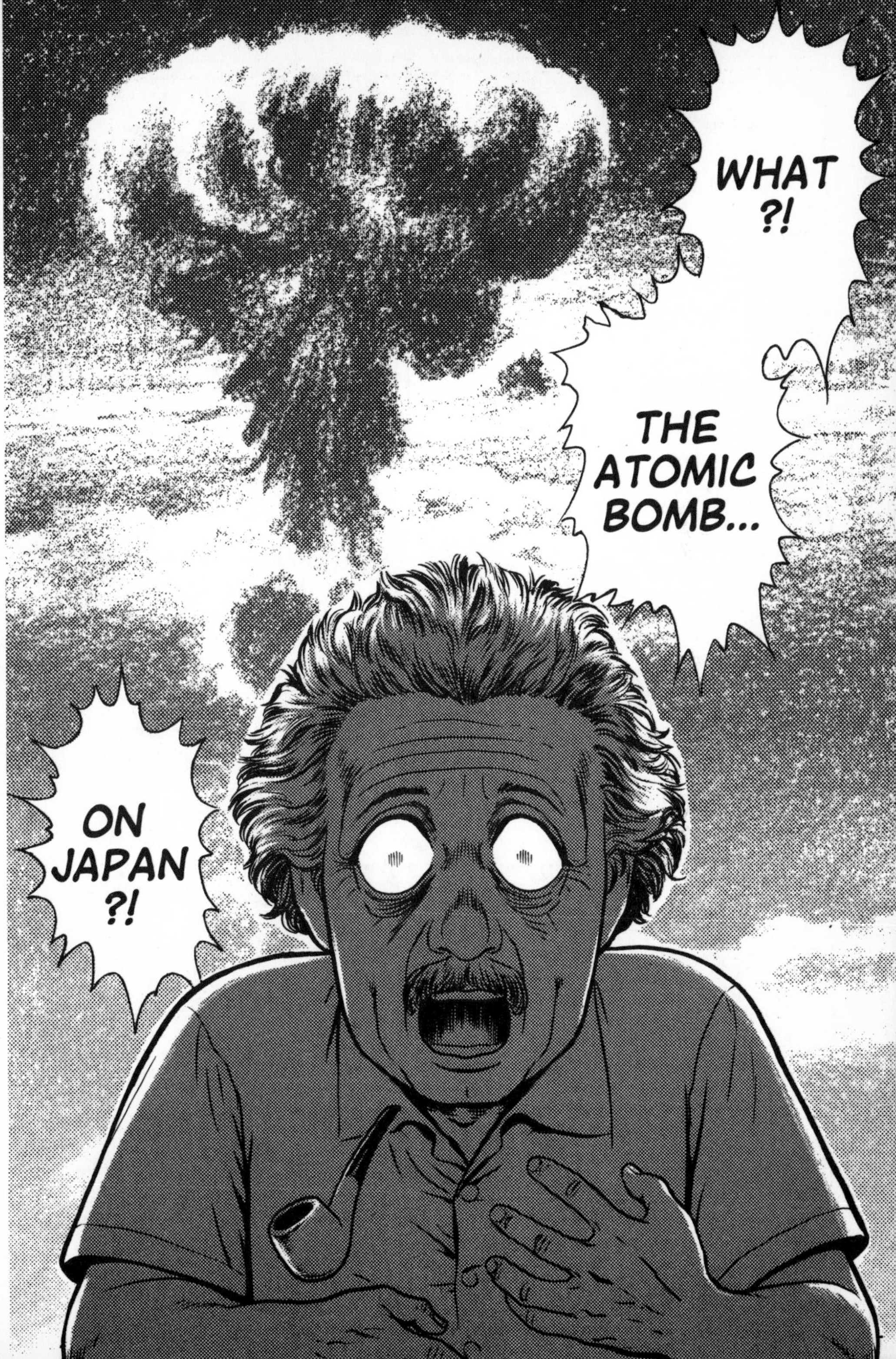
WHAT ?!
THE ATOMIC BOMB...
ON JAPAN ?!

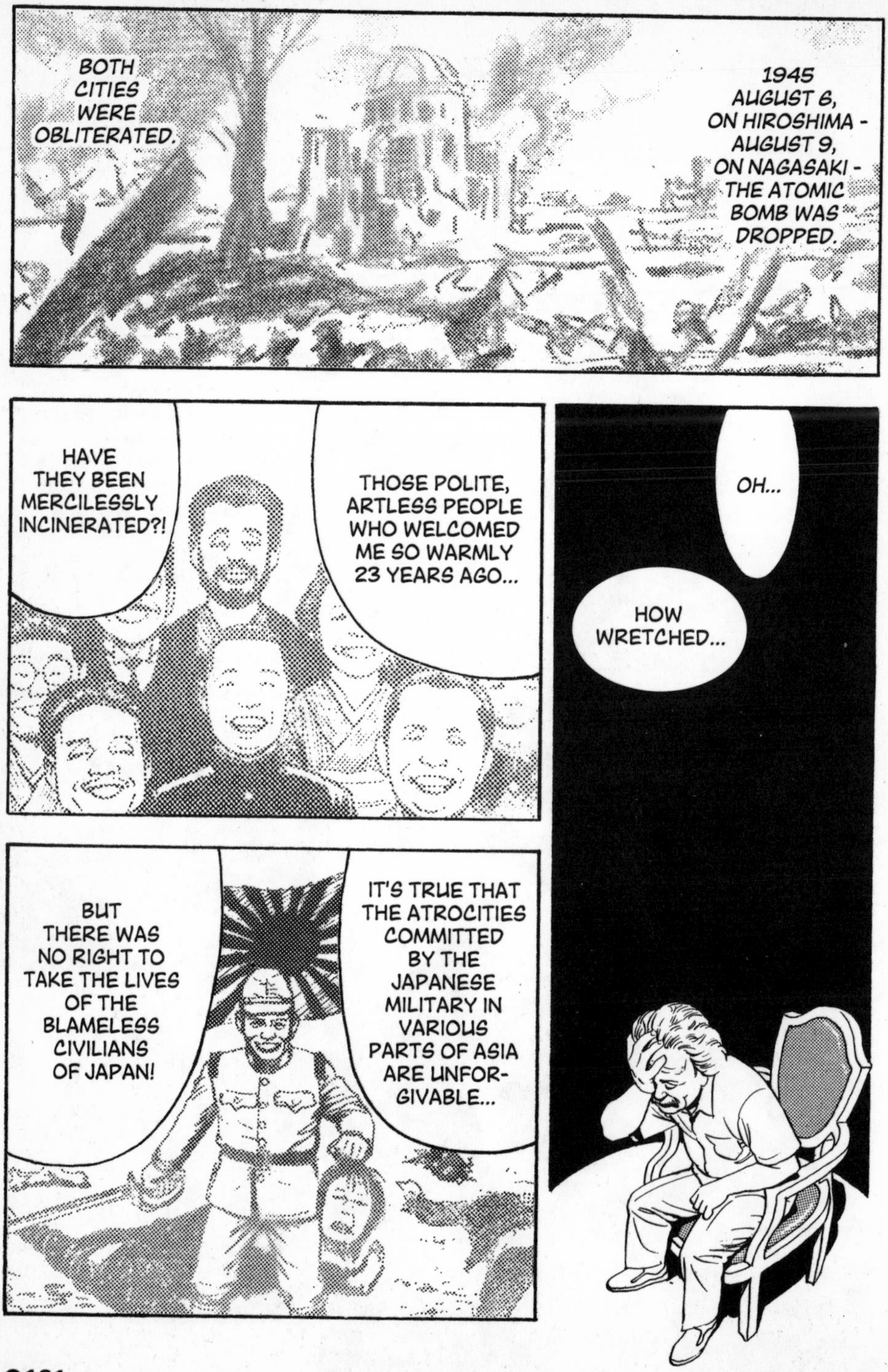
1945 AUGUST 6, ON HIROSHIMA - AUGUST 9, ON NAGASAKI - THE ATOMIC BOMB WAS DROPPED.
BOTH CITIES WERE OBLITERATED.
OH...
HOW WRETCHED...
THOSE POLITE, ARTLESS PEOPLE WHO WELCOMED ME SO WARMLY 23 YEARS AGO...
HAVE THEY BEEN MERCILESSLY INCINERATED?!
IT'S TRUE THAT THE ATROCITIES COMMITTED BY THE JAPANESE MILITARY IN VARIOUS PARTS OF ASIA ARE UNFORGIVABLE...
BUT THERE WAS NO RIGHT TO TAKE THE LIVES OF THE BLAMELESS CIVILIANS OF JAPAN!

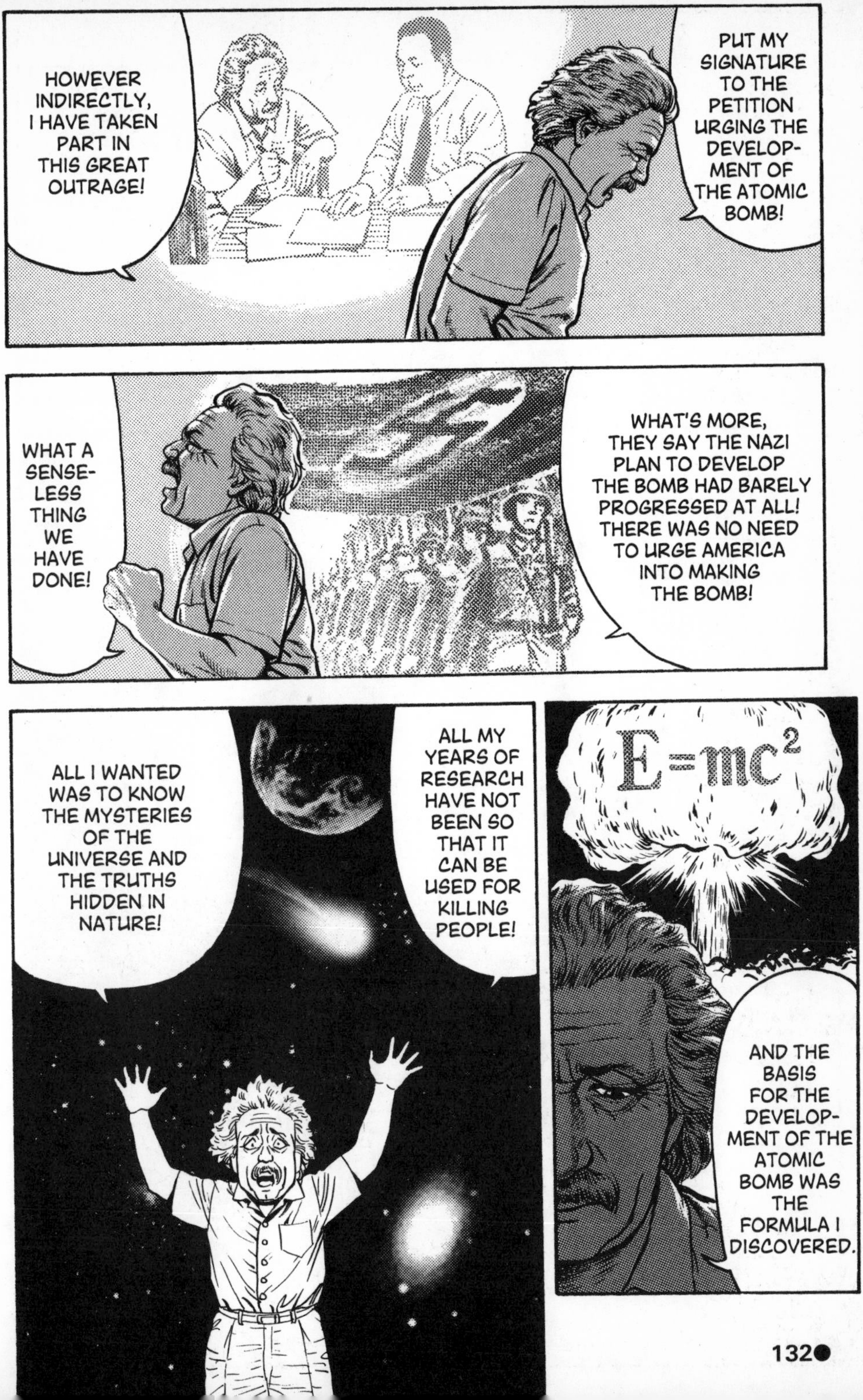
PUT MY SIGNATURE TO THE PETITION URGING THE DEVELOPMENT OF THE ATOMIC BOMB!
HOWEVER INDIRECTLY, I HAVE TAKEN PART IN THIS GREAT OUTRAGE!
WHAT'S MORE, THEY SAY THE NAZI PLAN TO DEVELOP THE BOMB HAD BARELY PROGRESSED AT ALL! THERE WAS NO NEED TO URGE AMERICA INTO MAKING THE BOMB!
WHAT A SENSELESS THING WE HAVE DONE!
E=mc²
AND THE BASIS FOR THE DEVELOPMENT OF THE ATOMIC BOMB WAS THE FORMULA I DISCOVERED.
ALL MY YEARS OF RESEARCH HAVE NOT BEEN SO THAT IT CAN BE USED FOR KILLING PEOPLE!
ALL I WANTED WAS TO KNOW THE MYSTERIES OF THE UNIVERSE AND THE TRUTHS HIDDEN IN NATURE!

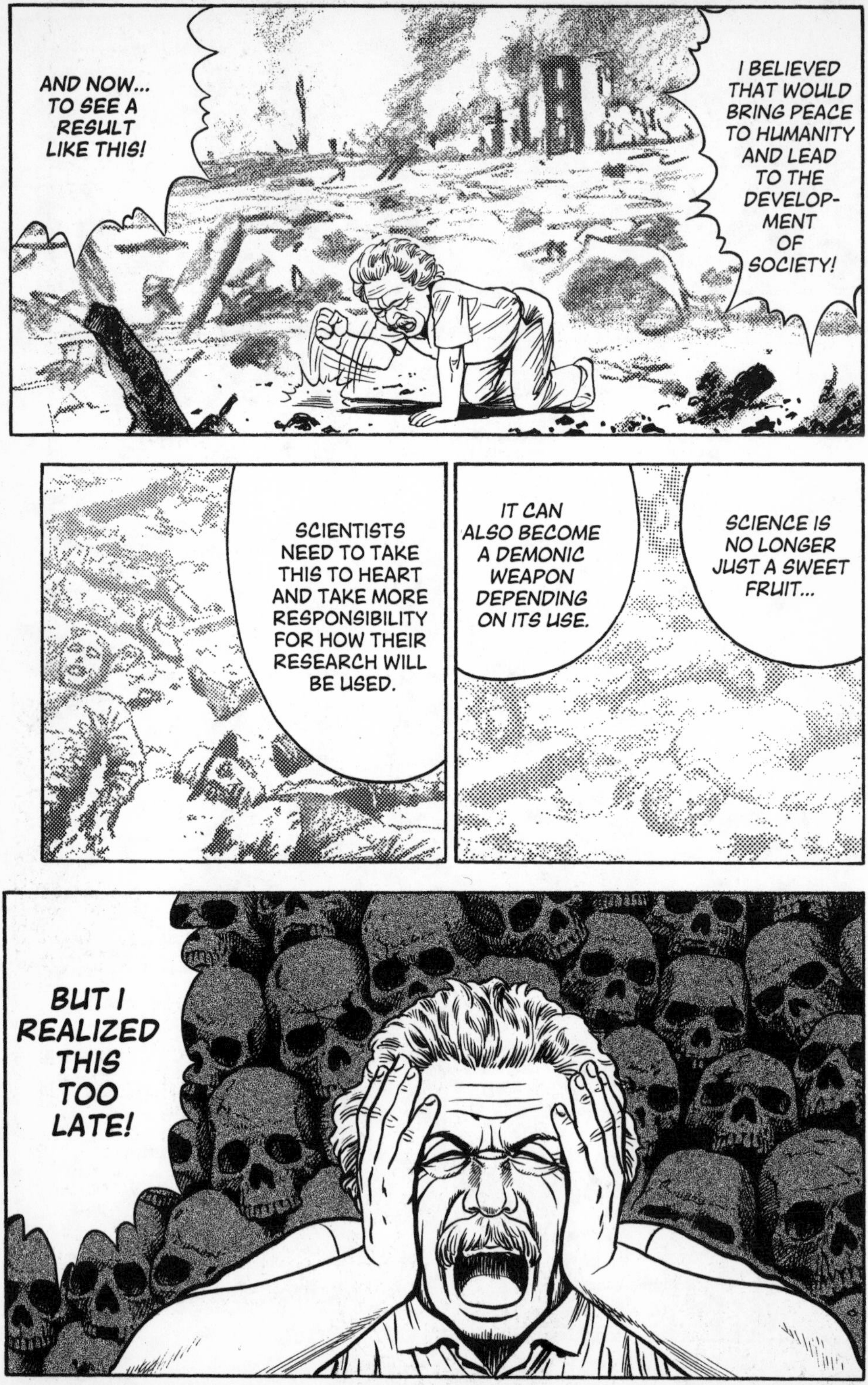
I BELIEVED THAT WOULD BRING PEACE TO HUMANITY AND LEAD TO THE DEVELOP-MENT OF SOCIETY!
AND NOW... TO SEE A RESULT LIKE THIS!
SCIENCE IS NO LONGER JUST A SWEET FRUIT...
IT CAN ALSO BECOME A DEMONIC WEAPON DEPENDING ON ITS USE.
SCIENTISTS NEED TO TAKE THIS TO HEART AND TAKE MORE RESPONSIBILITY FOR HOW THEIR RESEARCH WILL BE USED.
BUT I REALIZED THIS TOO LATE!

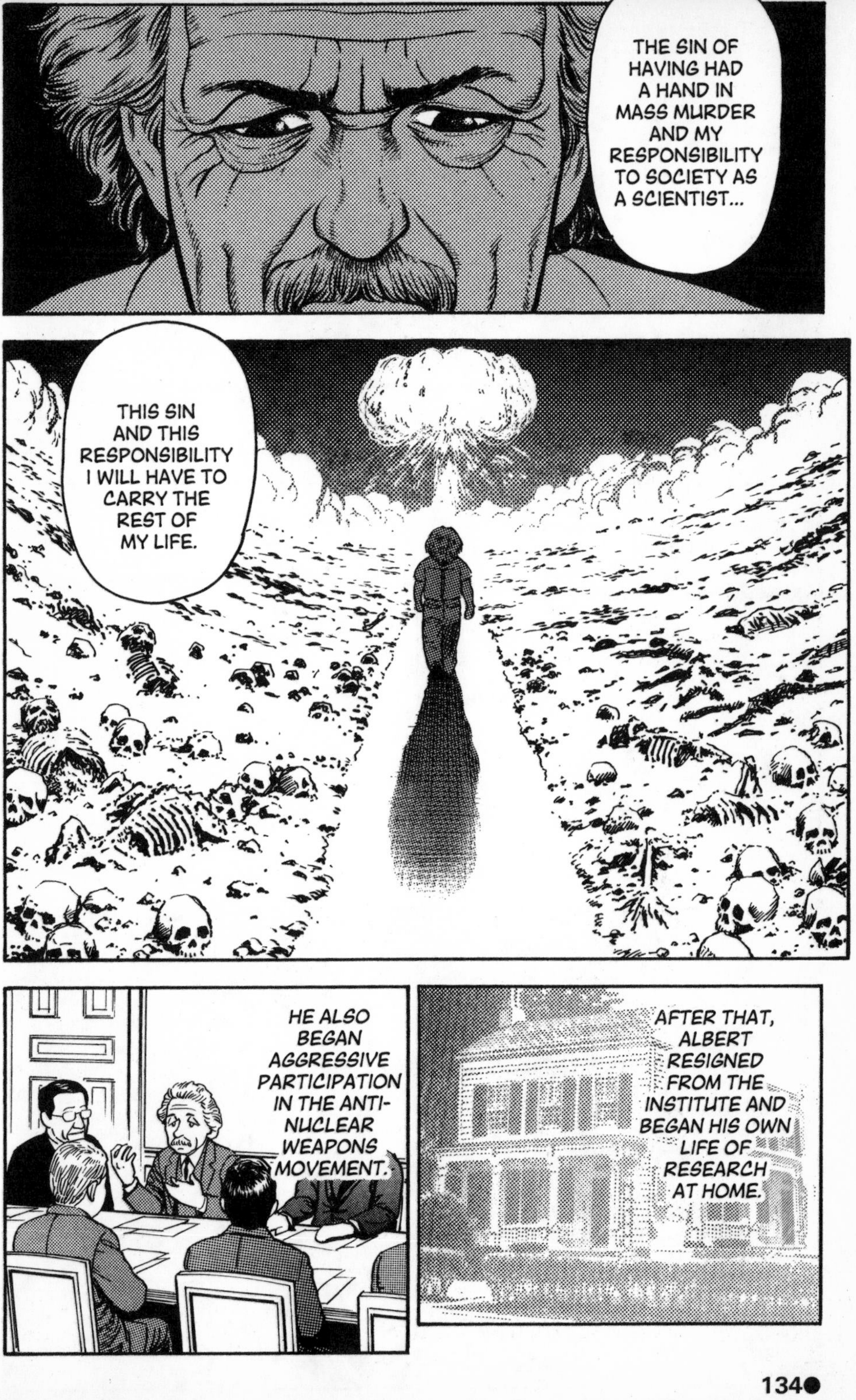
THE SIN OF HAVING HAD A HAND IN MASS MURDER AND MY RESPONSIBILITY TO SOCIETY AS A SCIENTIST...
THIS SIN AND THIS RESPONSIBILITY I WILL HAVE TO CARRY THE REST OF MY LIFE.
AFTER THAT, ALBERT RESIGNED FROM THE INSTITUTE AND BEGAN HIS OWN LIFE OF RESEARCH AT HOME.
HE ALSO BEGAN AGGRESSIVE PARTICIPATION IN THE ANTI-NUCLEAR WEAPONS MOVEMENT.

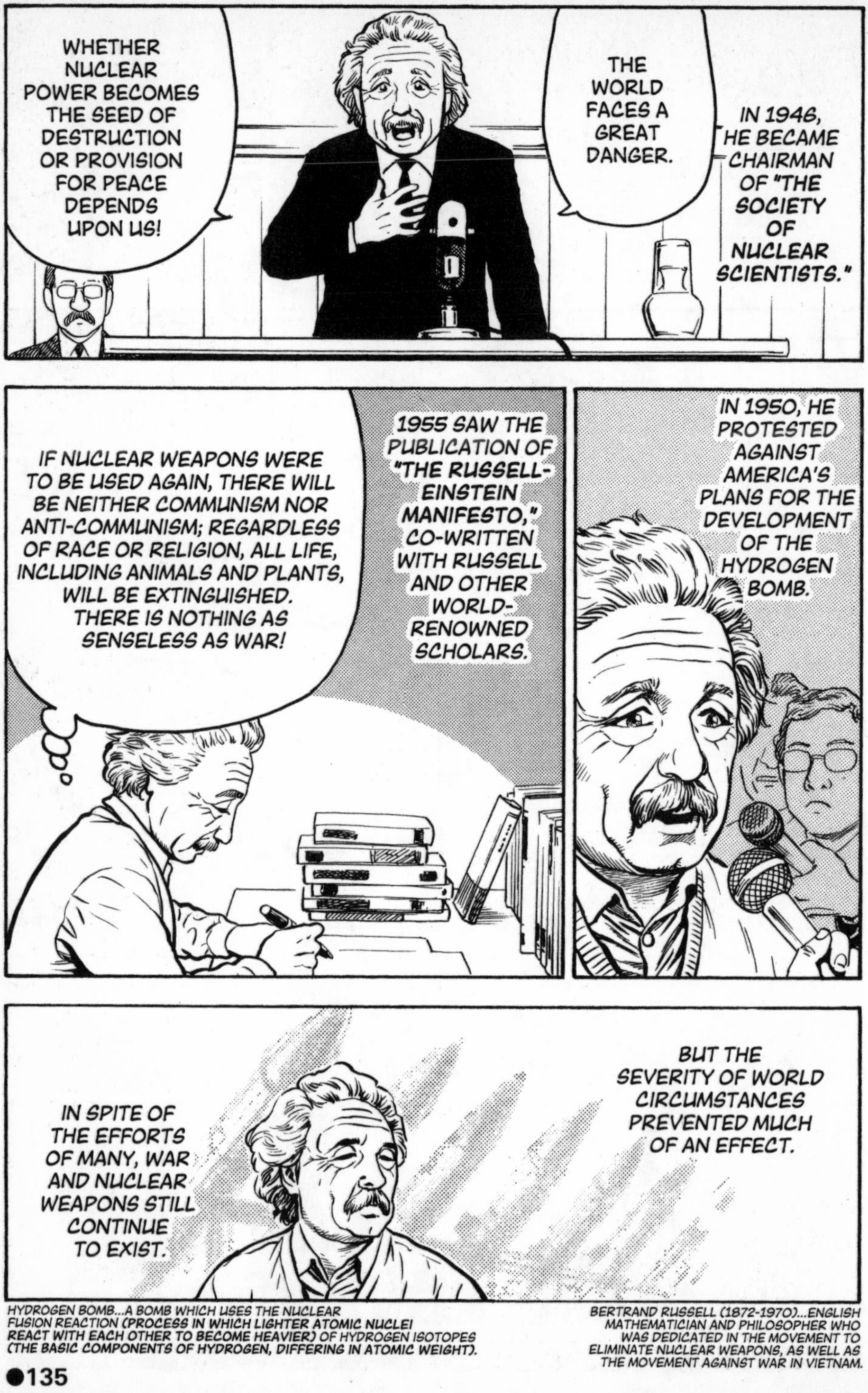
IN 1946, HE BECAME CHAIRMAN OF "THE SOCIETY OF NUCLEAR SCIENTISTS."
THE WORLD FACES A GREAT DANGER.
WHETHER NUCLEAR POWER BECOMES THE SEED OF DESTRUCTION OR PROVISION FOR PEACE DEPENDS UPON US!
IN 1950, HE PROTESTED AGAINST AMERICA'S PLANS FOR THE DEVELOPMENT OF THE HYDROGEN BOMB.
1955 SAW THE PUBLICATION OF "THE RUSSELL-EINSTEIN MANIFESTO," CO-WRITTEN WITH RUSSELL AND OTHER WORLD-RENOWNED SCHOLARS.
IF NUCLEAR WEAPONS WERE TO BE USED AGAIN, THERE WILL BE NEITHER COMMUNISM NOR ANTI-COMMUNISM; REGARDLESS OF RACE OR RELIGION, ALL LIFE, INCLUDING ANIMALS AND PLANTS, WILL BE EXTINGUISHED. THERE IS NOTHING AS SENSELESS AS WAR!
BUT THE SEVERITY OF WORLD CIRCUMSTANCES PREVENTED MUCH OF AN EFFECT.
IN SPITE OF THE EFFORTS OF MANY, WAR AND NUCLEAR WEAPONS STILL CONTINUE TO EXIST.

HYDROGEN BOMB...A BOMB WHICH USES THE NUCLEAR FUSION REACTION (PROCESS IN WHICH LIGHTER ATOMIC NUCLEI REACT WITH EACH OTHER TO BECOME HEAVIER) OF HYDROGEN ISOTOPES (THE BASIC COMPONENTS OF HYDROGEN, DIFFERING IN ATOMIC WEIGHT).

BERTRAND RUSSELL (1872-1970)...ENGLISH MATHEMATICIAN AND PHILOSOPHER WHO WAS DEDICATED IN THE MOVEMENT TO ELIMINATE NUCLEAR WEAPONS, AS WELL AS THE MOVEMENT AGAINST WAR IN VIETNAM.

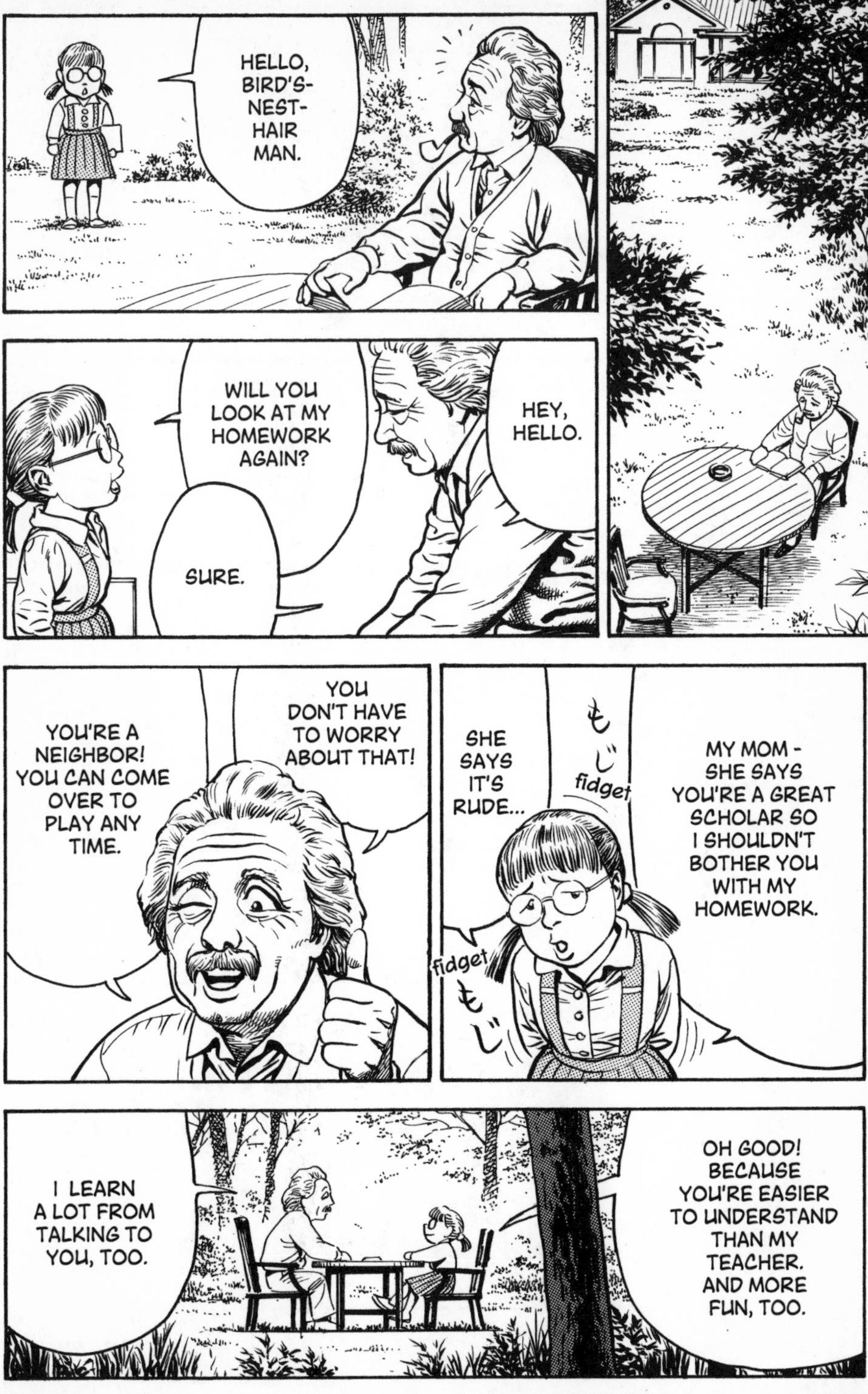
HELLO, BIRD'S-NEST-HAIR MAN.
HEY, HELLO.
WILL YOU LOOK AT MY HOMEWORK AGAIN?
SURE.
MY MOM - SHE SAYS YOU'RE A GREAT SCHOLAR SO I SHOULDN'T BOTHER YOU WITH MY HOMEWORK.
もじ fidget
SHE SAYS IT'S RUDE...
fidget もじ
YOU DON'T HAVE TO WORRY ABOUT THAT!
YOU'RE A NEIGHBOR! YOU CAN COME OVER TO PLAY ANY TIME.
OH GOOD! BECAUSE YOU'RE EASIER TO UNDERSTAND THAN MY TEACHER. AND MORE FUN, TOO.
I LEARN A LOT FROM TALKING TO YOU, TOO.

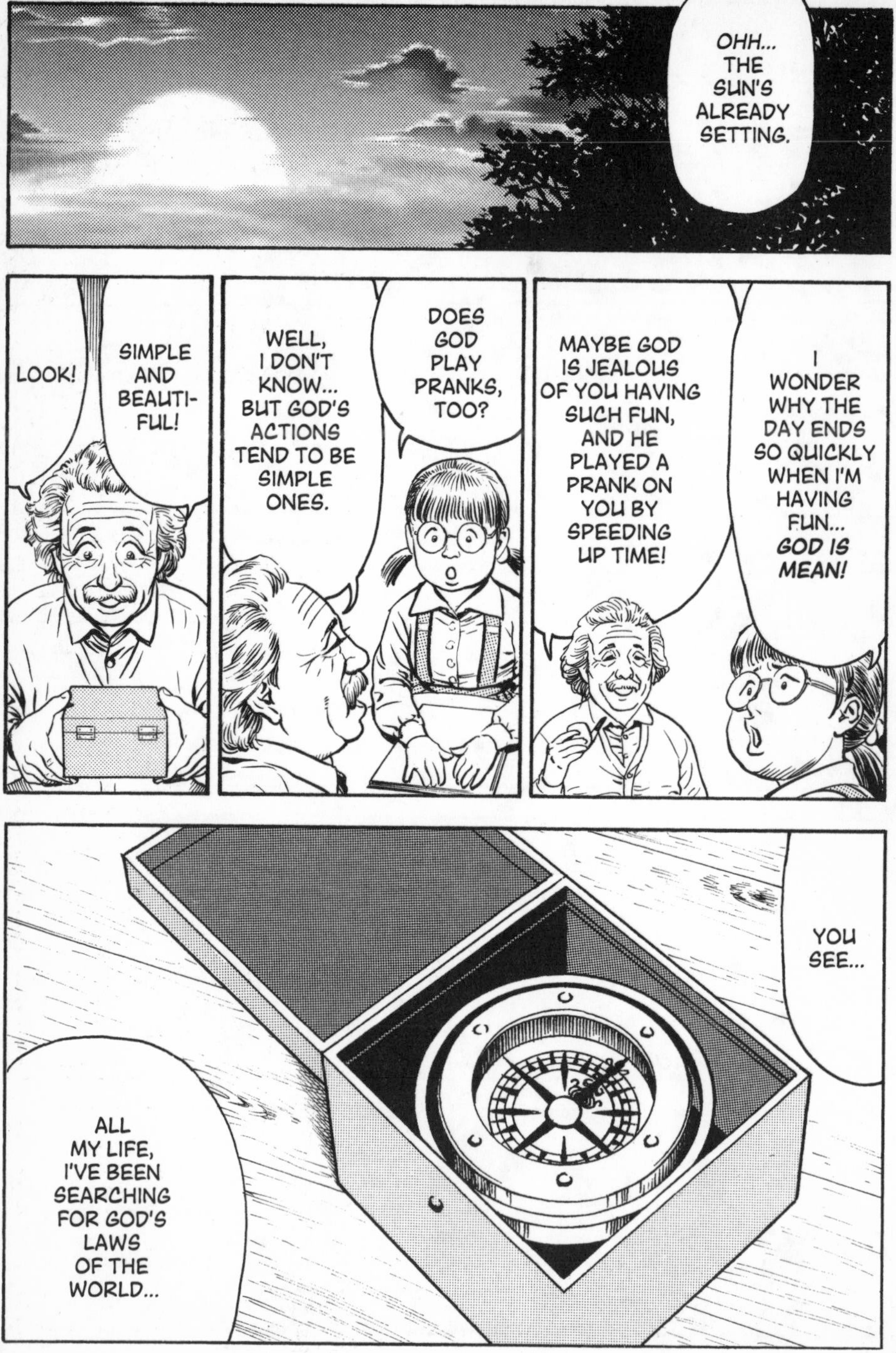
OHH... THE SUN'S ALREADY SETTING.
I WONDER WHY THE DAY ENDS SO QUICKLY WHEN I'M HAVING FUN... *GOD IS MEAN!*
MAYBE GOD IS JEALOUS OF YOU HAVING SUCH FUN, AND HE PLAYED A PRANK ON YOU BY SPEEDING UP TIME!
DOES GOD PLAY PRANKS, TOO?
WELL, I DON'T KNOW... BUT GOD'S ACTIONS TEND TO BE SIMPLE ONES.
SIMPLE AND BEAUTI-FUL!
LOOK!
YOU SEE...
ALL MY LIFE, I'VE BEEN SEARCHING FOR GOD'S LAWS OF THE WORLD...

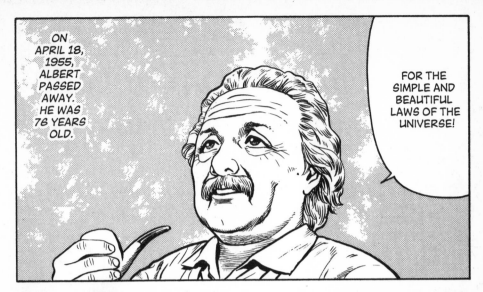

FOR THE SIMPLE AND BEAUTIFUL LAWS OF THE UNIVERSE!
ON APRIL 18, 1955, ALBERT PASSED AWAY. HE WAS 76 YEARS OLD.
WITH CHILDLIKE INNOCENCE, HE SPENT HIS LIFE IN THE PURSUIT OF NATURE'S TRUTH.
THE TURMOIL OF THE ERA IN WHICH HE LIVED DID NOT GRANT HIM THE FREEDOM OR PEACE HE HAD WISHED FOR...
BUT HIS ACCOMPLISHMENTS HAVE BEEN PASSED DOWN IN MANY WAYS, AND CONTINUE TO LIVE ON TODAY.

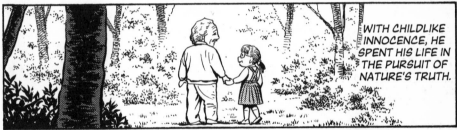

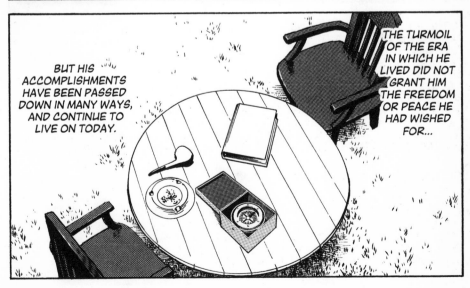

WHAT WAS EINSTEIN LIKE AS A CHILD?

ASTRO: WHAT WAS GERMANY LIKE AT THE TIME DR. EINSTEIN WAS BORN?

DR.ELEFUN: GERMANY HAD JUST BEEN UNIFIED INTO A NEW COUNTRY IN 1871. UNTIL THEN, IT HAD CONSISTED OF A FEDERATION OF ABOUT 40 SMALL INDEPENDENT COUNTRIES, UNIFIED AROUND THE THEN MOST POWERFUL PRUSSIA. AT THE TIME EINSTEIN WAS BORN, GERMANY WAS TRYING VERY HARD TO BECOME A STRONG COUNTRY ABLE TO COMPETE WITH THE LIKES OF ENGLAND, RUSSIA AND FRANCE. PLANS FOR NATIONAL ENRICHMENT AND SECURITY WERE PUT INTO ACTION, AND RIGOROUS REGULATIONS AND MILITARISM WERE FORCED UPON THE PEOPLE. EVEN AS A CHILD, ALBERT SEEMS TO HAVE DISLIKED UNREASONABLE COERCION.

ASTRO: I'VE HEARD THAT HE WAS HOT-TEMPERED.

DR.ELEFUN: HE WAS A CHILD THAT WAS ABLE TO PLAY QUIETLY FOR HOURS ALONE, BUT WHEN SUDDEN TANTRUMS HIT, HE WOULD THROW THINGS AND BECOME COMPLETELY UNMANAGEABLE. THERE WERE TIMES WHEN EVEN HE WAS UNABLE TO CONTROL HIMSELF. HOWEVER, THESE FITS SEEM TO HAVE SUBSIDED BY THE TIME HE ENTERED THE FIRST GRADE.

ASTRO: WHAT GOT HIM INTERESTED IN SCIENCE?

DR.ELEFUN: THE FIRST THING TO COME TO MIND IS THE MAGNETIC COMPASS HE RECEIVED FROM HIS FATHER...THE ORDINARY KIND THAT ALWAYS POINTS TO THE NORTH. WITH THIS, ALBERT MUST HAVE PERCEIVED THAT THERE IS A STRANGE, UNSEEN FORCE IN NATURE. ALSO, WHEN HE WAS TWELVE, ALBERT SEEMS TO HAVE BEEN DEEPLY IMPRESSED AFTER READING A BOOK ON EUCLIDEAN GEOMETRY. THIS WAS A BOOK OF THEOREMS ESTABLISHED AROUND THE YEAR 300 A.D. IN ANCIENT GREECE BY THE MATHEMATICIAN EUCLID. FOR EXAMPLE, THERE IS THE THEOREM THAT SAYS, "PERPENDICULAR LINES DRAWN FROM THE THREE TIPS [*"vertices"] OF A TRIANGLE ALWAYS MEET [*"intersect"] AT A SINGLE POINT." TO THE YOUNG ALBERT, BEING ABLE TO EXPLAIN NATURAL PHENOMENA IN SIMPLE FORMULAS AND THEOREMS MUST HAVE BEEN A DELIGHTFUL CONCEPT.

ASTRO: WHAT WAS HE LIKE AT SCHOOL?

DR.ELEFUN: AT THE TIME, EVEN THE SCHOOLS FOLLOWED A STRICT, MILITARISTIC COURSE. THE YOUNG ALBERT HATED THIS METHOD OF "KNOWLEDGE BY FORCE." HE ESPECIALLY HATED BEING FORCED TO MEMORIZE INFORMATION. ON THE OTHER HAND, HE STUDIED THE SUBJECTS OF PHYSICS AND MATH ON HIS OWN, ON A LEVEL FAR GREATER THAN WHAT WAS BEING TAUGHT AT SCHOOL.

HOW DID EINSTEIN PROGRESS IN HIS RESEARCH?

ASTRO: *HE SEEMS TO HAVE BEEN A PERSON WHO WORKED AT HIS OWN PACE.*

DR.ELEFUN: EVER SINCE HE WAS A CHILD, ALBERT WAS THE TYPE TO THINK THINGS DEEPLY THROUGH TO HIS SATISFACTION BEFORE PRODUCING AN ANSWER. WHEN HE WAS SIXTEEN, ALBERT HAD THIS THOUGHT ABOUT LIGHT: "LET'S SAY A RAY OF LIGHT IS RECEDING FROM ME. IF I CHASED AFTER IT IN A VESSEL GOING AT THE SAME SPEED AS THE LIGHT, HOW WOULD IT LOOK TO ME?" AFTER TEN YEARS OF PURSUING THIS THEME, HE CAME UP WITH THE GREAT "THEORY OF RELATIVITY." IT'S VERY IMPORTANT TO NEVER GIVE UP IN ANYTHING, AND KEEP IN DOGGED PURSUIT.

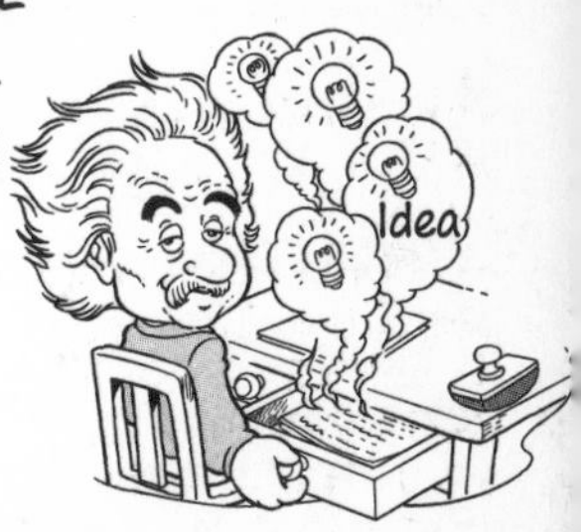
Idea

ASTRO: *WHAT DID HE STUDY AT THE UNIVERSITY?*

DR.ELEFUN: HE WAS ABLE TO ENROLL IN THE ZURICH UNIVERSITY AS HE HAD WISHED, BUT THE CONTENTS OF THE LECTURES - EVEN IN HIS FAVORITE SUBJECT OF PHYSICS - WERE SO CLASSICAL AND OUTDATED THAT HE BECAME BORED. THE PROFESSORS WOULDN'T EVEN DEAL WITH HIM WHEN HE QUESTIONED THEM ABOUT THE LATEST SCIENTIFIC THEMES IN WHICH HE WAS INTERESTED. SO HE HAD NO CHOICE BUT TO CONDUCT HIS RESEARCH AND EXPERIMENTS ON HIS OWN. FOR THIS REASON, ALBERT'S RELATIONSHIP WITH THE PROFESSORS SUFFERED, AND HE WAS NOT ABLE TO OBTAIN THE POSITION OF ASSISTANT HE HAD HOPED FOR AFTER GRADUATION.

ASTRO: *WHAT KIND OF RESEARCH WAS HE DOING WHILE WORKING AT THE PATENT OFFICE?*

DR.ELEFUN: MUCH OF HIS WORK AT THE PATENT OFFICE CONCERNED THE NOTIONS OF SCIENCE IN WHICH EINSTEIN WAS SO INTERESTED, AND THIS JOB SUITED HIM WELL. HE THOUGHT OF HIS "ELEVATOR THOUGHT EXPERIMENT" WHILE RIDING ON THE ELEVATORS HERE AT WORK. THIS EXPERIMENT GOES SOMETHING LIKE THIS: "AN ELEVATOR IS FLOATING IN THE ZERO GRAVITY OF SPACE. IF AN ANGEL WERE TO PULL THIS ELEVATOR ALONG AT AN ACCELERATION OF 980 CM PER SECOND, THE PERSON INSIDE THE ELEVATOR WOULD BE ABLE TO STAND ON THE FLOOR THE SAME AS IF HE WERE ON EARTH, AND IF AN APPLE WAS DROPPED, IT WOULD FALL TO THE FLOOR." WHILE HE CARRIED ON HIS WORK AT THE PATENT OFFICE, IN HIS FREE TIME HE ENJOYED FREQUENT DEBATES ON SUBJECTS LIKE SCIENCE, PHILOSOPHY AND LITERATURE WITH HIS FRIENDS AND THUS STIMULATED HIS IMAGINATION. MANY SCIENTIFIC IDEAS WERE BORN FROM SUCH DISCUSSIONS WITH HIS FRIENDS, AND HE WOULD PROBE THESE IDEAS UNTIL THEY BECAME FINISHED THEORIES.

"THE THEORY OF RELATIVITY" – WHAT DID IT CHANGE, AND HOW?

ASTRO: WHAT WAS THE THOUGHT ON SPACE AND TIME BEFORE THE THEORY OF RELATIVITY WAS PUBLISHED?

DR.ELEFUN: MOST SCIENTISTS BELIEVED IN THE THEORIES THAT ISAAC NEWTON HAD FORMULATED IN THE 17TH CENTURY. OF SPACE AND TIME, NEWTON THEORIZED THAT, "TIME AND DISTANCE REMAIN THE SAME, NO MATTER WHO MEASURES THEM, OR WHERE."

ASTRO: I KNOW THE LENGTH OF TIME CHANGES WITH THE SITUATION, BECAUSE TIME SEEMS TO GO FASTER WHEN I'M HAVING FUN.

DR.ELEFUN: WELL, I THINK THAT'S A LITTLE DIFFERENT... BUT EVEN DR. EINSTEIN HAS HUMOROUSLY EXPLAINED, "WHEN ONE IS SPEAKING TO A BEAUTIFUL GIRL, AN HOUR FEELS LIKE ONE MINUTE. THAT IS RELATIVITY." IN OTHER WORDS, HE THEORIZED THAT TIME AND SPACE FLUCTUATE IN RELATION TO THE SITUATION OF THE OBSERVER. NEWTON'S THEORY WAS A DARING BUT IDEALIZED VERSION OF SPACE AND TIME, AND AS EINSTEIN PONDERED WHETHER THERE WASN'T A MORE ACCURATE WAY TO EXPLAIN EVERYDAY INCIDENTS, HE CONCLUDED, "THERE IS NO ABSOLUTE IN SPACE."

ASTRO: WHAT WAS THE THINKING ON LIGHT?

DR.ELEFUN: AT THE TIME, LIGHT WAS THOUGHT TO BE A WAVE THAT TRAVELED THROUGH A UNIVERSAL SUBSTANCE CALLED "ETHER." IN OPPOSITION TO THIS THEORY, EINSTEIN DECLARED, "ETHER DOES NOT EXIST. MOREOVER, THE SPEED OF LIGHT ALWAYS REMAINS THE SAME." THIS IS HOW THE FAMOUS FORMULA, "$E=MC^2$" WAS BORN. THIS FORMULA BECAME AN EFFECTIVE TOOL FOR REVEALING MANY MYSTERIES OF NATURAL PHENOMENA.

ASTRO: WHAT KINDS OF THINGS, FOR EXAMPLE?

DR.ELEFUN: WE WERE ABLE TO UNDERSTAND HOW THE UNIVERSE BEGAN, HOW IT WORKS, AND WHETHER THERE IS A FINITE EDGE OF SPACE. EVEN NOW, THE UNIVERSE IS SAID TO BE EXPANDING, BUT IN QUESTIONING WHETHER THE UNIVERSE WILL CONTINUE TO EXPAND OR SHRINK INTO A SINGLE POINT, THE THEORY OF RELATIVITY IS CRUCIAL. ALSO, USING THIS THEORY, OTHER RESEARCH - SUCH AS LOOKING INTO THE EXACT NATURE OF A BLACK HOLE OR THE POSSIBILITY OF BUILDING A TIME MACHINE - IS BEING CONDUCTED. THE IMPORTANCE OF THE ROLE EINSTEIN HAS PLAYED IS INESTIMABLE.

WHAT KIND OF MAN WAS EINSTEIN?

ASTRO: *WHAT KIND OF LIFE DID HE LIVE?*

DR.ELEFUN: EINSTEIN HELD THE BELIEF THAT, "THE TRUTH IS BEAUTIFUL AND SIMPLE," AND LIVED IN THIS SAME WAY. HE ONLY POSSESSED THINGS OF BASIC NEED. HIS HAIR WAS ALWAYS TUSSELED, AND HIS SUITS AND CLOTHING DISSHEVELED -HE RARELY EVER PUT ON A NECKTIE. HE HAD ABSOLUTELY NO INTEREST IN FASHION.

ASTRO: *DID HE HAVE OTHER INTERESTS BESIDES RESEARCH IN PHYSICS?*

DR.ELEFUN: HE LOVED TO PLAY THE VIOLIN, AND HE SOMETIMES HELD RECITALS AMONG FRIENDS. HE ALSO HAD A SMALL SAILBOAT OF HIS OWN, WHICH HE SAILED WHENEVER HE FOUND THE TIME. HE MUST HAVE GREATLY ENJOYED BEING SWEPT ALONG THE WATER BY THE BREEZE.

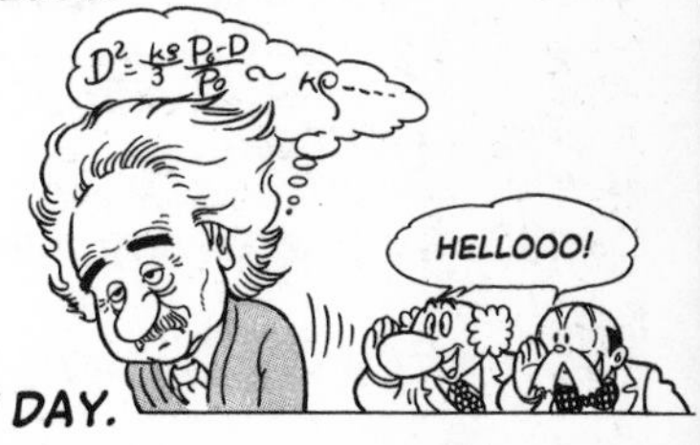
HELLOOO!

ASTRO: *HE MUST HAVE BEEN VERY BUSY EVERY DAY.*

DR.ELEFUN: AFTER HIS NAME BECAME WORLD FAMOUS, HE RECEIVED MANY REQUESTS FOR LECTURES FROM ALL OVER THE WORLD, AND HE NO LONGER HAD ANY TIME TO SETTLE DOWN WITH HIS RESEARCH. EVEN THEN, HE SOMEHOW FOUND THE TIME TO ANSWER THE LETTERS OF AS MANY PEOPLE AS HE COULD. HE NEVER LET HIS FAME MAKE HIM VAIN OR CONCEITED.

ASTRO: *HE WAS ALSO ACTIVE IN THE PEACE MOVEMENT.*

DR.ELEFUN: IN 1914, EUROPE WAS DRAGGED INTO WORLD WAR ONE. EINSTEIN COULD NOT WATCH IDLY WHILE MANY PEOPLE WERE MEANINGLESSLY KILLED. BEGINNING WITH HIS SIGNING THE NEXT YEAR OF "A MANIFESTO TO EUROPE," A PETITION WHICH CALLED FOR AN INTERNATIONAL PEACEKEEPING UNION, HE BECAME A LIFELONG ACTIVIST FOR PEACE. HE WAS ESPECIALLY DEVASTATED BY THE DROPPING OF THE ATOMIC BOMB ON JAPAN, SINCE HE HIMSELF HAD ADVOCATED THE DEVELOPMENT OF SUCH A BOMB. FROM THEN ON, HE AGGRESSIVELY CAMPAIGNED FOR THE MOVEMENT AGAINST NUCLEAR ARMS. JUST SEVEN DAYS BEFORE HIS DEATH, HE PUT HIS SIGNATURE TO THE "RUSSELL-EINSTEIN MANIFESTO," A DOCUMENT WHICH RELATED THE HORROR THAT NUCLEAR WEAPONRY POSED TO THE WORLD. AS MUCH AS HE LOVED SCIENCE WITH ALL HIS HEART, HE ALSO ACCEPTED THE OBLIGATION TO FULFILL HIS RESPONSIBILITIES AS A SCIENTIST.

TIME LINE: THE LIFE OF EINSTEIN 1879–1955

A.D.	AGE	THE LIFE OF EINSTEIN
1879		MARCH 14, BORN IN ULM, A CITY IN SOUTHERN GERMANY.
1880	1	EINSTEIN FAMILY MOVES TO MUNICH.
1884	5	RECEIVES PORTABLE MAGNETIC COMPASS FROM FATHER.
1885	6	ENROLLS IN ELEMENTARY SCHOOL. BEGINS TO PLAY THE VIOLIN.
1891	12	BEGINS TO SHOW INTEREST IN GEOMETRY AND CALCULUS.
1894	15	FAMILY MOVES TO ITALY, LEAVING ALBERT BEHIND IN GYMNASIUM IN MUNICH.
1895	16	DROPS OUT OF GYMNASIUM. ATTENDS SCHOOL IN AARAU, SWITZERLAND.
1896	17	RENOUNCES GERMAN CITIZENSHIP. ENROLLS IN ZURICH FEDERAL POLYTECHNIC ACADEMY.
1902	23	BEGINS EMPLOYMENT AT SWISS PATENT OFFICE IN BERN. FATHER HERMANN DIES.
1903	24	MARRIES MILEVA MARIC.
1904	25	ELDEST SON, HANS ALBERT IS BORN.
1905	26	PUBLICATION OF *"SPECIAL THEORY OF RELATIVITY"* AND *"QUANTUM THEORY OF LIGHT."*
1907	28	PUBLICATION OF THEORY REGARDING *"QUANTUM MECHANICS."*
1909	30	RESIGNS FROM PATENT OFFICE AND BECOMES ASSOCIATE PROFESSOR AT ZURICH UNIVERSITY.
1910	31	SECOND SON, EDUARD IS BORN.
1911	32	APPOINTED PROFESSOR AT GERMAN UNIVERSITY OF PRAGUE, CZECH REPUBLIC.
1914	35	APPOINTED PROFESSOR AT BERLIN UNIVERSITY. FAMILY MOVES TO BERLIN. WIFE AND CHILDREN IMMEDIATELY RETURN TO ZURICH AND SEPARATION PERIOD BEGINS.
1915	36	COMPLETES GENERAL THEORY OF RELATIVITY.
1919	40	DIVORCES MILEVA. MARRIES COUSIN ELSA LOEWENTHAL. EINSTEIN BECOMES WORLD FAMOUS.
1920	41	MOTHER PAULINE DIES.
1922	43	ON THE BOAT TO JAPAN, LEARNS OF WINNING NOBEL PRIZE IN PHYSICS.
1929	50	AWARDED THE MAX PLANCK MEDAL.
1933	54	CROSSES TO AMERICA. APPOINTED PROFESSOR AT PRINCETON INSTIUE FOR ADVANCED STUDY.
1936	57	WIFE ELSA DIES.
1939	60	SIGNS PETITION "REGARDING THE DEVELOPMENT OF THE ATOMIC BOMB" ADDRESSED TO PRESIDENT ROOSEVELT.
1945	66	LEARNS OF ATOMIC BOMB DROPPED ON JAPAN.
1946	67	CALLS FOR THE FORMATION OF "A WORLD GOVERNMENT TO ERADICATE WAR."
1955	76	SIGNS THE "RUSSELL-EINSTEIN MANIFESTO" THE ELIMINATION OF NUCLEAR ARMS. DIES APRIL 18, 1:15 AM.

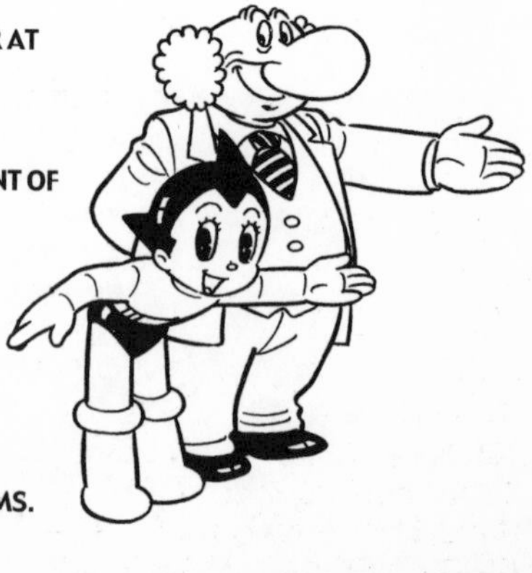

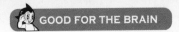

GOOD FOR THE BRAIN

EDU·MANGA™
ALBERT EINSTEIN

ILLUSTRATED BY KOTARO IWASAKI
STORY BY ISAO HIMURO

TRANSLATION	SACHIKO SATO
LETTERING	DAN NAKROSIS
GRAPHIC DESIGN/LAYOUT	ERIC ROSENBERGER/FRED LUI
EDITOR IN CHIEF	FRED LUI
PUBLISHER	HIKARU SASAHARA

ENGLISH EDITION PUBLISHED BY
DIGITAL MANGA PUBLISHING
A DIVISION OF DIGITAL MANGA, INC.
1487 W 178TH STREET, SUITE 300
GARDENA, CA 90248

WWW.DMPBOOKS.COM

FIRST EDITION: DECEMBER 2006
ISBN: 1-56970-975-0
LCCN: 2006934125

1 3 5 7 9 10 8 6 4 2

PRINTED IN CHINA

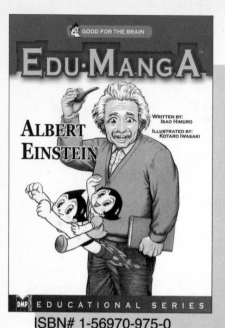

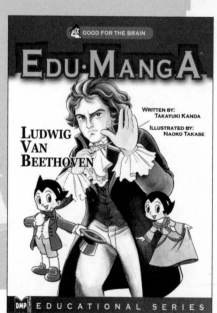

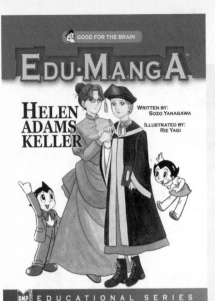
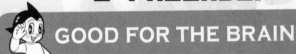
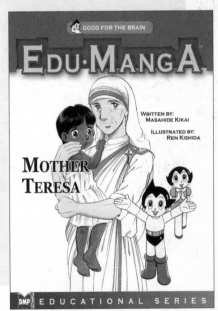

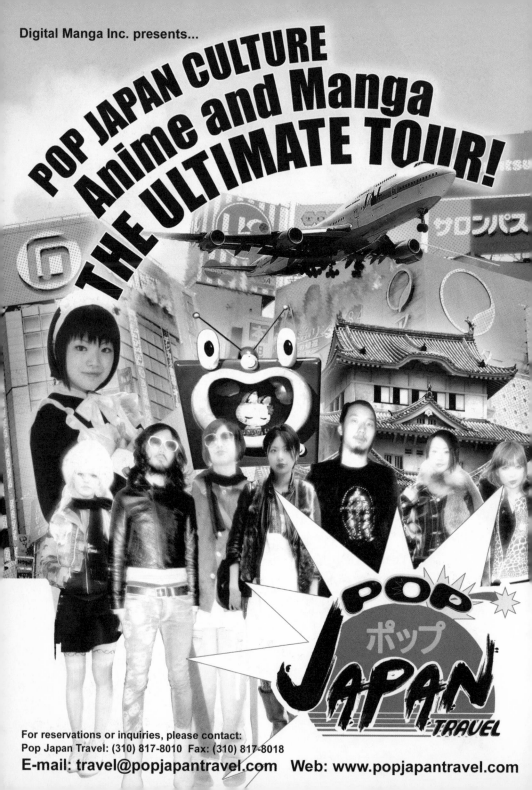

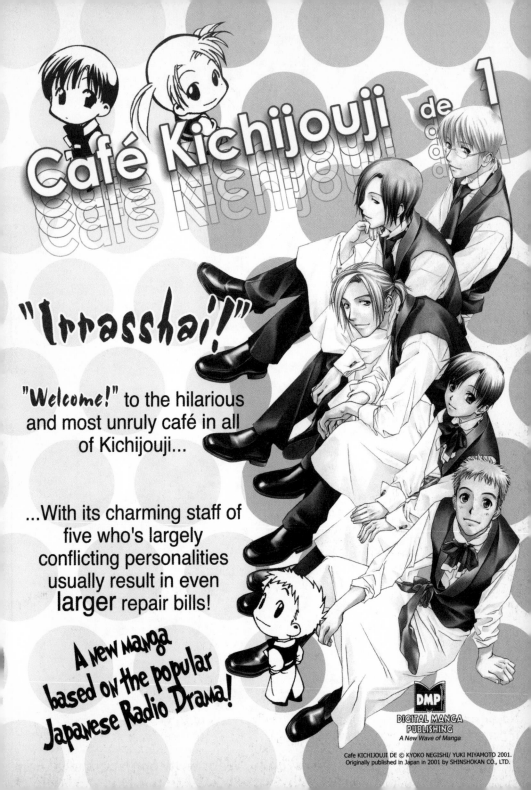

Café Kichijouji de 1

"Irrasshai!"

"Welcome!" to the hilarious and most unruly café in all of Kichijouji...

...With its charming staff of five who's largely conflicting personalities usually result in even **larger** repair bills!

A new manga based on the popular Japanese Radio Drama!

DMP
DIGITAL MANGA
PUBLISHING
A New Wave of Manga

PROJECT X
240Z
challengers

Written and Illustrated by:
Akira Yokoyama

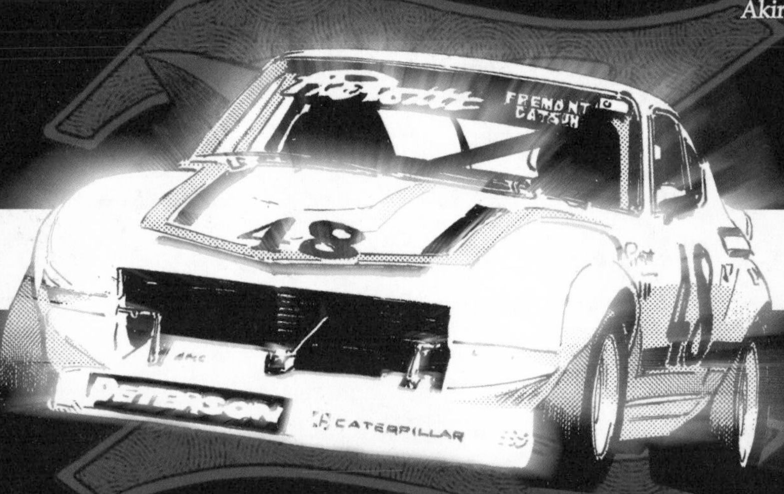

We Mean Business.
Building a world class Japanese sports car...
it ain't easy!!

ISBN: 1-55970-957-2 $12.95

Project X - The Challengers - Nissan 240Z
© NHK/Akira Imai/Akira Yokoyama. Originally published in Japan in 2003 by Ohzora Publishing Co.

DMP
DIGITAL MANGA
PUBLISHING
www.dmpbooks.com

PROJECT X

challengers

CUP NOODLE

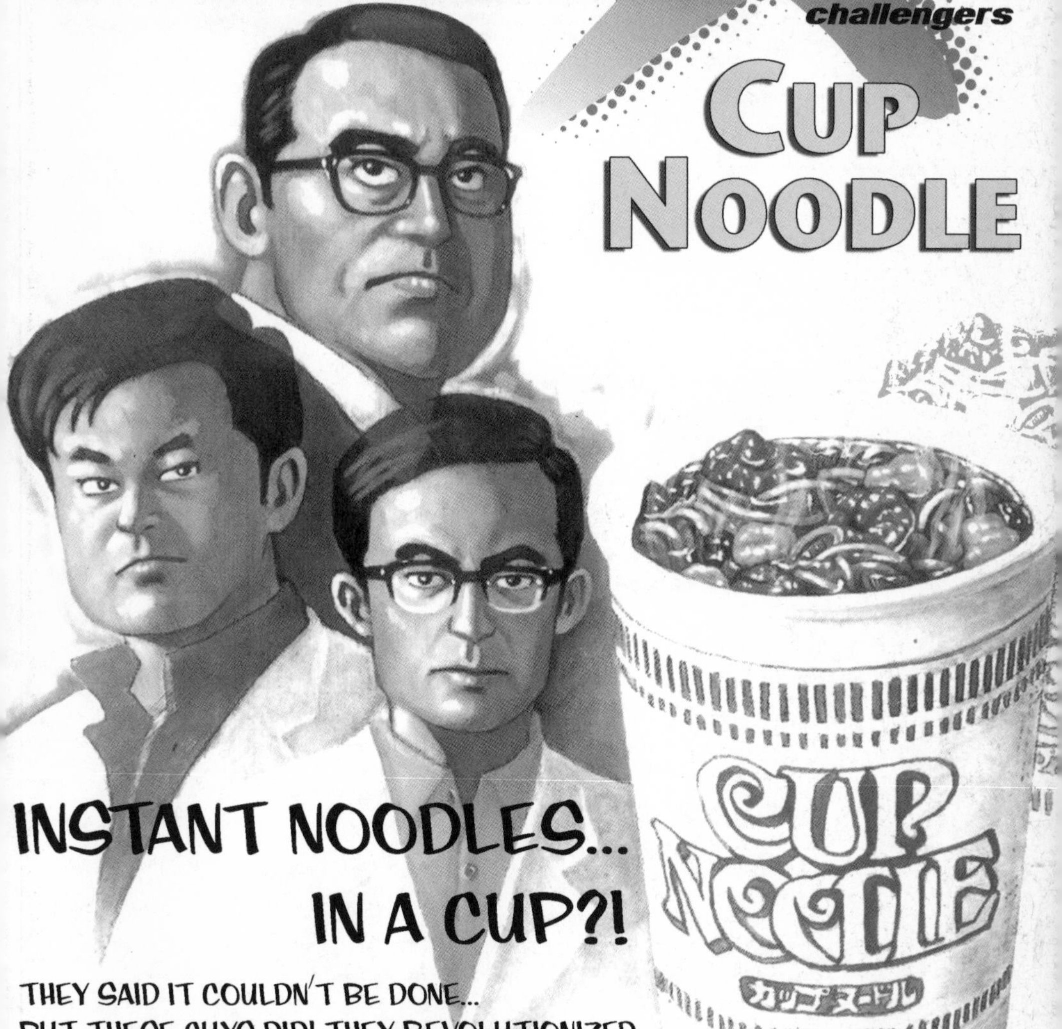
CUP NOODLE
カップヌードル

INSTANT NOODLES...

IN A CUP?!

THEY SAID IT COULDN'T BE DONE...
BUT THESE GUYS DID! THEY REVOLUTIONIZED
THE JAPANESE FOOD INDUSTRY WITH
THEIR NEW INNOVATION FOR NOODLES.

ISBN# 1-56970-959-9 $12.95

DMP
DIGITAL MANGA PUBLISHING

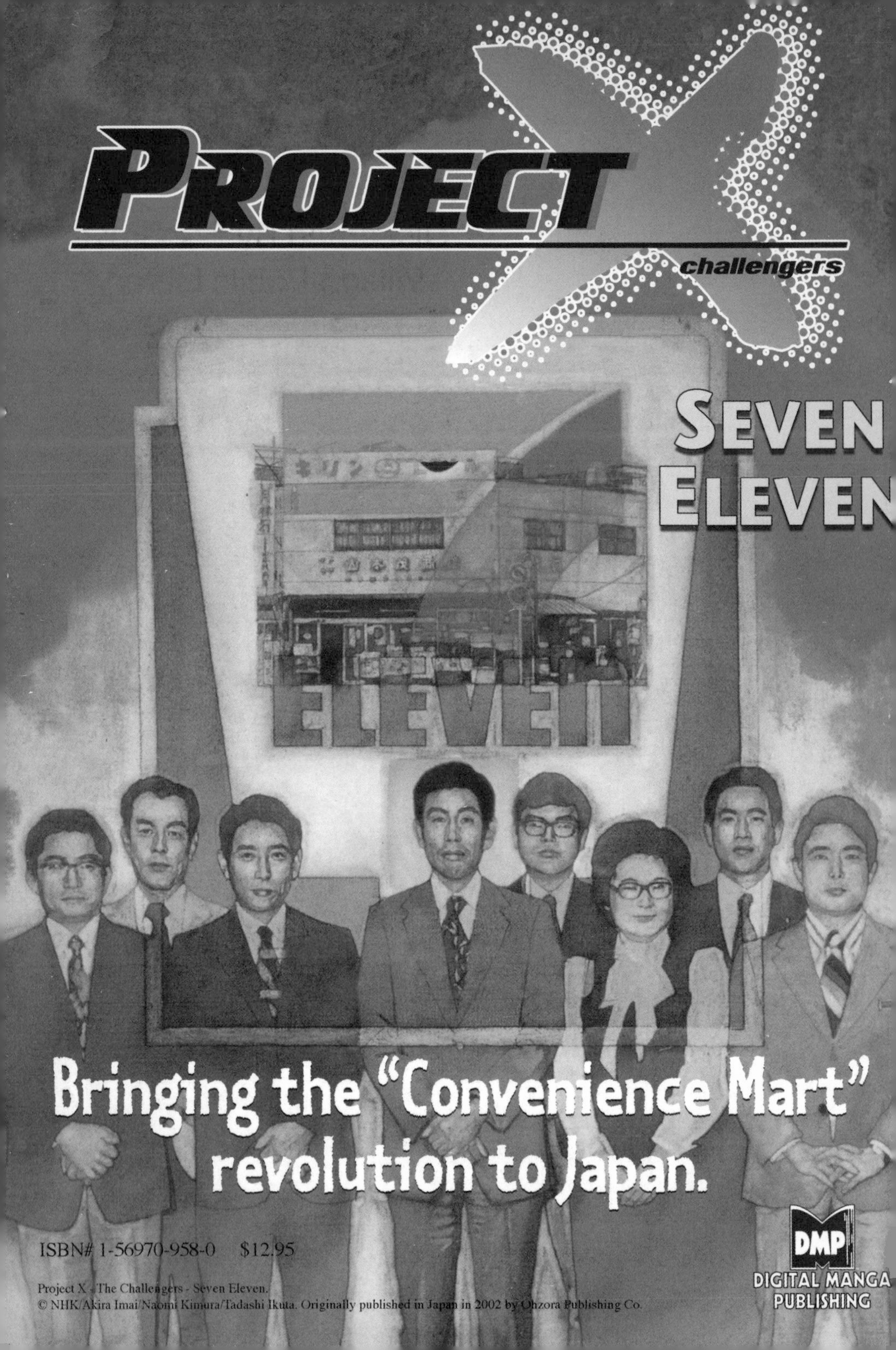
PROJECT X
challengers
SEVEN ELEVEN
ELEVEN
Bringing the "Convenience Mart" revolution to Japan.
ISBN# 1-56970-958-0 $12.95
Project X - The Challengers - Seven Eleven.
© NHK/Akira Imai/Naomi Kimura/Tadashi Ikuta. Originally published in Japan in 2002 by Ohzora Publishing Co.
DMP
DIGITAL MANGA PUBLISHING

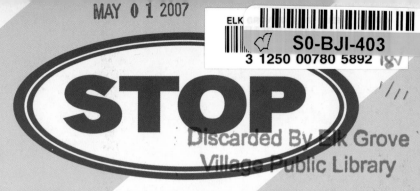

STOP

This is the back of the book! Start from the other side.

NATIVE MANGA
readers read manga from *right to left*.

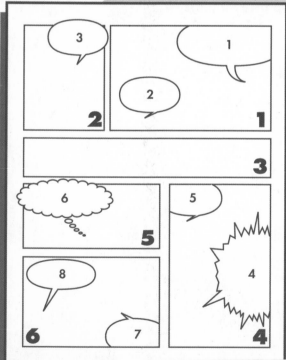

If you run into our *Native Manga* logo on any of our books... you'll know that this manga is published in it's true original native Japanese right to left reading format, as it was intended. Turn to the other side of the book and start reading from right to left, top to bottom.

Follow the diagram to see how its done. *Surf's Up!*

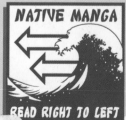

NATIVE MANGA
READ RIGHT TO LEFT